Lynda Weinman's | Hands-On Training

Macromedia®

Flash®
Professional 8

Includes Exercise Files and Demo Movies

lynda.com

By James Gonzalez

Macromedia® Flash® Professional 8 Hands-On Training

By James Gonzalez

lynda.com/books | Peachpit Press
1249 Eighth Street • Berkeley, CA • 94710
800.283.9444 • 510.524.2178 •
510.524.2221(fax)
http://www.lynda.com/books
http://www.peachpit.com

lynda.com/books is published
in association with Peachpit Press,
a division of Pearson Education
Copyright ©2006 by lynda.com

ISBN: 0-321-29388-6

0 9 8 7 6 5 4 3 2

Printed and bound in the
United States of America

H•O•T Credits

lynda.com Director of Publications: Tanya Staples

Editor: Karyn Johnson

Production Editor: Myrna Vladic

Compositor: Jonathan Woolson

Copyeditor: Darren Meiss

Proofreader: Liz Welch

Interior Design: Hot Studio, San Francisco

Cover Design: Don Barnett, Owen Wolfson

Cover Illustration: Bruce Heavin (bruce@stink.com)

Indexer: Julie Bess, JBIndexing Inc.

Video Editors and Testers: Rosanna Yeung, Scott Cullen, Eric Geoffroy

H•O•T Colophon

The text in *Macromedia Flash Professional 8 H·O·T* was set in Avenir from Adobe Systems Incorporated. The cover illustation was painted in Adobe Photoshop and Adobe Illustrator.

This book was created using QuarkXPress and Microsoft Office on an Apple Macintosh using Mac OS X. It was printed on 60 lb. Influence Matte at Courier.

Table of Contents

Introduction

A Note from Lynda Weinman

Most people buy computer books to learn, yet it's amazing how few books are written by teachers. James Gonzalez and I take pride that this book was written by experienced teachers, who are familiar with training students in this subject matter. In this book, you'll find carefully developed lessons and exercises to help you learn Flash Professional 8—one of the most powerful and popular animation and authoring tools for the Web.

This book is targeted to the beginning- to intermediate-level Web designers and Web developers who need a tool for creating powerful, compelling, and highly interactive digital content for the Web. The premise of the hands-on approach is to get you up-to-speed quickly with Flash Professional 8 while actively working through the lessons in this book. It's one thing to read about a program, and another experience entirely to try the product and achieve measurable results. Our motto is, "Read the book, follow the exercises, and you'll learn the program." I have received countless testimonials and it is our goal to make sure it remains true for all our hands-on training books.

This book doesn't set out to cover every single aspect of the Flash Professional 8 program, nor does it try to teach you everything this extremely powerful application can do. What we saw missing from the bookshelves was a process-oriented tutorial that teaches readers core principles, techniques, and tips in a hands-on training format.

I welcome your comments at **fl8hot@lynda.com**. If you run into any trouble while you're working through this book, check out the technical support link at **http://www.lynda.com/books/HOT/fl8**.

James Gonzalez and I hope this book will improve your skills in Flash. If it does, we have accomplished the job we set out to do!

—Lynda Weinman

About lynda.com

lynda.com was founded in 1995 by Lynda Weinman and Bruce Heavin in conjunction with the first publication of Lynda's revolutionary book, *Designing Web Graphics*. Since then, lynda.com has become a leader in software training for graphics and Web professionals and is recognized worldwide as a trusted educational resource.

lynda.com offers a wide range of Hands-On Training books, which guide users through a progressive learning process using real-world projects.

lynda.com also offers a wide range of video-based tutorials, which are available on CD-ROM and DVD-ROM and through the **lynda.com Online Training Library**. lynda.com also owns the **Flashforward Conference and Film Festival**.

For more information about lynda.com, check out **http://www.lynda.com**. For more information about the Flashforward Conference and Film Festival, check out **http://www.flashforwardconference.com**.

Register for a FREE 24-hour Pass

Register your copy of Flash Professional 8 Hands-On Training today and receive the following benefits:

- **FREE 24-hour pass to the lynda.com Online Training Library™** with over 10,000 professionally

produced video tutorials covering over 150 topics by leading industry experts and teachers

- news, events, and special offers from lynda.com

- the lynda.com monthly newsletter

To register, visit **http://www.lynda.com/register/ HOT/fl8**.

Additional Training Resources from lynda.com

To help you master and further develop your skills with Flash 8, Web design, and Web development, register to use the free, 24-hour pass to the **lynda.com Online Training Library** and check out the following training resources:

Flash Professional 8 Beyond the Basics Hands-On Training
by Shane Rebenschied
lynda.com/books and Peachpit Press
ISBN: 0321293878

Flash Professional 8 Essential Training
with Shane Rebenschied

Flash Professional 8 New Features
with Shane Rebenschied

Flash Professional 8 Beyond the Basics
with Shane Rebenschied

Flash 8 User Experiences Best Practices
with Robert Hoekman Jr.

Flash Professional 8 and Photoshop CS2 Integration
with Michael Ninness

Studio 8 Web Workflow
with Abigail Rudner

About the Author

James Gonzalez is a computer applications and digital communications professor at the College of Marin, near San Francisco, California, where he teaches courses in interactive media design, eLearning, and Web technologies. His current professional focus is on the application of digital media in online instructional environments.

James has over 17 years of classroom teaching experience. He has spent the majority of this time designing, developing, and implementing various technology-focused instructional programs. He has taught courses nationwide on the use of digital media software and their applications in instructional environments and has also published numerous works on these subjects, including half a dozen recent video and Web-based instructional courses covering the use of Macromedia Flash, Dreamweaver, and Director and Adobe Premiere Pro.

When not teaching or writing, James provides consulting and technical services on the applications of multimedia and telecommunications technologies for training and education. James travels extensively; he tries to get away as often and as widely as his RV, Internet technology, and his busy schedule will allow, most frequently to Europe and Brazil.

Acknowledgments from James Gonzalez

Many individuals have made significant contributions to the book you hold in your hands. First and foremost are the various authors who have written previous editions of either the Flash Hands-On Training books or one of the other titles in the series. Together, all these folks have developed and refined an instructional method and presentation style that really works.

However, I would like to thank by name, two of these individuals that I have had the pleasure to work with personally: **Tanya Staples**, the Director of Publications for lynda.com and the developmental editor of this book; and **Rosanna Yeung**, the author of the previous edition of this book.

Tanya has made significant contributions throughout the planning, writing, video recording, beta testing, copy editing, and final proofing of this book. Thanks, Tanya, for your deep commitment to this project, your attention to detail, your exceptional management of each phase of the production, your timely advice, and your consistent professionalism. You're the best!

As the previous author of this book and a beta tester on this one, Rosanna has also made strategic and valuable contributions throughout the planning, writing, and editing of the book, even rewriting Chapter 17 when time was running out and I needed all the help I could get! Thanks, Rosanna, for your gracious and generous support and for your insightful comments and observations during the planning and beta testing. I think we actually implemented almost every suggestion you made!

Darren Meiss had the unenviable job of editing my copy for this book. Thank you for being so good at those things at which I am not. (That sounds funny, but you get the drift, and besides, Darren will clean this right up if it's wrong!) As Rosanna wrote in the last edition, "Your attention to detail is amazing." I second this.

I would also like to thank my other beta tester, **Scott Cullen**, for all your hard work and quick turnaround of each chapter and for making sure our Mac readers would not miss out on anything.

Thanks are also owed to **Garrick Chow**, who updated Chapter 19, and **Michael Cooper** (**cureforgravity.ca**), whose wonderful Flash artwork you can see in the new material on Flash filters and blends.

Jonathan Woolson (thinkplaydesign.com) was the compositor; his skills put all the pieces together into the final copy you have in your hands. Thank you.

Paavo Stubstad, the chief video editor at lynda.com, who did such a good job of cleaning up my umms, uhhs, and duhhs, and editing out my other mistakes for the videos on the HOT CD-ROM.

Special thanks to **Domenique Sillett**, who did the original artwork and designs and Patrick Miko (**miko@ultrashock.com**) of **www.ultrashock.com** for allowing us to use his collection of audio files for the exercises and videos.

And finally, I would like to send my thanks and love to my wife, Elisabeth, for graciously agreeing to assume the role of a "book widow" during the production of this project. Thanks for putting up with all the long hours and never complaining (well, maybe once) about the loss of your companion in life, even while on vacation at the beach! I love you, and I owe you one.

How to Use This Book

This section outlines important information to help you make the most of this book:

The Formatting in This Book

This book has several components, including step-by-step exercises, commentary, notes, tips, warnings, and video tutorials. Step-by-step exercises are numbered. Filenames, folder names, commands, keyboard shortcuts, and URLs are bolded so they pop out easily: **filename.htm**, **images** folder, **File > New**, **Ctrl+click**, **http://www.lynda.com**.

Commentary is in dark gray text.

This is commentary text.

Interface Screen Captures

Most of the screen shots in the book were taken on a Windows computer using Windows XP Professional, as I do much of my design, development, and writing in the Windows operating system. I also own, use, and love my Mac computers, and I note important differences between the two platforms when they occur.

What's on the HOT CD-ROM?

You'll find a number of useful resources on the HOT CD-ROM, including the following: exercise files, video tutorials, and information about product registration. Before you begin the hands-on exercises, read through the following section so you know how to set up the exercise files and video tutorials.

Exercise Files

The files required to complete the exercises are on the HOT CD-ROM in a folder called **exercise_files**. These files are divided into chapter folders, and you should copy each chapter folder onto your **Desktop** before you begin the exercises for that chapter. For example, if you're about to start Chapter 5, copy the **chap_05** folder from the **exercise_files** folder on the **HOT CD-ROM** onto your **Desktop**.

On Windows, when files originate from a CD-ROM, they automatically become write-protected, which means you cannot alter them. Fortunately, you can easily change this attribute. For complete instructions, read "Making Exercise Files Editable on Windows Computers" below.

Video Tutorials

Throughout the book, you'll find references to video tutorials. In some cases, these video tutorials reinforce concepts explained in the book. In other cases, they show bonus material you'll find interesting and useful. To view the video tutorials, you must have QuickTime Player installed on your computer. If you do not have QuickTime Player, you can download it for free from Apple's Web site: **http://www.apple.com/quicktime**.

To view the video tutorials, copy the videos from the **HOT CD-ROM** onto to your hard drive. Double-click the video you want to watch, and it will automatically open in QuickTime Player. Make sure the volume on your computer is turned up so you can hear the audio content.

If you like the video tutorials, refer to the instructions earlier in this chapter and register to receive a free pass to the **lynda.com Online Training Library**, which is filled with over 10,000 video tutorials covering over 150 topics.

Making Exercise Files Editable on Windows Computers

By default, when you copy files from a CD-ROM to a Windows computer, they are set to read-only (write-protected), which will cause a problem with the exercise files because you will need to edit and save many of them. You can remove the read-only property by following these steps:

1 Open the **exercise_files** folder on the **HOT CD-ROM**, and copy one of the subfolders, such as **chap_02**, to your **Desktop**.

2 Open the **chap_02** folder you copied to your **Desktop**, and choose **Edit > Select All**.

3 Right-click one of the selected files and choose **Properties** from the contextual menu.

4 In the **Properties** dialog box, select the **General** tab. Deselect the **Read-Only** option to disable the read-only properties for the selected files in the **chap_02** folder.

Making File Extensions Visible on Windows Computers

By default, you cannot see file extensions, such as .htm, .fla, .swf, .jpg, .gif, or .psd on Windows computers. Fortunately you can change this setting easily. Here's how:

1 On your **Desktop**, double-click the **My Computer** icon.

Note: If you (or someone else) changed the name, it will not say **My Computer**.

---

2 Choose **Tools > Folder Options** to open the **Folder Options** dialog box. Select the **View** tab.

---

3 Deselect the **Hide extensions for known file types** option to makes all file extensions visible.

Flash Professional 8 System Requirements

Windows

- 800 MHz Intel Pentium III processor (or equivalent) and later
- Windows 2000, Windows XP
- 256 MB RAM (1 GB recommended to run more than one Studio 8 product simultaneously)
- 1024 x 768, 16-bit display (32-bit recommended)
- 710 MB available disk space

Macintosh

- 600 MHz PowerPC G3 and later
- Mac OS X 10.3, 10.4
- 256 MB RAM (1 GB recommended to run more than one Studio 8 product simultaneously)
- 1024 x 768, thousands of colors display (millions of colors recommended)
- 360 MB available disk space

Getting Demo Versions of the Software

If you'd like to try demo versions of the software used in this book, you can download demo versions from the following Web page:

http://www.macromedia.com/downloads/

1

Getting Started

Most likely, if you've purchased a copy of Macromedia Flash 8, you already know why you want to use the program. You might have experience building Web pages or using other graphics programs and want to increase your software skills for today's job market. However, some of you might not know the benefits of using Flash 8 rather than HTML for authoring a Web site. This chapter outlines the Flash 8 product line, including the differences between Flash Basic 8 and Flash Professional 8, and answers the question, "Why use Flash 8?" It also contains a summary of the notable new features in Flash 8, and it outlines some of the ways you can extend Flash 8 content using other technologies such as CGI, XML, and JavaScript.

Introducing the Macromedia Flash 8 Product Line

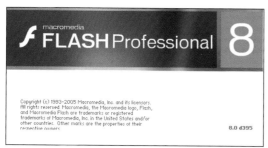

Macromedia has again developed the program into two distinct solutions: **Flash Basic 8** and **Flash Professional 8**. Although this book was written using Flash Professional 8, you can complete many of the exercises in Flash Basic 8. The following material, however, requires Flash

Professional 8: Chapter 7, "*Filters and Blending Modes*," Exercises 5, 8, and 9 of Chapter 8, "*Motion Tweening and Timeline Effects*," and Exercise 5 of Chapter 16, "*Video.*"

Flash Basic 8 was designed with an emphasis on the creation, import, and manipulation of many types of media (audio, video, bitmaps, vectors, text, and data).

Flash Professional 8 was created for both advanced Web designers and application builders. It is particularly suitable for large-scale, complex projects deployed using Flash Player along with a hybrid of HTML content. Flash Professional 8 includes all the features of Flash Basic 8, along with several powerful new tools. It provides new expressiveness tools for optimizing the look and feel of your Flash files, external scripting capabilities for handling dynamic data from databases, and more.

You may be asking yourself "Which program is right for me?" This chapter includes a quick summary of the new and enhanced features of each program and a list of features found only in Flash Professional 8.

Why Use Flash 8?

Flash has several key benefits, including small file sizes, fast downloading speed, precise visual control, advanced interactivity, the capability to combine bitmap and vector graphics and include video and/or animation, and scalable and streaming content.

Download Speed

If you want to design a Web site containing an abundance of visual content, download speed can be a major problem. As most of you know, nothing can be more frustrating than a slow-loading

site. Even limited use of compressed bitmap graphic file formats (GIF and JPEG) can result in slow Web sites that frustrate visitors. Because of this, Web developers are often forced to use less visual but faster-downloading designs.

Flash content is often smaller than HTML content because it uses its own compression scheme, which optimizes vector and bitmap content differently than GIFs or JPEGs. For this reason, Flash 8 has become the delivery medium of preference for graphic-intensive Web sites.

Visual Control

Another benefit of Flash 8 is that it frees Web designers from many of the restraints of traditional HTML (**H**yper**T**ext **M**arkup **L**anguage). Flash 8 gives you complete and accurate control over position, color, fonts, and other aspects of the screen regardless of the delivery platform (Mac or Windows) or browser (Explorer, Firefox, Netscape, Safari, and others). This is a radical and important departure from traditional HTML authoring, which requires precise planning to ensure that graphics and content appear reliably and consistently on different computer platforms and with various Web browsers. Flash 8 lets designers focus on design instead of HTML workarounds.

Enhanced Interactivity

Although Flash 8 is often known as an animation program, it also provides powerful interactivity tools that allow you to create buttons or free-form interfaces for site navigation that include sound and animation. Flash 8 provides powerful scripting capabilities that make it possible to create complex presentations well beyond the capability of standard HTML or JavaScript. This book covers interactivity in a number of later chapters.

Combine Vectors and Bitmaps

Most graphics on the Internet are bitmap images, such as GIFs or JPEGs. The size of a bitmap file depends on the number of pixels it contains; as the image dimensions increase, so does the file size and download time. In addition to file-size disadvantages, bitmap images that are enlarged beyond their original size often appear distorted, out of focus, and pixilated.

In contrast, graphics created within Flash 8 are composed of **vectors**. Vector images use mathematical formulas to describe the images; bitmaps record information pixel by pixel and color by color. Vector graphics offer much smaller file sizes and increased flexibility for certain types of images, such as those with solid color fills and typographic content. Some images will have a smaller file size as bitmaps, and some will be smaller as vectors. The great thing about Flash 8 is that you can use either type of image.

A bitmap graphic, shown in the illustration on the left, is built pixel by pixel and color by color; a vector graphic, shown in the illustration on the right, is built from mathematical formulas. Vector graphics remain the same file size regardless of their physical dimensions, whereas bitmap graphics increase and decrease depending on their size. As a result, you can use Flash 8 to create and display large vector images and animations without increasing file size.

Video

Embedding video inside SWF files is a huge plus for creating media-rich Web sites, and Macromedia has enhanced the video capabilities even further in this release of Flash. Incorporating video opens the floodgates even further for the types of projects you can create using Flash 8. You will get the chance to learn about the video features in Flash 8 in Chapter 16, "*Video.*"

Scalability

Because Flash 8 movies can use vectors, they can be resized in any Web browser window and still retain their original scale and relative position. Most important, the file size of vector graphics is independent of their display size, making it possible to create full-screen vector animations displaying at any resolution that are only a fraction of the file size of a comparable bitmap graphic.

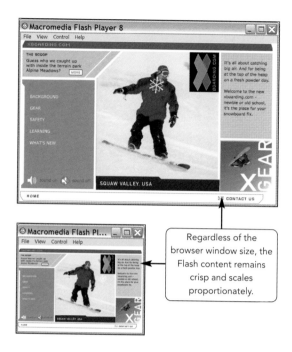

Regardless of the browser window size, the Flash content remains crisp and scales proportionately.

Flash 8 content can be set to scale dynamically within the browser window, as shown in the illustration here.

Does all of this mean you should use only vectors in your Flash 8 movies? Absolutely not. Although Flash 8 is known for its vector capabilities, its support of bitmap images is excellent and far exceeds the support offered by HTML. Specifically, if you scale a bitmap image larger than its original size in HTML, the graphic will become distorted and unattractive. Flash 8 lets bitmaps scale, animate, and transform (skew, distort, and so on) without much image degradation, which means you can, and often will, combine bitmap and vector images in your movies. Delivering both bitmap and vector graphics together lets you create movies that look good at different resolutions and still deliver a bandwidth-friendly file size. You can even use Flash 8 to convert bitmap images into vectors, which you will learn to do in Chapter 9, "Bitmaps."

Streaming Content

Vectors are not the only way Flash 8 makes itself more bandwidth-friendly. Flash 8 files download to Web browsers in small units, which lets the files display some content while the rest is still downloading in the background. Ideally, the content will play more slowly than it downloads, so that the viewing experience is not interrupted. This method of playing one part of an entire Web site while the rest is still downloading is called **streaming**. It differs significantly from the way HTML files are downloaded and displayed in a browser, which takes place one page at a time.

With HTML, all content is organized into pages (HTML files). When you load a page, all the parts of its content are downloaded to the browser and then displayed. Flash 8 movies, on the other hand, can be organized in a very different way.

Imagine a Web site with four or five pages. If it were a pure HTML site, each time you traveled from one page to another you would have to wait for the new page to download before being displayed. With a site built in Flash 8, however, all of the "pages" could be contained in a single movie. When you visit the site, the first page would download and be displayed. While you were reading the first page, the other pages would be downloading in the background. When you clicked on a link to go to another page, it would be displayed immediately! This is the real beauty of streaming. When used correctly, it lets you build a site that eliminates a lot of unwanted waiting that plagues much of the Internet. You'll learn more about how to optimize your Flash 8 content for streaming in Chapter 17, "*Publishing and Exporting.*"

What's New in Flash 8?

Flash 8 offers many upgraded and new features providing a more efficient workflow, greater control over the look and feel of your finished projects, enhanced text support, scripting improvements, and improved video support. The following table outlines the new features:

Flash 8 New Features		
Feature	Flash Basic 8	Flash Professional 8
Gradient enhancements: New, simplified controls allow you to apply more complex gradients containing up to 16 different colors. You can also control gradient focal points more precisely. (See Chapter 3, *"Using the Drawing and Color Tools."*)	✓	✓
Object drawing model: Provides more control and flexibility when creating multiple or overlapping objects. You can now create shapes directly on the Stage that do not interfere with other shapes. Creating a shape with the new object drawing model does not cause changes to other shapes that exist underneath the new shape. (See Chapter 3, *"Using the Drawing and Color Tools."*)	✓	✓
Flash type: Text objects now have a more consistent appearance across both the Flash authoring tool and Flash Player. See Chapter 13, *"Working with Text."*)	✓	✓
Scripting improvements: A new Script Assist mode in the Actions panel lets you create scripts without knowledge of ActionScript. (See Chapter 12, *"ActionScripting Basics and Behaviors."*)	✓	✓
Expanded work area: Macromedia expanded the work area around the Stage and renamed it the Stage pasteboard. You can now store more graphics and other objects on the Stage pasteboard without having them appear during playback of the SWF file. (See Chapter 2, *"Understanding the Interface."*)	✓	✓
Mac document tabs: On the Macintosh only, you can now open multiple Flash files and choose among them from document tabs at the top of the window. (See Chapter 2, *"Understanding the Interface."*)	✓	✓
Enhanced user interface: Macromedia reorganized and streamlined the design of the Preferences dialog box, making it easier to understand and use. (See Chapter 2, *"Understanding the Interface."*)	✓	✓
Single Library panel: You can now view multiple Flash libraries simultaneously in a single Library panel. (See Chapter 11, *"Movie Clips."*)	✓	✓

continues on next page

Flash 8 New Features *continued*		
Feature	Flash Basic 8	Flash Professional 8
Easier publishing: Macromedia streamlined the Publish Settings dialog box, making it easier to publish your Flash projects. (See Chapter 17, *"Publishing and Exporting."*)	✓	✓
Object-level undo mode: You can now track file changes on a per-object basis. When you use this mode, each object on the Stage and in the Library has its own undo list, which lets you undo the changes you make to an object without having to undo changes to any other object.	✓	✓
Blending modes: Flash Professional 8 contains image compositing effects called blending modes. Blending is a method of mixing the color information of a graphic object with the color information of graphic objects beneath it. You can use blending modes to change the appearance of an image on the Stage by combining it in interesting and varied ways with the color content of objects beneath it. (See Chapter 7, *"Filters and Blending Modes."*)		✓
Custom easing controls: New tween animation controls provide improved control over the rate of change at the start, end, and middle of a tween. With these new controls, you can create more complex and realistic tween animations. (See Chapter 8, *"Motion Tweening and Timeline Effects."*)		✓
New video encoder: A new stand-alone video encoder application, Flash 8 Video Encoder, significantly improves video production workflow by providing an easy way to convert video files into the Flash Video (FLV) format. This encoder application can also perform batch processing of video files. (See Chapter 16, *"Video."*)		✓
8-bit alpha support: Flash Professional 8 supports 8-bit alpha channels at video runtime, allowing you to overlay video composited with a transparent or semi-transparent alpha channel over other Flash content. (See Chapter 16, *"Video."*)		✓
Enhanced text anti-aliasing: Improved anti-aliasing settings makes normal and small-sized text appear clearer and easier to read. (See Chapter 13, *"Working with Text."*)		✓
Bitmap smoothing: Bitmap images now look much better on the Stage when greatly enlarged or reduced and also maintain more consistency between the Flash authoring tool and the Flash Player. (See Chapter 9, *"Bitmaps."*)		✓

Project, Player, or Projector?

Flash as a term can be confusing. Macromedia uses the word interchangeably to include Flash as an authoring tool, Flash as a player, and Flash as a stand-alone projector. The following table should help set the groundwork for understanding the differences among the authoring tool, the player, and the stand-alone projector:

Macromedia Flash Applications	
Application	**Description**
Flash authoring tool	The Flash software application creates and edits artwork, animation, sound, and interactive elements, storing the results in the FLA file format. Any changes to the Flash movie must be edited in the production FLA file. It's also the file you need to export the SWF file format, which is embedded into an HTML document and published to the Web.
Flash Player	The Flash Player must be installed in users' Web browsers to see Flash 8 content in the SWF file. This player comes preinstalled in current Web browsers. If, for some reason, you do not have the Flash Player, you can download it from the Macromedia Web site for free.
Flash Projector	You can also store Flash 8 content in stand-alone projectors that do not require a Web browser in order to play. You can distribute these files via email, on CD-ROMs, or on disk, but not typically over the Web. The file extension for a Flash 8 projector is .exe (Windows) or .hqx (Mac).

File Types Associated with Flash 8

You can save and output Flash 8 media in many formats. The most common types of Flash 8 files are project files, movie files, and projector files. The file types can become very confusing, because all of these are commonly referred to as "movies." The following list explains the three most prominent Flash 8 formats. You will learn about all the file types that Flash 8 can produce in detail in Chapter 17, "*Publishing and Exporting.*"

Flash File Types		
Icon	**File Type**	**Description**
Untitled-1.fla	**Projector file (.fla)**	The master project file format, sometimes referred to as the *production file*, stores all the settings and resources for your Flash 8 project. You can reopen and reedit the FLA file at any time using the Flash 8 Authoring Tool. (.fla stands for **FLA**sh.)
Untitled-1.swf	**Movie file (.swf)**	The movie format, sometimes referred to as the *published file* and/or the *optimized file*, can be embedded in Web pages for Web-based Flash 8 presentations. These files are generally not editable. (.swf stands for **S**mall **W**eb **F**ile.)
Untitled-1.exe Untitled-1 Projector	**Windows Projector file (.exe) and Mac Projector file (.hqx)**	A stand-alone projector file that can play on any computer without the need for the Flash Player. Flash 8 writes both Windows and Mac format projector files.

Caution: Player Required!

Flash 8 content is not visible in a Web browser unless either the Macromedia Flash Player or the Shockwave Player has been installed in that browser. In the past, this has been seen as a serious limitation of the format, although over the past few years the number of Internet users who have the player has increased exponentially because current Web browsers now come with the Flash Player preinstalled.

Macromedia has hired an independent consulting firm to maintain an estimate of the number of

Macromedia Flash Players that are in use. At the time of this writing, the Flash player was installed on over 600 million desktops and mobile devices globally, and new versions reach 80 percent of computers on the Web in approximately 12 months. The Macromedia Flash Player 8 comes preinstalled on all new browsers shipped by AOL, CompuServe, Microsoft, and Netscape. Additionally, all versions of Microsoft Windows 98 and newer and Apple OS 8 and newer operating systems include the plug-in.

Macromedia Players	
Flash Player	The Macromedia Flash Player is used for viewing Macromedia Flash content on the Web. You can download the latest version of the Macromedia Flash Player at **http://www.macromedia.com/downloads/**. This player installs inside the player folder for your Web browser of choice.
Shockwave Player	The Shockwave Player is used for viewing Macromedia Director content on the Web. You can download the latest version of the Shockwave Player at **http://www.macromedia.com/downloads/**.

Beyond Flash 8

Flash 8 is an incredibly powerful tool by itself. However, there are a few functions it can't perform. Here are some of the Web technologies you should know about if you want to extend Flash 8 beyond its basic capabilities.

What's CGI?
A CGI (**C**ommon **G**ateway **I**nterface) script is a program that defines a standard way of exchanging information between a Web browser and a Web server. You can write CGI scripts in any number of languages (Perl, C, ASP, and others). If you plan to create a complex Web application that requires the use of something like CGI, I recommend you work with a Web engineer who has experience creating these kinds of scripts. Flash 8

can communicate with CGI scripts, although that topic is beyond the scope of this book.

For further information on using CGI, please check out the following URLs:

http://www.cgidir.com/

http://www.cgi101.com/

http://www.icthus.net/CGI-City/

What's XML?
XML (**EX**tensible **M**arkup **L**anguage) is a standard that handles the description and exchange of data. XML enables developers to define markup languages that define the structure and meaning of information. Therefore, an XML document is much

like a database presented in a text file. You can transform XML content into a variety of different formats, including HTML, WML, and VoiceXML.

XML differs from HTML in that it is not predefined—you create the tags and attributes. You can also use XML to create your own data structure and modify it for the data you want it to carry. In Flash 8, you can use the XML object to create, manipulate, and pass that data. Using ActionScripting, a Flash 8 movie can load and process XML data. As a result, an XML-savvy Flash 8 developer can develop a movie that dynamically retrieves data from the external XML document instead of creating static text fields within a project file.

Just as HTML provided an open, platform-independent format for distributing Web documents, XML has become the open, platform-independent format for exchanging any type of electronic information. Like CGI, XML is also a topic beyond the scope of this book.

For further information on XML, take a look at the following URLs:

http://www.ait-usa.com/xmlintro/xmlproject/article.htm

http://www.xml.com/

http://www.xmlfiles.com/

JavaScript and Flash 8

The Flash 8 scripting language is ActionScript, which is based on JavaScript, another scripting language. Although they share a similar syntax and structure, they are two different languages. One way to tell them apart is that ActionScript uses scripts that are processed entirely within the Macromedia Flash Player, independently of the browser that is used to view the file. JavaScript, on the other hand, uses external interpreters that vary according to the browser used.

You can use ActionScript and JavaScript together because Flash 8 lets you call JavaScript commands to perform tasks or to send and receive data. A basic knowledge of JavaScript can make learning ActionScript easier, because the basic syntax of the scripts and the handling of objects is the same in both languages. However, this is not a requirement for learning ActionScripting.

You will be introduced to ActionScripting in Chapter 12, "ActionScript Basics and Behaviors," which gives you hands-on experience in applying the powerful scripting language. For further information and tutorials about JavaScript and how to use it in conjunction with Flash 8, check out the following URLs:

http://www.javascript.com/

http://javascript.internet.com/

http://www.flashkit.com/links/Javascripts/

That's a wrap for this chapter. You've familiarized yourself with the Flash 8 product line, the new features of Flash 8, and how to extend Flash content using various technologies. Now it's time to learn more about the Flash interface. On to the next chapter!

2

Understanding the Interface

If you are new to Flash 8, don't skip this chapter. Although you might be tempted to jump right in with the hands-on exercises, take the time to read through this chapter first so you can get a "big picture" look at the Flash 8 interface.

This chapter begins with an overview of the main interface elements: the Timeline, the Stage, the Stage pasteboard, and the various panels in Flash 8. This will be a relatively short overview so you can get to the actual exercises as quickly as possible. After all, hands-on exercises are the best way to learn how these tools work.

If you are a veteran of Flash MX 2004, feel free to skim this chapter, but be sure to check out the new features in the Actions panel and the toolbar.

The Document Window

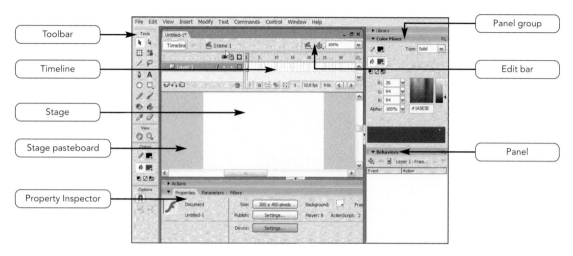

The Document window contains six main elements: the Timeline, Stage, Stage pasteboard area, edit bar, toolbar, and panels, plus the Property Inspector.

Each time you create a new document in Flash 8, you are presented with a blank Document window, which is divided into six main components:

Timeline: The Timeline controls all the elements in a project file, including layers, frames, the playhead, and the status bar. You'll learn more about these features later in this chapter. By default, the Timeline is docked above the Stage, but you can undock and move the Timeline to any location onscreen. You'll learn how later in this chapter.

Stage: The Stage displays your animations, images, and other content. It is the area visible to users after you publish or export a finished project. You'll learn how to modify the properties of the Stage, such as size, color, and frame rate, in Chapter 4, "*Animation Basics*," and how to export and publish projects in Chapter 17, "*Publishing and Exporting*."

Stage pasteboard: The Stage pasteboard—newly expanded in Flash 8—is the light-gray area around the Stage. The contents of the Stage pasteboard are not visible to users when you export or publish your projects. As a result, you can place objects here and animate them onto the Stage so they enter and exit from offstage. You can also

store objects with no graphic representation, such as data elements, on the Stage pasteboard, keeping the Stage uncluttered.

Edit bar: The edit bar displays your current location inside the project file, including the name of the current scene. It also provides controls for editing scenes and symbols and lets you change the magnification using the Zoom box. The edit bar changes location depending on whether the Timeline is docked or undocked. (You'll learn how to dock and undock the Timeline later in this chapter.)

Toolbar: The toolbar contains tools for creating and editing artwork. This long vertical bar gives you access to just about every tool you need to create and modify objects.

Panels: Each panel has a unique set of tools or information for viewing or modifying specific file elements. For example, the contents of the Property Inspector change based on the object selected on the Stage, letting you make changes to the current selection quickly, right inside the panel. You'll learn more about panels later in this chapter.

The Timeline

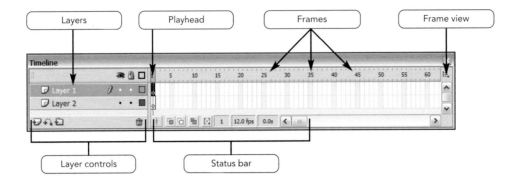

Layers   Playhead   Frames   Frame view

Layer controls   Status bar

The Timeline controls and displays the static and moving elements of a project over time. In this section, you'll learn about the main elements of the Timeline. You'll get more in-depth, hands-on experience with the Timeline as you complete the exercises throughout in this book.

Playhead: The playhead indicates which frame in the Timeline is currently displayed on the Stage. Once you have two or more frames of artwork on the Stage (which you'll learn to do in Chapter 3, "*Using the Drawing and Color Tools*"), you can click and drag the playhead to move it to a specific frame. You can also scrub (scan) through the Timeline to quickly preview animations. You'll get a lot of practice doing this in the animation sections of this book.

Layer controls: The layer controls let you add, organize, hide, and lock layers. They also let you display the contents of layers as outlines. You'll learn more about the layer controls later in this chapter.

Status bar: The status bar gives you feedback about the current frame, the frame rate in frames per second (fps), and the elapsed time of your movie. It also contains tools that let you perform onion skinning and edit multiple frames. You'll learn about these features in Chapter 4, "*Animation Basics.*"

Frame view: This pop-up menu lets you control the appearance of the Timeline. You can change the appearance of the individual frames or the entire size of the Timeline itself. As you'll see in

Chapter 14, "*Sound,*" changing the Timeline's appearance can be very helpful with certain types of projects.

Docking and Undocking the Timeline

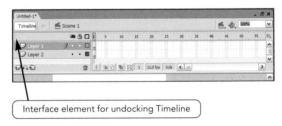

Interface element for undocking Timeline

If you have the luxury of working with a large monitor or multiple monitors, you can easily dock and undock the Timeline from the main document window, which gives you more flexibility in arranging your work environment. For example, you can place the Stage on one monitor and stash all the Flash 8 panels on your second monitor, giving you an uncluttered view of your work.

You can dock and undock the Timeline easily: Position your cursor over the gripper (the grid of dots) in the upper-left corner of the Timeline until the cursor changes to an icon with four arrows. Click and drag to undock the Timeline. As you click and drag, you'll see a thin outline around the perimeter of the Timeline, indicating you are moving it.

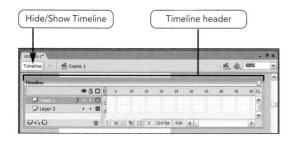

Hide/Show Timeline

Timeline header

When you release the mouse, the Timeline is undocked from the Document window, and it will appear as its own window. Once it is undocked, you can click and drag the Timeline header to drag it to any location onscreen.

If you want to redock the Timeline to the Document window, you can dock it in the default position above the Stage, or on the right, left, or bottom portion of the Document window.

To redock the Timeline, click and drag the Timeline header to the desired location. When you release the mouse, the Timeline will dock automatically.

Tip: If you want to reposition the Timeline without docking to one of the positions just listed, hold down the **Ctrl** (Windows) key or **Cmd** (Mac) key as you reposition the Timeline.

One other handy Timeline interface feature is the **Hide/Show Timeline** button. Click the button to toggle the Timeline display on or off.

The Layer Controls

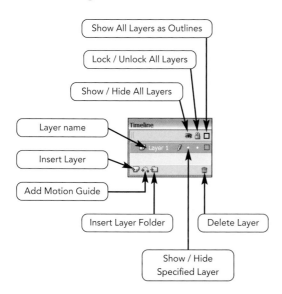

Show All Layers as Outlines

Lock / Unlock All Layers

Show / Hide All Layers

Layer name

Insert Layer

Add Motion Guide

Insert Layer Folder

Delete Layer

Show / Hide Specified Layer

Like most graphics applications, Flash 8 has an excellent set of tools for working with layers. The Timeline's layer controls play an important role in your workflow. You'll use them to add, modify, delete, and organize layers, and hide, lock, and control the appearance of the layer contents. As

you add layers in Flash 8, the artwork on the topmost layer in the Timeline stacks on top of artwork on lower layers. At any time, you can rearrange the stacking order of the artwork by dragging and dropping the layers in the layer controls area. The following list explains the layer controls in more detail:

Layer name: The default layer names are Layer 1, Layer 2, and so on. Double-click a layer name to rename it. Give your layers short, descriptive names to help you easily identify the contents on each layer.

Insert Layer button: Click this button to add new layers to your projects. Each time you add a new layer, it is automatically created on top of the currently selected layer.

Add Motion Guide button: Click this button to add a guide layer on top of the currently selected layer. A guide layer contains objects you can animate along a path drawn on the guide layer. You'll work with guide layers in Chapter 8, "Motion Tweening and Timeline Effects."

Insert Layer Folder button: Click this button to create a layer folder. Layer folders help you organize your layers into groups that you can easily expand and collapse.

Delete Layer button: Click this button to delete the currently selected layer. If you accidentally delete a layer, you can undo your actions by choosing **Edit > Undo Delete Layer**.

Show/Hide All Layers button: Toggle the eye icon to hide and show the artwork on the Stage and the contents of all layers in the Timeline. Toggle the eye icon on a specific layer to hide the contents of that layer. **Note:** Hiding layers does not hide your artwork in the published movie. To hide the contents of layers in a finished movie, place the artwork in the Stage pasteboard area.

Lock/Unlock Layers button: Click the padlock icon to lock the currently selected layer, making it

impossible to edit the contents of the layer. You'll find this feature useful when you start working with multiple layers—especially ones with overlapping content—because it will prevent you from accidentally making changes to the layer. **Tip:** To lock all layers except the currently selected layer, **Alt+click** (Windows) or **Option+click** (Mac) the padlock column of the currently selected layer.

Show All Layers as Outlines button: Click the outline icon to display the contents of the layers in the Timeline in Outline view. Outline view represents solid shapes as outlined shapes with no solid fill. You'll find this feature helpful when you're working with multiple layers with overlapping content—it lets you see the content more clearly. Displaying your content as outlines also increases the speed at which Flash 8 can redraw the screen, especially during complex animation sequences.

The Edit Bar

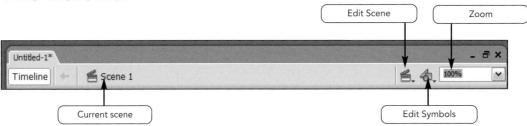

The edit bar provides quick, visual feedback about where you are located in your movie. It contains buttons and a pop-up menu and provides quick access to the scenes and zoom levels. Here is a brief description of each feature in the edit bar:

Current scene: The scene currently open on the Stage appears on the edit bar. You'll learn about scenes in Chapter 12, "*ActionScript Basics and Behaviors.*"

Edit Scene pop-up menu: If your movie contains more than one scene, the Edit Scene pop-up menu displays a list of all the scenes in your project file. You'll learn how to use multiple

scenes in Chapter 12, "*ActionScript Basics and Behaviors.*" You'll find this readout indispensable for determining exactly where you are in the Flash authoring environment.

Edit Symbols pop-up menu: The Edit Symbols pop-up menu displays all of the symbols in your project. You'll learn about symbols in Chapter 6, "*Symbols and Instances.*"

Zoom box: The Zoom box lets you zoom in and out of the Stage.

The Toolbar

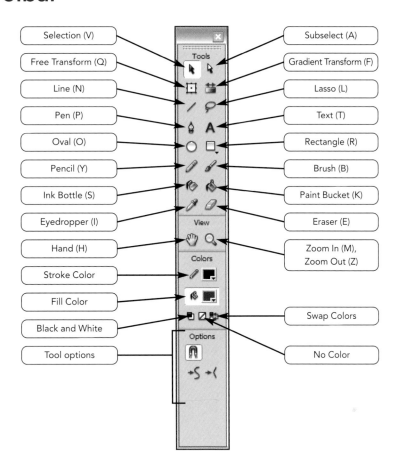

Selection (V)	Subselect (A)
Free Transform (Q)	Gradient Transform (F)
Line (N)	Lasso (L)
Pen (P)	Text (T)
Oval (O)	Rectangle (R)
Pencil (Y)	Brush (B)
Ink Bottle (S)	Paint Bucket (K)
Eyedropper (I)	Eraser (E)
Hand (H)	Zoom In (M), Zoom Out (Z)
Stroke Color	
Fill Color	
Black and White	Swap Colors
Tool options	No Color

The toolbar contains tools for creating and editing artwork. Each of the main tools has an associated keyboard shortcut, which is listed in parentheses next to the tool name in the illustration. You will learn more about the various tools in the toolbar in Chapter 3, "Using the Drawing and Color Tools," and in various exercises throughout the book.

When you hover over a toolbar icon, a small tooltip appears with the name and keyboard shortcut for the tool. You can disable the tooltips feature in the General Preferences dialog box by choosing **Edit > Preferences > General** (Windows) or **Flash Professional > Preferences > General** (Mac).

WARNING: | **Docking the Toolbar on Windows vs. Macintosh**

By default, the toolbar is located in the upper-left corner of the application window. You can click and drag to reposition the toolbar anywhere onscreen. In Windows, you can dock the toolbar vertically along either side of the application window. On a Mac, you can reposition the toolbar anywhere inside the application window, but you can't dock it.

The Panels

Panels are windows containing tools and information to help you work in your project file more efficiently. You can use each panel to view and modify elements within your project file. The options within the panels let you change settings, such as color, type, size, rotation, and many others. You can display, hide, move, resize, group, and organize the panels in any way you wish. In the next few sections, you'll learn how to dock, resize, and work with panels. At the end of this section, you'll find a quick reference describing the panels in Flash 8.

Undocking and Docking Panels

You can easily dock and undock panels to create new combinations that better fit your workflow preferences.

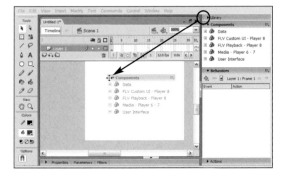

To undock a panel, position your cursor over the gripper in the upper-left corner of the panel title bar. Notice the pointer becomes an icon with four arrows. Click and drag to undock the panel to any location onscreen.

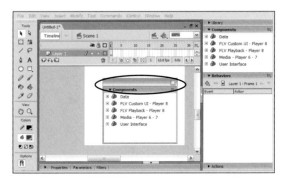

After you undock a panel, you can move it around the work area by clicking and dragging the panel's title bar.

To redock a panel or add it to another panel group, position your cursor over the panel's gripper. Click and drag the panel onto another panel until you see a dark outline over the panel. When you release your mouse, the panel is added to the panel group.

Resizing Panels

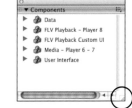

Windows panel   Macintosh panel

You can resize panels by clicking and dragging the panel's border (Windows) or by dragging the lower-right corner (Mac), as shown in the illustration here.

Note: Some of the panels, such as the Property Inspector and the toolbar, cannot be resized. In the case of the Property Inspector (but interestingly, not the toolbar), the cursor will not turn into the resize arrows when you move it over the border (Windows), or you will not see the lines in the lower-right corner of the panel (Mac), which indicates you cannot resize the panel.

Expanding, Collapsing, Hiding, and Closing Panels

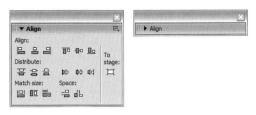

Panel expanded   Panel collapsed

To expand and collapse the contents of a panel, click the triangle next to the panel name. **Tip:** To show or hide all of the panels in your document, press **F4** or choose **Window > Hide Panels** to close all of the panels.

Using the Panel Options Menu

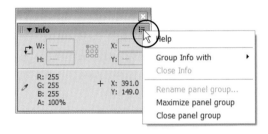

Many panels have a menu in the upper-right corner, as shown in the illustration here. To display the contents of the menu, simply click it. **Note:** If a panel is collapsed, you cannot open this menu.

Creating and Saving Workspace Layouts

Flash 8 lets you create custom workspace layouts, which you can save and use at any time. This feature lets you quickly organize your workspace for specific tasks. For example, you can create different workspace layouts for drawing, animation, or working with ActionScripts. The following steps walk you through the process of saving a custom workspace layout:

1. Choose **Window > Workspace Layout > Save Current** to open the **Save Workspace Layout** dialog box.

2. Type a name in the **Name** field and click **OK**. That's all there is to it!

Switching Workspace Layouts

To switch between different workspace layouts, choose **Window > Workspace Layout** and choose a workspace layout. **Note:** To return the panels to their default locations, choose **Window > Workspace Layout > Default**.

Renaming and Deleting Workspace Layouts

You can rename or delete workspace layouts from the **Manage Workspace Layouts** dialog box.

1. Choose **Window > Workspace Layout > Manage** to open the **Manage Workspace Layouts** dialog box.

2. To delete a workspace layout, select it and then click **Delete**. Click **OK**.

3. To rename a workspace layout, select it and then click **Rename**. This opens the **Rename Workspace Layout** dialog box. Type a new name in the **Name** field and click **OK** to close the dialog box. Click **OK** again to close the **Manage Workspace Layouts** dialog box.

Defining the Panels

This section briefly describes the panels in Flash 8. As you navigate through the exercises in this book, you'll work in-depth with each of these panels.

You can open panels in one of two ways: choosing it from the Window menu or using the associated keyboard shortcut. (See the "Panel Keyboard Shortcuts in Flash 8" table later in this chapter.)

Here is a description of each of the panels in Flash 8:

Main panel (Window > Toolbars > Main): Lets you perform simple tasks such as creating, saving, and opening Flash movies, and printing movie frames.

Note: The Main panel appears in Windows only.

Controller panel (Window >Toolbars > Controller): Provides one way of previewing your movie. The Controller panel contains features similar to those on a remote control, letting you stop, rewind, fast-forward, and play your movie.

Edit bar (Window > Toolbars > Edit Bar): Gives you quick visual feedback about your current location, lets you navigate to different scenes in your Flash movie, and contains a pop-up menu for zooming into or out of the Stage. It's a good idea to keep the edit bar open at all times while authoring in Flash 8.

Property Inspector (Window > Properties > Properties): Is a one-stop panel for displaying and changing the most commonly used attributes of

the current selection on the Stage. This context-sensitive panel lets you modify the current selection using only one panel, rather than having to open several panels. This is another panel you'll want to keep open at all times while authoring your movies.

Timeline (Window > Timeline): Controls and displays the static and moving elements of your Flash 8 projects. The layers represent the depth of the objects in your movie; the frames represent how they change over time.

Toolbar (Window > Tools): Contains tools for drawing, painting, selecting, and modifying artwork. The toolbar is another important one you'll use frequently. For a listing of the keyboard shortcuts to the tools, refer to the "Toolbar" section earlier in this chapter.

Library panel (Window > Library): Provides a location for you to store and organize specific assets within your project, including symbols, imported artwork, sound files, and video files. You will learn about the Library panel in Chapter 6, *"Symbols and Instances."*

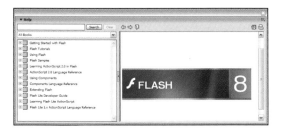

Help panel (Help > Help): Lets you access all Help information within the program and provides context-sensitive reference and tutorials, including information about ActionScript usage and syntax. The Help panel is an essential tool for learning both Flash and ActionScript.

Align panel (Window > Align): Gives you access to several different alignment and distribution options.

Color Mixer panel (Window > Color Mixer): Lets you create new colors in one of three different modes—RGB (red, green, blue), HSB (hue, saturation, brightness), or HEX (hexadecimal). The Color Mixer panel also lets you add alpha and work with different types of gradients.

Color Swatches panel (Window > Color Swatches): Displays a file's color palette. The default color palette is the Web-safe palette of 216 colors, but you can add colors by using the **Color Mixer** panel.

The **Color Swatches** panel also lets you import and export palettes between Flash files, as well as between Flash and other applications, such as Macromedia Fireworks and Adobe Photoshop. Use the **Color Swatches** panel to duplicate colors, remove colors, change the default palette, reload the Web-safe palette (if you have replaced it), or sort the palette according to hue.

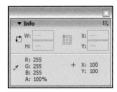

Info panel (Window > Info): Contains numerical information about the size, position, and color of the selected object. The Info panel is very helpful when you need specific positions and measurements.

Scene panel (Window > Other Panels > Scene): Displays a list of all the scenes in your movie. The Scene panel lets you quickly add, duplicate, delete, name, or rename scenes, and it also provides a way to jump to different scenes in your project.

Transform panel (Window > Transform): Lets you numerically transform (rotate, scale, and skew) an object. This panel also lets you create a transformed copy of an object.

Actions panel (Window > Actions): Lets you add and modify actions for a frame, button, or movie

clip. You will learn all about the Actions panel in Chapter 12, *"ActionScript Basics and Behaviors."*

Behaviors panel (Window > Behaviors): Lets you add interactivity to your Flash movies without the need for explicit coding in the Actions panel. Using the Behaviors panel, you can quickly perform common actions such as stopping and starting playback of audio and video or moving the playback head to a specified frame. You will learn more about behaviors in Chapter 12, *"ActionScript Basics and Behaviors."*

Components panel (Window > Components): Organizes your move components—movie clips containing complex ActionScript elements. Components save time and effort by letting you add powerful functionality to your movies without the need to learn advanced ActionScripting. Flash 8 features several new components. You will learn more about components in Chapter 15, *"Components and Forms."*

Component Inspector (Window > Component Inspector): Lets you set the parameters (attributes) of a component after you add an instance of that component to your movie.

Debugger panel (Window > Debugger): Checks and displays errors while a movie is playing in the Flash Player.

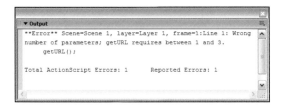

Output panel (Window > Output): Provides assistance during troubleshooting by displaying feedback information after you test your movie.

Accessibility panel (Window > Other Panels > Accessibility): Gives you options to help make your movies more accessible to people with visual or auditory disabilities. Also, support for third-party plug-ins lets you offer improved solutions for screen reading and closed captioning. You will learn more about creating accessible content in Chapter 19, "*Integration.*"

History panel (Window > Other Panels > History): Lets you track the steps you've completed in your Flash document and convert those steps into reusable commands to automate repetitive tasks.

Movie Explorer panel (Window > Movie Explorer): Displays the contents of your movie, organized in a hierarchical tree. Use this panel to quickly locate specific elements within your project file. You will learn about the Movie Explorer panel in Chapter 18, "*Putting It All Together.*"

Web Services panel (Window > Other Panels > Web Services): Lets you view, refresh, add, or delete Web services. After a Web service—such as the results of a database search query or search results from Google—has been added, the service is available to any Flash application you create.

Strings panel (Window > Other Panels > Strings): Assists in deploying text content into multiple languages. This is an advanced feature and is outside of the scope of this book. For more information about the **Strings** panel, refer to the Flash 8 Help and search for "strings panel".

Common Library panels (Window > Common Libraries): Provides access to sample libraries included with Flash 8. These libraries contain pre-made buttons, learning interactions, and sounds you can use in your movies.

Keyboard Shortcuts

If you're a keyboard shortcut junkie, you'll want to add these shortcuts to the various panels under your belt. For a listing of the keyboard shortcuts for each of the tools in the toolbar, refer to the "Toolbar" section earlier in this chapter.

Panel Keyboard Shortcuts in Flash 8

Panel	Windows	Macintosh
Property Inspector	Ctrl+F3	Cmd+F3
Timeline	Ctrl+Alt+T	Option+Cmd+T
Tools	Ctrl+F2	Cmd+F2
Library	Ctrl+L	Cmd+L
Align	Ctrl+K	Cmd+K
Color Mixer	Shift+F9	Shift+F9
Color Swatches	Ctrl+F9	Cmd+F9
Info	Ctrl+I	Cmd+I
Scene	Shift+F2	Shift+F2
Transform	Ctrl+T	Cmd+T
Help	F1	F1
Actions	F9	Option+F9
Behaviors	Shift+F3	Shift+F3
Components	Ctrl+F7	Cmd+F7
Component Inspector	Alt+F7	Option+F7
Debugger	Shift+F4	Shift+F4
Output	F2	F2
Accessibility	Alt+F2	Option+F2
History	Ctrl+F10	Cmd+F10
Movie Explorer	Alt+F3	Option+F3
Strings	Ctrl+F11	Cmd+F11
Web Services	Ctrl+Shift+F10	Cmd+Shift+F10

EXERCISE

1 | Creating a New Custom Keyboard Shortcut Set

To further streamline your workflow, you can create, modify, duplicate, and delete sets of custom keyboard shortcuts. Flash 8 has an entire interface dedicated to making this process easier. One of its niftiest features lets you assign keyboard shortcuts in Flash 8 that match those used in other programs, including Fireworks, Freehand, Photoshop, and even earlier versions of Flash! You may be thinking, "Hey, this is only for power users," but you'll be a power user in no time, right?

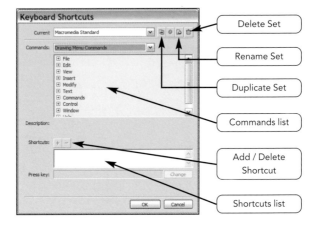

The following steps outline the process of creating, modifying, and deleting custom keyboard shortcuts. This isn't an exercise that you have to complete now; if you'd like, just make a mental note of it for later use.

---

1 Choose **Edit > Keyboard Shortcuts** (Windows) or **Flash > Keyboard Shortcuts** (Mac) to open the **Keyboard Shortcuts** dialog box.

---

2 In the upper-right corner of the dialog box, click the **Duplicate Set** button to open the **Duplicate** dialog box. From here, you can create a copy of the current keyboard shortcut set, ensuring you don't make permanent changes to the original keyboard shortcut set.

---

3 Type a name for new the keyboard short-cut set in the **Duplicate name** field. Try to stick to a meaningful name you can recall later. Click **OK**.

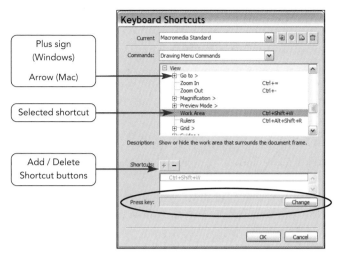

Plus sign
(Windows)

Arrow (Mac)

Selected shortcut

Add / Delete
Shortcut buttons

4 Back in the **Keyboard Shortcuts** dialog box, choose an option from the **Commands** pop-up menu. If necessary, click the **plus** (+) sign (Windows) or the **arrow** (Mac) next to a command to drill down and display additional keyboard shortcuts. Click to select the keyboard shortcut you want to change.

---

5 Click the **Add Shortcut** or **Delete Shortcut** button to add or delete the currently selected keyboard shortcut.

---

6 Press the keys you want to use as the keyboard shortcut to assign it to the option. Notice the shortcut key appears in the **Press key** text box. Click **Change** to confirm your selection and assign it to the menu item.

Note: If the key combination you selected is already in use, you will get an error message at the bottom of the dialog box.

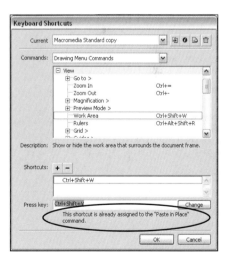

Well, that's a quick run-through of the Flash 8 interface. Now that you are more familiar with the "big picture," let's narrow the focus to specific interface elements. In the next chapter, you'll work with the drawing and coloring tools in the tool-bar. Flash 8 has a powerful set of graphics tools for creating any kind of artwork and animation imaginable. So go ahead, turn to the next page and get started.

3

Using the Drawing and Color Tools

Flash 8 has a powerful set of drawing and color tools to help you create artwork for your animations. In addition to creating drawings from scratch, you can also import existing artwork into Flash 8 from other programs such as FreeHand, Fireworks, Photoshop, or Illustrator. You'll learn how in Chapter 19, *"Integration."*

In this chapter, you'll learn how to create drawings from scratch in Flash 8 using the drawing and color tools. You'll also learn how to apply complex gradients to objects, and you'll learn about the new object drawing model, which makes it easier to work with and modify shapes.

Drawing Tools Defined

Flash 8 contains a set of powerful drawing tools. Although many of them may be familiar to you from other programs, you'll find some tools are quite unique. The following chart outlines the behavior of each drawing tool, including the associated keyboard shortcuts, which may be familiar to you from Chapter 2, "*Understanding the Interface.*" Don't feel compelled to read through everything here. If you want to jump into the exercises, go right ahead. Either way, you'll be comfortable drawing in Flash 8 in a very short time!

Drawing Tools in Flash 8		
Icon	**Name**	**What Does It Do?**
▶	**Selection (V)**	Selects, moves, and edits shapes and drawings.
▶	**Subselection (A)**	Modifies the anchor points and tangent handles of a shape's path or outline.
⊡	**Free Transform (Q)**	Freely transforms objects, groups, instances, or text blocks. With this tool, you can move, rotate, scale, skew, and distort individual transformations or combine several transformations all at once.
▤	**Gradient Transform (F)**	Modifies the gradient fills of shapes. With this tool, you can adjust the size, direction, or center of the fill; precisely control the location of the gradient focal point; and apply other parameters to your gradients.
╱	**Line (N)**	Draws straight lines. Holding down the Shift key lets you constrain the lines to 45-degree angles. You can modify the lines drawn with this tool with the Ink Bottle tool or by using the controls in the Property Inspector.
◔	**Lasso (L)**	Creates irregular-shaped selections of your artwork by drawing a freehand selection around it. Use the Lasso options to fine-tune and adjust your selections.
✎	**Pen (P)**	Creates straight or curved line segments and is the only drawing tool in Flash 8 that lets you create Bézier curves, which gives you precise control of your line segments.
A	**Text (T)**	Creates static text or text fields. With text fields, you can accept user input and even display HTML-formatted text that's been loaded from an external text file into a movie.
○	**Oval (O)**	Creates circles and ovals composed of fills and strokes, just fills, or just strokes. Holding down the Shift key lets you create perfect circles. Holding down the Alt key (Windows) or the Option key (Mac) lets you draw a circle or oval from the center.

continues on next page

Drawing Tools in Flash 8 *continued*

Icon	Name	What Does It Do?
	Rectangle (R)	Creates rectangles and squares composed of strokes and fills, just strokes, or just fills. Holding down the Shift key creates perfect squares. Holding down the Alt key (Windows) or the Option key (Mac) lets you draw a rectangle or square from the center.
	Pencil (Y)	Creates lines in one of three different modes: Straighten, Smooth, and Ink.
	Brush (B)	Creates shapes with fills only. You can adjust the size, style, and behavior of the brush by adjusting the tool options or by using the Property Inspector.
	Ink Bottle (S)	Changes the color or width of a line or adds a stroke to a shape. The Ink Bottle has no effect on the fill of a shape.
	Paint Bucket (K)	Adds a fill inside a shape and can change the color of a fill. The Paint Bucket has no effect on the stroke of a shape.
	Eyedropper (I)	Copies the fill or stroke attributes of an object so you can apply them to another object. This tool is especially useful when you want to copy the exact color of one object and use it on another object.
	Eraser (E)	Removes any unwanted image areas on the Stage. Holding down the Shift key lets you erase in perfect horizontal and vertical lines.

Lines, Strokes, and Fills Defined

In addition to learning how each of the drawing tools behave, you need to understand the difference between fills, strokes, lines, and shapes. These differences can be confusing because the interface refers to both lines and strokes. The following chart provides an example and a brief explanation of each:

Lines, Strokes, and Fills		
Lines and strokes		Create line drawings with the Pencil, Pen, and Line tools. Create strokes or outlines with the Rectangle and Oval tools. The terms *stroke* and *fill* are used interchangeably in the Flash 8 documentation and throughout this book because you can modify both shapes and strokes using the same tools. Lines and strokes are independent of fills, and you can modify them using the Ink Bottle, the Color and Tool modifiers in the toolbar, the Color Mixer panel, or using the Stroke Color in the Property Inspector.
Fills		Create fills with the Brush and Paint Bucket tools. You can create fills without strokes, as shown in the illustration here. You can modify fills using the Paint Bucket, the Color and Tool modifiers in the toolbar, the Color Mixer panel, or the Property Inspector.
Strokes, lines, fills, and shapes		Attach strokes and lines to fills, as shown in the illustration here, with the Ink Bottle tool. Modify them using the Ink Bottle, the Color and Tool modifiers in the toolbar, the Color Mixer panel, or the Property Inspector. Flash 8 refers to strokes, lines, fills, or a combination thereof, as *shapes*. Shapes appear as a dotted mesh on the Stage and display the word *shape* in the Property Inspector.

1 | Drawing with the Pencil Tool

The Pencil tool creates freehand line drawings. By selecting one of the three modes—Straighten, Smooth, or Ink—you can control how the lines are drawn. In this exercise, you will draw a circle with the Pencil tool using each of the three modes, so you can better understand how each one behaves.

---

1 Copy the **chap_03** folder from the **HOT CD-ROM** to your **Desktop**. Open **pencil.fla** from the **chap_03** folder.

As you can see, **pencil.fla** is a blank file with the Stage dimensions set to 400 x 200 pixels, which should be enough space for you to draw some shapes.

---

2 Select the **Pencil** tool from the **toolbar** and choose **Straighten** from the **Options** pop-up menu.

As you can see, the Options section of the toolbar is context-sensitive based on the tool selected in the toolbar.

NOTE:

About the Pencil Tool Modes

In Flash 8, the Pencil tool is similar to tools in other graphics programs, such as Adobe Illustrator and Adobe Photoshop. One of the great features of the Pencil tool in Flash 8 is the different drawing modes—Straighten, Smooth, and Ink—which give you more precise control over your drawings.

Straighten
Perfect look

Smooth
Smooth look

Ink
Hand-drawn look

As you can see in the illustration here, drawing with the Straighten mode creates perfect, geometric shapes, drawing with the Smooth mode smoothes out the edges of shapes, and drawing with the Ink mode represents the line exactly as you draw it, giving it the most hand-drawn appearance of the three modes.

The circles as you draw in Straighten mode   *The circle when you finish drawing in Straighten mode*

3 Click and drag to draw a circle on the **Stage**.

Notice when you release the mouse, the shape automatically snaps to a perfect circle. The Straighten mode guesses what shape you are trying to draw and automatically creates a perfect, geometric shape.

4 In the **toolbar**, choose **Smooth** from the **Options** pop-up menu.

The circle as you draw in Smooth mode   *The circle when you finish drawing in Smooth mode*

5 Click and drag to draw another circle on the **Stage**.

Notice when your release the mouse, the circle gets smoother, but the change is less significant than when you used Straighten mode.

The circle as you draw in Ink mode   *The circle when you release the mouse button*

6 In the **toolbar**, choose **Ink** from the **Options** pop-up menu. Click and drag to draw a third circle on the **Stage**.

Notice when using the Ink mode there is very little change in the circle when you release the mouse.

7 Tired of drawing circles? Go ahead and practice drawing other simple shapes, such as squares, triangles, polygons, and so on, with each of the different **Pencil** options. You'll get an even better idea of how each drawing mode works and how they can help you create artwork in Flash 8.

Tip: To clear the **Stage**, press **Ctrl+A** (Windows) or **Cmd+A** (Mac) to select everything on the **Stage**, then press the **Delete** key.

8 When you are done playing with the **Pencil** tool, close **pencil.fla**. You don't need to save your changes.

2 | Using the Oval and Rectangle Tools

The Oval and Rectangle tools are ideal for creating geometric shapes, such as ovals, circles, rectangles, and squares. You can create simple shapes with independent lines and fills quickly and effortlessly. In this exercise, you'll learn how to use these tools.

1 Open **shapes.fla**, which is a blank file you can use to draw shapes, from the **chap_03** folder.

2 Select the **Oval** tool from the **toolbar**. At the bottom of the **toolbar** are two options: **Object Drawing**, which lets you choose which drawing model to use (you will learn about drawing models later in this chapter), and **Snap to Objects**, which makes it easier to align objects on the **Stage**. Click the **Snap to Objects** button.

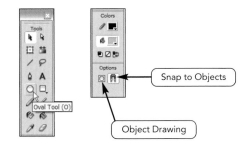

In this exercise, you'll learn how to create shapes using the merge drawing model (the default drawing model) and the Snap to Objects feature. Later in this chapter, you'll create shapes using the new object drawing model.

3 Hold down the **Shift** key and click and drag to draw a circle on the **Stage**.

Holding down the Shift key while drawing creates a perfect circle. Notice Flash 8 automatically uses the current fill and stroke colors to create the circle.

4 Click and drag to create an oval on the **Stage**.

Notice when you don't hold down the Shift key while drawing, Flash 8 doesn't constrain the shape as a perfect circle. Also notice the drawing pointer is different than it was in Step 3. The pointer change is a visual clue that you are drawing an oval or a circle.

5 Select the **Rectangle** tool from the **toolbar**. In the **Options** area of the toolbar, leave the **Snap to Objects** button turned on and the **Object Drawing** button turned off.

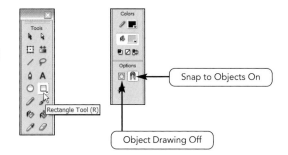

Snap to Objects On

Object Drawing Off

---

6 Hold down the **Shift** key and click and drag to create a square on the **Stage**.

Notice the pointer indicates you are drawing a "perfect shape," the same as it did when you created a circle in Step 3. Again, just as when you created the circle and oval, Flash 8 uses the selected fill and line colors.

Take a look at the corners of the square you just drew. Notice they are square, 90 degree corners. What if you want to create rounded corners? Not to worry, you can easily create rounded corners using the Set Corner Radius feature. You'll learn how in the next steps.

---

7 At the bottom of the **toolbar**, click the **Set Corner Radius** button to open the **Rectangle Settings** dialog box.

Set Corner Radius

---

8 Type **25** in the **Corner radius** field and click **OK**.

This option will add rounded corners with a 25-point radius to the next rectangle you draw. You can enter a value between 0 and 999 in the Rectangle Settings dialog box. The higher the number, the more rounded the corners.

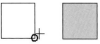

---

9 Click and drag to draw another rectangle on the **Stage**.

Notice the corners of the rectangle are rounded, reflecting the value you entered in the Rectangle Settings dialog box. Nice!

Rounding Corners As You Draw

You may find it difficult to determine the exact radius of the corners you want before you draw a rectangle and, unfortunately, you can't use the Set Corner Radius option after you draw a rectangle. Luckily, a handy keyboard shortcut helps you interactively create rounded corners as you draw rectangles in Flash 8. As you click and drag to draw a rectangle, press the **down** arrow to increase the corner radius or press the **up** arrow to increase the corner radius. This is a very cool little shortcut you'll use often!

Oval and Rectangle Settings

If you want to create a specific-sized oval or rectangle, you may find it difficult to do so with the Oval tool or Rectangle tool. Fortunately, you can also specify the width and height of ovals and rectangles, as well as the corner radius of rectan-

gles, by using the controls in the Oval Settings and Rectangle Settings dialog boxes.

With either the **Oval** tool or **Rectangle** tool selected in the **toolbar**, **Alt+click** (Windows) or **Option+click** (Mac) an empty area of the **Stage** where you want to create the oval or rectangle. In the **Oval Settings** or **Rectangle Settings** dialog box, specify your settings and click **OK**. Flash 8 automatically draws an appropriate-sized oval or rectangle where you clicked.

10 Save your changes to **shapes.fla**; you will need this file again in Exercise 6. Close the file.

3 | Using the Brush Tool

You can use the Brush tool to paint shapes with solid colors, gradients, and even bitmaps fills. In this exercise, you'll learn how to use the Brush tool to create and modify shapes.

---

1 Open **paint.fla**, which is a blank file you can use to paint shapes, from the **chap_03** folder.

---

2 Select the **Brush** tool from the **toolbar**.

Notice there are several options for the Brush tool—Object Drawing, Lock Fill, Brush Mode, Brush Size, and Brush Shape. You'll learn about these options in this exercise.

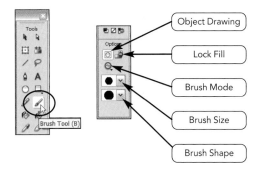

---

3 Draw a circle on the **Stage**.

Notice Flash 8 uses the fill color for this shape, not the stroke color. The Brush tool creates shapes that are fills and, therefore, only uses the fill color.

---

4 At the bottom of the **toolbar**, click to expand the contents of the **Brush Size** pop-up menu. Select the fourth size from the top.

As you can see from the preview, this is a smaller brush tip than the default brush tip you worked with in Step 3. You'll see how it works in the next step.

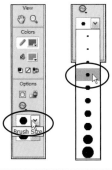

---

5 Draw a smaller circle inside the large one on the **Stage**.

Notice the smaller brush size creates a narrower fill shape than the shape you drew in Step 3.

---

6 At the bottom of the **toolbar**, click to expand the contents of the **Brush Shape** pop-up menu. Select the fifth shape from the bottom.

As you can see from the preview, this tip has a different shape than the default, round brush you've been working with. You'll see how it works in the next step.

7 Draw another circle on the **Stage**.

Notice the different result between this brush shape and the one you used in Steps 3 and 5. You can produce some very nice calligraphy effects with this brush shape because it changes thickness depending on the direction of your brush stroke—just like working with a calligraphy pen or a flat paintbrush.

TIP: | **Working with a Wacom Tablet**

Flash 8 offers support for most pressure-sensitive graphics tablets, including Wacom tablets. Using a tablet can help you create natural-looking shapes with a hand-drawn look. As you increase pressure on the tablet, the width of the shape will increase, whereas less pressure will create a thinner shape. For more information, refer to the Wacom Web site: **www.wacom.com**.

---

8 Experiment with the other brush shapes and sizes so you are more comfortable with the **Brush** tool. If you have a graphics tablet, try out the pressure sensitivity with the **Brush** tool.

TIP: | **Adding Strokes to Brush Shapes**

Because the Brush tool creates shapes that are fills, you can use the Ink Bottle to easily add a stroke to the shapes you create. You'll learn how to use the Ink Bottle in Exercise 4.

9 When you are done experimenting with the **Brush** tool, close **paint.fla**. You don't need to save your changes.

VIDEO: | **painting.mov**

In the last exercise, you learned how to create and edit brush strokes. There are a number of other useful features you can use with the Brush tool, such as Paint Fills, Paint Selections, Paint Behind, and Paint Inside. To learn more about these features, check out **painting.mov** in the **videos** folder on the **HOT CD-ROM**.

4 | Modifying Lines and Shapes

In the last three exercises, you learned how to draw lines and create shapes with the Brush, Oval, and Rectangle tools. You'll learn how modify these shapes in the next two exercises. In this exercise, you'll learn how to use the Property Inspector and Ink Bottle to modify the appearance of existing lines. In addition, you will learn some of the nuances involved in selecting lines and when to use the Ink Bottle versus the Property Inspector.

1 Open **strokes.fla** from the **chap_03** folder.

This file contains shapes created with lines and fills, which you'll use to modify lines and add strokes to shapes.

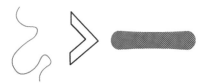

2 Select the **Selection** tool from the **toolbar**, and click the squiggle drawing to select it.

Notice when you select the line, it gets a bit thicker, and a dotted mesh appears over it, indicating the line is selected.

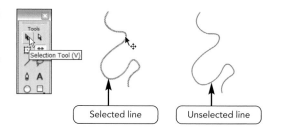

Selected line   Unselected line

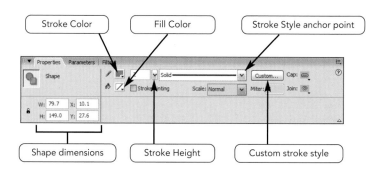

Stroke Color   Fill Color   Stroke Style anchor point

Shape dimensions   Stroke Height   Custom stroke style

3 Make sure the **Property Inspector** is visible. If it's not, choose **Window > Properties > Properties**.

Note: You must select a line before you can modify its stroke settings using the Property Inspector.

The Property Inspector

When you're work-
ing in Flash 8, you'll
constantly use the
Property Inspector
because it conve-

niently displays, and lets you change, the settings associated with the currently
selected object on the Stage, including text, symbols, video, frames, and even tools,
all in one easy-to-use interface.

4 With the line still selected, choose
the dotted line from the **Stroke Style**
pop-up menu (the fourth style from the
top). Click a blank area of the **Stage** to
deselect the line so you can clearly see
the change you just made.

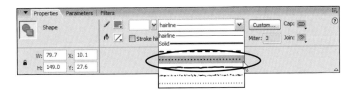

Deselect the line to see the
change in Stroke style

Use the Property Inspector as a quick, easy way to
modify selected artwork. When you have a line
selected, the Property Inspector displays the current
settings for that line. This is helpful when you need to
know what the line settings are for a particular object.
The default stroke settings are a 1-point, solid black line.

Hiding Selections

When lines are selected, it can be hard to see the changes you've made. To temporarily hide the dotted mesh so you can better see the changes, press **Ctrl+H** (Windows)
or **Shift+Cmd+E** (Mac) to hide and show the selection.

5 With the line still selected on the
Stage, click the arrow next to **Stroke
Height** in the **Property Inspector** to
reveal the **Stroke Height** slider. Click
and drag the slider to a setting of **4** to
increase the thickness of the line. (You
can choose a line thickness from **0.25**
to **10**.) Deselect the line by clicking a
blank area of the **Stage** to clearly see
the changes.

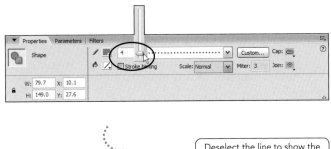

Deselect the line to show the
change in the stroke height.

6 Click to select the line on the **Stage**. In the **Property Inspector**, click the **Stroke Color** box and choose another color. As you can probably guess, changing the stroke color changes the color of the line. Deselect the line by clicking a blank area of the **Stage** to clearly see the changes.

You've now learned how to select and modify the style, height, and color of an entire stroke. Next you'll learn how to modify these properties for just a line segment.

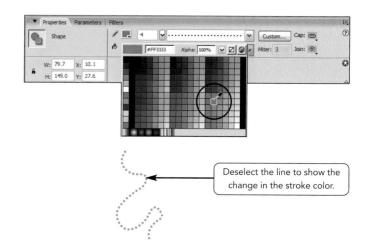

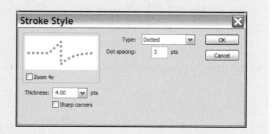

Deselect the line to show the change in the stroke color.

TIP:

Creating Custom Line Styles

You can create your own custom line styles in the Stroke Style dialog box. With the line selected on the **Stage**, click the **Custom** button in the **Property Inspector**. When the **Stroke Style** dialog box opens, you can create your own line style using the different options. The changes you make to the settings here are temporary, and they will return to their default settings once you quit Flash 8.

---

7 With the **Selection** tool selected in the **toolbar**, position your pointer over the bottom line of the arrow.

As you position the pointer over the line, notice the pointer changes to an arrow with a short, curved line, indicating you're over a line segment.

---

8 Click the lower-right line segment.

Notice a dotted mesh appears over the line segment you selected.

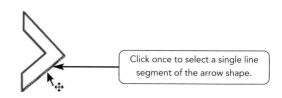

Click once to select a single line segment of the arrow shape.

9 In the **Property Inspector**, use the **Stroke Height** slider to change the line width to **5**.

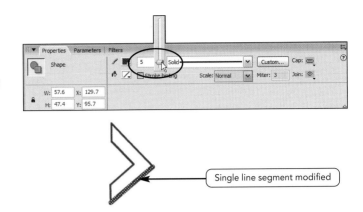

Notice only the selected line segment changed. In order to modify a line segment, you must select it before you change the settings in the Property Inspector. In this case, you selected only one of the six line segments of the arrow shape.

Single line segment modified

TIP: | **Selecting Line Segments**

Unlike other drawing programs, Flash 8 breaks lines with hard angles into separate line segments. For example, clicking the bottom line of the arrow shape selects only the bottom portion of the shape because the shape has six hard angles, creating six separate lines. If you want to select the entire shape, *double-click* only one of the line segments.

---

10 With the line segment still selected, type **2.75** in the **Stroke Height** field in the **Property Inspector**.

If you know the exact value you want to use, you can change the width of a line by entering a specific numeric value in the field next to the Stroke Height slider.

---

11 Click anywhere on the **Stage** to deselect the line segment. Double-click any part of the arrow to select all six line segments.

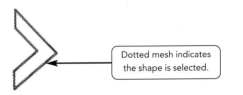

Dotted mesh indicates the shape is selected.

This shortcut is essential when you need to select entire shapes composed of multisegmented lines.

---

12 Practice changing the style, width, and color of the selected lines using the controls in the **Property Inspector**. Choose any setting you like—the point here is to become more comfortable with selecting lines and line segments and changing their properties with the **Property Inspector**.

Now you know how to modify an existing line using the Property Inspector, but what do you do when your object doesn't have a line or a stroke? You add one using the Ink Bottle tool. You'll learn how in the following steps.

13 Select the **Ink Bottle** tool from the **toolbar.**

The Ink Bottle tool lets you add a stroke around an object with no stroke or make changes to the color, width, and texture of existing lines. With the Ink Bottle tool, you can set the stroke color using the Property Inspector or the Stroke Color options in the toolbar. Since you have used the Property Inspector quite a bit in this exercise, next you'll get a chance to use the color settings in the toolbar.

NOTE:

Property Inspector or Toolbar?

In Flash 8, there are often several ways to access and work with the same tools. In most situations, you'll find the Property Inspector will streamline your workflow, because it gives you quick access to the properties of the currently selected object or tool, in one convenient panel.

In contrast to the Property Inspector, which is useful for modifying the properties of existing shapes, you can use the toolbar to set object properties before creating new shapes.

14 In the **toolbar**, click the **Stroke Color** box and choose a **light gray** from the color palette.

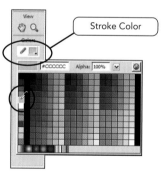

15 Click the outer edge of the snowboard shape to add a stroke to the outside of the shape.

The Ink Bottle tool

The Ink Bottle tool serves many purposes. You can add a stroke to an object, as you did in the last step, or you can modify the color, size, and style of the stroke for several objects at once. To modify more than one object, hold down the **Shift** key or the **Ctrl** (Windows) or **Cmd** (Mac) key to multiple-select the objects on the Stage. You'll find multiple-selecting objects saves you a lot of time when you have several objects to add or modify.

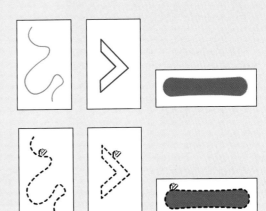

Stroke selected

Stroke deleted

16 Select the **Selection** tool from the **toolbar** and double-click to select the stroke around the snowboard shape. The dotted mesh appears, confirming you have selected the stroke. Press the **Delete** key to remove the stroke.

Now you know how to add and remove strokes—it's that easy!

Complex Artwork

Complex objects containing numerous lines and shapes add to the file size of your final movie, so if your design allows, use complex artwork sparingly.

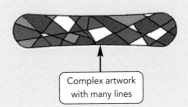

Complex artwork with many lines

17 Close **strokes.fla**. You don't need to save your changes.

5 | Modifying Strokes and Fills

There are several ways to change the stroke and fill of a shape. You can specify the stroke and fill colors before you create the shape; you can use the Paint Bucket tool to modify fill colors and the Ink Bottle tool to modify strokes; or you can use the Color Mixer panel to create solid, gradient, and bitmap strokes and fills, which you can apply to the shapes you create. In this exercise, you'll learn how to use the Paint Bucket tool and the Color Mixer panel to modify strokes and fills of a shape.

1 Open **modifyFills.fla** from the **chap_03** folder.

As you can see, this file contains one layer with a vector graphic of a snowboard.

2 Select the **Selection** tool from the **toolbar**. Click to select the blue background of the snowboard.

When a shape is selected, a dotted mesh appears over the shape.

3 Choose **Window > Color Mixer** to open the **Color Mixer** panel.

What Is the Color Mixer Panel?

The Color Mixer panel gives you precise control over color, all in one panel. The next exercise will show you how to use the Color Mixer panel to create gradient fills.

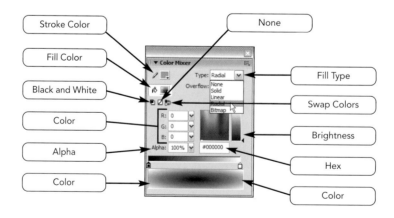

4 In the **Color Mixer** panel, click the **Fill Color** box and select a shade of red from the palette.

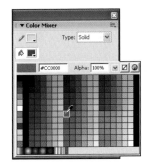

Notice the background color of the snowboard changes to red. Unfortunately, the insides of the letters are still blue. Not to worry, you'll fix this in the next step.

NOTE:

Why Didn't Everything Turn to the Color I Selected?

Flash 8 treats shapes that are one continuous color as a single shape. Each time a new color appears, it is a new shape, which means you must modify it individually. In the previous step, the middle parts of the letters were treated as separate shapes because they were surrounded by white. Next, you will learn how to quickly fill these remaining blue shapes with the Paint Bucket tool.

---

5 Select the **Paint Bucket** tool from the **toolbar** and click each of the blue shapes inside the letters to change the color to match the currently selected color (the red background color you selected in Step 4).

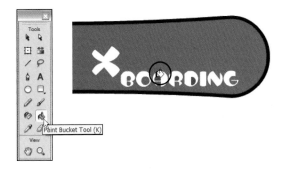

Unlike the Color Mixer panel method, you don't need to select the artwork before you color it with the Paint Bucket tool. If you are having trouble clicking on the small blue regions inside the type, you may want to magnify the contents of the Stage using the Zoom tool. You can also use short-cut keys to zoom in and out by pressing **Ctrl+** or **Ctrl–** (Windows) or **Cmd+** or **Cmd–** (Mac).

Tip: As a safeguard, you can always press **Ctrl+Z** (Windows) or **Cmd+Z** (Mac) to undo any mistakes you make.

TIP:

Applying Fills

Using the Fill Color box in the Color Mixer panel or using the Paint Bucket tool in the toolbar are two ways to change the solid fill color of an object. Both methods yield the same results, but using the Property Inspector can help speed up your workflow, since you can change and access many features using only one panel. You will use this third method of changing fill colors shortly, but note that you *must* have the object selected first if you want to change the fill color using the Property Inspector.

6 Select the **Selection tool** from the **toolbar**. Click the letter **B** on the snowboard to select it. You'll know it's selected when you see the dotted mesh.

You could select and change the color of each letter individually, but that would be a time-consuming process. Instead, you'll use the **Shift** key to multiple-select all the letters in the word *BOARDING* so you can fill all the letters at the same time.

---

7 Hold down the **Shift** key and click each of the remaining letters in the word **BOARDING** to multiple-select all the letters. If you make a mistake and want to start over, press the **Esc** key to clear all selections, or click a blank area of the **Stage** to deselect.

---

8 Make sure the **Property Inspector** is visible. If it's not, choose **Window > Properties > Properties**. In the **Property Inspector**, click the **Fill Color** box and select **black** from the **Fill Color** palette.

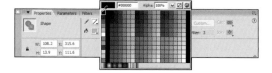

Notice all the letters changed to the new color you selected! Now that you've mastered changing fills, it's time to learn how to modify strokes. You'll learn how in the next few steps.

---

9 With the **Selection** tool still selected in the **toolbar**, double-click the snowboard to select it.

Double-clicking will select the entire object, including both strokes, the one around the snowboard, and also the one around the yin and yang design.

Tip: To select a single stroke, double-click the stroke itself.

---

10 In the **Property Inspector**, click the **Stroke Color** box and select a shade of **yellow** from the **Stroke Color** palette. Choose a different stroke style from the **Stroke Style** pop-up menu. When you're finished, click a blank area of the **Stage** to deselect your artwork so you can see your changes clearly.

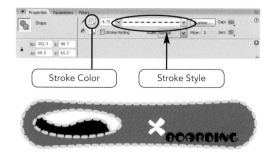

---

11 Double-click the stroke of the yin and yang design on the snowboard to select it. In the **Property Inspector**, select a new **Stroke Color** and **Stroke Height** for the outline. When you're finished, click a blank area of the **Stage** to deselect your artwork so you can see your changes clearly.

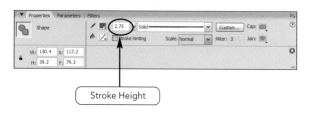

Stroke Height

12 Close **modifyFills.fla**. You don't need to save your changes.

Understanding the Flash Drawing Models

Now that you've mastered how to use the drawing tools in Flash 8, it's time to learn about the two drawing models in Flash 8: the merge drawing model and the object drawing model. The drawing models define how multiple shapes interact with each other, particularly when you create overlapping shapes.

The merge drawing mode, which has been the default drawing model in previous versions of Flash, automatically merges overlapping shapes. As a result, if you create overlapping shapes and then move the shapes away from the each other, you end up with broken or merged shapes. For many users, the merge drawing model was difficult to understand because it was so different from models in other drawing programs.

Fortunately, Flash 8 has a new drawing model—the object drawing model—which provides more control and flexibility when creating multiple or overlapping objects. The object drawing model behaves the way models in other drawing programs behave. Before you get started with the hands-on exercises, take some time to review the following chart, which will help you understand the differences and benefits of each of the two drawing models:

Flash Drawing Models Defined

Merge Drawing Model	Object Drawing Model	Description
Selecting Objects		
Selection displayed as dotted mesh	Selection displayed as bounding rectangle	When selecting a shape created with the merge drawing model, the selection appears as a dotted mesh. When you select a shape created using the object drawing model, Flash 8 surrounds the shape with a rectangular bounding box.
Overlapping Objects		
Shapes on the same layer interact with each other.	Shapes on the same layer do not interact with each other.	The merge drawing model automatically merges shapes when they overlap. The object drawing model creates separate objects you can manipulate individually and that do not automatically merge together when overlapped.
Stroke and Fill		
Stroke and fill independent	Stroke and fill integrated together	Merge shapes contain separate strokes and fills, which you can manipulate independently. Object shapes contain integrated strokes and fills. To manipulate them, double-click the shape to enter object drawing mode.

6 | The Merge and Object Drawing Models

In this exercise, you will create shapes with each drawing model using the Oval tool to learn the differences, benefits, and nuances of working with each.

---

1 Open a new file in Flash 8 (**File > New > Flash Document**). Chose a light-gray color in the **Fill Color** palette in the **toolbar**. Select the **Oval** tool. You will draw two ovals in the merge drawing model next, so make sure **Object Drawing** is deselected. Draw two ovals on the **Stage**.

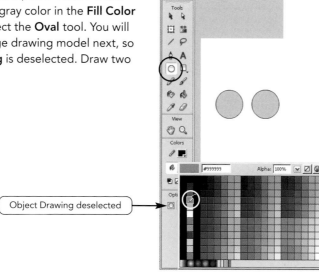

Object Drawing deselected

---

2 Select the **Selection** tool from the **toolbar**. Double-click one of the oval shapes on the **Stage** to select it. Click and drag to reposition the oval so it overlaps the other oval.

Dotted mesh designates a selected merge shape.

The merge drawing model is the default drawing model. When selected, the merge object displays a dotted mesh.

---

3 Deselect the oval by clicking anywhere on the **Stage**. Double-click the oval to select it again and click and drag it away from the circle shape.

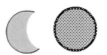

Notice the selected oval left a hole in the other oval where the two shapes overlapped. When you overlap objects using the merge drawing model, they automatically merge to create a single shape. When you move the shapes apart, the shapes do not return to their original, unmerged state. If you want to keep the objects as separate, unmerged objects when overlapped, you must use the new drawing model in Flash 8—the object drawing model. You will do this next.

---

4 Choose a green color from the **Fill Color** palette. Select the **Oval** tool from the **toolbar**. At the bottom of the **toolbar**, click the **Object Drawing** button to switch from the default merge drawing model to the new object drawing model.

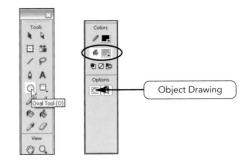

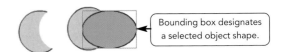

Object Drawing

5 Click and drag with the **Oval** tool to create a third oval, adjacent to the first two, on the **Stage**.

You've just created an object shape. Object shapes behave a bit differently than the merge shapes you have worked with up to this point.

6 Select the **Selection** tool from the **toolbar**. Click the green oval to select it. Move it so it overlaps one of the gray merge object ovals.

Notice the green oval shape, which was created using the object drawing model, is surrounded by a rectangular bounding box, rather than the dotted mesh you saw for the gray merge object ovals.

Bounding box designates a selected object shape.

7 Click and drag the green oval away from the gray oval. Deselect the green oval by clicking anywhere on the **Stage**.

Unlike in Step 3, the objects did not merge where they overlapped. When you create shapes with the object drawing model, they behave independently from other shapes.

8 Double-click the green oval.

The other gray ovals on the Stage dim, and you cannot select them! Notice the edit bar indicates you are no longer in Scene 1 but are in something called a "Drawing Object."

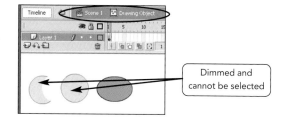

Dimmed and cannot be selected

9 Click the green oval and move it around the **Stage**.

The bounding rectangle is replaced by a dotted mesh, and the stroke is left behind. The shape no longer looks or behaves as an object shape, but as a merge shape! When you double-click an object shape, you automatically exit the object drawing model and enter into the merge drawing model. As a result, object shapes are automatically converted to merge shapes, which in some circumstances are easier to work with. However, this isn't a permanent change—you can return merge shapes back to object shapes very easily. You'll learn how in the next step.

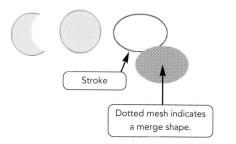

Stroke

Dotted mesh indicates a merge shape.

10 In the edit bar, click the **Scene 1** button to return to the object drawing model. The shape no longer behaves as a merge shape but as an object shape. See for yourself by manipulating the graphics on the **Stage** again.

You now have a good overview of the differences between the two drawing models in Flash 8. If you're new to Flash, you may think the object drawing model is the best way to create your Flash artwork, since it behaves like the models in most other graphics programs and because usually you won't want objects merging with each other. However, you can achieve some interesting effects using the merge drawing model, which you'll learn about in the following tip.

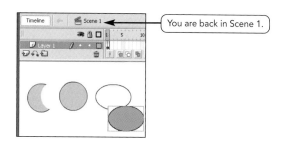

You are back in Scene 1.

11 Close your Flash file. You don't need to save your changes.

TIP:

Creating Negative Space with Merge Objects

You can use the unique behavior of merge objects described in this last exercise to create some interesting artwork, such as artwork that takes advantage of "negative" space. For example, if you place a different colored merge object shape over the glove shape, deselect it, reselect it, and then move it away, it will cut an X shape in the fill of the glove, as illustrated here. This is a quick and easy way to add an interesting logo to the snowboarding glove!

Note: If the X shape were exactly the same color as the glove, it would not have cut through the glove and made an X shape. Instead, it would have just combined with the glove into one shape.

Other than starting out with object drawing model shapes, there are additional ways of overlapping shapes without having them cut into or combine with one another. You can convert the shapes to symbols, which you will learn more about in Chapter 6, "Symbols and Instances." You can also select multiple shapes and group them (**Modify > Group**), which you will learn about in the next exercise. Grouping shapes also makes it easier to work with shapes you want to keep together or modify in the same way.

7 | Grouping Objects

Now that you have a good idea of how the drawing features behave in Macromedia Flash 8, this exercise shows you how to group objects so you can modify and work with them all together.

---

1 Open **multiple.fla** from the **chap_03** folder. This file contains some simple shapes created with the merge object model that you will combine into a group.

---

2 Double-click the blue glove object to select both its shape and fill. Notice that it displays a dotted mesh. **Shift+double-click** the boot to select its stroke and fill as well. Choose **Modify > Group**. A thin blue line appears around both shapes, indicating they are part of the same (grouped) object. You can also group an object by using the keyboard shortcuts, **Ctrl+G** (Windows) or **Cmd+G** (Mac).

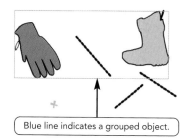

Blue line indicates a grouped object.

---

3 Select the **Selection** tool from the **toolbar**. Drag the group over one of the other merge objects on the **Stage**.

The two shapes move as one grouped object on the Stage.

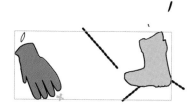

---

4 Deselect the group by clicking on any blank area of the **Stage**. Click the group again and move it off the objects. Notice that the grouped objects do not interact with the other merge drawing objects on the **Stage**.

As you can see, grouping objects, even single objects, is a quick way of protecting them from being affected by or affecting other objects. In addition to being able to move grouped objects together, you can also modify them as a single object, which you'll learn how to do next.

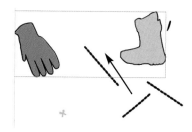

---

5 Choose the **Free Transform** tool from the **toolbar** and click the group to select it. Position the mouse over the lower-right corner of the selection bounding box until the pointer changes to a double-headed arrow. Click and drag down toward the lower right to scale both objects in the group.

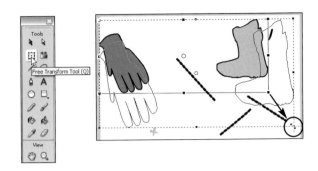

You can also rotate, skew, flip, and make other modifications to all the members of a selected group. Next, you will learn how to modify single elements of a group, independent of the other members of the group.

---

6 Double-click the blue glove with the **Selection** tool. Flash exits out of **Scene 1** and enters into the edit window for the group. Select just the glove so only it is highlighted with a dotted mesh (which indicates you can now edit the object independent of the other objects in the group). Select a different color from the **Fill Color** palette. Notice only the glove changes color.

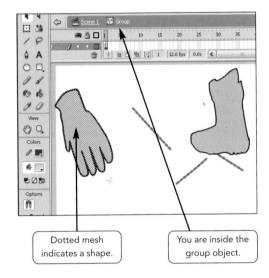

Dotted mesh indicates a shape.

You are inside the group object.

---

7 Click the **Scene 1** link above the **Timeline** to exit out of the group edit window and return to **Scene 1**. The group should still be selected. Choose **Modify > Ungroup** to return each object back to its original ungrouped status.

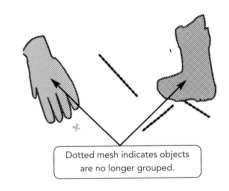

The ease at which you can group and ungroup combinations of shapes (objects shapes as well as merge shapes) and the power and flexibility provided by this grouping capability makes this an important workflow-enhancing skill.

Dotted mesh indicates objects are no longer grouped.

---

8 Save and close **multiple.fla**—you won't need it again.

---

8 | Creating Gradients

Gradients help you create cool and interesting effects. Flash 8 lets you create two types of gradient fills: linear and radial. In this exercise, you'll learn how to use the Color Mixer panel and Color Swatches panel to create, apply, and change the shape and color of linear and radial gradients. Flash has really beefed up its gradient capabilities in version 8, both in the Color Mixer and in the Gradient Transform tool.

---

1 Open **newGradient.fla** from the **chap_03** folder.

This file contains one layer with two snowboards. You will be applying gradients to both of these shapes in this exercise.

---

2 Select the **Selection** tool from the **toolbar**. Click the blue fill on the snowboard on the left to select it.

---

3 Make sure the **Color Mixer** panel is open. If it is not, choose **Window > Color Mixer**. Choose **Radial** from the **Type** pop-up menu.

As you can see, the selected shape is now filled with a radial gradient, using black and white, which are the default colors. A radial gradient radiates outward from the center. In this case, black is in the center and the gradient radiates to white.

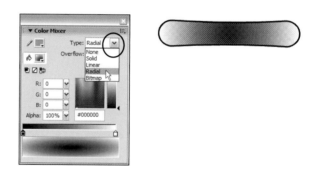

---

4 Double-click the black pointer in the **Color Mixer** panel. The pointer selects the black color point of the gradient and opens a color palette that lets you define the fill color for the selected pointer.

Tip: You may need several tries to get the color palette to appear. Double-click the black pointer carefully!

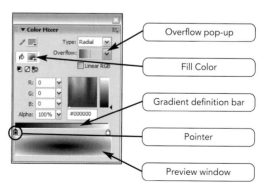

Overflow pop-up

Fill Color

Gradient definition bar

Pointer

Preview window

---

5 Select a shade of red from the color palette.

As you can see, the appearance of the radial gradient changes to range from red to white instead of ranging from black to white. You have just created your first custom gradient! Next you will use the Gradient Transform tool to edit the appearance of gradient.

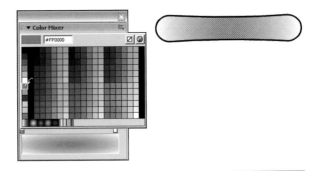

---

6 Select the **Gradient Transform** tool from the **toolbar**. Use the various edit handles to change the center point, width, radius, rotation, and focal point of the gradient fill. Experiment with each of the edit handles to get the hang of how each controls the appearance of the gradient fill.

Next you will make a linear gradient.

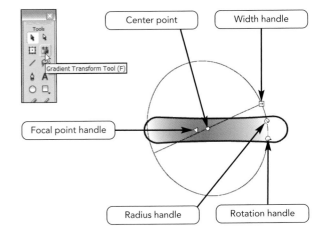

---

7 Select the **Selection** tool from the **toolbar**. Click the blue fill on the snowboard on the right side of the **Stage** to select it.

---

8 In the **Color Mixer** panel, choose **Linear** from the **Type** pop-up menu.

As you can see, this option creates a linear gradient, using the same colors you used for the previous gradient.

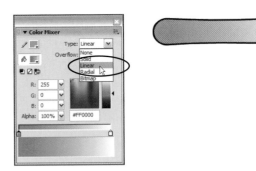

9 Make sure the **Color Swatches** panel is visible. If it's not, choose **Window > Color Swatches**. Choose **Add Swatch** from the **Color Mixer** panel menu to save the currently selected gradient in the **Color Swatches** panel so you can access it easily.

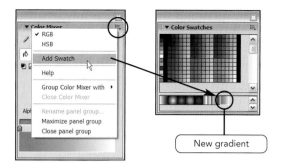

New gradient

10 Select the **Gradient Transform** tool from the **toolbar**. Modify the width, rotation, and center point handles to become familiar with how they modify the appearance of the linear gradient fill.

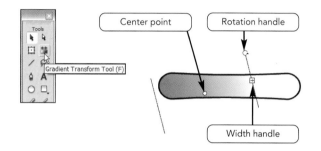

Center point

Rotation handle

Width handle

11 When you're finished, close **newGradient.fla**. You don't need to save your changes.

NOTE:

New Gradient Features in Flash 8

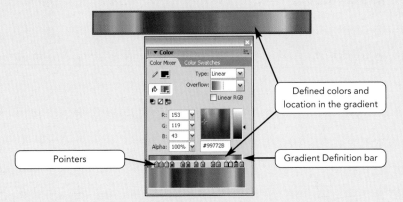

Defined colors and location in the gradient

Pointers

Gradient Definition bar

In addition to new features in the Gradient Transform tool, Flash 8 now supports the use of gradients containing up to 16 colors, which lets you create much more complicated and colorful gradients. Create additional colors in your gradients by clicking below the Gradient Definition bar in the Color Mixer panel. A new color, represented by the color pointer, will appear after each click.

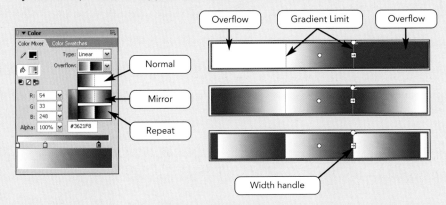

Overflow   Gradient Limit   Overflow

Normal

Mirror

Repeat

Width handle

Flash 8 provides three new options for controlling how gradient overflow, the colors that extend beyond the limits of the gradient, should be handled. The options are **Normal** (Windows) or **Extend** (Mac), which is the default; **Mirror** (Windows) or **Reflect** (Mac); or **Repeat**. You can generate an overflow in your gradients by selecting them with the Gradient Transform tool and decreasing their width by clicking and dragging the width handle.

9 | Drawing with the Pen Tool

The Pen tool creates more complex shapes by combining both straight and curved lines in the same shape. Shapes created with the Pen tool consist of paths, anchor points, and tangent handles, which you can modify with the Subselection tool, which you'll learn about in Exercise 10.

If you've used other vector-based drawing programs, such as Macromedia FreeHand or Adobe Illustrator, you'll be instantly comfortable with the Pen tool in Flash 8 because it works the same way. If you haven't used the Pen tool before, it can take some getting used to. You'll probably need plenty of practice before you become really comfortable with it.

In this exercise, you will start by learning how to use the Pen tool to draw a few basic geometric shapes. By the end of this exercise, you will be more comfortable working with the Pen tool to create more complex shapes of your own.

---

1 Open **pen.fla** from the **chap_03** folder.

As you can see, this file has two layers: the shapes layer contains a series of outlines you'll use as a guide for drawing shapes in this exercise; the draw here layer is an empty layer you'll use to draw shapes with the Pen tool. The shapes layer is locked so you can't edit the artwork, but have fun drawing on the draw here layer.

Note: Since you will be using the Pen tool in this exercise, it will be easier to see the results if you use the default settings for this tool. If you just completed the previous exercises in this chapter, use the **Property Inspector** to set the stroke settings to their default values (**black**, **solid**, **1 point**).

---

2 Click the **draw here** layer in the **Timeline** to select it. You'll know it's selected when you see a pencil icon next to the layer name.

---

3 Select the **Pen** tool from the **toolbar**.

---

4 Move your mouse to the lower-left corner of the triangle outline and click.

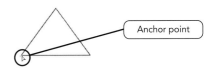

A small circle appears. This is the first anchor point, indicating the beginning of your line. Line segments are created between pairs of anchor points to create shapes.

---

5 Click the top corner of the triangle to add the second
anchor point.

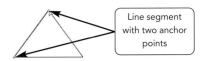

The line segment appears as a red line with two square
anchor points on either end on top of the line segment,
which is the stroke color in the Property Inspector and in
the toolbar which you set in Step 1. The red line indicates
the line segment is selected.

---

6 Click the lower-right corner of the triangle to create a
second line segment between the upper- and lower-right
anchor points.

---

7 Position the pointer over the lower-left corner of the
triangle where you created the first anchor point in Step 4.
A small circle appears beside the pointer, indicating the
path will be closed if you click. Click to close the path and
create the shape. When you close a path, the shape automatically fills with the currently selected fill color in the
Property Inspector or on the **toolbar**.

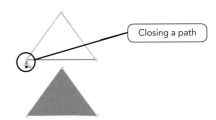

Next, you'll learn to draw a circle with the Pen tool, which can be a bit more complicated than drawing a
triangle and may take some time to master. Don't worry if you have to do this exercise a few times
before you get the hang of things.

TIP: | **Pen Preferences**

When you are working with the Pen tool, there are a number of preferences you can change to make using it a bit easier. Choose **Edit > Preferences** to open the **Preferences** dialog box. Select the **Drawing** category to see the **Pen** preferences. There are three you may find helpful:

Show pen preview (off by default) lets you preview the line segments as you draw with the Pen tool. A stretchy line will appear as a preview of the line segment you will create when you click.

Show solid points (off by default) displays selected anchor points as solid points and unselected anchor points as hollow points when you use the Subselection tool.

Show precise cursors (off by default) causes the Pen pointer to appear as a crosshair. This can be helpful for precise drawing and works great with the grid feature.

---

8 Using the **Pen** tool, click at the top center of the circle outline to create the first anchor point.

---

9 Click the middle-right edge of the circle and drag down to add another anchor point. As you drag, you will see two tangent handles appear. Move the mouse around and watch how the angle of the line changes as you do this. Don't release the mouse button just yet.

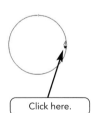

Click here.

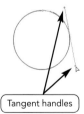

Tangent handles

---

10 Drag down toward the lower right until the line segment seems to match the outline of the circle. Now release the mouse button. The circle you draw doesn't have to be perfect here; just try to get yourself comfortable working with the **Pen** tool.

11 Click the middle-bottom edge of the circle to add another anchor point. The line will curve when you add the third anchor point, to complete half of the circle shape.

12 Click and drag up on the middle-left edge of the circle to add another anchor point. As you drag, you will see two tangent handles appear. Don't release the mouse just yet.

13 Drag up toward the top left until the line segment seems to match the outline of the circle. Release the mouse button.

14 Move the pointer to the first anchor point you created at the top of the circle. When you see the small circle appear next to the **Pen** tool pointer, click to close the path and fill the circle with the currently selected fill color.

15 Save your changes and keep **pen.fla** open for the next exercise. Don't worry if the circle you created it isn't perfect.

Next you'll learn how to modify lines using the shapes you just made.

10 | Modifying Paths

In the last exercise, you learned how to create shapes using the Pen tool. Next, you'll learn how to reshape them using the Selection and Subselection tools to modify paths using their anchor points or tangent handles.

---

1 If you just completed Exercise 9, **pen.fla** should still be open. If it's not, go back and complete Exercise 9.

---

2 Select the **Selection** tool from the **toolbar**.

---

3 Position the pointer over the left side of the triangle.

Notice the pointer changes to a small curved line. This line indicates you are over a line segment.

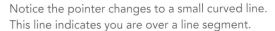

---

4 Click and drag the line segment to the left. The shape will start to distort and stretch as you continue to drag the mouse. When you release the mouse, notice both the line and the fill have changed their shape.

The Selection tool offers a free-form way of transforming shapes. Although it can be fun to use, it lacks the precision you sometimes need when creating complex shapes. When you need pinpoint precision, use the Subselection tool, which lets you manipulate the anchor points and tangent handles of paths after you have added them.

---

5 Select the **Subselection** tool from the **toolbar**

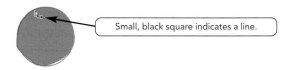

6 Position the pointer over the edge of the circle shape. A small black square appears, indicating you are over a line.

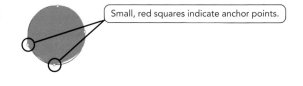

Small, black square indicates a line.

7 Click the edge of the circle to select it. Notice the anchor points are now visible. The anchor points are represented by small red squares along the line of the circle.

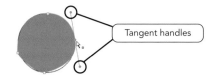

Small, red squares indicate anchor points.

Note: Flash 8 adds anchor points, if necessary, to create curves, which is why you might see more than four anchor points on your artwork.

8 Position the pointer over the middle-right anchor point. A small white square appears next to the pointer when you are directly over the anchor point.

9 Click to select the middle-right anchor point. When you do, the tangent handles for that anchor point appear.

Tangent handles

10 Click and drag the top tangent handle of the middle-right anchor point to the right. When you release the mouse, you'll notice the top and bottom portions of the curve change together. This is the normal behavior of tangent handles.

11 Click to select the middle-left anchor point.

12 Hold down the **Alt** key (Windows) or **Option** key (Mac) and click and drag the top tangent handle of the middle-left anchor point over to the left. When you release the mouse, you'll notice only the top portion changes.

As you can see, holding down the Alt (Windows) or Option (Mac) key lets you modify one part of a curve without affecting the other.

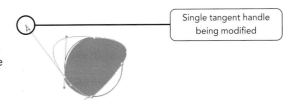

Single tangent handle being modified

13 Click the anchor point on the middle right of the circle and drag down to try to match the circle image in the background. You can click and drag an anchor point to make the circle more perfect in shape.

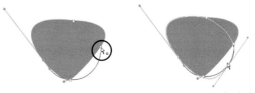

Now you know how to use the Selection and Subselection tools to modify the lines you create in Flash 8. With the Selection tool, you can reshape straight or curved lines by dragging the lines themselves. The Subselection tool lets you reshape by clicking and moving the anchor points and tangent handles. Next you will learn how to add, remove, and convert anchor points.

14 Select the **Pen** tool from the **toolbar**.

In addition to drawing shapes, the Pen tool can add anchor points to a line.

15 Position the **Pen** tool over the rounded side of the triangle shape. Click to select the path. Notice that when you move the **Pen** tool directly over the path, a small **+** symbol appears next to the pointer. Click to add a new anchor point.

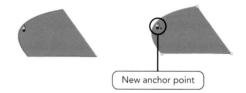

New anchor point

Converting curves to straight lines is a rather simple process and one you should know how to do. You'll learn how in the following steps.

16 Position the pointer over the newly added anchor point and notice that a small caret (^) symbol appears, indicating you will convert the curve point to a corner point if you click.

17 Click the anchor point to convert the anchor point to a corner point, transforming the curve into a straight-edged shape. Because you converted the anchor point to a corner point, you'll no longer have access to any tangent handles.

Converting a corner point to a curve point is even easier to do—you'll do that next.

18 Select the **Subselection** tool from the **toolbar**. Click the anchor point to select it. Hold down the **Alt** (Windows) or **Option** (Mac) key and click and drag the anchor point you just modified up a bit. When you do this, you will convert the corner point back to an anchor point.

Note: Make sure the anchor point is still selected before you drag it. Selected anchor points are red.

---

19 With the anchor point still selected, press **Delete** to remove the anchor point.

---

20 Close **pen.fla.** You don't need to save your changes.

By now, you should feel pretty comfortable working with the drawing and color tools in Flash 8. If you don't feel quite there yet, feel free to practice and play some more with the different tools and color settings. You might try drawing some artwork for a project you want to create in Flash 8. Nothing will ever replace good old-fashioned practice.

4

Animation Basics

Flash has a reputation as a powerful and robust animation tool. If you know other animation tools, such as Macromedia Director or Adobe After Effects, you might be looking for similarities. It's actually easier to learn the animation capabilities of Flash 8 if you don't know other animation programs, because you have no preconceived notions of how you think it might work.

This chapter introduces you to the Timeline, which plays a significant role in producing animations. The Timeline lets you work with keyframes, blank keyframes, frame-by-frame animation, and onion skinning. If these are new terms to you, they won't be for long. This chapter also covers setting the frame rate (and how it affects playback speeds). By the end of this chapter, things should really get moving for you, all puns intended!

The Timeline

Understanding and working with the Timeline is essential to creating animations in Flash 8. This illustration identifies the elements of the Timeline you'll be working with in this chapter.

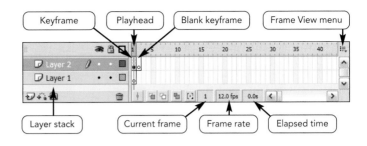

The following chart describes the features in the Timeline.

Timeline Features	
Feature	**Description**
Keyframe	Defines the moment in the Timeline when actions or animation changes occur. Keyframe content remains unchanged until another keyframe or a blank keyframe occurs in the Timeline.
Playhead	The playhead—a red rectangle with a long, red line—indicates the currently selected keyframe. Click and drag (or *scrub*) the playhead back and forth in the Timeline to quickly preview your animation.
Blank keyframe	You can either add content to blank keyframes or use them to intentionally break up or make changes to an animation.
Frame View menu	Gives you several different options for changing the size and therefore the number of frames visible at one time in the Timeline. The default view, Normal, displays the frames at an appropriate size for most projects. However, when you start creating longer animations, you will need to set the Frame view to Small or Tiny, so you can see more frames at one time.
Layer stack	Organizes the elements of an animation and controls the order in which they stack on top of each other. As a result, you can animate layers independent of and in front of or behind other layers. Each layer has options for hiding or showing the layer, locking it, and displaying its contents as outlines. You'll learn more about layers in Chapter 5, "*Shape Tweening.*"
Current frame	Displays the current position of the playhead and the frame number of the currently selected frame.
Frame rate	Displays the number of **f**rames **p**er **s**econd (fps) at which the movie attempts to play on the user's browser or computer. Double-clicking the frame rate value is a quick way to access the Document Properties dialog box.
Elapsed time	Displays the time elapsed from Frame 1 to the current playhead location at the currently selected frame rate.

1 | Document Properties

The document properties are general specifications—such as Stage dimensions, background color, and frame rate—that affect your entire project. When you start a new project in Flash 8, you should set the document properties. Here's an exercise to show you how.

---

1 Copy the **chap_04** folder from the **HOT CD-ROM** to your **Desktop**. Choose **File > New** to create a new file. Choose **File > Save**. In the **Save**

dialog box, name the file **movie.fla** and save it in the **chap_04** folder. Make sure the **Property Inspector** is visible. If it's not, choose **Window > Properties**.

Notice the following default document properties: the default Stage dimensions are 550 x 400 pixels, the default movie background is white, and the default frame rate is 12 frames per second. You'll learn how to change each setting in the following steps.

---

2 In the **Property Inspector**, type **24** in the **Frame rate** field.

For every second of your animation, 24 frames play. You'll learn more about frame rates in the next exercise.

---

3 In the Property Inspector, click the **Background** box to display the default color palette. Select a **light blue** to change the background color of your movie.

---

4 In the Property Inspector, click the **Size** button to open the **Document Properties** dialog box, which lets you give a title and brief description of your movie, as well as set frame rate preferences, movie dimensions, background color, and rule measurements for your entire movie.

---

5 Type **700** in the **width** field and **350** in the **height** field.

These fields control the absolute pixel dimensions of the Stage. You will learn other ways to control the size of your movie in Chapter 17, "*Publishing and Exporting.*"

6 Click the **Ruler units** pop-up menu, which contains several ways to display the ruler units on your **Stage**. Leave this option set to the default—**Pixels**.

7 Click **OK** to close the **Document Properties** dialog box.

Notice the values in the **Property Inspector**—the dimensions, background color, and frame rate changed to reflect the settings you specified in the **Document Properties** dialog box.

You can quickly use the Property Inspector at any point to change the movie's background color or frame rate. In addition, you can use the Size button to access the Document Properties dialog box, where you can change the Stage dimensions and ruler units. However, avoid changing dimensions once you have started adding content to your Stage. Changing Stage dimensions at this point offsets the position of your artwork, which can be difficult to fix.

8 Save your changes and leave **movie.fla** open for the next exercise.

Understanding Keyframes and Frames

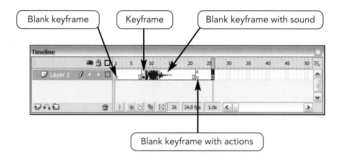

Blank keyframe | Keyframe | Blank keyframe with sound

Blank keyframe with actions

Before you start creating animations, you need to understand two terms—*frames* and *keyframes*. In Flash 8, the Timeline represents the passing of time, with each slot in the Timeline representing an individual frame. Keyframes are a special type of frame that represent a change in content. For example, if you have artwork in Frame 1, and you don't change it until Frame 20, the image in Frame 1 will persist until Frame 20. In order to change the appearance of an animation, you must

add a new keyframe. For example, if you have artwork in Frame 1, and you want to change it in Frame 2, you must add a new keyframe in Frame 2, indicating the change. A keyframe indicates a change in content between two frames.

If you've never worked with animation before, these concepts may seem foreign to you. Not to worry, you'll have lots of opportunities to work with frames and keyframes in this chapter.

Before you start the hands-on exercises, you need to identify and create frames and keyframes in the Timeline. The following chart describes each in more detail, including the keyboard shortcuts where available.

Working with Frames and Keyframes	
Feature	**Description**
Frame	Just like film, Flash 8 divides lengths of time into frames. The frame rate determines how much time each frame takes up. For example, if your movie's frame rate is 12 fps, one frame will take up 1/12 of 1 second. If an object is on the Stage for 24 frames, it will appear visible for 2 seconds in the movie. You'll learn more about frame rate later in this chapter.
	Although the Timeline in Flash 8 has *slots* for frames, you have to define them as frames or keyframes in order for the content to exist at that point in the movie. Different layers can have different numbers of frames. For example, Layer 1 could have 10 frames while Layer 2 has only one.
	When you define a frame, all of the previous slots are also defined as frames. If you have artwork on the Stage, it will continue to exist when you add frames to the Timeline.
	If you insert frames between keyframes, you will lengthen the time of your animation.
	To define or insert frames, select any slot(s) and/or frame(s) in the **Timeline** and press **F5** or choose **Insert > Timeline > Frame**.
Keyframe	A keyframe indicates a change in content or motion between frames. A keyframe containing artwork is represented by a solid, black circle. By default, when you add a new keyframe in Flash 8, the content (except for actions and sounds) is copied from the previous keyframe. (If there is no previous keyframe, the layer will be blank up and until the new keyframe.) To make a change to the artwork in the new keyframe, you select the keyframe before you alter the artwork on the Stage. Simply adding a keyframe will not change the artwork.
	To insert a new keyframe, select any slot or frame in the Timeline to select it and press **F6** (Windows only) or choose **Insert > Timeline > Keyframe**.
Clear keyframe	Clearing a keyframe removes the contents of the keyframe but leaves the frame itself. This process will not reduce the number of frames on a layer but will simply remove the keyframe and change it to a regular frame. The content from the previous keyframe will then continue through the existing frames. If the previous keyframe is a blank keyframe, there will be no content through the existing frames (in this case, you may want to remove frames instead; see **Remove frames** below).

continues on next page

	Working with Frames and Keyframes *continued*
Feature	**Description**
Remove frames	If you need to delete frames, keyframes, or blank keyframes, select the frames in the **Timeline** and press **Shift+F5** or choose **Edit > Timeline > Remove Frames** (Windows only). You can also remove frames by **right-clicking** (Windows) or **Ctrl+clicking** (Mac) a frame and choosing **Remove Frames** from the pop-up menu.
Blank keyframe	A blank or empty keyframe indicates there is no artwork on the Stage. By default, when you create a new document, the Timeline contains one blank keyframe, which you can identify by the empty circle icon. As soon as you create or place artwork on the Stage, the empty circle icon changes to a solid, black circle, indicating the keyframe contains artwork. Once you have artwork on a keyframe, any new keyframe or frame you create will also include the artwork from the previous keyframe. A blank keyframe, however, will remove any content, including actions and sounds, from the Stage on that layer at that point.
	If you insert a blank keyframe into an empty slot after a keyframe or frame, the previous empty slots will be defined as frames.
	Although a blank keyframe contains no artwork, it *can* contain sound and actions. You will learn more about sound in Chapter 14, "*Sound*," and more about actions in Chapter 12, "*ActionScript Basics and Behaviors*."
	To insert a blank keyframe, select any slot(s) and/or frame(s) in the **Timeline** and press **F7** (Windows only) or choose **Insert > Timeline > Blank Keyframe**.

2 | Frame-by-Frame Animation with Keyframes

A common animation technique is to make a word appear as though it is being written before your eyes. You can achieve this effect easily using keyframes. When you insert a keyframe, Flash 8 copies the content of the previous keyframe to the newly created keyframe, which you can then change to create an animation. In this exercise, you'll learn how to make the word *xboard!* animate on the Stage using frame-by-frame animation.

1 Open **movieFinal.fla** from the **chap_04** folder.

The easiest way to understand animations is to look at a finished example, such as the one in **movieFinal.fla**.

2 Press **Enter** (Windows) or **Return** (Mac) to preview the animation on the **Stage**.

Notice the animation creates the word *xboard!* magically before your eyes! Although it may seem complicated, you'll see how easy it is to create a frame-by-frame animation with keyframes in this exercise.

3 Close **movieFinal.fla**. If you completed Exercise 1, **movie.fla** should still be open. If it's not, open the **movie.fla** file you saved in Exercise 1 or go back and complete Exercise 1.

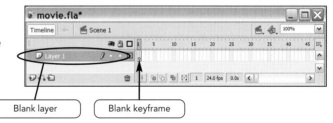

Blank layer   Blank keyframe

Notice **movie.fla** contains a single layer with a single blank keyframe. This is the minimum you need to start drawing, and this is the way all new documents appear by default.

4 In the **Timeline**, double-click the **Layer 1** name. When the bounding box appears, rename the layer **xboard!** and press **Enter** (Windows) or **Return** (Mac).

Naming layers keeps them recognizable and organized.

5 Select the **Brush** tool from the **toolbar**. From the **Color** and **Options** sections of the toolbar, select any size, shape, and color (other than **white**—you'll see why in Step 11).

The Brush tool only paints fills, not strokes, so you want to change the color in the Fill Color well.

Over the next few steps, you'll write the word *xboard!*, one letter at a time, in a series of keyframes.

---

6 With the **Brush** tool selected in the **toolbar**, and **Frame 1** selected in the **Timeline**, draw the first part of the letter **x** on the left side of the **Stage**, as shown in the illustration here.

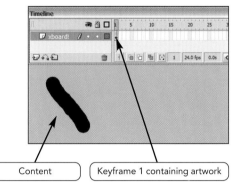

Content   Keyframe 1 containing artwork

Notice Frame 1 now contains a small black dot, indicating it contains artwork. Frame 1 is now referred to as a keyframe, rather than a blank keyframe, because it is no longer empty.

To make a change in the Timeline, you must place a keyframe where you want the change to occur. Now that you have filled in the first keyframe of Layer 1, you are going to add another keyframe at Frame 2 so you can draw the second frame of your animation. Adding a new keyframe after the last one will copy all the content from the previous keyframe to the new keyframe. You will draw another stroke in this new keyframe to create a change in your animation.

---

7 In the **Timeline**, click **Frame 2** to select it and choose **Insert > Timeline > Keyframe** or press **F6**.

This adds a new keyframe at Frame 2. Notice the contents of Frame 1 are the same as the contents of Frame 2. You'll add artwork to Frame 2 in the next step.

Tip: In Windows, remember the **F6** keyboard shortcut, because you will be using it often to insert keyframes.

---

8 With the **Brush** tool still selected and **Frame 2** selected in the **Timeline**, draw the second part of the **x** in the new keyframe.

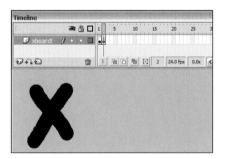

9 Choose **Insert > Timeline > Keyframe** to add a new keyframe to the **Timeline** in **Frame 3**.

Notice Frame 3 has the same contents as Frame 2.

---

10 With the **Brush** tool still selected and **Frame 3** selected in the **Timeline**, draw a **b** on the **Stage**. Click and drag (scrub) the **playhead** back and forth in the **Timeline** to quickly preview the animation. You'll see the **x** and **b** being drawn directly on the **Stage**.

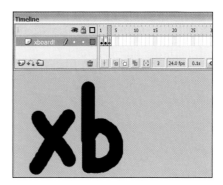

---

11 Choose **Preview in Context** from the **Frame View** menu to display a thumbnail preview of the contents of each keyframe.

Viewing the Timeline with black dots representing keyframes with artwork might seem somewhat abstract to you. The Frame View menu has several options for displaying the contents of your individual frames in the Timeline.

You'll find the Preview in Context view helpful when creating frame-by-frame animations.

Note: Do you remember when you chose a color for the brush in Step 6, and you were asked to choose any color other than white? Now you can see why. If you had chosen white for the brush color, you would not see the artwork in Preview in Context view because the Timeline frames are also white.

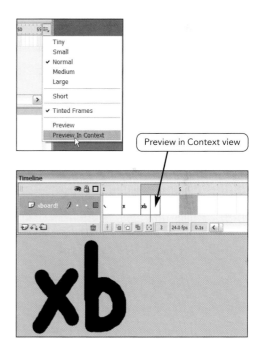

Preview in Context view

---

12 With **Frame 3** selected in the **Timeline**, choose **Insert > Timeline > Keyframe** to insert another keyframe into **Frame 4**.

---

13 With the **Brush** tool still selected, draw an **o** on the **Stage**. As you draw, you'll see the contents of **Frame 4** appear in the **Timeline** preview.

As you continue to spell out the word *xboard!*, you don't have to draw the whole letter in each keyframe. Instead, you can draw a part of the letter (just as you did with the *x*) in one keyframe, choose **Insert > Timeline > Keyframe** to insert the next keyframe, and draw the remaining parts of the letter in that keyframe to create a more realistic animation.

14 Using the techniques you learned in this exercise, use the **Brush** tool and add new keyframes to finish drawing the word *xboard!*. When you are done, your **Timeline** should look like the one shown in the illustration here.

15 Scrub the **playhead** across the **Timeline** to preview the animation on the **Stage**.

16 Press **Enter** (Windows) or **Return** (Mac) to play the animation once.

Unlike scrubbing the playhead, when you press Enter (Windows) or Return (Mac) to preview the animation on the Stage, you see an accurate preview of the frame rate for the animation, which you set to 24 fps in Exercise 1.

17 Choose **Control > Loop Playback** and press **Enter** (Windows) or **Return** (Mac) to repeat the animation continuously. Looping repeats the animation until you choose to stop it.

Notice how fast the animation plays. Next, you'll learn how to slow down the animation by adjusting the frame rate, which defines how many frames your animation plays per second. Due to varying processor speeds, there is no guarantee your movie will always play back at the specified frame rate on every computer. Keep this in mind when you're designing and testing animations. If possible, always test your movies on a variety of computers with varying processor speeds so you can get an accurate idea of the range of results your viewers will see.

18 Press **Enter** (Windows) or **Return** (Mac) to stop the animation.

19 Choose **Normal** from the **Frame View** menu to change the **Timeline** back to **Normal** view so you see keyframes in the **Timeline** instead of a preview of the artwork.

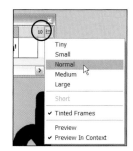

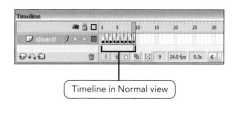

Timeline in Normal view

---

20 Make sure the **Property Inspector** is visible. If it's not, choose **Window > Properties**.

---

21 In the **Frame rate** field, decrease the frame rate to **12**. As you learned in Exercise 1, 12 fps is the default frame rate when you create a new movie in Flash 8.

---

22 Press **Enter** (Windows) or **Return** (Mac).

Notice the animation plays slower. The movie is taking twice as long to play the same number of frames. The lower the frame rate, the slower the animation plays (and vice versa). Go ahead and experiment with other frame rates. When you're finished experimenting, return the frame rate to its default setting of 12 frames per second so you're ready for the next exercise.

---

23 Save and close **movie.fla**.

What Is the Frame Rate?

The frame rate determines the number of frames your movie plays per second. This rate corresponds directly to the length of time your animation takes to play.

Here's how to use the frame rate to calculate the playback time of your animation. Start with the total number of frames in the Timeline and divide it by the frame rate; the result is the number of seconds it will take to view your movie.

For example, if your Timeline has 36 frames, and your frame rate is set to 12 fps, your animation

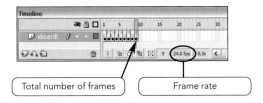

Total number of frames   Frame rate

length will be 3 seconds. The following chart gives examples of how the frame rate affects the duration of the animation. Next, you will learn how to create more than one animation in the same movie and have them play at different speeds.

Frame Rate

Number of Frames	÷	Frame Rate	=	Duration
24 frames	÷	12 fps	=	2 seconds
36 frames	÷	12 fps	=	3 seconds
48 frames	÷	24 fps	=	2 seconds

Recommended Frame Rates

When you set a frame rate in Flash 8, you're setting the maximum frame rate for your movie, or how quickly the movie "tries" to play. The actual playback frame rate depends on several factors, including the download speed and processor speed of the computer used to view the movie. If the frame rate is set higher than the computer can display, the movie will play as fast as the computer's processor will allow. If you set the frame rate to 200 (which is really high), the average computer will not be able to display the movie at this rate. Also, frames with more objects, colors, or

transparency than others take more time for the computer to render. Thus, the actual frame rate can vary during playback due to the rendering requirements from one frame to another.

Based on these factors, use a frame rate of at least 12 fps and not more than 25 fps, so the average computer can display your movie as you intended. A frame rate of 15 to 20 fps, which is similar to the 24 fps used in motion pictures, works well most of the time.

3 | Inserting and Deleting Frames

As you learn to create animations, you'll want to adjust the speed of your animations. In the previous exercise, you learned how to adjust the frame rate to increase and decrease the speed of an animation. But what do you do if you want only certain sections of your movie to play faster or slower than other sections? In this exercise, you will learn how to insert and remove frames in the Timeline so different sections of an animation play at different speeds, even though they all share the same frame rate.

1 Open **frames.fla** from the **chap_04** folder.

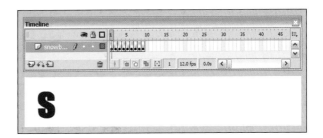

As you can see, the file contains one layer with a simple frame-by-frame animation using text. You'll get a chance to work with text in Chapter 13, "*Working with Text.*"

2 Press **Enter** (Windows) or **Return** (Mac) to preview the animation on the **Stage**.

As you can see, the animation plays so fast you almost lose the effect of the text appearing one letter at a time. Adjusting the frame rate to slow down this animation will affect the entire movie, which could be problematic because you may want other sections of your movie to play at a different speed. For example, in this project you may want the word *snow* to appear slowly and the word *board* to appear quickly. You can solve this problem easily by inserting duplicate frames at strategic points to lengthen parts of the animation.

3 In the **Timeline**, click **Frame 1** to select it. Choose **Insert > Timeline > Frame (F5)**, which duplicates the contents of Frame 1 and extends the **Timeline** by one frame.

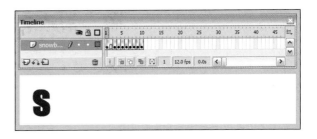

When you add a new frame, Flash 8 creates a duplicate of the preceding frame. You aren't going to change this content; if you wanted to change the duplicate content, a keyframe would have been a better choice.

4 With **Frame 1** still selected in the **Timeline**, press **F5** to insert another frame. Each time you choose **Insert > Timeline > Frame** or press **F5**, you will insert one frame to extend the **Timeline**.

What Do Those Dots Mean?

As you start adding content to your project, you'll notice different icons in the Timeline. The black dots indicate keyframes with content. The light-gray frames without icons indicate frames (no change in content).

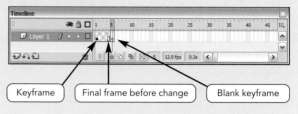

Keyframe | Final frame before change | Blank keyframe

For example, in the illustration here, Frames 2, 3, and 4 have the same content as Keyframe 1. The white rectangle indicates the last frame in a frame range, which means the next frame will be either a blank keyframe (empty) or a keyframe (with content). In this example, the empty circle icon indicates a blank keyframe.

5 With **Frame 1** still selected in the **Timeline**, press **F5** eight more times (giving you a total of 11 additional frames between the first two keyframes).

By adding more frames, you are extending the distance between the first two keyframes in the Timeline. The additional frames slow down the speed of the animation because the content of Keyframe 1 will display for a longer period of time.

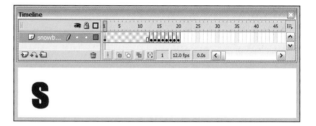

6 Press **Enter** (Windows) or **Return** (Mac) to preview the animation on the **Stage**.

Notice there is a significant delay between the letters *s* and *n*—about one second—because 12 frames divided by 12 fps = 1 second. Even though you changed the delay between the letters *s* and *n*, you didn't affect the speed of the rest of the animation. As you can see, this is a great trick to use when you want to play different sections of an animation at different speeds.

7 In the Timeline, click **Frame 13** to select it.

Frame 13 is the new location of the second keyframe. It was originally in Frame 2 before you added more frames in Steps 3, 4, and 5.

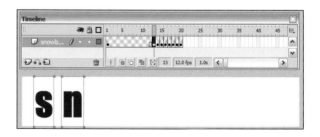

8 Press **F5** 11 times to insert 11 frames in the **Timeline**.

Each added frame contains the same content as Frame 13, creating another pause between the letters *n* and *o*.

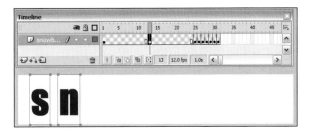

---

9 Using the techniques you learned in Steps 7 and 8, add frames between the letters *o* and *w*.

---

10 Press **Enter** (Windows) or **Return** (Mac) to preview the animation on the **Stage**.

Notice how much slower the word *snow* animates compared to the word *board*. As you can see from this exercise, you can control the timing of an animation without having to adjust the frame rate of the entire movie. Inserting frames slows down specific sections in the animation. The inverse is also true— you can speed up an animation by deleting frames. You'll learn how in the next few steps.

---

11 In the **Timeline**, click **Frame 2** to select it. **Right-click** (Windows) or **Ctrl+click** (Mac) and choose **Remove Frame**s from the contextual menu or use the Windows shortcut key **Shift+F5** to remove the currently selected frame.

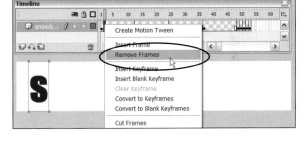

As you can see, you shortened the Timeline by one frame and decreased the amount of time between the letters *s* and *n* in your animation.

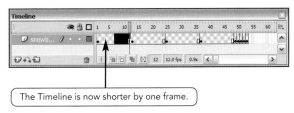

The Timeline is now shorter by one frame.

---

12 Click and drag **Frames 7** through **11** to multiple-select the frames.

---

13 With **Frames 7** through **11** selected, choose **Edit > Timeline > Remove Frames** (or use the Windows shortcut key **Shift+F5**) to remove the selected frames and shorten your **Timeline** by five frames.

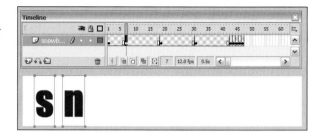

14 Using the techniques you learned in Steps 11, 12, and 13, reduce the number of frames so there are only five frames between the *s*, *n*, *o*, and *w* keyframes.

15 Press **Enter** (Windows) or **Return (Mac)** to preview your animation on the **Stage**.

As you can see, the word *snow* now plays faster than it did in Step 10, but still slower than the letters in the word *board*. The animation plays at two speeds because there are more frames between the keyframes in the word *snow* but fewer frames between the keyframes for the word *board*. Adding frames is a great technique for speeding up or slowing down the timing of animations without changing the frame rate of the entire movie.

16 Close **frames.fla**. You don't need to save your changes.

4 | Copying and Reversing Frames

Creating a looping animation (one that repeats indefinitely) can be a lot of work if you have to draw each frame over and over. In Flash Professional 8, you can copy, paste, and reverse a sequence of frames to create a looping animation. You will learn how in this exercise.

1 Open **loopingFinal.fla** from the **chap_04** folder. Choose **Control > Loop Playback** to set the playback option to **Loop**, or repeat indefinitely. Press **Enter** (Windows) or **Return** (Mac) to preview the animation on the **Stage**.

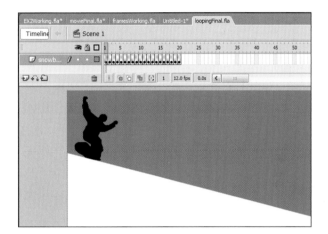

This is the completed version of the animation you'll create in this exercise. As you can see, the snowboarder cruises down and up the mountain slope over and over. You will create this same animation technique without having to draw all the frames over again.

2 Choose **Control > Loop Playback** to stop the animation from looping. Press **Enter** (Windows) or **Return** (Mac) to stop previewing the animation on the **Stage**. Close **loopingFinal.fla**

3 Open **looping.fla** from the **chap_04** folder.

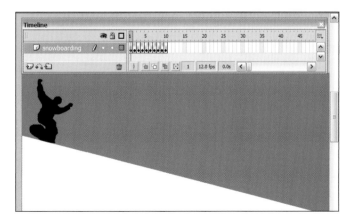

The file contains a single layer named snowboarding, which contains a sequence of 10 keyframes. In each keyframe, the boarder is a little further down the slope, creating the illusion that the boarder is moving down the slope when the sequence is played back.

4 In the **Timeline**, click the **snowboarding** layer to select all the frames.

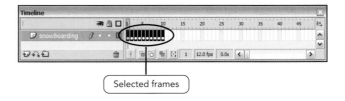

Selecting a layer in the Timeline is an easy way to multiple-select the frames on a layer. Next, you'll make a copy of the selected frames.

Selected frames

---

5 Position your pointer over the selected frames. Click and drag the frames to the right, inside the **Timeline**. Don't release the mouse just yet!

Notice as you click and drag the frames a light-gray outline indicates the selected frames and where they'll be moved when you release the mouse button.

---

6 Without releasing the mouse, hold down the **Alt** (Windows) or **Option** (Mac) key.

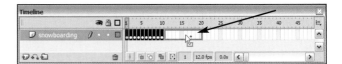

Notice the small plus sign appears to the right of the pointer indicating you will duplicate (or copy), not move (or cut), the frames when you release the mouse.

---

7 Release the mouse to create a copy of the selected frames in **Frames 11** through **20**.

---

8 Press **Enter** (Windows) or **Return** (Mac) to preview the movie on the **Stage**.

Notice the animation does not look correct. The boarder reaches the bottom of the slope and jumps back up to the top, which is not the same as the single fluid motion you saw in the finished animation. In traditional animation, you'd have to redraw all the frames in reverse order to achieve this effect. Fortunately in Flash 8, you can save yourself that manual process and simply duplicate and reverse the existing frames in the animation. You'll learn how in the next steps.

9 Click **Frame 11** and then **Shift+click Frame 20** to select **Frames 11** through **20**. Choose **Modify > Timeline > Reverse Frames**.

You won't see a change in the Timeline, but you will notice the change on the Stage when you test the movie.

---

10 Press **Enter** (Windows) or **Return** (Mac) to preview your animation on the **Stage**. As you can see, the snowboarder races down the hill and goes back up the hill, as if you were rewinding the film to view an instant replay! Nice! If you choose **Control > Loop Playback**, you can watch the animation preview loop endlessly.

---

11 Close **looping.fla**. You don't need to save your changes.

---

5 | Using Onion Skinning

Now that you have created a couple of frame-by-frame animations, it's a good time to add a few new tricks to your bag. First, you'll learn to use the Onion Skinning feature, which lets you to see a ghost image of the previous frame so you can see where you want to place the artwork in relation to the preceding frames. You will also learn to use the Free Transform tool, which allows you to scale, rotate, skew, and distort your artwork.

1 Open **onionFinal.fla** file from the **chap_04** folder. Choose **Control > Loop Playback** to set the playback option to loop, or repeat indefinitely. Press **Enter** (Windows) or **Return** (Mac) to preview the animation on the **Stage**.

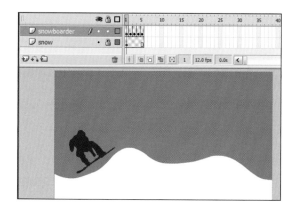

This is the completed version of the animation you'll create in this exercise. In this animation, you'll see the snowboarder catching some air! You will create this same animation technique without having to draw all the frames over again.

2 Choose **Control > Loop Playback** to stop the looping. Press **Enter** (Windows) or **Return** (Mac) to stop previewing the animation on the **Stage**. When you're finished viewing the animation, close **onionFinal.fla**.

3 Open **onion.fla** from the **chap_04** folder.

This file contains one keyframe with the snowboarder beginning his jump on the top layer and one keyframe with the snow on the bottom layer. The snow layer has been locked so that you don't accidentally select something on it. You will be modifying the artwork and creating the frame-by-frame animation on the snowboarder layer in the next few steps.

4 Click **Frame 2** of the **snowboarder** layer to select it and choose **Insert > Timeline > Keyframe** to add a keyframe.

Frame 2 now contains a small black dot, indicating it contains content. As you know from Exercise 2, when you create a new keyframe, it copies the content from the previous keyframe—in this case, Frame 1.

Tip: If you try to add a keyframe without first selecting a frame, nothing happens. Why? When you have more than one layer in your document, you have to select the frame so Flash 8 knows where to insert the keyframe.

---

5 With the playhead on **Frame 2**, click the snowboarder artwork on the **Stage** to select it. You'll know it's selected when you see the dotted mesh. Click and drag the snowboarder up and to the right, as though he is advancing in his jump.

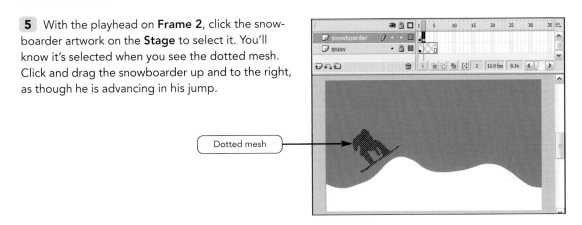

Dotted mesh

---

6 Click the **Onion Skin** button.

Onion Skin button

Notice the faint ghost image showing the content of Frame 1 on the Stage. Onion skinning lets you see the artwork in the previous keyframes and change the artwork relative to the ghost images.

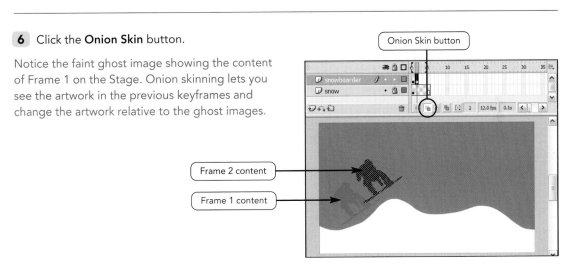

Frame 2 content

Frame 1 content

Onion Skin Markers

After you click the Onion Skin button, a gray bar with a draggable bracket on each end appears at the top of the Timeline. These are called onion skin markers. The start onion skin marker (the one on the left) is on Frame 1 (the first frame of your animation), and the end onion skin marker (the one on the right) is on Frame 5 (the last frame of your animation). If you click and drag your playhead to the right or left, the start onion skin marker will move along with it. You can also drag either of the onion skin markers to the left or right to include more frames if they are spanning fewer keyframes than you have in the Timeline.

Onion Skin markers

---

7 Select the **Free Transform** tool from the **toolbar**.

The Free Transform tool lets you modify selected artwork by changing the size, rotation, skew, and distortion. To learn more about the Free Transform tool, check out the chart at the end of this exercise.

---

8 Make sure the **playhead** is on **Frame 2**, and click the snowboarder on the **Stage** to select it.

Notice a bounding box appears around the artwork, indicating you can transform the artwork. If you position the pointer near or over the handles (the squares in the corners and on the edges of the bounding box), the pointer changes, indicating the transform options.

---

9 Position your pointer just outside the upper-right corner of the bounding box until it changes to the **rotate** icon (a round arrow). Click and drag to the right to rotate the snowboarder slightly to make the jump look more realistic.

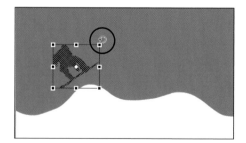

---

10 Click **Frame 3** to select it and choose **Insert > Timeline > Keyframe** to insert another keyframe.

---

11 Click the snowboarder artwork with the **Free Transform** tool to select it. Click and drag to move the snowboarder to the right. Using the technique you learned in Step 9, click and drag to rotate the snowboarder.

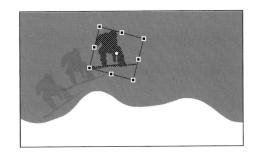

12 Repeat Steps 10 and 11 twice more, adding keyframes to Frames 4 and 5, positioning, and rotating the artwork in each keyframe. When you're finished, the artwork on the **Stage** should match the artwork shown in the illustration here.

13 Choose **Control > Loop Playback**. Press **Enter** (Windows) or **Return** (Mac) to preview the movie on the **Stage**. When you're finished, choose **Control > Loop Playback** to stop the movie from repeating and press **Enter** (Windows) or **Return** (Mac) to stop the movie.

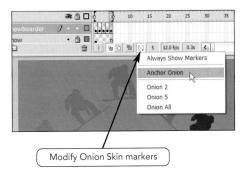

Modify Onion Skin markers

As you can see, the snowboarder is catching some air— just like in the final movie you looked at in Step 1!

If you do not want the onion skin markers to move when you move the playhead or click a frame in the Timeline, you can choose **Anchor Onion** from the **Modify Onion Markers** button pop-up menu to lock the onion skinning span where it is until you unlock it again or manually drag the start or end onion skin markers.

14 Experiment with the **Free Transform** tool to create more effects. Try resizing, rotating, and skewing using the editing nodes.

You'll get a chance to work with the Free Transform tool again in Chapter 6, "*Symbols and Instances*."

15 When you are finished experimenting, close **onion.fla**. You don't need to save your changes.

VIDEO: | **onion.mov**

To learn more about onion skinning, check out **onion.mov** in the **videos** folder on the **HOT CD-ROM**.

NOTE: | **The Free Transform Tool**

The Free Transform tool lets you modify objects in several ways. As you position the pointer over the bounding box of a selected object, it will change to indicate what type of transformation is available. As you click and drag, you will see a preview of the transformation you are about to make. The following chart lists how you can use the Free Transform tool to transform objects.

Free Transform Tool Features	
	Clicking and dragging up or down on a corner transform handle rotates the object. The pointer icon changes to a round arrow, indicating that you can rotate the object.
	Clicking and dragging diagonally on one of the corner transform handles modifies the scale of the object. The pointer changes to a diagonal double-pointed arrow when you can perform this transformation.
	Clicking and dragging one of the middle side transform handles modifies the width or height of the object. The pointer changes to a horizontal (or vertical depending on which side you are on) double-pointed arrow when you can perform this transformation.
	Clicking and dragging between any two transform handles skews the object. The pointer changes, indicating that you can skew the object.
	Clicking and dragging one of the middle side transform handles to the other side of the object flips the object. The pointer changes to a horizontal or vertical double-pointed arrow depending on which side you are on.
	Clicking and dragging the center registration point modifies the center point of the object. After you alter the center point, all transformations will rotate or move in relation to the new center point location.

6 | Testing Movies

So far, you've been testing your movies by previewing them on the Stage. This is a great way to test the frame rate, but there are other ways to test your work. In this exercise, you will learn how to preview the movie file as a SWF file—the format you would use to publish the movie to the Web—with the Test Movie feature. You'll learn a really easy way to produce the HTML file required to view the SWF file in a Web browser. You'll also learn how to preview the movie in a browser with the Preview in Browser feature. This exercises covers the basics—you'll find more in-depth information about publishing Flash 8 content in Chapter 17, "*Publishing and Exporting.*"

---

1 Open **frames_Test.fla** from the **chap_04** folder.

It is important to know where your project file (FLA) has been saved before you use the Test Movie and Preview in Browser features because Flash 8 generates new files and automatically saves them in the same location as your project file (FLA). If you saved your file in a different location, just make sure you know where it is. In this case, you're working with **frames_Test.fla**, which is included in the **chap_04** folder.

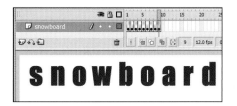

---

2 Choose **Control > Test Movie** or press **Ctrl+Enter** (Windows) or **Cmd+Return** (Mac) to preview the movie file in a new window as a SWF file.

When you test the movie, Flash 8 automatically previews the movie as a SWF file, which is exactly what you'd see if you exported the file as a SWF.

Tip: You can click and drag the resize handle

Resize handle

of the preview window to change its size. Although the size of the window changes, the snowboard letters stay the same size. You'll learn how to make content scalable using the publish settings in Chapter 17, "*Publishing and Exporting.*"

TIP:

Loop-de-loop

At this point, you're probably wondering why your animation is looping (playing over and over). This is the default behavior of all movies in Flash 8, although you don't see it when you simply press Enter (Windows) or Return (Mac) to preview your movie (unless you've turned on the Loop Playback option). If you upload the published file to the Web, it would loop. You will learn to control the looping in your final movie (SWF) file in Chapter 12, "*ActionScript Basics and Behaviors*," when you learn how to add actions to frames. If all this looping is making you dizzy, you can choose **Control > Loop Playback** to toggle this feature off.

3 With the preview window still open, choose **Window > Toolbars > Controller** to open the **Controller** toolbar.

This handy little gadget is especially useful with longer movies—it lets you easily stop, restart, or step back one frame at a time in the Timeline.

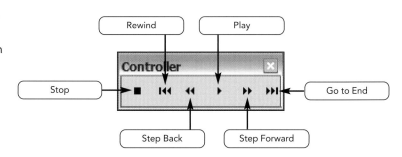

4 Click the **Stop** button to stop your animation.

5 Click the **Play** button to play the animation. If you'd like, experiment with the other buttons on the **Controller** toolbar.

Although you didn't see it happen, when you tested the movie in Step 2, Flash 8 automatically created the SWF for the movie and saved it in the same location as your project (FLA) file. You'll locate this file next.

6 Open the **chap_04** folder.

Notice the **frames_Test.swf** file inside this folder. This file was automatically generated by Flash 8. Also notice the SWF file has a different icon than the FLA files, which can be helpful visual feedback, especially if your file extensions are turned off. The SWF file is the file you'd use on a Web page in the same manner you would use a GIF or JPG.

7 Return to Flash 8 and close the preview window.

---

8 Choose **File > Publish Preview > Default – (HTML)** or press **F12** to launch your default browser with a preview of your movie file (SWF).

Previewing the SWF file in a browser is a quick and easy way to see what the movie looks like and how it plays back in a browser. Although this technique is great for previewing your movies, you'll learn better ways to publish the final SWF file in Chapter 17, "*Publishing and Exporting.*"

NOTE: | **Defining a Default Browser**
If you have several browsers installed on your computer, you can specify which one Flash uses as the default browser. There's a great explanation of how to define default browsers in Windows and on a Mac on Macromedia's Web site: **http://www.macromedia.com/support/flash/ts/documents/browser_pref.htm**.

---

9 Hide Flash 8 and navigate to the **chap_04** folder.

Notice there is a **frames_Test.html** file inside the **chap_04** folder. When you published a preview of the file in Step 8, Flash 8 generated the HTML file automatically, which is what lets you view the SWF file in a browser.

At this point, all the files necessary to publish to the Web have been generated for you automatically. More thorough instructions and details about this process will be provided in Chapter 17, "*Publishing and Exporting.*" The purpose of this exercise was to demonstrate a quick and easy way to preview your projects.

---

10 Return to Flash 8. Close **frames_Test.fla**. You don't need to save your changes.

Congratulations—you just completed a long, but essential, part of your animation training! The next three chapters focus on more complex and specific animation topics, such as shape tweening, symbols and instances, and motion tweening. Now would be a great time for a break. You've worked through a lot of material, and you deserve one!

5

Shape Tweening

No doubt you've seen animations on the Web or on television showing an object transforming (or morphing) from one shape into another. You can create this effect in Flash 8 using a technique called shape tweening.

The exercises in this chapter offer a thorough introduction to shape tweening. By working through them, you will expand your Flash 8 skill set to include shape tweening, shape hinting, and multiple shape tweening.

What Is Shape Tweening?

Shape tweening lets you gradually transform, or morph, a shape into another shape. For example, you can start with a circle and gradually transform, or morph, it into a square by creating a series of shapes in-between that slowly change from a circle to a square.

In traditional animation, a *lead* or *key* animator creates *extremes*, such as the starting frame (in this case the circle) and the ending point (in this case the square). A second animator, the *in-betweener*, performs the tedious task of creating the transitional frames between the start and end point so the animation slowly morphs from the square to the circle.

In computer animation, the process is similar—you begin with a starting frame and an ending frame. Fortunately, the computer generates the in-between frames, saving you the time-consuming task of creating them yourself. The process of generating the in-between frames is called *tweening*.

Before moving on to the hands-on exercises, take some time to familiarize yourself with some key terms—shape, keyframes, and tweening—which are described in the following chart:

Shape Tweening Terms and Definitions

Terms	Definition
Shape	In Flash 8, shapes are vector-based objects or a series of vector-based objects. You can create shapes in Flash 8 using any of the drawing tools with either the merge drawing model or new object drawing model you learned about in Chapter 3, "*Using the Drawing and Color Tools*," or you can import shapes into Flash 8 from other vector-creation programs, such as Adobe Illustrator or Macromedia Freehand. In order for a shape to be suitable for shape tweening, it cannot be composed of grouped objects, bitmaps, or symbols. (You will learn about symbols in Chapter 6, "*Symbols and Instances*.") You can shape tween with type if it's first converted to a shape, which is called "breaking apart." You will learn how to break type apart later in this chapter.
Keyframe	In traditional animation, "key" or "lead" animators draw "extremes," or the important frames that define motion or transition. In the example here, the key animator would create two keyframes—the first with a circle and the second with a square.
Tweening	The term *tweening* is borrowed from traditional animation terminology and is slang for *in-betweening*. In traditional animation, a second animator, referred to as the "in-betweener" takes the "extremes" created by the key animator and creates transitional frames between the starting point and the ending point to describe the motion. In this example, the "in-betweener" uses circle and square frames and draws a series of transitional shapes morphing from the circle to the square. As you can imagine, it requires a lot of precision and attention to detail to develop these frames. Fortunately, Flash 8 creates the in-between frames for you.

Flash 8 can also shape tween lines into shapes, or shapes into lines, regardless of differences in the colors or gradients between the starting and end points. Here is one example:

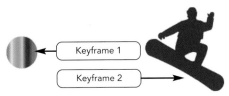

The first step in creating a shape tween is to create two unique keyframes.

Next, apply a shape tween to the keyframes. Flash 8 interpolates the difference between the keyframes and automatically generates all of the in-between frames.

Shape tweening is the only process in Flash 8 that lets you quickly animate from one distinct shape to another. You can also use shape tweening to animate from one gradient to another, from one color to another, and/or from one position on the Stage to another. The possibilities and limitations of shape tweening in Flash 8 are as follows.

What shape tweening can do:

- Tween the shape of an object

- Tween the color of an object (including a color with transparency

- Tween the position of an object

- Tween scale, rotation, and skew of an object

- Tween text that has been broken apart

- Tween gradients

What shape tweening can't do:

- Tween grouped objects

- Tween symbols

- Tween text that has not been broken apart

1 | Shape Tweening

In this exercise, you'll learn the basics of shape tweening by creating an animation of a snowboard changing into the letter *X*.

---

1 Copy the **chap_05** folder from the **HOT CD-ROM** to your **Desktop**. Open **textTween_Final.fla** from the **chap_05** folder. Press **Enter** (Windows) or **Return** (Mac) to preview the animation. When you're finished previewing the final animation, close **textTween_Final.fla**.

Notice the animation of the snowboard gradually morphs into the letter *X*. You'll learn how to create this animation with the shape tweening features in the following steps.

---

2 Open **textTween.fla** from the **chap_05** folder.

As you can see, the file contains two layers: one named **boarding text** with the word *boarding* on it and one named **tween** with the snowboard shape on it. You will be working on the tween layer.

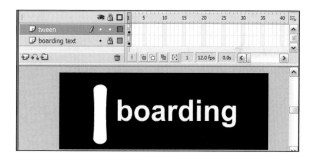

---

3 With the **tween** layer selected, click **Frame 12** to select it and press **F7** to add a blank keyframe.

By adding a blank keyframe rather than a keyframe, you can create new artwork on Frame 12. This is in contrast to copying the artwork from Frame 1, which you learned about in Chapter 4, "*Animation Basics.*"

Notice Frame 12 is blank—it contains neither the snowboard nor the word *boarding*. Take a

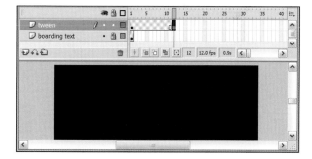

look at the Timeline closely. Notice the boarding text layer has only one frame, and the tween layer now has 12 frames. In order for the word *boarding* to appear throughout the entire animation, the boarding text layer must also contain 12 frames. You'll fix this in the next step.

4 On the **boarding text** layer, click **Frame 12** and press **F5** to add frames up to **Frame 12**.

Tip: Layers are not at all related to frames. Layers represent the relationship of objects in space (one object on top or below another object), whereas frames represent the relationship of objects in time (one object appearing after or before another object).

5 In the **toolbar**, select the **Text** tool. On the **tween** layer, click **Frame 12** to select it. Position your pointer on the **Stage**, click once, and type the capital letter *X*.

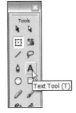

Note: The letter *X* uses the following text options in the Property Inspector: Arial font, size 86, white, and bold type, but you can use whatever options you like. You will learn more about the text options in Chapter 13, "*Working with Text*."

6 In the toolbar, select the **Selection** tool. Click the *X* you created in the last step to select it. Drag the *X* to position it as shown in the illustration here.

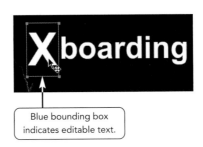

When you create text using the Text tool, the text is still in an editable format, which means you can double-click it and change the letters to something else. If you deselect the text and use the Selection tool to select it again, you'll see a blue bounding box and no dotted mesh, indicating it is still editable text. To shape tween it, you have to convert it from editable text to an editable shape by breaking it apart; you cannot use editable text as the source of a shape tween. Although you may not think of type as a grouped object, you must break it to become a shape. You'll learn more about working with text in Chapter 13, "*Working with Text*."

Blue bounding box indicates editable text.

7 With the *X* still selected, choose **Modify > Break Apart**, or press **Ctrl+B** (Windows) or **Cmd+B** (Mac), to break apart the text and convert it to a shape.

The dotted mesh indicates you're now working with a shape, which you can use to shape tween.

Dotted mesh indicates selection is a shape.

---

8 Click anywhere between the two keyframes to select a frame. Any frame will work—just do not select a keyframe.

---

9 Make sure the **Property Inspector** is open. If it is not, choose **Window > Properties > Properties**. In the **Property Inspector**, choose **Shape** from the **Tween** pop-up menu to apply a shape tween between the keyframes.

After you apply a shape tween between two keyframes, you'll see green shading between the keyframes on the Timeline, indicating the shape tween is active and working.

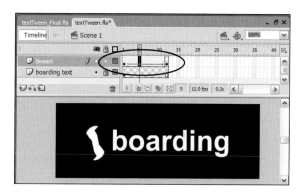

---

10 Hold down the **Shift** key and click **Frame 24** on the **tween** and **boarding text** layers to multiple-select both frames. Press **F5**. Flash adds 12 more frames for you, extending the animation out to **Frame 24**.

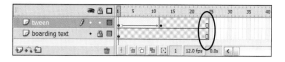

Adding these additional 12 frames adds one more second to the animation (provided the frame rate is set to the default setting of 12 frames per second) before it loops again, making the total length of the animation about two seconds.

11 Choose **Control > Test Movie** to view the movie in a preview window.

You'll see the snowboard morph into the letter *X*. If the animation does not morph the way you expected, don't worry, you'll learn how control it more precisely with shape hints in the upcoming exercise.

---

12 When you are finished testing, close the preview window and return to Flash 8. Save **textTween.fla** and keep it open for the next exercise.

WARNING:

Fixing Broken Tweens

As you work more with shape and motion tweens, you'll sometimes encounter a broken (dashed) line in your Timeline instead of a solid arrow. The broken line indicates your tween is not working, making it easy to spot problems with your animations.

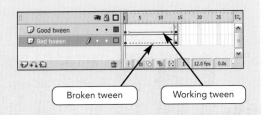

Here are some tips for troubleshooting broken tweens:

- Make sure the objects in each keyframe are shapes and not grouped objects.

- Make sure the text has been broken apart.

Sometimes, you may even need to erase the tween and start over from the first keyframe. You'll learn more about the causes of broken shape tweens when you learn about symbols in future chapters.

2 | Using Shape Hints

When creating shape tweens, Flash 8 automatically determines how one shape will change into the next shape. This process is automatic, so you don't have complete control over how the tween is constructed. Shape hinting helps you regain some control over a tween, and you'll use it primarily to fix a shape tween that doesn't tween quite to your liking. In this exercise, you'll use the animation you created in Exercise 1 and add shape hints to better control how the snowboard morphs in to the X.

1 If you just completed Exercise 1, **textTween.fla** should still be open. If it's not, go back and complete Exercise 1. Press **Enter** (Windows) or **Return** (Mac) to preview the shape tween.

Notice as the shape tween progresses, the snowboard unnaturally appears to crumple up like a piece of paper and then all of a sudden pop into the letter X. In this exercise, you'll learn how to make the tween appear more fluid and natural.

2 Click the **tween** layer to select it and position the **playhead** over **Frame 1**.

When you add shape hints, you must start on the first frame of your animation.

3 Choose **Modify > Shape > Add Shape Hint**.

Notice the red circle with an *a* appears in the middle of the snowboard, indicating it is a shape hint.

4 In the **toolbar**, select the **Selection** tool, and drag the shape hint to the upper-left corner of the snowboard.

5 Position the **playhead** over **Frame 12**, which is the last frame of the shape tween.

Just as in Step 3, you'll see a shape hint appear in the middle of the shape, in this case the *X*. You'll position the shape hint in the next step.

6 Drag the shape hint to the upper-left, inside corner of the *X*. Moving the shape hint ensures the upper-left corner of the snowboard ends up as the upper-left corner of the letter *X*.

When you release the mouse, the shape hint is supposed to change from red to green but these color changes are not always reliable. This color change is Flash's way of telling you the shape hint has been accepted. If your shape hint doesn't turn green on the final keyframe of the tween, you did not place it in the same (or in a similar) location as the first shape hint, and you'll need to make some adjustments. You may need to reposition shape hints to fine-tune a shape tween—sometimes just a small adjustment will help Flash 8 get the hint (pun intended)!

According to the Flash 8 documentation, shape hints should be yellow in the starting keyframe, green in the ending keyframe, and red when they are not on a curve (the edge of a shape), although this is not always the case. Since these color changes are not reliable, your best bet is to place shape hints in similar locations on each keyframe and pay more attention to how the tween animates than to the color of the shape hints.

7 Position the **playhead** back over **Frame 1** and press **Enter** (Windows) or **Return** (Mac) to preview the animation with the shape hint.

Notice the shape tween is already more smooth and natural. Next, you'll add more shape hints to improve it some more.

8 On the **Timeline**, make sure the **playhead** is positioned over **Frame 1**. Choose **Modify > Shape > Add Shape Hint** to add another shape hint to the snowboard.

Notice the second shape hint icon has a small *b*, indicating it is the second shape hint.

9 Drag the second shape hint to the upper-right corner of the snowboard.

10 Position the **playhead** over **Frame 12** (the last keyframe of your shape tween). Drag the second shape hint (*b*) to the upper-right, outside corner of the *X*.

11 Position the **playhead** over **Frame 1** and press **Enter** (Windows) or **Return** (Mac) to preview your work.

As you can see, the transition is getting more and more natural looking!

12 On the **Timeline**, make sure the **playhead** is over **Frame 1**. Repeat Steps 8, 9, and 10 two more times to add two more shape hints, moving them to the remaining corners of the snowboard and the *X*. When you are finished, **Frame 1** and **Frame 12** should match the illustration shown here.

13 Press **Enter** (Windows) or **Return** (Mac) to test the shape tween.

Experiment with adjusting the positions of the shape hints. Moving them even slightly can give a completely different look to your shape tween.

Although adding hints helps smooth out a shape tween, there may be times when you want to remove shape hints. You'll learn how in the next few steps.

14 Position the **playhead** over **Frame 1**. **Right-click** (Windows) or **Ctrl+click** (Mac) on shape hint *d*. Choose **Remove Hint** from the contextual menu to remove the shape hint.

15 Press **Enter** (Windows) or **Return** (Mac) to see how removing the shape hint affects the animation. Remove another shape hint and notice how it affects the animation.

16 When you are finished experimenting, save your changes and close **textTween.fla**.

3 | Creating Multiple Shape Tweens

So far, you've learned how to create single shape tweens. In this exercise, you'll learn how to create multiple shape tweens by placing them on separate layers using the Distribute to Layers feature. Working with multiple layers is the only way to choreograph animations with multiple tweens. This exercise will also introduce the layer folder feature, which is a wonderful way to organize and consolidate animations containing many different layers.

1 Open **mutplShpTwn_Final.fla** from the **chap_05** folder. Press **Enter** (Windows) or **Return** (Mac) to preview the movie. If you can't see the entire **Stage**, choose **View > Magnification > Show All** so you can see the whole animation, complete with multiple shape tweens. When you're finished viewing the animation, close the file.

In this exercise, you'll re-create this animation by shape tweening the alpha, or transparency, and size of multiple shapes. On the Timeline, notice the folder with all the layers inside. The folder icon represents a layer folder, which you'll learn about near the end of this exercise.

2 Open **mutplShpTwn.fla** from the **chap_05** folder.

As you can see, this file contains one layer with five different shapes. Although you can tween one shape into many shapes using just a single layer, the tween you will create in the next few steps requires each of the five shapes to be animated on its own separate layer.

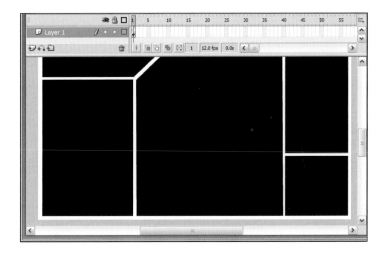

3 With **Layer 1** selected, click **Frame 1** to select all the shapes and choose **Modify > Timeline > Distribute to Layers**.

The Distribute to Layers feature places each of the selected shapes on its own layer. If you

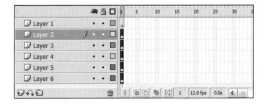

click any of the shapes on the Stage, you'll see the corresponding layer highlighted on the Timeline.

4 Double-click **Layer 2**. When the bounding box appears, rename the layer to **Left bottom** and press **Enter** (Windows) or **Return** (Mac). Rename **Layer 2** to **Left bottom**, **Layer 3** to **Left top**, **Layer 4** to **Middle**, **Layer 5** to **Right bottom**, and **Layer 6** to **Right top**.

Renaming layers with descriptive names makes it easier to identify which shape is on each layer.

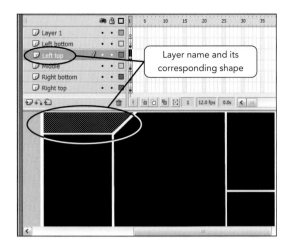

Layer name and its corresponding shape

TIP :

Resizing the Timeline

Use the scroll bar at the base of the Timeline to reveal more layers. Use the scroll bar to the right to extend the Timeline to reveal more of the layer names.

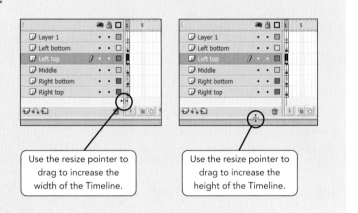

Use the resize pointer to drag to increase the width of the Timeline.

Use the resize pointer to drag to increase the height of the Timeline.

---

5 On the **Left bottom** layer, click **Frame 12** to select it. **Shift+click Frame 12** of the **Right top** layer to select **Frame 12** on all the layers.

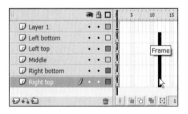

6 Choose **Insert > Timeline > Keyframe** on **Frame 12** of each of the currently selected layers to add a keyframe to each.

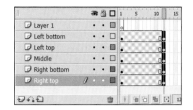

Inserting a keyframe copies the artwork from Frame 1 of each layer, which will serve as the ending keyframe of your shape tween animation.

---

7 Position the **playhead** over **Frame 1**.

Next, you'll prepare the beginning point of the shape tween animation by altering the size of each shape in Frame 1.

---

8 On the **Timeline**, click the **Lock/Unlock All Layers** button, next to the **eye** icon, to lock all the currently selected layers. On the **Left bottom** layer, click the **lock** icon to unlock just that layer.

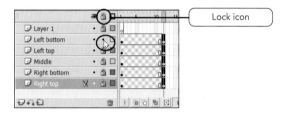

Locking layers makes it easier to work on just a single layer's shapes without affecting any of the other shapes.

---

9 On the **Left bottom** layer, click **Frame 1** to select it. In the **toolbar**, select the **Free Transform** tool. Position your pointer over the upper-right corner of the rectangle. When the resize pointer appears, drag toward the lower-left portion of the **Stage** to resize the shape, as shown in the illustration here. This will be the starting point of the animation for the **Left bottom** layer.

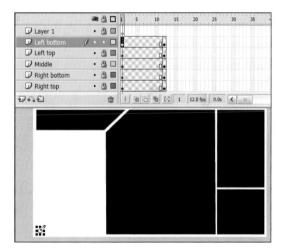

Tip: To scale the shape keeping the same proportion (or aspect ratio), hold down the **Shift** key as you drag the resize pointer.

---

10 On the **Left bottom** layer, click the dot in the **lock** column to lock the layer. Click the **lock** icon for the **Middle** layer to unlock the layer.

Next, you'll resize the shape on the **Middle** layer.

11 On the **Middle** layer, click **Frame 1** to select it. With the **Free Transform** tool still selected in the **toolbar**, hold down the **Shift+Alt** (Windows) or **Shift+Option** (Mac) keys and drag down and toward the lower left of the **Stage**, as shown in the illustration here.

Holding down the **Shift+Alt** (Windows) or **Shift+Option** (Mac) keys scales the shape down from its center, rather than one of the corners, creating the starting point for the animation in the center of the Middle layer.

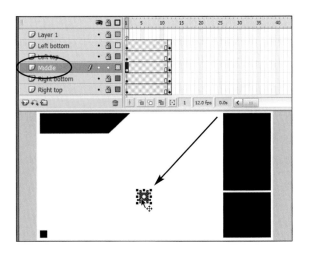

12 Repeat Steps 10 and 11 to select and resize the **Left top**, **Right bottom**, and **Right top** layers.

When you are finished, the shapes on the layers on Frame 1 should match the illustration shown here. If necessary, use the Selection tool to reposition the shape on the Middle layer near the center of the Stage.

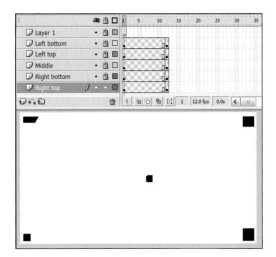

13 Click the **Lock/Unlock All Layers** button to unlock all the layers on the **Timeline**. Position the **playhead** over **Frame 1**. Make sure the **Color Mixer** is visible; if it's not, choose **Window > Color Mixer**.

Next, you'll use the Color Mixer to set all the keyframes to an alpha of 0%. The alpha setting lets you set the transparency of an object. In this case, you will set the transparency to 0% to make it invisible.

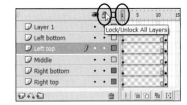

14 With the **Selection** tool, click the shape on the upper-left corner of the Stage to select it. You will change the alpha of this shape using the **Color Mixer** panel next.

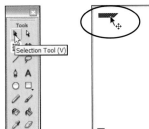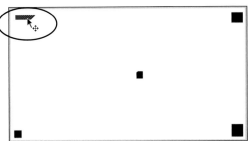

---

15 In the **Color Mixer** panel, make sure the **Fill color** button is selected. Type **0%** in the **Alpha** field or drag the slider to **0%**. To see the changes to the shape on the **Stage**, deselect the shape by clicking a blank area of the **Stage**.

Since an Alpha setting of 0% means the object is completely transpar-

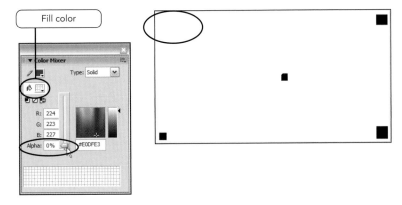

ent, the shape should now be invisible. Later, you will add a keyframe, change the Alpha to 100% (completely visible), and create a tween the make the shape fade into view.

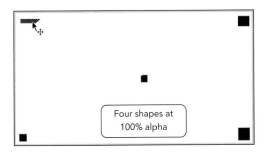

Four shapes at 100% alpha

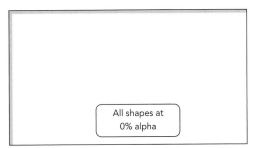

All shapes at 0% alpha

16 Hold down the **Shift** key and click the remaining four shapes on the **Stage**—**Left bottom**, **Middle**, **Right top**, and **Right bottom**—to select them. In the **Color Mixer**, type **0%** in the **Alpha** field and press **Enter** to change the alpha for all four shapes at the same time.

When you are finished, the Stage should appear as though it is blank. Don't worry, the shapes are still there—they are just completely transparent. Next, you'll add a shape tween to fade in the shapes from 0% to 100% alpha.

17 On the **Left bottom** layer, click **Frame 5** to select it. **Shift+click Frame 5** of the **Right top** layer to select **Frame 5** of all the layers.

18 In the **Property Inspector**, choose **Window > Properties**. Choose **Shape** from the **Tween** pop-up menu to generate a shape tween between each of the two keyframes on the currently selected layers.

Notice the solid arrow and the green tint between the keyframes, which signifies the tween is active and working.

19 Press **Enter** (Windows) or **Return** (Mac) to see the shape tween in action! Cool!

Notice the shapes fade in from invisible to visible, while increasing in size at the same time. Next, you'll extend the last set of keyframes for two more seconds.

20 On the **Left bottom** layer, click **Frame 36** to select it. **Shift+click Frame 36** of the **Right top** layer to select **Frame 36** on all the layers.

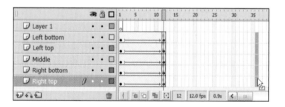

21 Press **F5** to add an additional 24 frames to the **Timeline**.

Provided the frame rate is set to the default of 12 frames per second, the final animation will be about 3 seconds long (36 frames ÷ 12 fps = 3 seconds). The shapes will tween from 0% to 100% alpha in the first second and remain on the Stage for another two seconds before looping again.

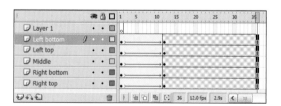

22 Choose **Control > Test Movie** to view the movie in a preview window and see the shape tweens in action again! When you're finished viewing the movie, close the preview window.

Notice the shapes in the animation fade in from 0% to 100% alpha, then remain on the Stage for about two more seconds before looping again. By using a multiple shape tween, you can have different animations on different layers all happening at the same time. In this case, each shape fading in and out is a separate animation.

What about that layer folder you saw in the finished version of this file? Next you'll learn how to put the shape tween layers into a layer folder.

23 Double-click the **Layer 1** icon to open the **Layer Properties** dialog box. Type **container** in the **Name** field and select the **Folder** option. This changes **Layer 1** to a **Layer folder**. Click **OK**.

For more information about the options in the Layer Properties dialog box, refer to the chart at the end of this exercise.

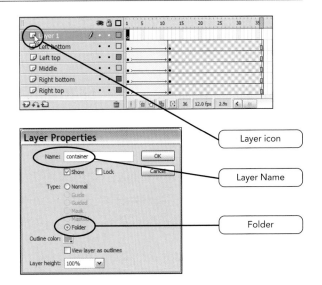

Layer icon

Layer Name

Folder

NOTE:

What Is a Layer Folder?

Layer folders let you store layers in an organized folder structure. Note that you cannot have artwork in a layer folder—the layer folder's sole purpose is to hold multiple layers so you can keep the Timeline compact and organized.

24 On the **Timeline**, hold down the **Shift** key and click the **Left bottom** and **Right top** layers to multiple-select the layers in-between but not the **container** layer folder. Drag the selected layers onto the **container** layer folder to place the layers in the layer folder.

Notice the layers are all indented under the **container** layer folder, indicating they are part of the layer folder.

Layers outside folder

Layers inside folder

25 Click the triangle to the left of the **container** layer name to collapse the folder.

Now you see the layers, now you don't! Now this is organization! You will come to appreciate layer folders when you work on projects with dozens of layers.

Layer folder expanded

Layer folder collapsed

---

26 Choose **Control > Test Movie** to view the movie file in a preview window. When you're finished viewing the movie, close the preview window.

Although you've moved the layers into a layer folder, the animation is left untouched. Layer folders are simply an organizational tool and do not alter the animation in any way.

---

27 Close **mutplShpTwn.fla**. You don't need to save your changes.

VIDEO: | **multiple_shape_tween.mov**

For more information about multiple shape tweening, check out **multiple_shape_tween.mov** in the **videos** folder on the **HOT CD-ROM**.

Understanding Layer Properties

The Timeline offers a number of ways of controlling layers, but other options are available in the Layer Properties dialog box. The following chart describes these additional options:

Layer Properties	
Option	**Description**
Guide	A guide layer lets you use the contents of a layer as a tracing image (or guide), which helps you create artwork on other layers. Guide layers are the only layers that are not exported with the movie.
Guided	A guided layer contains the objects that will animate by following the path defined on the guide layer. To create this animation, the guided layer is created first and then linked to the guide layer. Chapter 8, "*Motion Tweening and Timeline Effects*," will give you hands-on experience working with guided layers.
Mask	A mask layer hides and reveals portions of artwork located in layers directly beneath the mask layer. You will learn more about mask layers in Chapter 9, "*Bitmaps*."
Masked	Masked layers contain the artwork that is hidden or revealed by the mask layer above it. You will learn how to work with masked layers in Chapter 9, "*Bitmaps*."
Folder	The Folder option lets you convert a normal layer into a layer folder. When converted, all content on the layer is automatically deleted. Layer folders contain one or more normal layers, making it easier to work with and organize projects with dozens of layers.
Outline color	When the **View layer as outlines** option is selected on the Timeline, Flash displays the contents of the layer as outlines on the Stage. The **Outline color** option lets you specify the color of these outlines. By default, each layer will use a different color; this option provides an additional degree of organizational control.
Layer height	This option lets you change the height at which a layer or folder is displayed on the Timeline The default view is 100%, but Flash also provides two enlarged views (200% or 300%) which are especially useful for working with sounds.

With the exercises in this chapter, you've gained a solid foundation on the basics and subtle nuances of shape tweening. As you gain experience with Flash 8, you'll find shape tweening a useful technique for accomplishing many different types of effects. Next, you'll learn about symbols and instances.

6

Symbols and Instances

Effective Flash 8 movies, even simple ones, often use symbols and instances. So, what are symbols and instances and what can they do for you? Symbols let you create content once and use it over and over in your movies. This very powerful feature has several benefits. Symbols let you create complex movies from simpler components that are easier to create and update and that download faster. How? Symbols download only once, regardless of how many copies (called *instances*) you have in your movie. For example, if you have a symbol of a snowflake, and you add 50 instances of that snowflake to the Stage, the file size would be not be significantly larger because the snowflake only has to download once. However, if, instead, you draw 50 separate snowflakes, 50 snowflakes would have to download, which would increase the file size dramatically.

The concept of symbols and instances takes practice to fully comprehend. This chapter will give you that practice so you can better understand how to create and work with symbols and instances to create effective Flash projects.

The Symbol and Instance Structure

Think of a Flash symbol as a master object or stamp. You create a symbol once—it can be a simple shape or something very complex—and use it multiple times throughout your movie. Each time you reuse a symbol in your project file, it is called an instance, which is a copy of a symbol.

The concept of symbols and instances is the key to reducing the file size and download weight of your Flash 8 documents. Symbols need to be downloaded, but instances are simply described in a small text file by their attributes (scale, color, transparency, animation, and so on), which is the reason they add so little to the final file size of your movie. The best way to reduce file sizes is to create symbols for any object you'll use more than once in your movie. In addition to reducing file

size and download time, symbols and instances also help you make quick updates to objects across your entire project file—a real time-saver! Later in the book, as you learn about more advanced animation techniques, you'll see symbols and instances play a very important dramatic role in animation, too!

There are three types of symbols in Flash 8: graphic symbols, button symbols, and movie clip symbols. In this chapter, you'll only be working with graphic symbols. Button and movie clip symbols are covered in later chapters.

Here's a handy chart defining some new terms you'll encounter in this chapter:

Symbol Definitions	
Term	**Definition**
Symbol	A reusable object that serves as a master, which you can use to create copies (instances). When you create a symbol, it automatically becomes part of the project file's Library.
Instance	A copy of the original symbol. You can alter the color, size, shape, and position of an instance without affecting the original symbol.
Graphic symbol	One of the three types of symbols consisting of static or animated artwork. The graphic symbol Timeline is dependent on the main Timeline—it plays only while the main Timeline is playing. You'll learn more about this behavior as you work through the exercises in this book.

Symbol Naming Conventions

As you start creating symbols and instances, you'll need to name them. In more complex projects that include ActionScript, instance names become very important, especially for movie clip symbols. For this reason, you need to adhere to some guidelines when naming symbols, instances, and document files in Flash 8. Following these rules will keep you out of a lot of trouble:

Do Use

Lowercase letters (a–z) and numbers (1–9) only. Symbol names starting with numbers or upper-case letters can confuse ActionScript. For this reason, start symbol names with a lowercase letter. You can use numbers for symbol names but not as the first character. Restricting your names to only lowercase letters makes them easier to remember.

Descriptive names. Try to use descriptive, easy-to-remember names. For example, use gfxLogoBkgd rather than symbol6. When using multiword names, capitalize the first letter of each word (except the first word) so you can read it easier. However, remember that when you refer to an object in ActionScripting, you must reference the symbol with the same capitalization you used in its name.

Don't Use

Special characters. Special characters such as ! @ # & $, and many others, are forbidden. Many of these special characters have a specific meaning to Flash 8 and can cause problems with ActionScript. To avoid accidentally using a special character, avoid altogether anything other than numbers or letters.

Spaces. Never use spaces in your names. Instead, string your words together or use underscores. For example, instead of *my first symbol*, use myFirstSymbol, or even better, my_first_symbol (no uppercase letters to remember!).

Periods. Never put periods in your file or symbol names (other than the three-letter extension). For example, **snow.boarder.fla** will cause problems. Instead use **snow_boarder.fla**.

Forward slashes. Forward slashes are misinter-preted as path locations on a hard drive. Never use them. For example, my/new/symbol would be interpreted as the object symbol located in the **new** folder located in the **my** folder.

Important Timeline Vocabulary Terms

This chapter reintroduces the Timeline; in the following exercises, you'll learn that symbols contain their own Timelines. Therefore, you may have a single project with several different Timelines.

The following chart will help you further understand the distinctions among the various types of Timelines.

Timeline Definitions	
Term	**Definition**
Main Timeline	When you open a Macromedia Flash 8 project (FLA), it defaults to the Timeline of Scene 1. This is also called the main Timeline. The main Timeline is visible when you're inside a scene. (You will learn more about scenes in Chapter 12, "*ActionScript Basics and Behaviors.*")
Graphic symbol Timeline	Each symbol has its own Timeline. The Timeline for a graphic symbol and the scene in which the symbol is placed must have the same number of frames, or the symbol's animation will not play properly. This is a unique behavior of the graphic symbol; button and movie clip symbols do not behave the same way. You'll learn about button and movie clip symbols in later chapters.
Scene's Timeline	Every Flash 8 project (FLA) has a main Timeline in the form of the Scene 1 Timeline. You'll see in later chapters that Flash 8 projects can have multiple scenes. In those cases, each scene is considered part of the main Timeline. Learning the difference between a scene's Timeline and a symbol's Timeline is one of the key concepts to working successfully with Flash 8.

1 | Creating Graphic Symbols

Symbols are used for many purposes in Flash 8. Before you can learn the power and potential benefits of symbols, you'll need to know how to create them. This first exercise shows you how to create a graphic symbol.

1 Open **graphicSymbol.fla** from the **chap_06** folder you copied to your **Desktop**.

This file contains one layer with a snowflake in Frame 1. You'll convert this shape into a graphic symbol in the following steps.

2 Choose **Window > Library**, or press **Ctrl+L** (Windows) or **Cmd+L** (Mac), to open the **Library** panel.

Notice the project filename displayed at the top of the Library panel.

Project filename   The Library

NOTE:

What Is the Library?

The Library is a container where Flash 8 stores and organizes symbols, bitmap graphics, sound clips, video clips, and fonts. Since each media has a different icon associated with it, it's easy to identify the different Library assets at a glance. For designers, it can be one of the most useful and frequently used interface elements in the program. The Library is attached to the movie you're working with. If you give your project file (FLA) to someone else, he or she will see the same Library you see when you have the file open.

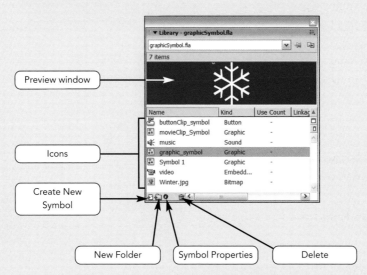

Inside the Library, you can sort the contents by name, kind, use count, and linkage. As your files become more complex, create folders within your Library to help separate your symbols into different categories. Since you will frequently work with the Library, learn the shortcut to open it: **Ctrl+L** (Windows) or **Cmd+L** (Mac). You will get an in-depth look at the Library and all its functions in later chapters.

3 Using the **Selection** tool, select the **snowflake** on the **Stage**. Notice the dotted mesh, indicating you have selected a shape. Drag the **snowflake** into the lower half of the **Library** panel to open the **Convert to Symbol** dialog box.

Note: Instead of dragging the shape into the Library, you can also select the shape and choose **Modify > Convert to Symbol**, or press **F8**, to open the Convert to Symbol dialog box.

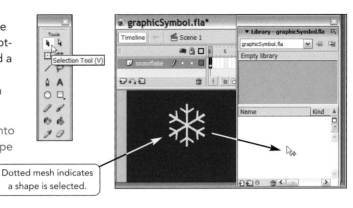

Dotted mesh indicates a shape is selected.

---

4 Type **snowflake** in the **Name** field, select **Behavior: Graphic**, and make sure the middle box of the **Registration** square is selected. Click **OK**.

Note: In later chapters, you'll learn about movie clip and button symbols, which are more complex to explain and require an understanding of graphic symbols first. For this reason, this chapter focuses exclusively on graphic symbols.

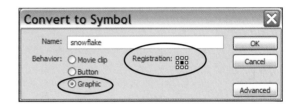

NOTE:

The Convert to Symbol Dialog Box

The Convert to Symbol dialog box offers two views: Basic (the default) and Advanced. To access the Advanced view, click the Advanced button. The Advanced view contains two extra sections: Linkage and Source. The Source section includes information and settings related to the source of the new symbol, such as its file location or if it should always be updated before publishing. The Linkage settings will be covered in Chapter 14, "*Sound.*" To return to Basic view, click the Basic button.

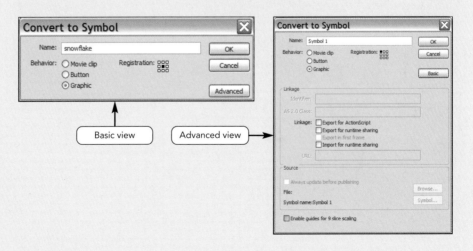

Basic view   Advanced view

Notice you now have two snowflakes in your project file: the snowflake symbol, which is located in the Library, and a snowflake instance (a copy of the original symbol) on the Stage. Instances are copies of symbols from the Library brought to the Stage.

Congratulations! You have just made your first graphic symbol!

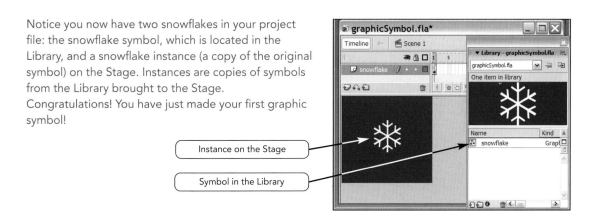

Instance on the Stage

Symbol in the Library

NOTE:

What Is a Registration Point?

When you convert a shape into a symbol, Flash 8 needs to know where you want the shape's center point to be located. Why? It becomes very important when you create animation using rotation because the symbol will rotate around its registration point.

Selected snowflake before converted to a symbol

Selected snowflake after converted to a symbol

Registration point

Once converted to a symbol, the snowflake on the Stage changed slightly. Notice the bounding box and the circle with a crosshair in the middle of the snowflake. This provides visual feedback that your snowflake is now a graphic symbol. The circle and crosshair act as a marker, telling you where the center (or registration point) of the symbol is. This is an important indicator because it affects how all of the instances of this symbol are rotated and scaled. You will learn how to rotate and scale instances later in this chapter.

5 With the **Selection** tool, click the **snowflake** instance on the **Stage** to select it.

6 Press the **Delete** key to delete the **snowflake** instance from the **Stage**.

Notice the snowflake is no longer on the Stage or on Frame 1 of the snowflake layer, and the keyframe has been replaced by a blank keyframe. Notice also, however, the snowflake graphic symbol is still safely stored in the Library.

Note: Don't worry if you delete an instance from the Stage; you can still find it in the Library. However, if you delete a symbol from the Library, it may be gone forever. If you accidentally do this, quickly undo the deletion by choosing **Edit > Undo Delete Library Item(s)** or press **Ctrl+Z** (Windows) or **Cmd+Z** (Mac). You can also choose **File > Revert** to return the project file back to the last time you saved it.

Instance of snowflake deleted

Snowflake graphic symbol in Library

7 In the **Library**, click the **snowflake** graphic symbol icon, and drag it onto the **Stage** to add a **snowflake** instance to the **Stage**.

Notice a keyframe is placed in Frame 1 of the snowflake layer.

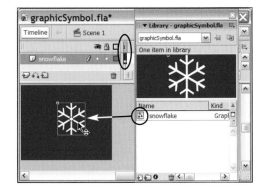

8 Save and close **graphicSymbol.fla**. You won't need to use this file again.

In the next exercise, you will learn to work with symbol instances.

Five Ways to Create a Symbol

There are five different ways to create a symbol either using artwork on the Stage or by creating a new symbol from scratch on a blank Stage:

- Select the artwork on the **Stage** and drag it into the **Library** to automatically turn the artwork you select into a symbol.

- Select the artwork on the **Stage** and choose **Modify > Convert to Symbol**, or use the shortcut key **F8**, to automatically turn the artwork you select into a symbol.

- Choose **Insert > New Symbol**, or use the shortcut key **Ctrl+F8** (Windows) or **Cmd+F8** (Mac), to go into symbol editing mode with a blank canvas ready for you to add or create artwork.

- Choose **New Symbol** from the **Library Options** menu (in the upper-right corner of the **Library**) to go into symbol editing mode with a blank canvas ready for you to add or create artwork.

- Click the **New Symbol** button (in the lower-left corner of the **Library**) to go into symbol editing mode with a blank canvas ready for you to add or create artwork.

2 | Creating Symbol Instances

In the last exercise, you learned how to create a symbol. In this exercise, you will learn how to create and modify instances of a symbol. Since instances are just copies of the master symbol, you can modify them individually without affecting the master symbol in the Library. You will learn how in the following steps.

1 Open **instances.fla** from the **chap_06** folder.

This file contains two layers: a layer named **background**, which contains a bitmap image, and a layer named **snowflake instances**, where you will place instances of the snowflake graphic symbol you created in the last exercise. The background layer has been locked so that you don't accidentally edit that layer.

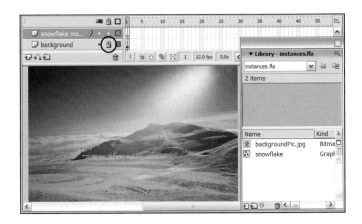

2 Click the **snowflake instances** layer to select it.

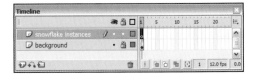

3 Make sure the **Library** is visible. If it's not, choose **Window > Library**, or press **Ctrl+L** (Windows) or **Cmd+L** (Mac).

Notice there are two items in the Library: the snowflake symbol and a bitmap image called **backgroundPic.jpg**. You might be wondering how those elements got there. The snowflake was converted to a symbol in this project file, after which it automatically appeared in the Library. The **backgroundPic.jpg** bitmap was imported into the Flash file. Anytime you import images into Flash 8, they automatically get added to the Library. As you know from the last exercise, the Library stores more than just symbols; it also stores bitmaps, sounds, and video clips. You'll learn more about importing images and other content into Flash 8 in Chapter 19, "*Integration.*"

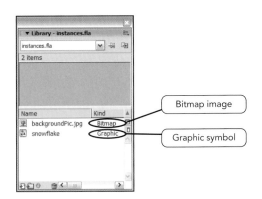

Bitmap image

Graphic symbol

4 In the **Library**, click and drag the **snowflake** graphic symbol icon onto the **Stage**.

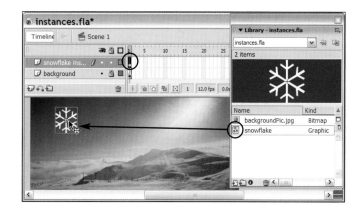

When you release the mouse, you'll see an instance of the snowflake on the Stage. Notice a keyframe is placed in Frame 1 of the snowflake instances layer.

Note: Symbols are stored in the Library, and instances are located on the Stage. From every symbol, you can create as many instances as you want on the Stage.

5 Click and drag seven additional snowflakes from the **Library** onto the **Stage**. When you're finished, you should have a total of eight **snowflake** instances on the **Stage**. **Tip:** You can also insert instances by clicking in the **Library's** preview window and dragging an instance onto the **Stage**.

Clicking and dragging from the Library is one way to create instances on your Stage, but you can also **Ctrl+drag** (Windows) or **Option+drag** (Mac) an instance on the Stage to create a duplicate of it without dragging it from the Library.

6 Save your changes and keep **instances.fla** open for the next exercise.

Next, you'll learn how to edit symbols.

3 | Editing Symbols

Instances on the Stage have a parent/child relationship with their corresponding symbols in the Library. One of the advantages of this special relationship is that if you change a symbol in the Library, all of the instances on your Stage update. As you can imagine, this feature can save a lot of time when you're making large updates across an entire project. This ability to make quick—and sometimes large—updates is one of the most powerful advantages of symbols. In this exercise, you'll modify the appearance of the snowflake symbol to change all eight instances on the Stage.

1 If you just completed Exercise 2, **instances.fla** should still be open. If it's not, go back and complete Exercise 2.

2 Make sure the **Library** is visible. If it's not, press **Ctrl+L** (Windows) or **Cmd+L** (Mac) to open it.

3 In the **Library**, double-click the **graphic symbol** icon to the left of the **snowflake** symbol name.

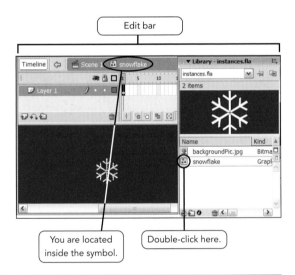

Edit bar

You are located inside the symbol.

Double-click here.

Notice the Stage changes; you are now in symbol editing mode, which means you're no longer working in the main Timeline. Notice the gray Stage pasteboard is gone, as is the blue bounding box around the symbol. When you're in symbol editing mode (inside a symbol) you won't see the pasteboard area, unless you are using the Edit in Place feature, which you'll learn about later in this exercise. Also notice the edit bar above the Stage shows two names: Scene 1 and snowflake, which is another indicator you are no longer working on the main Timeline but instead are inside the snowflake graphic symbol Timeline.

TIP: | **Frequently Check Your Location in the Edit Bar**

It's easy to get lost when moving into and out of symbol editing mode. You may not even be aware you have switched views. So, keep a watchful eye on the edit bar, which indicates where you are and which Timeline you are working on.

4 Select the **Ink Bottle** tool from the **toolbar**, and select black from the **Stroke Color** pop-up color palette. Click the **snowflake** to add a stroke to the shape.

The preview window in the Library updates instantly to reflect the change you made.

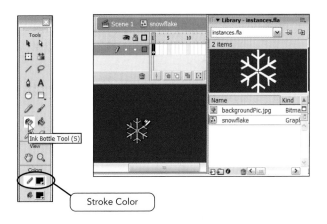

Stroke Color

5 In the edit bar, click the **Scene 1** link to return to the main **Timeline**. You should see the bitmap with the snow and sky.

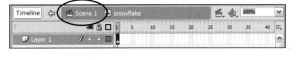

The gray Stage pasteboard appears again, and you see only the Scene 1 name, without the snowflake name next to it. Also notice how all of the instances of the snowflake have a black stroke around them. Every time you modify a symbol, it affects all of the instances you have in your project file. This can be a very powerful way to make project-wide changes to your Flash files.

Stage pasteboard

6 With the **Selection** tool, double-click a **snowflake** instance on the **Stage**.

Double-clicking an instance lets you edit the symbol in place, which means in the context of the other instances on the Stage. When you edit a symbol in place, the other objects on the Stage dim to differentiate them from the symbol you are editing. You can also edit the symbol in place by choosing **Edit > Edit in Place**.

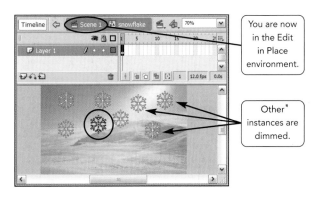

You are now in the Edit in Place environment.

Other instances are dimmed.

Techniques for Editing Symbols

Editing an instance in place (double-clicking the instance on the Stage) produces the same end result as editing the symbol in the Library (double-clicking the graphic symbol icon to the left of the symbol name in the Library). Both techniques change the appearance of the master symbol as well as all of its instances. The difference between the two techniques is that when you edit the symbol in the Library, you cannot see the main Timeline. When you edit an instance in place, you see a dimmed version of the Stage, and you can preview your changes in context with the rest of the objects on the Stage.

7 Select the **Selection** tool from the **toolbar** and double-click the stroke around the **snowflake** to select it. Press the **Delete** key to remove the stroke.

Notice the strokes on all the other snowflake instances have been deleted as well. Again, each time you edit a symbol, all the other instances of that symbol update as well. Next, you'll make a change to the fill of the snowflake symbol.

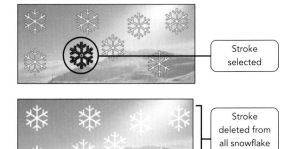

Stroke selected

Stroke deleted from all snowflake instances

8 With the **Selection** tool, click to select the **snowflake** instance on the **Stage**.

9 In the **Property Inspector**, click the **Fill Color** box and choose a shade of **blue**.

Because the snowflake was already selected, the fill color of the snowflake updated as soon as you selected a color. Again, all the other instances of the snowflake change color as well.

10 In the edit bar, click the **Scene 1** link to return to the main **Timeline**. You now see the background bitmap and the snowflake instances in full color.

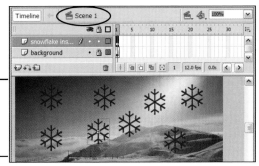

Snowflake instances updated with new fill color

11 Save your changes and keep **instances.fla** open for the next exercise.

4 | Editing Symbol Instances

In the last exercise, you learned how to modify a symbol to make changes to all of the instances on the Stage. What do you do if you want to change the color of one instance, or change the color of each instance individually? Not to worry, you select an instance on the Stage in the main Timeline and modify the color in the Property Inspector. The Property Inspector lets you change the tint, brightness, and alpha settings of symbol instances. This is the only way to change the color values of an instance because the Paint Bucket and Brush tools work only on shapes, not on symbol instances. In this exercise, you will use the Property Inspector and the Free Transform tool to change the appearance of instances—in this case individual snowflakes.

---

1 If you just completed Exercise 3, **instances.fla** should still be open. If it's not, go back and complete Exercise 3.

---

2 Select the **Selection** tool from the **toolbar**. Click the **snowflake** instance in the upper-left corner of the **Stage** to select it.

Make sure you just single-click the snowflake instance. If you double-click it accidentally, you'll enter symbol editing mode, which means you'll be editing the symbol, not the instance. If this happens, go back to the main Timeline by clicking the Scene 1 link in the edit bar.

Click once to select the snowflake instance.

---

3 Make sure the **Property Inspector** is visible. If it's not, choose **Window > Properties > Properties**, or use the shortcut **Ctrl+F3** (Windows) or **Cmd+F3** (Mac), to open it.

---

4 From the **Color** pop-up menu in the **Property Inspector**, choose **Brightness**. Click the slider to the right of the pop-up menu and drag it up to **100%** to increase the brightness level of the selected instance.

Note: The Brightness option controls the brightness value of the instance and has a range of –100% (completely black) to 100% (completely white).

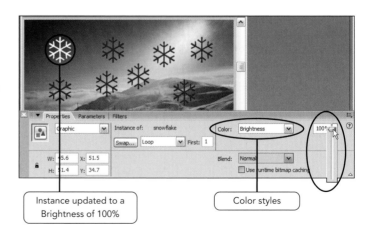

Instance updated to a Brightness of 100%

Color styles

5 With the **Selection** tool, click to select a different **snowflake** instance on the **Stage**. Select any snowflake you want.

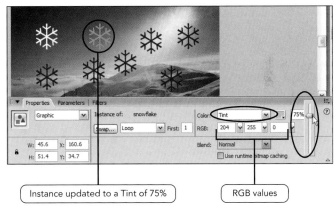

Tint color box

6 From the **Color** pop-up menu in the **Property Inspector**, choose **Tint** to apply a tint to the base color of your instance. Click the **Tint Color** box, and from the pop-up color palette, select a shade of **yellow**.

7 Click and drag the **Tint** slider up to **75%**.

As you drag the slider up, notice how the color becomes brighter. The Tint option has a range of 0% (no tint) to 100% (fully saturated). Tinting changes the amount of color applied to the instance. It also changes the RGB values in the Property Inspector.

Note: You control the color of the instance by modifying the percentage of the tint being applied and the indi-

Instance updated to a Tint of 75%   RGB values

vidual RGB (red, green, and blue) values. The Tint option is the only way you can change the color of an instance, other than setting the RGB values directly in the Advanced Effect dialog box, which you will do later in the exercise. This option also changes both the Fill and Stroke settings to the value you specify. You cannot change these settings separately when editing the instance; you can only edit Fill and Stroke settings when you are editing the symbol.

8 With the **Selection** tool, click to select another **snowflake** instance on the **Stage**. Select one that has not been modified yet.

9 From the **Color** pop-up menu in the **Property Inspector**, choose **Alpha**.

Alpha, which has a range of 100% (opaque) to 0% (transparent), lets you control the transparency value of the selected instance.

10 Click and drag the **Alpha** slider down to **0%** to decrease the transparency. Watch the selected snowflake disappear as you drag the slider down. Return the **Alpha** slider to **30%**.

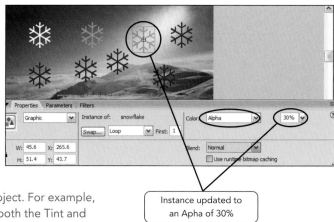

In the next few steps, you'll learn about the Advanced option in the Color pop-up menu, which lets you modify multiple settings for a selected object. For example, you can use this option to adjust both the Tint and Alpha settings of the selected instance. The best way to learn about the Color pop-up menu is to use it, so you'll do that next.

Instance updated to an Apha of 30%

---

11 With the **Selection** tool, click to select another unmodified **snowflake** instance on the **Stage**.

---

12 From the **Color** pop-up menu in the **Property Inspector**, choose **Advanced**. Click the **Settings** button.

---

13 In the **Advanced Effect** dialog box, click the arrow and drag the **Red** slider to **60%**, the **Blue** slider down to **10%**, and the **Alpha** slider to **50%**.

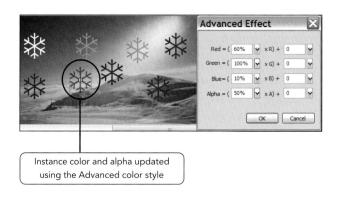

The left column of fields in the Advanced Effect dialog box lets you manipulate the colors using percentages, and the right column of fields lets you manipulate the colors using numbers that correspond with color values.

Instance color and alpha updated using the Advanced color style

14 For the remaining snowflakes, practice changing the **Brightness**, **Tint**, **Alpha**, or a combination of these, using the **Advanced** feature.

It never hurts to practice! If you'd like to learn more about the controls in the Color pop-up menu, check out the chart at the end of this exercise.

NOTE:

Removing Color Styles

Up to this point in the exercise, you have added many different color styles to the instances on the Stage. If you want to remove the styles you applied to an instance, you can simply select the instance and choose **None** from the **Color** pop-up menu to restore the instance to its original condition.

So far, you've changed symbol instances by modifying their brightness, tint, and alpha. However, you can also rotate, scale, and skew instances. In the following steps, you'll learn how using the Free Transform tool.

---

15 With the **Selection** tool, click to select any unmodified **snowflake** on the **Stage**.

---

16 Select the **Free Transform** tool from the **toolbar**.

When you select the Free Transform tool, notice a bounding box appears around the selected snowflake.

---

17 Position the pointer over the bottom-middle handle of the bounding box. When the pointer changes to the **scale** pointer, click and drag to increase the height of the **snowflake**.

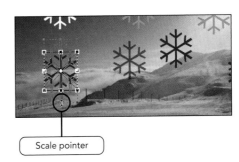

Scale pointer

18 Position the pointer between the bottom-left and middle handles (slightly above the handles) until you see the **skew** pointer. Then click and drag to the left to skew the selected **snowflake**.

Skew pointer

---

19 With the **Free Transform** tool, click to select another unmodified **snowflake** instance on the **Stage**.

---

20 Position the pointer over the bottom-left handle. When the pointer changes to the scale pointer, click and drag diagonally to scale the **snowflake** to a larger size.

Tip: If you hold down the **Shift** key while you drag one of the handles, the snowflake will scale proportionally on all sides.

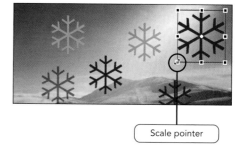

Scale pointer

---

21 With the **Free Transform** tool, click to select another unmodified **snowflake** instance on the **Stage**.

---

22 Position the pointer over a corner handle until the **rotate** pointer appears. Click and drag to rotate the selected **snowflake**.

Rotate pointer

NOTE:

Changing the Registration Point

When using the Free Transform tool, you'll notice each selected object has the circle in the center, which serves as an anchor from which position, rotation, and scale originate. You can move the center point (registration point) if you want to. Here's how:

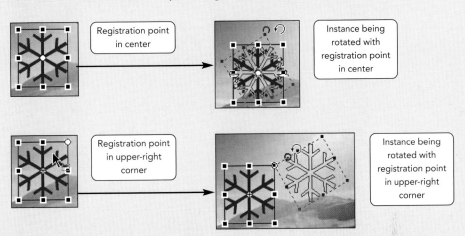

Registration point in center

Instance being rotated with registration point in center

Registration point in upper-right corner

Instance being rotated with registration point in upper-right corner

To change the **registration point**, select the instance with the **Free Transform** tool and click and drag the center circle to a new location. From then on, any transformations you make will originate from this new position. Use this technique when you want to rotate from a corner; you can even move the registration point off the image to rotate on a distant axis.

23 Using the **Free Transform** tool, click to select the last **snowflake** on the **Stage**. Apply any transformation you like.

Remember, practice makes perfect, so have some fun creating your own transformation to the last unchanged snowflake instance.

24 When you are finished experimenting, close **instances.fla**. You won't need this file again.

Color Styles

The following chart explains the different options available in the Color pop-up menu in the Property Inspector. As you learned in Exercise 4, you can use the color style options to change the color and alpha properties of an instance.

Color Style Options	
Option	**Description**
Brightness	Controls the brightness (lightness or darkness) of the selected symbol. The percentage slider goes from –100% (black) to 100% (white).
Tint	Tints a selected symbol with a specific RGB color. You can choose a color from the Tint color palette and use the slider to modify the percentage of that specific color. You can set the range from 100% (fully saturated at the specified color) to 0% (contains none of the specified color). You can also choose a color by moving the R, G, and B color sliders up and down.
Alpha	Changes the transparency of a selected instance. Using the slider, you can make instances completely opaque (100%), completely transparent (0%), or any value in-between.
Advanced	Adjusts both the tint and alpha of an instance. Experiment with the different settings to get the appearance you are looking for.

5 | Animating Graphic Symbols

Until now, you have been working with static graphic symbols. In this exercise, you'll learn how to create a graphic symbol containing an animation. When you use animated graphic symbols in Flash 8, the number of frames inside the symbol must be the same as the number of frames on the main Timeline. In this exercise, you will modify the snowflake graphic symbol and add a simple shape tween animation to its Timeline to convert it into an animated graphic symbol. The end result will be a snowflake that turns into a small snowball and then fades away.

---

1 Open **animSymbol_Final.fla** from the **chap_06** folder. Choose **Control > Test Movie** to preview the animation. When you're finished, close the preview window and close **animSymbol_Final.fla**.

It's snowing! In this exercise, you'll play Mother Nature and create this snowing animation.

---

2 Open **animSymbol.fla** from the **chap_06** folder.

This file contains two layers: one named **background**, which contains a bitmap background image, and one named **animSymbol**, where you will place the animated graphic symbol you are about to create. The background layer has been locked so you don't modify it accidentally.

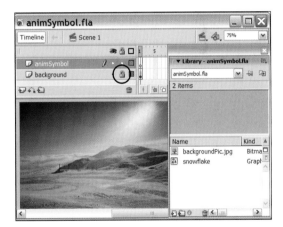

---

3 Make sure the **Library** is visible. If it's not, press **Ctrl+L** (Windows) or **Cmd+L** (Mac) to open it.

The Library contains two items: **backgroundPic.jpg**, which is the background image, and a snowflake graphic symbol, which you will animate in the next steps.

---

4 In the **Library**, double-click the **graphic symbol** icon to the left of the **snowflake** symbol name to enter symbol editing mode.

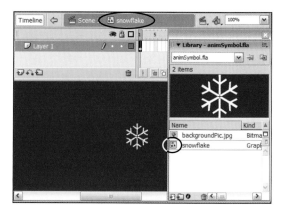

Notice that the contents of the Stage have changed and that the snowflake graphic symbol icon appears in the edit bar. These two clues indicate you are in symbol editing mode.

In the following steps, you will create a shape tween animation to make the snowflake look as though it is falling as it changes into a small snowball and then fades away. Keep in mind you are creating this animation of your snowflake on the graphic symbol Timeline, which is different from the main Timeline in Scene 1. As a result, the animation will affect all the instances of this symbol on the main Timeline because you are editing the master symbol.

---

5 In the **Timeline**, double-click **Layer 1**. When the bounding box appears, type **snowflake** and press **Enter** (Windows) or **Return** (Mac) to rename the layer. Press **F7** on **Frame 12** to add a blank keyframe.

Remember, a blank keyframe copies no artwork from the previous keyframe.

---

6 At the bottom of the **Timeline**, click the **Onion Skin** button. Make sure the **start onion skin** marker is anchored at **Frame 1** and the **end onion skin** marker is anchored at **Frame 12**.

By turning on onion skinning, you will be able to see a faint ghost image of the artwork in Frame 1 and add artwork relative to it.

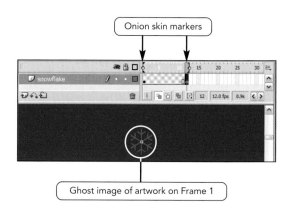

Onion skin markers

Ghost image of artwork on Frame 1

7 In the **toolbar**, select the **Oval** tool and set the **Stroke** to **none** and the **Fill** to **white**.

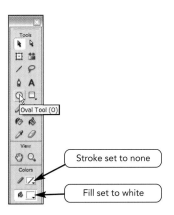

Stroke set to none

Fill set to white

---

8 Make sure the **playhead** is over **Frame 12**. With the **Oval** tool, draw a small **snowball** just below the ghost image of the **snowflake**.

Notice the new keyframe on Frame 12. You will create the tween between the two keyframes in the following steps.

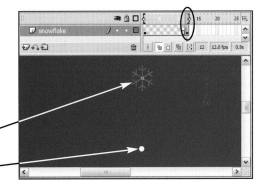

Artwork on Frame 1

Artwork on Frame 12

---

9 Make sure you are still in the **snowflake** graphic symbol **Timeline** (check the edit bar), and click anywhere between **Frame 1** and **Frame 12** to select one of the frames.

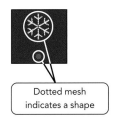

Dotted mesh indicates a shape

---

10 Make sure the **Property Inspector** is visible. If it is not, press **Ctrl+F3** (Windows) or **Cmd+F3** (Mac). Since the snowflake and the snowball are both shapes, choose **Shape** from the **Tween** pop-up menu.

11 Press **Enter** (Windows) or **Return** (Mac) to get a quick preview of what your animation will look like. Notice the snowflake turns into a snowball in about 1 second, provided your frame rate is set to the default setting of 12 frames per second (12 frames ÷ 12 fps = 1 second).

12 Press **F6** on **Frame 24** to add a keyframe. Select the **Selection** tool from the **toolbar**. Click an drag the **snowball** circle on **Frame 24** down, as shown in the illustration here.

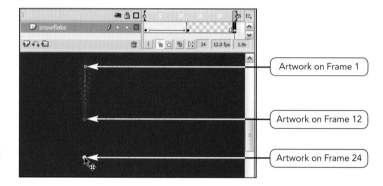

Artwork on Frame 1

Artwork on Frame 12

Artwork on Frame 24

Remember, a keyframe identifies a change in the Timeline and copies the artwork of the previous keyframe. In this case, you copied the artwork of the snowball on Frame 12 to Frame 24 and then moved the artwork down. Next, you'll make the snowball disappear.

13 Make sure the **Color Mixer** is visible. If it's not, choose **Window > Color Mixer** or press **Shift+F9**. With the **snowball** still selected on **Frame 24**, make sure the **Fill** color is selected in the **Color Mixer** panel and set the **Alpha** to **0%** to make the snowball in **Frame 24** transparent. Click anywhere off the **snowball** to deselect it, and you will see it disappear!

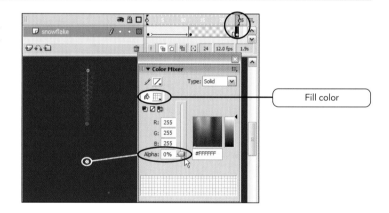

Fill color

You'll add a second tween in the next steps.

14 In the **snowflake** graphic symbol **Timeline**, click anywhere between **Frame 12** and **Frame 24** to select one of the frames.

15 In the **Property Inspector**, choose **Shape** from the **Tween** pop-up menu to add a second tween, showing the snowball falling and disappearing.

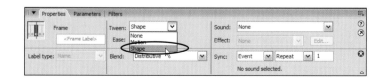

16 At the bottom of the **Timeline**, click the **Onion Skin** button to turn off onion skinning.

Notice the onion skin markers have disappeared.

---

17 Position the playhead over **Frame 1** and press **Enter** (Windows) or **Return** (Mac) to preview the entire animation. As the snowflake falls, it should turn into a snowball, and then the snowball should fade away, all in about 2 seconds (24 frames ÷ 12 fps = 2 seconds). Not bad!

TIP: | **Where Do I Change the Alpha Transparency?**

Use the Property Inspector to set alpha transparency of an instance (bounding box).

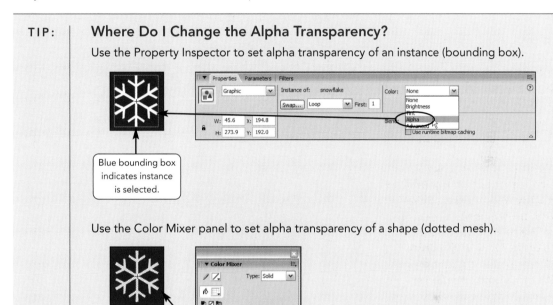

Blue bounding box indicates instance is selected.

Use the Color Mixer panel to set alpha transparency of a shape (dotted mesh).

Dotted mesh indicates a shape is selected.

---

18 When you are happy with the animation, click the **Scene 1** link in the **edit bar** to return to the main **Timeline**.

You'll add the snowflake animated graphic symbol to the main Timeline next.

---

19 Select **Frame 1** of the **animSymbol** layer. Click and drag the **snowflake** graphic symbol from the **Library** onto the **Stage** to add an instance of the animated **snowflake** graphic symbol to the main **Timeline**, **Scene 1**.

Notice there is now a keyframe in Frame 1 of the animSymbol layer.

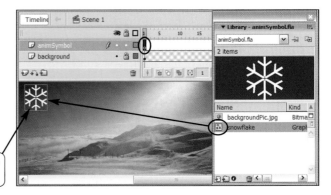

Instance of the snowflake graphic symbol

---

20 Choose **Control > Test Movie** to preview your movie. But wait, the snowflake is not animating! Why? You will learn how to fix this next. Close the preview window to return to the main **Timeline**.

The Timeline of the animated graphic symbol is directly related to the main Timeline (the current scene—in this case, Scene 1) of the project. If the animated graphic symbol is 24 frames long, the main Timeline also needs to be at least 24 frames long. Currently, the main Timeline is 1 frame long; therefore, only one frame is displayed. To fix this animation, you need to extend the main Timeline to at least 24 frames.

---

21 Click **Frame 24** of the **animSymbol** layer and **Shift+click Frame 24** of the **background** layer to select both frames.

---

22 Press **F5** to insert frames and extend the **Timeline** of both layers to **24** frames.

Frames 2 through 24 in both layers are now shaded gray because you added

frames. The main Timeline is now at least as long as the graphic symbol Timeline, and you'll see the entire animation play. Your snowflake is about to animate!

Note: You just extended both layers so that the content of these layers is displayed for the same length of time. For example, extending just the animSymbol layer would cause the background layer to disappear when the playhead reached Frame 2. Extending both layers to Frame 24 ensures that all layers are displayed for the same length of time.

---

23 Choose **Control > Test Movie** to preview your movie.

Cool—this time your snowflake is animating! Notice the animation starts out as a snowflake, turns into a snowball, and disappears as it falls towards the ground. Next, you'll add more instances of the snowflake graphic symbol to the Stage to create the effect of falling snow.

24 Close the preview window.

25 On the main **Timeline**, drag 10 more instances of the animated **snowflake** symbol onto the **Stage** to make a total of 11.

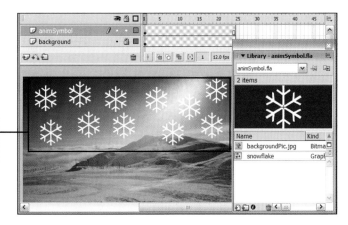

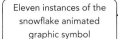

Eleven instances of the snowflake animated graphic symbol

26 Choose **Control > Test Movie** to open a new window with a preview of your movie.

Notice the snowflakes are all falling in unison, which doesn't look very natural. In the next few steps, you'll learn how to change the starting frames of each animated graphic symbol to create more realistic-looking snowfall.

27 Close the preview window.

28 Click to select a **snowflake** instance on the **Stage**.

29 Type a value between **1** and **24** in the **First** field of the **Property Inspector** to set the frame where you'd like the animation to begin. Since the snowflake animated graphic symbol has a total of 24 frames, you

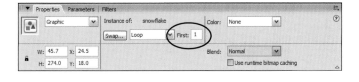

can enter any number between 1 and 24. Setting the animation to start playing partway through will give the effect of the snowflakes falling at different times, rather than in perfect unison.

30 Repeat this process for all of the **snowflakes** on the **Stage**, entering a different value in the **First** field of the **Property Inspector**.

Changing the starting frame of each animation changes the starting point of each animation, yielding a more realistic snowfall effect.

---

31 Choose **Control > Test Movie** to preview your movie. It's snowing! When you are done previewing your movie, close the preview window.

In Flash 8, you can often produce the same effect in a number of different ways. However, some methods are more efficient than others. The exercise you just completed outlines an efficient way of using one symbol to create several instances that look and behave differently. You could have created and animated each of the snowflakes separately to produce the same effect, but that would require much more work.

---

32 Save and close **animSymbol.fla**. You won't need this file again.

NOTE:

Looping

You might have noticed the 24-frame animation of the falling snowflakes played over and over again when you tested the movie. This type of behavior is called a loop, which is an animation sequence that repeats over and over. Flash 8 defaults to looping whatever is on the Stage, unless you use ActionScript to tell it not to. You will learn about ActionScript in Chapter 12, "ActionScript Basics and Behaviors."

Great job! You've made it this far; by now you should feel a lot more comfortable working with symbols and instances and understand the role they can play in your projects. But you aren't finished yet. Future chapters on buttons and movie clips will continue this learning process. So don't stop now—you are just getting to the good stuff.

7

Filters and Blend Modes

New to Flash Professional 8 is a collection of image compositing effects called blend modes and image special effects called filters, which you can use to create sophisticated, eye-catching graphic effects. In the past, you would have created this content in an image-editing program, such as Adobe Photoshop, and imported it into Flash, dramatically increasing the size of the project. Blend modes and filters let you create this content natively in Flash Professional 8, giving you more flexibility and control with much smaller file sizes.

Blend modes mix the color information of a graphic object with the color information of graphic object(s) beneath it. You can use blend modes to change the appearance of an image on the Stage by combining it in interesting and varied ways with the content of objects beneath it. For example, with the Lighten blending mode, you can make areas of an object appear lighter in color based on the colors of the objects beneath it.

Filters process the content of a graphic object to produce a special effect. For example, you can apply a bevel filter to an object to make its edges appear rounded, apply a blur filter to make edges of an object appear softer, or apply a drop shadow to cast a shadow behind an object.

This chapter introduces you to the blend modes and filters in Flash Professional 8; however, this will by no means be a comprehensive treatment. The various ways to use and combine these visual effects is limited only by your imagination and time. Experiment on your own beyond the material presented in this chapter to transform your Flash images.

What Are Blend Modes?

Flash Professional 8 has a variety of blend modes to help you achieve the look you want. If you've worked with image-editing applications, such as Adobe Photoshop, you may already be familiar with the concept of blend modes and how to use them to achieve interesting visual effects. Fortunately, blend modes work much the same way in Flash Professional 8. For example, you can create highlights or shadows, colorize a grayscale image, change the color of a symbol, and much, much more.

In order to use blend modes, you must have at least two objects on the Stage, and you must convert the objects to either buttons or movie clip symbols. Blend modes do not work with graphic symbols. You'll learn more about buttons and movie clip symbols, including the benefits of working with them, in later chapters. For now, just remember you can only use blend modes with buttons and movie clip symbols, not graphic symbols.

Blend modes let you alter how a current image or object blends with the images or objects underneath to create interesting effects.

The example on the left shows two images stacked on top of each other with no blending—a mountain scene and an orange opaque oval. The example on the right shows the same two images with the Overlay blend mode applied. As you can see, the orange oval on top is blending with the landscape below to produce an interesting visual effect to draw attention to the snowboarder. The orange oval has turned from fully opaque to partially transparent, allowing the landscape below to come through with some of the color of the original orange oval.

When you use blend modes, four important factors come into play:

- **Base object and color:** The object below the object you want to blend. In the preceding example, the base object is made up of shades of blues and gray in the mountain scene photograph.

- **Blend object and color:** The object you are blending or applying the blend mode to. In the preceding example, the blend object is the orange oval.

- **Result object or color:** The result of the blend mode on the base object or color. In the preceding example, the Overlay blend mode kept the base color of the blend object the same but adjusted the Opacity, which is what makes the photographic content from the base object and color visible through the orange.

- **Opacity:** The degree of transparency applied to the blend mode. Depending on the color of the blending object and the blend mode you choose, you'll get different levels of transparency. In the preceding example, the combination of the orange blend object and the Overlay blend mode yields a high degree of transparency.

Blend Mode Basics

If you've worked with blend modes in image-editing applications, you've probably done some experimenting to get the desired result. In some cases, experimentation can be very frustrating because the results can vary widely, depending on the color(s) of the base object and the color(s) of the blend object. This section helps you understand the different blend modes and, hopefully, eliminates some of the guesswork.

The blend modes in Flash Professional 8 are divided into categories, just like in image-editing applications, such as Adobe Photoshop. Understanding how these categories work will help you understand the results you'll get when using blend modes. This section provides detailed information about the most common blend modes you'll use in Flash 8 and how they work.

Normal and Layer Blend Modes

The Normal and Layer blend modes do not blend the objects. They maintain the original appearance of the objects stacked on top of each other. Using the Layer blend modes lets you stack multiple movie clips on top of each other without affecting the appearance.

Normal

Layer

In the examples here, you can see three squares—one black, one gray, and one white—on top of a photograph of a mountain scene. On the left is the Normal blend mode, which does not blend the black, gray, and white squares with the photograph below. On the right is the Layer blend mode. Like the Normal blend mode, the Layer blend mode does not blend the objects—it simply lets you stack multiple movie clips on top of each other without affecting the appearance of the movie clips.

Darken and Multiply Blend Modes

The Darken and Multiply blend modes ignore white, making objects darker.

Darken   *Multiply*

In the example on the left, the Darken blend mode eliminated the white square because the pixels are lighter than the photograph below. However it kept the black square intact because the pixels are darker than the photograph below. The gray square was eliminated in the areas that are darker in the photograph below but maintained in the areas that are lighter. As you can see, a small corner of the gray square is still intact because the pixels below the square in that small area are lighter than the photograph below.

In the example on the right, the Multiply blend mode also eliminated the white square because the pixels there are lighter than the photograph below but kept the black square intact because the pixels there are darker than the photograph below. Where you can see the difference between the Darken and Multiply blend modes is in the gray square. The Multiply blend mode darkened the gray and made the square transparent. Unlike the Darken blend mode, which simply cancels out pixels that are lighter, the Multiply blend mode multiplies the base color by the blend color, which results in darker, richer colors.

Darken   *Multiply*

When the blend object has a hue other than black, white, or gray, you can see the difference between Darken and Multiply. Because the Darken blend mode replaces only areas that are lighter than the blend color, it produces a greenish tinge over the darker areas. Because the Multiply blend mode multiplies the base color by the blend color, it produces a darker, richer result.

Lighten and Screen Blend Modes

The Lighten and Screen blend modes yield the opposite result of the Darken and Multiply blend modes—they ignore black, making objects lighter.

Lighten

Screen

In the example on the left, the Lighten blend mode eliminated the black square because the pixels are darker than the photograph below. It kept the white square intact because the pixels are lighter than the photograph below. The gray square was eliminated in the areas that are darker than the photograph below but was maintained in the areas that are lighter. As you can see, the lower-left corner of the gray square was eliminated because the pixels in that small area are darker than the photograph below.

In the example on the right, the Screen blend mode also eliminated the black square because the pixels are darker than the photograph below but kept the white square because the pixels are lighter than the photograph below. Where you can see the difference between the Lighten and Screen blend modes is in the gray square. The Screen blend mode lightened the gray and made the square transparent. Unlike the Lighten blend mode, which simply cancels out pixels that are darker, the Screen blend mode multiplies the base color by the inverse of the blend color, which results in lighter colors that appear bleached out.

Lighten

Screen

When the blend object has a hue other than black, white, or gray, it is easy to see the difference between Lighten and Screen. Because the Lighten blend mode replaces only areas that are darker than the blend color, it produces a pinkish tinge over the high-contrast areas, specifically in the shadows on the mountain. Because the Screen blend mode multiplies the inverse of the blend color with the base color, it produces a bleaching effect that is truer to the blend color.

Overlay and Hard Light Blend Modes

Where the Darken and Multiply blend modes ignore white and the Lighten and Screen blend modes ignore black, the Overlay and Hard Light blend modes ignore gray, which results in greater contrast and increased saturation.

Overlay

Hard Light

In the example on the left, the Overlay blend mode multiplies the blend color, thus eliminating the gray square and increasing the contrast and saturation over the areas where the black and white squares blend with the photograph. With the black square, the Overlay blend mode increased the contrast saturation, yielding a darker result than the photograph. With the white square, the Overlay blend mode decreased the contrast and saturation, yielding a lighter result than the photograph.

In the example on the right, the Hard Light blend mode also eliminated the gray square but had no effect on the black and white squares. Whereas the Overlay blend mode multiplies the colors depending on the *base* color, the Hard Light blend mode multiplies the colors depending on the *blend* color, which in this case results in no blending.

Overlay

Hard Light

When the blend object has a hue other than black, white, or gray, you can easily see the different results of the Overlay and Hard Light blend modes. The Overlay blend mode produces a more subtle effect because it uses the base color, whereas the Hard Light blend mode produces a more saturated result.

1 | Working with Blend Modes

When you work with blend modes in Flash Professional 8, you can only apply them to buttons and movie clip symbols—you cannot apply them to graphic symbols. This exercise shows you how to convert objects to a movie clip symbols and shows you how to apply blend modes. After completing this exercise, you'll have no trouble experimenting on your own!

1 Copy the **chap_07** folder from the **HOT CD-ROM** to your **Desktop**. Open the **blendBasics.fla** file from the **chap_07** folder.

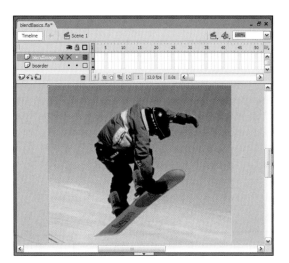 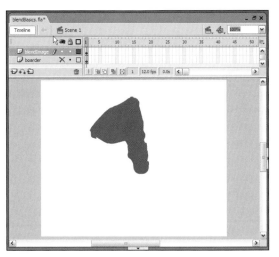

This file consists of two layers—a photograph of a snowboarder and a graphic that mimics the shape of the snowboarder's jacket. In this exercise, you'll apply blend modes to this colored shape to see how it interacts or blends with the original colors in the jacket below.

2 Select the **Selection** tool from the **toolbar**. Click the burgundy graphic (the blend image) to select it.

Before you can apply blend modes to an object, you must convert it to either a button or a movie clip symbol, which you'll do next.

Wondering what button and movie clip symbols are? Not to worry, you'll learn more about both in later chapters—they are more complex than the graphic symbols you have learned about up to this point. For now, just remember you can only apply blend modes to buttons and movie clip symbols.

3 Press **F8** to open the **Convert to Symbol** dialog box. Type **jacket** in the **Name** field. Make sure **Type: Movie clip** is selected. Click **OK** to convert the shape to a movie clip so you can start applying blend modes to it.

Take a look at the Property Inspector. Notice the Blend drop-down menu. Next, you'll apply a blend mode to the jacket.

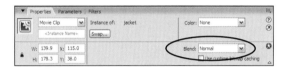

4 Choose **Multiply** from the **Blend** drop-down menu.

Notice the boarder's jacket is now shades of burgundy and purple. By applying the Multiply blend mode, you darkened the jacket using the shades of the burgundy shape. Next, you'll experiment with the Screen blend mode.

5 Choose **Screen** from the **Blend** drop-down menu.

Notice the boarder's jacket now has a bleached effect. Because the color of the blend object are darker than the screen, it created a very different result than working with the Multiply blend mode. Next, you'll experiment with the Overlay blend mode.

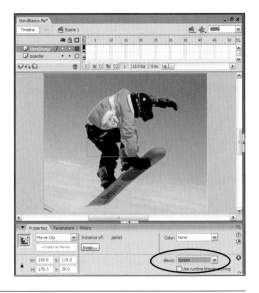

6 Choose **Overlay** from the **Blend** drop-down menu.

Notice the result is different yet again! This time, the boarder's jacket is shades of burgundy and white.

Which result is best? It depends on the result you're looking for.

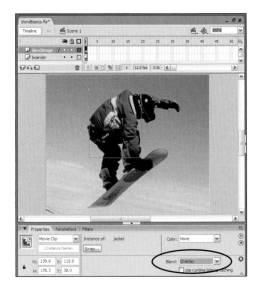

7 Experiment with the other blend modes in the **Blend** drop-down menu so you can see the wide range of results that are possible.

Note: You can also apply multiple overlapping blends by converting the boarder graphic to a movie clip and applying blends to it as well (which will blend colors with the underlying background image). Experiment with the other blends to achieve some interesting results. You can also experiment with the movie clip color and transparency settings, which can also have an effect on the blending results.

8 When you're finished experimenting, close **blendBasics.fla**. You don't need to save your changes.

About Filters

Filters are another new feature in Flash Professional 8. Using filters, you can make objects appear to glow, cast a shadow, become blurry, and more. In the past, the only way to add this type of look was by importing content from an image-editing application, such as Adobe Photoshop.

In Flash Professional 8, you can apply filters to text, buttons, and movie clips to create a variety of interesting visual effects. You can also animate filters using motion and shape tweens. For example, if you add a drop shadow to an object, you can simulate the look of the light source moving from one side of the object to another by changing the position of the drop shadow from its beginning and ending frames on the Timeline.

You can work with filters from a dedicated tab in the Property Inspector. From here you enable, disable, or delete filters. After you apply a filter, you can change its options anytime, or rearrange the order of filters to experiment with combined effects. When you remove a filter, the object returns to its previous appearance. View filters are applied to an object by selecting it, which automatically updates the filters list in the Property Inspector for the selected object.

The following table provides a handy summary of the seven filters available in Flash Professional 8:

Flash Professional 8 Filters

Filter	Description
Drop Shadow 	The Drop Shadow filter simulates the look of an object casting a shadow onto a surface, or cutting out a hole in the background in the shape of the object. In this example, you can see the Drop Shadow filter is simulating a light source shining from the upper left, casting a shadow on the lower-right areas of the graphic.
Glow 	The Glow filter applies a selected color around all the edges of an object, casting a soft glow. In this example, you can see an orange glow behind the gloves.

continues on next page

Filter	Description
Gradient Glow 	The Gradient Glow filter creates a glow using a gradient rather than just a single color. This filter requires one color at the start of the gradient with an alpha value of 0. You can choose any color, but you cannot move the position of this color. In this example, you can see the Gradient Glow filter casts a glow behind the gloves. Unlike the Glow filter, the Gradient Glow filter uses a gradient and can have multiple colors that fade from one to the next. In this example, the gradient glow fades from orange to green to white.
Bevel 	The Bevel filter applies a highlight effect along the edges of an object making it appear to be curved up above the background surface. Options include inner bevels, outer bevels, or full bevels. In this example, you can see the orange oval has a bevel, giving it a three-dimensional appearance.
Gradient Bevel 	The Gradient Bevel filter produces a raised look with a gradient color across the surface of the bevel that makes an object appear to be raised above the background. The gradient bevel requires one color in the middle of the gradient with an alpha value of 0. You cannot move the position of this color, but you can change its color. In this example, you can see the bevel is constructed using a gradient. Unlike the bevel you saw in the last example, the Gradient Bevel filter uses multiple colors that fade from one to the next. In this example, the gradient glow fades between shades of black and white.

continues on next page

Filter		Description
Blur	 	The Blur filter softens the edges and details of objects. In some cases, blur can make an object appear as if it is further in the background, or make an object appear to be in motion. The upper image shows the original; the lower image shows the same image with a blur.
Adjust Color	 	The Adjust Color filter adjusts the brightness, contrast, hue, and saturation of the selected button, movie clip, or text object. The upper image shows the original; the lower image shows the same image with the Adjust Color filter applied. As you can see, the colors have been adjusted to shades of green.

2 | Working with Filters

When you apply filters, you use a dedicated Filter tab in the Property Inspector to apply, disable, rearrange, and delete a sampling of filters. You can also apply multiple filters to an object, as you'll see in this exercise. Each time you add a new filter, it is added to the list of applied filters for that object in the Property Inspector, where you can modify the settings for each applied filter at any time.

1 Open the **filterBasics.fla** file from the **chap_07** folder.

This file consists of two layers: a text layer containing a text label and a buttons layer containing a simple button shape. In this exercise, you'll experiment with a variety of filter effects by applying them to both the text and button graphic. To start, you'll convert the button shape to a symbol.

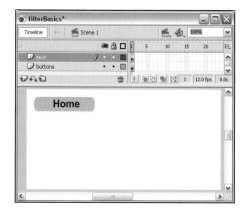

2 Click the button shape with the **Selection** tool to select it. Press **F8** to open the **Convert to Symbol** dialog box. Name the symbol **master_btn** and set **Type** to **Button**. Click **OK**.

You'll learn more about button symbols in Chapter 10, "*Buttons.*" They are more complex than the graphic symbols we have covered up to this point, but for now, just know that you can only apply filters to button symbols, movie clip symbols, or text.

3 Choose **Window > Properties > Properties** to open the **Property Inspector**, if it is not already open. Make sure the button instance is still selected on the **Stage**. Click the **Filters** tab. Click the **Add Filter** button and choose **Bevel** from the drop-down list.

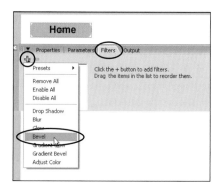

4 Set the **Strength** of the bevel filter to **50%**. Leave the rest of the settings at the default values.

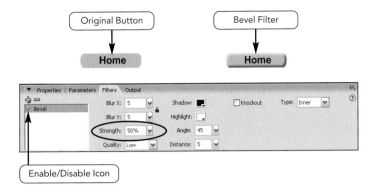

Take a look at the button; you have just applied your first filter effect! Next, you'll make some copies of the button so you can practice applying more filters.

Tip: To temporarily disable the filter so you can compare it with the original image, click the green checkmark next to the filter name in the filter list. (The green checkmark is replaced by a red X.) To turn the filter back on, click the red X.

---

5 Click **Frame 2** and drag down to select both the **text** and **button** layers. Press **F6** to add a keyframe to both layers.

This copies not only the button artwork and the text, but also the filter you added to the button in Step 3.

---

6 Click the button text label with the **Selection** tool to select it. In the **Filters** tab, click the **Add Filters** button. Choose **Glow** from the drop-down list, and set the values as shown in the illustration. Choose any **red** color from the color box to produce a soft, red glow around the letters of the text.

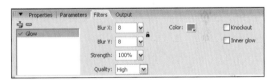

---

7 Click the button instance with the **Selection** tool to select it. In the **Filters** tab, click the **Add Filters** button. (Notice the **Bevel** filter you added in step 3 is also present in the filter list.) Choose **Drop Shadow** from the drop-down list. Set the **Strength** to **70%**. Leave the other settings at their default values.

Move the playback head back and forth between Frame 1 and Frame 2 to simulate this animation. Not a bad animation for the small effort you expended!

8 On the **buttons** layer, click **Frame 2** to select it. Notice the **Drop Shadow** filter assumes the second position in the filter list. Click and drag the **Drop Shadow** filter above the **Bevel** filter in the list.

You can move filters up and down in the list to change their order, resulting in subtle to major changes to the appearance of the object. In this case, rearranging the order did yield a small difference, as the illustration demonstrates.

In addition to temporarily disabling or rearranging the filters, you can also erase them, which you'll do next.

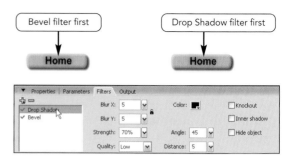

9 With **Frame 2** still selected on the **buttons** layer, select the **Bevel** filter from the filter list. Click the **Delete Filter** button to remove the filter from the button, changing its appearance on the **Stage**.

10 Click **Frame 3** and drag down to select both the **text** and **button** layers. Press **F6** to add a keyframe to both layers, which provides you with another button (without the **Bevel** filter but still containing the **Drop Shadow** filter) to explore the remaining filters. Experiment by adding additional filters to the button and text.

After working a bit with filters, you'll probably develop some favorites. Luckily, you can save filter settings as preset libraries, which you can easily apply to additional buttons, movie clips, and text objects. You'll do this next.

11 In the **Filters** tab, select a filter from the filter list. Click the **Add Filter** button, and choose **Presets > Save As** from the drop-down list.

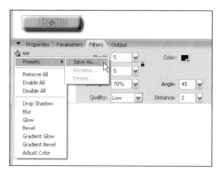

12 In the **Save Preset As** dialog box, type a descriptive name for your filter preset and click **OK**.

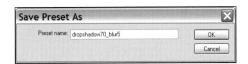

You may start to accumulate quite a few filter presets, so give them descriptive names. **Note:** You cannot use spaces or special characters in preset names.

---

13 To use the saved preset, select a button, movie clip, or text on the **Stage**. Click the **Add Filter** button, and choose **Presets** from the drop-down list. Your saved presets appear at the base of the submenu.

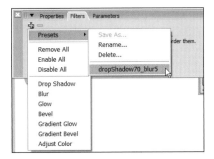

---

14 To delete a filter preset, click the **Add Filter** button, and choose **Presets > Delete** from the drop-down list to open the **Delete Preset** dialog box. Select the preset you want to remove, and click **Delete**.

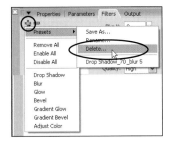

---

15 Close **filterBasics.fla**. You do not need to save your changes.

TIP:

Creating Preset Filter Libraries

You can also share your filter presets with other users by providing them with the filter configuration file. The filter configuration file is an XML file saved in the Flash Configuration folder, which is in the following location:

C:\Program Files\Macromedia\Flash 8\en\Configuration\Filters\filters.xml

Colorizing a Grayscale Image

In this exercise, you'll apply both a blend and a filter to colorize a grayscale image. You'll also learn how to resize and precisely position Stage elements and get an introduction to the Info panel, which contains size and position information of an object on the Stage.

---

1 Open **colorizing.fla** from the **chap_07** folder.

As you can see, **colorizing.fla** has a single frame and two layers: **overlay** on the top and **bw pic** on the bottom. The **overlay** layer is blank. The **bw pic** layer contains a grayscale image of a boarder. You'll be working in the **overlay** layer; the **bw pic** layer is locked.

---

2 Press **Ctrl+L** (Windows) or **Cmd+L** (Mac) to open the **Library**.

There are two bitmap images in the library: A grayscale photo and a stylized colored rendering of this photo labeled **theOverlay**.

Shortly, you'll add an Overlay blend to an instance of the colored rendering to accomplish a coloring effect on the underlying grayscale photo. But first, you need to position the image on the Stage and convert it to a movie clip symbol, which you'll do next.

---

3 On the **overlay** layer, select **Frame 1**. Drag a copy of **theOverlay** onto the Stage.

Notice that the image is too big and extends beyond the edges of the Stage. You'll fix this by resizing the image next.

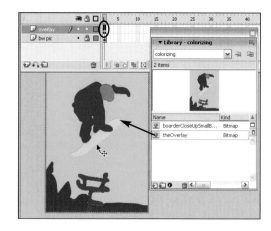

---

4 Choose **Window > Info** to open the **Info** panel.

This handy panel contains the current information of a selected object, including object dimensions and location. You'll use this panel to resize and position the overlay image.

---

5 Make sure that **theOverlay** is still selected. In the **Info** panel, set **W** (the width) to **225**, and set **H** (the height) to **300**. Set both the **X** and **Y** values to **0.0**. Press **Enter** (Windows) or **Return** (Mac) to accept the settings.

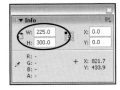

These settings resize the overlay image to the same size and location as the photograph underneath it. You're almost ready to add a blend and a filter to the overlay. First, you must convert the bitmap to a movie clip symbol, which you'll do next.

---

6 Make sure **theOverlay** is still selected. Press **F8** to open the **Convert to Symbol** dialog box. Enter **overlay_mc** in the **Name** field and set the **Behavior** (Windows) or **Type** (Mac) to **Movie clip**.

---

7 In the **Property Inspector**, choose **Overlay** from the **Blend** drop-down menu.

The photo is instantly colorized! Flash is blending color information of the colored overlay onto the grayscale image underneath. Next, you'll add a filter to the overlay.

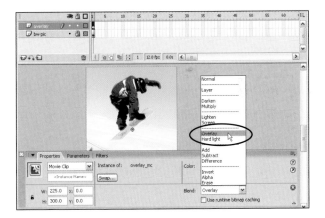

8 In the **Property Inspector**, click the **Filters** tab. Click the **Add Filter** button, and choose **Blur** from the drop-down list.

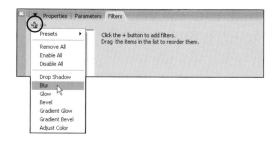

9 Set both the **Blur X** and **Blur Y** properties to **20**. Leave the **Quality** setting at its default.

The colorized image now has a Blur effect superimposed on top of it. This is a great example of combining blends and filters to quickly and easily produce an interesting image.

10 Save and close **colorizing.fla**.

You'll work with a very similar file in the next chapter, when you learn how to animate this Blur filter!

NOTE: | **Filters and Flash Player Performance**

Many aspects of filters can affect the performance of Flash Shockwave (SWF) files during playback. Specifically, the type, number, and quality of the filters you apply to objects will all have a direct impact on playback performance. The simple rule is that the more filters you apply to an object, the greater the number of calculations the Flash Player must process to correctly display the visual effects, and the slower the playback performance will be. For this reason, apply only the minimum number of filters necessary to achieve the visual effect desired.

In addition, each filter includes settings that let you control the strength and quality of the applied filter. Use lower settings to improve performance on slower computers or for projects requiring a lot of filter processing.

You've now completed this chapter providing an introduction to blend modes and filter effects in Flash Professional 8. These image tools will enable you to create a broad range of interesting visual imagery and effects to text, buttons, and movie clips. A unique feature of Flash is that you can animate the filters you apply using motion and shape tweens, which will be the topic of the next chapter.

8

Motion Tweening and Timeline Effects

Similar to shape tweening, motion tweening is a method of animation that takes the position and attributes of an object in a start keyframe, and the position and attributes of an object in an end keyframe, and calculates the animation that will occur between the two. However, unlike shape tweening, motion tweening requires you to use symbols, groups, and text blocks, rather than shapes, to create animation. In addition to position, motion tweens can animate scale, tint, transparency, rotation, and distortion. Throughout the following exercises, you will learn much more than simple motion tweening. You will learn how to edit multiple frames, how to use motion guides, how to use Timeline effects, and how to animate filters, which is new to Flash 8.

Flash 8 ships with eight Timeline Effects grouped into three categories: Assistants, Effects, and Transform/Transition. These Timeline Effects automate routine Timeline tasks, making your work easier and faster. Flash 8 also provides capabilities for animating its new graphic filters. You will get a chance to work with both effects and filters later in the chapter, but first it's important to gain an understanding of the nuances of motion tweening so you can quickly start creating your own animations.

Shape Tweening vs. Motion Tweening

When you start working in Flash 8, you might be confused about which type of tween to choose: motion or shape. You might waste time trying to figure out why your animation isn't working when in fact you simply selected the wrong type of tween to start with. The basic distinction between the two types of tweening is that shape tweens use shapes to morph one shape into another (turning a red square into a blue circle), whereas motion tweens use groups, text, or symbols to animate the position or attributes of an object. Use the following chart to help you decide which type of tween to use:

Tween Types Simplified

Element	Shape Tween	Motion Tween
Merge shape 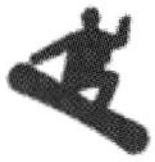	Yes	No
Object shape 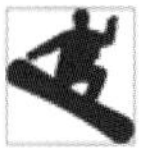	Yes	Yes
Group 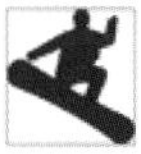	No	Yes
Symbol 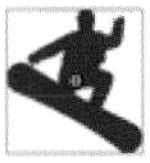	No	Yes
Text blocks Xboard Xboard	No	Yes
Broken-apart text Xboard	Yes	No

1 | Understanding Basic Motion Tweening

This exercise demonstrates how to create a basic motion tween using a graphic symbol. Motion tweens work only with symbols, grouped objects, and editable text. They are quite simple, especially once you've learned shape tweening. The big difference is not in the technique but in understanding when to use which of the five tween object types: shapes, groups, symbols, text blocks, or broken-apart text. You may find yourself often referring back to the "Tween Types Simplified" chart, because remembering the rules of objects and tweening is harder than the process itself.

---

1 Copy the **chap_08** folder from the **HOT CD-ROM** to your **Desktop**. Open **motionTween_Final.fla** from the **chap_08** folder. Choose **Control > Test Movie** to preview the motion tween animation you are about to create.

The snowboarder begins on the left side of the Stage, travels up to the peak of the slope, completes a jump off the lip of the peak and flips counterclockwise down to the right side of the Stage. Also notice the snowboarder changes in size and color. In the next two exercises, you will tween the snowboarder's position, size, and color.

---

2 When you are finished previewing the animation, close the preview window as well as **motionTween_Final.fla**. Open **motionTween.fla** from the **chap_08** folder.

This file contains two layers: a layer named snowboarder, which will contain the motion tween, and a layer named background, which contains a bitmap image of the snow slope. The background layer is locked to prevent you from editing it. In the Library, there is only a bitmap image of the slope called **jump.jpg**. Next, you'll convert the snowboarder shape to a graphic symbol.

---

3 Select the **Selection** tool from the **toolbar**. Click the snowboarder to select it. Notice the dotted mesh, which indicates you selected the shape successfully. Drag the snowboard shape to the bottom half of the **Library** to open the **Convert to Symbol** dialog box.

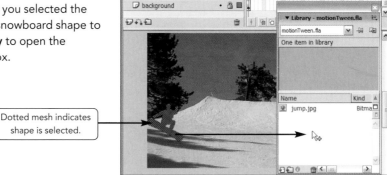

Dotted mesh indicates shape is selected.

4 In the **Convert to Symbol** dialog box, type **snowboarder** in the **Name** field. Select **Behavior: Graphic**. For the **Registration Point**, make sure **center** (the middle square) is selected. Click **OK**.

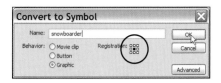

After you convert the shape of the snowboarder into a symbol, the dotted mesh is replaced by a blue bounding box around the snowboarder. Also, in the Library, there is a new graphic symbol called snowboarder. You are now ready to create your first motion tween.

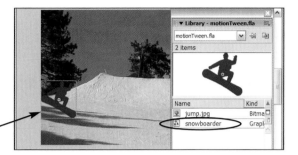

Blue bounding box indicates symbol is selected.

---

5 With the **Selection** tool still selected in the toolbar, click and drag the snowboarder instance off the **Stage** into the lower-left corner of the **pasteboard** (the gray area surrounding the **Stage**).

Dragging the snowboarder off the Stage will make the snowboarder enter the Stage from the left.

Stage pasteboard

---

6 On the **Timeline**, select **Frame 12** of the **snowboarder** layer and press **F6** to add a keyframe to copy the contents of **Frame 1** to **Frame 12**. On the **background** layer, select **Frame 12** and press **F5** to add frames up to **Frame 12**. You will move the position of the **snowboarder** instance on **Frame 12** next.

---

7 On the **Timeline**, select the keyframe on **Frame 12** of the **snowboarder** layer. Move the instance of the snowboarder from the **pasteboard** to just above the slope peak on the **Stage**.

You will add the motion tween in the following steps.

8 On the **Timeline**, click anywhere between **Frame 1** and **Frame 12** to select a frame.

9 Make sure the **Property Inspector** is open. If it's not, choose **Window > Properties > Properties**, or press **Ctrl+F3** (Windows) or **Cmd+F3** (Mac). Choose **Motion** from the **Tween** pop-up menu to set a motion tween for the range of frames between **Frame 1** and **Frame 12** of the **snowboarder** layer.

Notice the blue tint and the solid arrow between those frames, indicating a motion tween is active.

Arrow means motion tween is active.

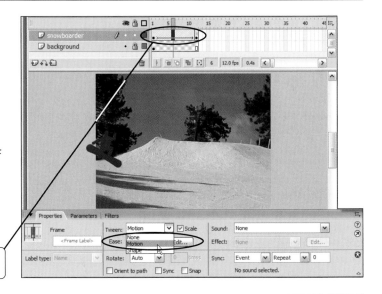

10 Move the **playhead** back to **Frame 1** and press **Enter** (Windows) or **Return** (Mac) to view the motion tween.

The snowboarder enters from the left of the Stage and animates up to the peak of the slope. All you did was set up the beginning and ending keyframes and turn on motion tweening—Flash 8 did all the rest!

Note: You can also scrub (move) the playhead back and forth to view the motion tween or press the less-than (<) or greater-than (>) sign on the keyboard to advance the playhead forward or backward one frame at a time.

11 On the **Timeline**, select **Frame 36** of the **snowboarder** layer and press **F6** to add a keyframe and to copy the contents of **Frame 12** to **Frame 36**.

On the **background** layer, select **Frame 36** and press **F5** to add frames up to **Frame 36**.

Next, you will move the position of the snowboarder instance on Frame 36.

---

12 On the **Timeline**, select the keyframe on **Frame 36** of the **snowboarder** layer. Click and drag to move the instance of the snowboarder from the slope peak to the lower-right corner of the pasteboard.

You will add the last motion tween in the following steps.

---

13 On the **Timeline**, click anywhere between **Frame 12** and **Frame 36** to select a frame.

---

14 In the **Property Inspector**, choose **Motion** from the **Tween** pop-up menu to set another motion tween on the **snowboard** layer for the range of frames between **Frame 12** and **Frame 36**.

Again, notice the blue tint and the solid arrow between those frames, indicating a motion tween is active.

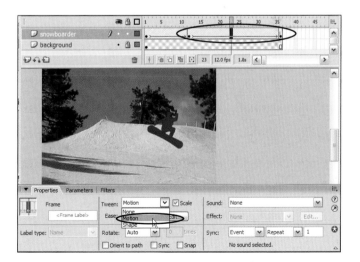

15 Press **Enter** (Windows) or **Return** (Mac) to view the motion tween.

The snowboarder enters from the bottom left of the Stage, animates up to the slope peak, and then slides down the slope to the lower-right corner of the Stage pasteboard.

Congratulations, you have created your first motion tween—two motion tweens to be exact!

___

16 Save your changes and keep **motionTween.fla** open for the next exercise.

___

2 | Using Tweening Effects

Surprisingly, despite its name, a motion tween isn't used solely for tweening motion. You can also tween the alpha, tint, brightness, size, position, and skew of a symbol. This exercise shows you how to do just that, and opens the door for you to create a wide range of animated effects—far beyond simply moving an object from one location to another.

---

1 If you just completed Exercise 1, **motionTween.fla** should still be open. If it's not, go back and complete Exercise 1.

---

2 Make sure the **playhead** is over **Frame 1** on the **Timeline**.

To make this animation a bit more realistic, you will rotate and scale the instance of the snowboarder in the following steps.

---

3 Select the **Free Transform** tool from the **toolbar**. On the **Stage**, click the **snowboarder** instance to select it.

You will scale the snowboarder instance next.

Snowboarder instance selected with the Free Transform tool

---

4 Move the cursor over the upper-right corner handle until the scale icon appears. Click and drag diagonally to scale the snowboarder to a smaller size.

Next you'll rotate the snowboarder instance.

Tip: If you hold down the **Shift** key while you drag one of the handles, the snowboarder will scale proportionally on all sides.

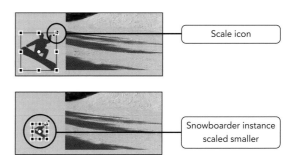

Scale icon

Snowboarder instance scaled smaller

---

5 Move the cursor over the upper-left corner handle of the **snow-boarder** instance until the rotate icon appears. Click and drag down until the board in the **snowboarder** instance is pointing upwards.

You will rotate the snowboarder instance on Frame 12 next.

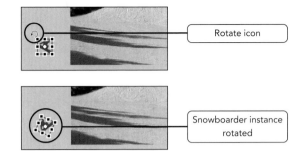

Rotate icon

Snowboarder instance rotated

---

6 On the **Timeline**, select the keyframe in **Frame 12** of the **snow-boarder** layer. With the **Free Transform** tool still selected in the **toolbar**, move the cursor over the upper-left corner handle of the **snow-boarder** instance until the rotate icon appears. Click and drag down until the board in the **snowboarder** instance is pointing upward.

You will make the snowboarder instance do a jump in the following steps.

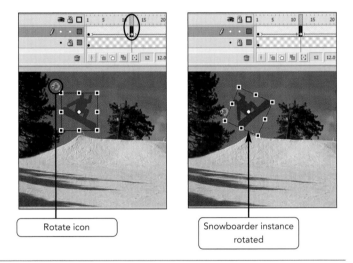

Rotate icon

Snowboarder instance rotated

---

7 On the **Timeline**, select any frame between **Frame 12** and **Frame 36** of the **snowboarder** layer to select the second motion tween. In the **Property Inspector**, choose **CCW** for the **Rotate** option to make the snow-boarder rotate counterclockwise one time during the last motion tween.

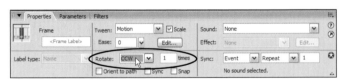

8 Press **Enter** (Windows) or **Return** (Mac) to preview the animation.

Now that's a jump! You're almost done—you will scale and change the tint of the snowboarder instance on the last keyframe in the following steps.

9 On the **Timeline**, select the keyframe on **Frame 36**. With the **Free Transform** tool still selected in the **toolbar**, move the cursor over the upper-right corner handle until the scale icon appears. Click and drag diagonally to scale the snowboarder to a smaller size.

Remember, holding down the **Shift** key while you drag will maintain the original aspect ratio of the image. You'll change the tint color of the snowboard instance next.

10 Move the **playhead** to **Frame 36**. Select the **Selection** tool in the **toolbar**. On the **Stage**, click the **snowboarder** instance.

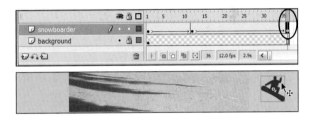

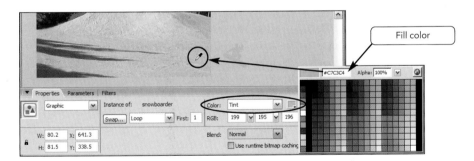

Fill color

11 In the **Property Inspector**, set **Color** to **Tint**. Click the **Fill Color** box and notice the pointer changes to an eyedropper. Move the **eyedropper** to the background image to sample a color from the snow.

You'll see the snowboarder update to the color you have sampled—in this case a shade of gray.

12 Choose **Control > Test Movie** to preview your animation.

The snowboarder enters the Stage from the left side, starts off small, and gets larger as he moves toward the peak of the slope. When he reaches the peak, the snowboarder jumps the lip and rotates counter-clockwise once until he reaches the bottom of the slope. At the same time the size is tweening, the tint of the snowboarder is also changing as he moves! You are now tweening the tint and scale (not to mention the position) in a motion tween!

---

13 Experiment by making changes to the keyframes in the motion tween with the **Free Transform** tool or by modifying the **Color** in the **Property Inspector**.

---

14 When you are finished experimenting, close **motionTween.fla.** You don't need to save your changes.

EXERCISE

3 | Editing Multiple Frames

Suppose you create a motion tween but then decide you would rather have the animation occur in a different position on the Stage. Can you imagine repositioning the items one frame at a time? With the Edit Multiple Frames feature, you can bypass this tedious chore. The following exercise shows you a method to move the entire animation with ease.

1 Open **editMultipleFrames.fla** from the **chap_08** folder.

This file contains one layer with a background image. The background layer is locked so you don't accidentally edit it.

Tip: If you can't see the whole background image, choose **View > Magnification > Show All**.

2 On the **Timeline**, click the **Insert Layer** button to add a new layer to the **Timeline**. Double-click **Layer 2**, rename the layer **tween**, and press **Enter** (Windows) or **Return** (Mac).

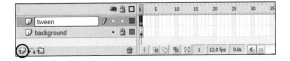

3 Press **Ctrl+L** (Windows) or **Cmd+L** (Mac) to open the **Library**. Click the **boarder** graphic symbol in the **Library** and drag it to the **tween** layer in the upper-left corner of the sky in the background image.

This is where the boarder will start the animation.

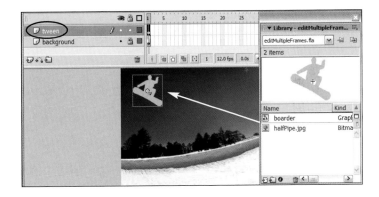

4 On the **tween** layer, select **Frame 12** and press **F6** to add a keyframe. This copies the contents of **Frame 1** to **Frame 12**. On the **background** layer, select **Frame 12** and press **F5** to add frames to that layer as well. This makes the background image visible throughout the motion tween.

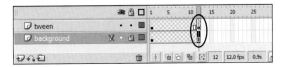

5 With the **playhead** over **Frame 12** and the **Selection** tool selected in the **toolbar**, drag the boarder to the right side of the **Stage** in the sky.

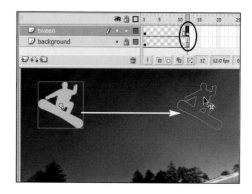

This spot will serve as the end point for your animation.

---

6 On the **Timeline**, click anywhere between the two keyframes on the **tween** layer to select a frame between **Frame 1** and **Frame 12**.

---

7 In the **Property Inspector**, choose **Motion** from the **Tween** pop-up menu. Choose **CCW** from the **Rotate** pop-up menu, which will make the boarder rotate counterclockwise one time during the motion tween.

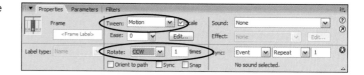

---

8 Press **Enter** (Windows) or **Return** (Mac) to preview the motion tween.

Notice this looks good, but for a more realistic look, the animation should occur in the snow rather than in the sky. You will change this next.

---

9 At the bottom of the **Timeline**, click the **Edit Multiple Frames** button.

Note: When you click the Edit Multiple Frames button, you'll see two markers—which look very similar to the

onion skinning markers you learned about in Chapter 4, "Animation Basics"—at the top of the Timeline. However, don't be fooled by the similarities. Editing multiple frames is quite different from onion skinning. The onion skinning bar represents the range of frames visible at the same time on your Stage. The Edit Multiple Frames markers represent the range of keyframes you can edit at the same time.

---

10 Position the starting point and ending point of the markers (representing your **Edit Multiple Frames** range) to span from **Frame 1** to **Frame 12**. If either the starting point or ending point is not over the correct frame, click and drag the bar over the correct frame. By doing this, you are defining which keyframes to edit simultaneously.

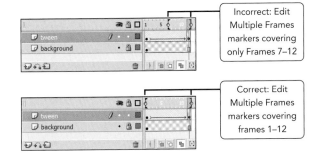

Incorrect: Edit Multiple Frames markers covering only Frames 7–12

Correct: Edit Multiple Frames markers covering frames 1–12

Next, you will move your entire animation to the bottom part of the Stage, so you want to make sure all the frames are covered by the Edit Multiple Frames bar. Since your animation is composed of two keyframes (Frame 1 and Frame 12), these are the frames you need the bar to cover.

---

11 Click the **tween** layer name to select the entire layer.

Notice you can see the boarder on the first keyframe and the boarder on the last keyframe. Unlike with onion skinning, you won't see ghosted representations of all of the frames between the two keyframes. Also, notice both boarders are selected (they have a border around them), which means you can move both at the same time.

---

12 With the **Selection** tool, click either one of the boarders on the **Stage** and drag downward. Notice both boarders move as you drag.

---

13 Turn off **Edit Multiple Frames** by clicking the **Edit Multiple Frames** button.

It's very important to turn off Edit Multiple Frames after you have completed your task. If you leave Edit Multiple Frames turned on and continue to work in your movie, Flash 8 will become confused as to which frame you're working in, and your movie will produce unexpected results. If you do make this mistake, remember that by default you can undo the previous 100 steps.

14 Press **Enter** (Windows) **or Return** (Mac) to preview the animation.

Now the whole animation has been moved to the bottom of the Stage, and the boarder is moving across the snow rather than in the air.

Note: The Edit Multiple Frames feature is a great technique to use when you need to move the contents of many frames all at once. It is also the only way to move an entire animation together at one time.

---

15 Close **editMultipleFrames.fla**. You don't need to save your changes.

This exercise shows you how to create a motion tween using a motion guide. A motion guide is a special layer on which you can draw a path, allowing a symbol to animate along the path, rather than traveling a straight line between two keyframes. In Flash 8, this is the only way to make a motion tween follow a curved path, so it is an important technique.

---

1 Open **motionGuide_Final.fla** from the **chap_08** folder. Choose **Control > Test Movie** to view the movie (SWF) file.

This file is a finished version of the file you are about to create. Notice how the snowflake moves from side to side in a downward direction before reaching the bottom of the screen. Using a motion guide, you will create this same effect next.

---

2 When you are finished previewing the animation, close the preview window and close the project file **motionGuide_Final.fla**. Open **motionGuide.fla** from the **chap_08** folder.

Notice the file contains one layer with the background image. The background layer is locked to prevent you from editing that layer. You'll be adding the falling snowflake in the following steps.

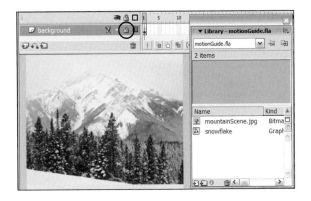

---

3 On the **Timeline**, click the **Insert Layer** button to add a new layer to the **Timeline**. Double-click **Layer 2** and rename the layer **snowflake** and press **Enter** (Windows) or **Return** (Mac).

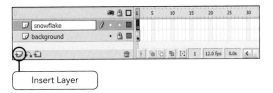

Insert Layer

4 In the **Library**, drag an instance of the **snowflake** graphic symbol to the upper-left corner of the **Stage**. Close the **Library** by pressing **Ctrl+L** (Windows) or **Cmd+L** (Mac) to make your workspace less cluttered.

This spot will be the starting position of the animation—notice the keyframe in Frame 1 of the snowflake layer.

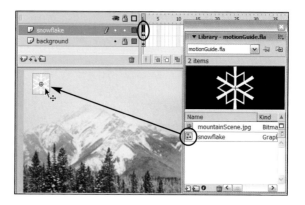

5 On the **Timeline**, click **Frame 48** of the **background** layer and press **F5** to add frames out to **Frame 48**.

This step will make sure the background shows throughout the snowflake animation, which you will create next.

6 On the **snowflake** layer, click **Frame 48** and press **F6** to add a new keyframe and to copy the contents of **Frame 1** to **Frame 48**. With the playhead over **Frame 48**, click the **snowflake** instance and drag it to the lower-right corner of the screen.

This spot will be the ending position of the animation.

7 On the **Timeline**, click anywhere between **Frame 1** and **Frame 40** to select a frame between the two keyframes.

8 In the **Property Inspector**, choose **Motion** from the **Tween** pop-up menu.

Notice the blue tint and the solid arrow between Frame 1 and Frame 48 of the snowflake layer, indicating that a motion tween is active.

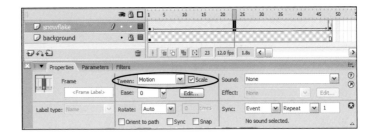

9 Press **Enter** (Windows) or **Return** (Mac) to test the motion tween animation.

Notice the snowflake move from the upper-left corner of the Stage down to the lower-right corner of the Stage in a linear motion. Next you'll make the snowflake follow a motion guide so that it moves across the Stage from right to left in a side-to-side fashion before reaching the ground. But first, you will add the motion guide.

10 Click the **snowflake** layer to select it. At the bottom of the Timeline, click the **Add Motion Guide** button to add a motion guide layer to the **snowflake** layer.

Notice this new layer has automatically been named Guide: snowflake. Also, notice the icon in front of the motion guide layer. This icon provides visual feedback that this layer is now a guide layer. The snowflake layer is also indented below the guide layer. This means the snowflake layer is taking instructions from the guide layer. The snowflake layer contains the motion tween, and the guide layer contains the path for the tween to follow. Before it can follow the path, however, you'll have to draw one, which you'll do soon, so keep following along.

11 Lock the **snowflake** layer to avoid editing it and click the **Guide: snowflake** layer to select it.

12 Select the **Pencil** tool from the toolbar. Choose **Smooth** from the **Pencil Mode** pop-up menu. Make sure **Object Drawing** is deselected in the **toolbar**.

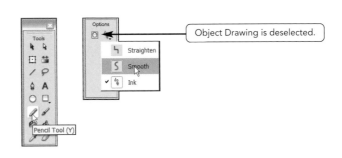

This option smoothes out irregularities as you draw the path for the snowflake to follow.

13 On the **Stage**, draw a curved line, similar to the one shown in the illustration here.

This line will serve as the path the snowflake will follow. It doesn't matter what color or stroke width you choose, because this line will not show in the final animation. Flash 8 is concerned only with the path of the line.

14 Unlock the **snowflake** layer. Lock the **Guide: snowflake** layer because you're done with it, and you want to avoid accidentally moving or editing it.

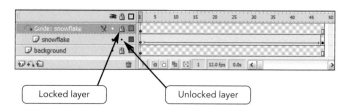

Locked layer   Unlocked layer

15 Position the **playhead** over **Frame 1**. Select the **Selection** tool from the **toolbar**, and click the **snowflake** instance to select it. Click the **registration point** in the center and drag the snowflake to the beginning of the path you drew on the guide layer. When you get close to the path, the snowflake will "snap" to it, and the **registration point** will turn into a small circle. This is where the snowflake will start following the path.

Note: To get the motion guide working properly, it's important to grab the snowflake symbol instance from the registration point. You'll know you have done this correctly when the registration point turns into an open circle, as shown in the illustration here.

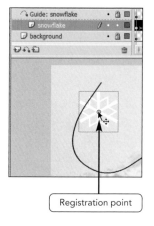

Registration point

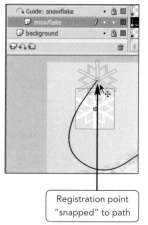

Registration point "snapped" to path

16 Move the **playhead** to **Frame 48**, the last keyframe of the animation. Click and drag the **registration point** of the snowflake instance to the bottom of the path you drew on the guide layer.

This is where the snowflake will stop following the path. That's it! Your animation is ready!

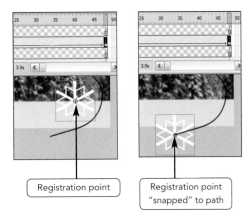

Registration point

Registration point "snapped" to path

---

17 Press **Enter** (Windows) or **Return** (Mac) to preview the snowflake animation.

Notice the snowflake now follows the path you drew on the guide layer.

---

18 Choose **Control > Test Movie**.

You don't see the line at all because the contents of your motion guide layer are never displayed in the final movie (SWF) file. However, your snowflake will still continue to follow the path.

Wouldn't it be nice if the snowflake rotated in the direction of its movement, instead of always facing in the same direction? In other words, if the snowflake is moving down, it should be pointing down, don't you think? In the next exercise, you'll learn about the new custom ease controls in Flash 8 to do just that!

---

19 Save your changes and keep **motionGuide.fla** open for the next exercise.

---

5 | Using the Custom Ease Controls

Flash 8 has new custom ease controls that give you greater control over the speed and pacing of your tween animations. Before, Flash's ease controls gave you control over just the start and ending speeds. With this new functionality, you now have control over the start, ending, and middle parts of your animations.

---

1 If you just completed Exercise 4 **motionGuide.fla** should still be open. If it's not, go back and complete Exercise 4.

In this exercise, you will use the visual Custom Ease In / Ease Out graph to achieve a high level of control over the speed of all parts of your tween animations.

---

2 Click anywhere in the motion tween of the **snowflake** layer. In the **Property Inspector**, select the **Orient to path** option.

With this option selected, Flash 8 will do its best to face the snowflake in the direction it's moving.

---

3 Choose **Control > Test Movie** to view the snowflake animation.

As the snowflake falls, it faces the direction of the path. Nice!

To make this animation a bit more realistic, you'll use the new custom ease controls in Flash 8 to vary the snowflake's speed as it falls toward the ground, simulating a gust of wind.

---

4 Click anywhere in the tween of the **snowflake** layer to select the motion tween. In the **Property Inspector**, click the **Edit** button to open the **Custom Ease In / Ease Out** dialog box.

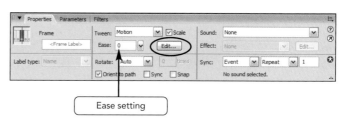

Ease setting

The Custom Ease In / Ease Out dialog box displays a graph representing the degree of motion over time. Frames are represented on the horizontal axis, and the percentage of change (in this case, the percentage of the entire animation) is represented by the vertical axis.

The Ease setting in Flash 8 lets you control the speed at the start and end of a tween. The custom easing graph also lets you set up easing in the middle of a tween! In the next steps, you'll use the controls in this window to add more realism to your falling snowflake by altering its speed during its descent.

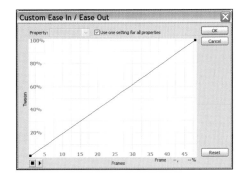

NOTE:

Understanding Ease In and Ease Out

Ease In and Ease Out relate to the speed of an animation. The term *easing* is used because when an animation begins slowly and then speeds up, it is considered to have been "eased in" to its motion. When slowing an animation at the end, it is said to be "eased out." Leaving the Ease setting at its default of None will produce animations with a linear motion, meaning all frames move at the same speed. With the new custom ease controls in Flash 8, you can speed up and slow down portions of the animation.

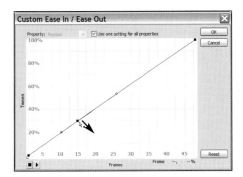

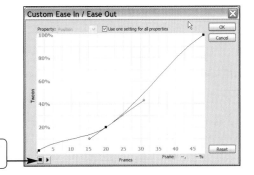

Stop and Play buttons

5 In the **Custom Ease In / Ease Out** dialog box, **Ctrl-click** (Windows) or **Cmd-click** (Mac) the diagonal line where it crosses **Frame 15** in the horizontal axis and approximately **30%** in the vertical axis to add a new control point to the line. Click and drag the line down to the **20% Tween** point on the vertical axis, while keeping it at **Frame 15** or **20** on the horizontal axis. (You don't need to be exact.)

The line is now a complex curve.

6 Test your work by moving the **Custom Ease In / Ease Out** window (so you can see the **Stage**) and clicking the **Play** and **Stop** buttons.

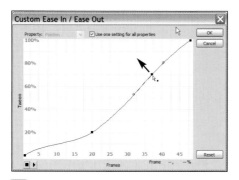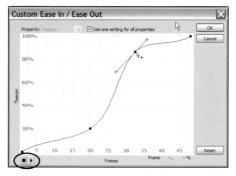

7 In the **Custom Ease In / Ease Out** dialog box, **Ctrl-click** (Windows) or **Cmd-click** (Mac) the diagonal line where it crosses **Frame 37** in the horizontal axis and **70%** in the vertical axis to add a second control point to the line. Click and drag the line up to about the **90% Tween** point on the vertical axis, while keeping it at **Frame 30** or **35** on the horizontal axis.

---

8 Test your work again by clicking the **Play** and **Stop** buttons.

You've created a more complex easing curve than the straight line you started with. This change will cause the tween to start slow, speed up in the middle, and then slow again at the end. Next, you'll test the movie to preview your work.

---

9 Click **OK** to close the **Custom Ease In / Ease Out** dialog box. Choose **Control > Test Movie** to preview your work.

The custom easing curve you defined in Steps 4 and 5 creates an animation that simulates your snowflake getting caught in a gust of wind as it descends to the ground. Experiment by adding more control points and using them to modify the shape of the graph.

Altering the ease speed of the snowflake in the Custom Ease In / Ease Out dialog box gave a more realistic look to the snowflake's movement. The motion guide, **Orient to path**, and **Ease** settings, when used in combination, are a terrific (and easy) way to create tween animations involving complex movements well beyond the linear visual effects you have used up to this point.

---

10 Close **motionGuide.fla**. You don't need to save your changes.

VIDEO: | **customEase.mov**

To learn more about the new custom ease controls in Flash 8, check out **customEase.mov** in the **videos** folder on the **HOT CD-ROM**.

6 | Animating Text

In this exercise, you'll create the effect of a word exploding on the screen. In the process, you'll get a chance to practice creating a symbol from text, breaking apart the letters, and distributing them to layers.

---

1 Open **explode_Final.fla** from the **chap_08** folder.

---

2 Choose **Control > Test Movie** to test the animation.

The words explode before your eyes! When you are finished previewing, close the file. You will create this animation next.

---

3 Open **explode.fla** from the **chap_08** folder.

This file has a blue background with a frame rate of 20 frames per second.

---

4 On the **Timeline**, double-click **Layer 1** and rename it **big air**. Press **Enter** (Windows) or **Return** (Mac).

You will add the text to this layer in the following steps.

---

5 Select the **Text** tool from the toolbar. In the **Property Inspector**, choose **Verdana** from the **Font** pop-up menu, choose **96** from the **Font Size** pop-up menu, choose a dark blue color from the **Fill Color** box, and click the **Bold** button.

---

6 Click anywhere on the **Stage** and type the words **big air**.

Notice there is now a keyframe in Frame 1 of the big air layer.

---

7 With the **big air** text selected, choose **Modify > Break Apart (Ctrl+B)** to break the text box into six individual text boxes, one box for each letter.

Text box before being broken apart

Text box after being broken apart

NOTE:

Motion Tweening Text

You don't have to convert a regular text block to a symbol to use it as the artwork for a motion tween. However, you are limited in the effects you can apply to text boxes. With a text block, you can animate the position and scale, rotation, skew, and flip. However, with a graphic symbol with text inside, you can animate color styles, such as color, brightness, alpha, and tint. With a symbol, you have more options for creating effects in your motion tween than you have using a regular text block.

---

8 With all six text boxes still selected, choose **Modify > Timeline > Distribute to Layers**.

This technique places each letter on a separate layer. This step is important because in order to create several motion tweens occurring at once, each tween must reside on its own layer. Likewise, each symbol (which you will create next) must reside on a separate layer.

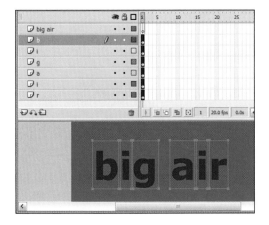

---

9 Select the **Selection** tool from the **toolbar**, and click anywhere off the **Stage** to deselect all six letters. Select the letter **b** and press **F8** to convert it into a symbol. In the **Convert to Symbol** dialog box, type **letter_b** in the **Name** field and choose **Behavior: Graphic**. Make sure the **Registration Point** is in the **center**. Click **OK**.

---

10 Select the letter **i**. Press **F8** to convert it into a symbol. In the **Convert to Symbol** dialog box, type **letter_i** in the **Name** field and choose **Behavior: Graphic**. Make sure the **Registration Point** is in the **center**. Click **OK**.

11 Repeat Step 10 to convert the letters **g**, **a**, and **r** to symbols. In the **Convert to Symbol** dialog box, name the symbols **letter_g**, **letter_a**, and **letter_r**, respectively. Do not convert the letter **i** in the word **air**.

You will learn to replace the letter *i* with an instance of the graphic symbol letter_i by using the Info panel next.

Note: You might be wondering why you didn't convert the letter *i* in the word *air* into a symbol. Since you already created a letter_i graphic symbol in Step 10, you will use that graphic symbol to create another instance of the letter_i. This is the beauty of symbols: create just one symbol, and use it to produce multiple instances on the Stage, without increasing the file size or download time.

---

12 Choose **Window > Info** to open the **Info** panel. With the **Selection** tool still selected in the **toolbar**, click the letter **i** in the word **air** on the **Stage** to select it.

Take note of the X and Y coordinates in the Info panel. In the example here, the coordinates are set to 319.4 and 74.8, respectively. Yours may be different if the text is located at a different location on the Stage, but don't worry—you can still follow along with the exercise. With 0,0 being the coordinates for the upper-left corner of the Stage, X = 319.4 means the letter *i* is 319.4 pixels from the left side of the Stage; Y = 74.8 means *i* is 74.8 pixels down from the top of the Stage.

Note: You can also get the X and Y position of an element in the Property Inspector. However, with the Info panel, you can access additional information, such as the registration point, the RGB values, and alpha transparency values.

---

13 Delete the letter **i** in the word **air** from the **Stage**.

Notice the keyframe in Frame 1 of the second i layer is now a blank keyframe. Next, you will place an instance of the letter_i graphic symbol in this blank keyframe.

14 Press **Ctrl+L** (Windows) or **Cmd+L** (Mac) to open the **Library**. Click and drag an instance of the **letter_i** graphic symbol to the **Stage**.

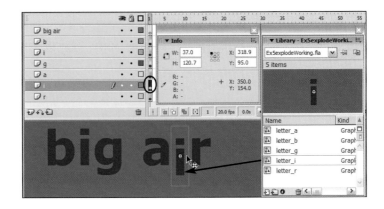

Notice Frame 1 of the second i layer now has a keyframe. Don't worry about positioning it precisely. You will use the Info panel to do that next.

15 Make sure the letter **i** in the word **air** is still selected. In the **Info** panel, change the **X** and **Y** value to the values you noted in **Step 12**.

Notice the letter *i* in the word *air* is now in its original position. You now have two instances of the letter_i graphic symbol instead of one. If you'd like, you can close the Info and Library panels.

16 On the **Timeline**, click **Frame 20** and Shift+click each of the six layers containing a symbol to select the frames. Press **F6** to add a keyframe at **Frame 20** on all six layers. Using the same technique, add a keyframe on **Frame 40** to all six layers.

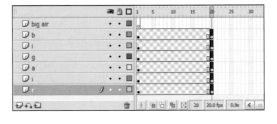

Frame 40 is where the letters are going to finish their animation.

17 Click anywhere off the **Stage** to deselect all the symbols. Position the **playhead** over **Frame 40** and click and drag the **letter_b** instance off the left side of the **Stage** onto the pasteboard.

The letter *b* will end up in this position.

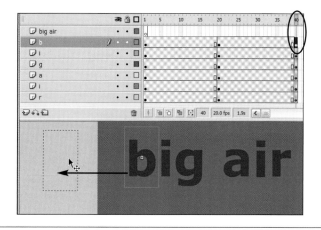

18 In the **toolbar**, select the **Free Transform** tool. Use this tool to rotate and scale the **letter_b** instance. You can use any degree of rotation and scale you like, or you can match what's shown in the illustration here.

19 In the **Property Inspector**, choose **Alpha** from the **Color** pop-up menu and set the amount to **0%**.

This step makes the letter *b* fade out completely by the end of the animation.

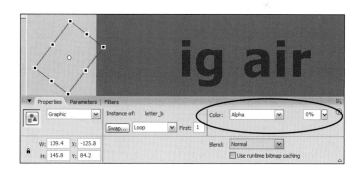

20 Repeat steps 17, 18, and 19 to modify the positions of the other graphic symbols on **Frame 40**, scaling, rotating, and adding an alpha effect to each one. Feel free to move, scale, rotate, or even flip and skew each letter in any way you want, but make sure to keep the **Alpha** setting at **0%** to ensure all the letters disappear at the same time.

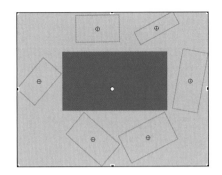

21 Click anywhere between **Frames 20** and **40** on the **b** layer. **Shift+click** the **r** layer to select all the layers on that frame. In the **Property Inspector**, choose **Motion** from the **Tween** pop-up menu and use the slider to increase the **Ease** to **80 Out**, which will add a motion tween to all the layers at once and make the motion tween start off fast and then slow down toward the end. This is a handy workflow shortcut.

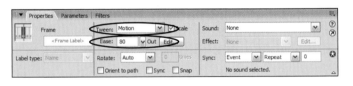

In the last exercise, you used the custom tween settings, accessible via the Edit button in the Property Inspector, to set up more complex speed changes in your motion tween animation. The basic Ease setting you used here is a quick, easy way to add a simple ease at the start or end of the tween.

22 Choose **Control > Test Movie**, or use the shortcut **Ctrl+Enter** (Windows) or **Cmd+Return** (Mac), to preview the animation.

Notice that the animation is a total of about 2 seconds and that the words *big air* stay on the Stage for about 1 second before exploding and fading away.

There are currently a large number of layers on the Timeline. If you find it difficult to work with so many layers, group the layers into a folder using the techniques you learned in Exercise 3 of Chapter 5, "*Shape Tweening.*"

23 Close **explode.fla**. You don't need to save your changes.

In the next exercise, you will learn to use a feature called Timeline effects to automate the creation of specific kinds of motion tween animations.

NOTE:

Motion Tweening Options and Limitations

Here are a few things that motion tweening can and cannot do.

For symbol instances, motion tweening can

- tween position
- tween brightness
- tween tint
- tween alpha
- tween scaling
- tween rotation
- tween skew
- tween filters

For symbol instances, motion tweening can't

- tween merge drawing model shapes
- tween broken-apart text
- tween multiple items on same layer

For grouped objects, text blocks, and object drawing model shapes, motion tweening can

- tween position
- tween scaling
- tween rotation
- tween skew
- tween filters (text blocks only)

NOTE:

What Are Timeline Effects?

Flash 8 includes prebuilt Timeline effects that can create common Timeline animations with just one step, reducing the need for excessive keyframing. You can modify Timeline effects repeatedly or undo them. Effects include Copy to Grid, Distribute Duplicate, Blur, Drop Shadow, Expand, Explode, Transition, and Transform. You can apply Timeline effects to text and graphics, including shapes, groups, graphic symbols, bitmap images (which you will learn about in Chapter 9, "*Bitmaps*"), button symbols (which you will learn about in Chapter 10, "*Buttons*"), and movie clips (which you will learn about in Chapter 11, "*Movie Clips*").

7 | Using Timeline Effect Assistants

This exercise shows you how to use Timeline effects to create animations that would otherwise require a lot of planning and time to create. You will learn how to use the Timeline effect assistants, Distributed Duplicate and Copy to Grid to duplicate and distribute an object multiple times on the Stage, as well as how to create a grid of lines painlessly and in little time.

---

1 Open **assistants_Final.fla** from the **chap_08** folder.

This file is the finished version of the project you'll be building in this exercise.

---

2 Choose **Control > Test Movie** to preview the movie.

Although nothing plays in the movie, notice the vertical and horizontal lines and the snowboard outlines. In the following steps, you will draw each line once and learn how to use Timeline effect assistants to quickly duplicate the lines and distribute them across the Stage effortlessly.

---

3 When you are finished previewing the movie, close the preview window and close assistants_Final.fla file. Open **assistants.fla** from the **chap_08** folder.

Notice there are five layers, and the text and bkgd layers are locked so you won't accidentally edit them. You will learn how to duplicate and distribute the snowboard outline using the Distributed Duplicate Timeline effect in the following steps.

---

4 Select the **Selection** tool from the **toolbar**. On the **Stage**, click to select the snowboard outline and choose **Insert > Timeline Effects > Assistants > Distributed Duplicate** to open the **Distributed Duplicate** dialog box.

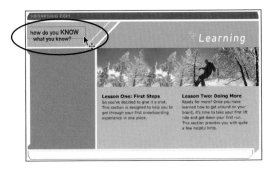

You will configure the settings here next.

5 In the **Distributed Duplicate** dialog box, type **2** in the **Number of Copies** field to duplicate the snowboard outline two more times for a total of three snowboard outlines on the **Stage**. For **Offset Distance X**, type **5**, and for **Y**, type **3**. Leave **Offset Rotation** and **Offset Start Frame** at **0** and make sure the **Change Color** option is deselected. The other settings should match those shown in the

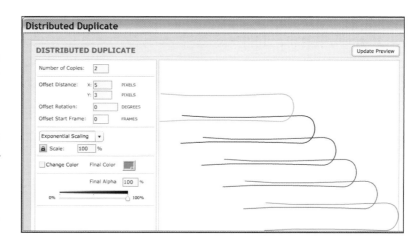

illustration. When you are done configuring your settings, click the **Update Preview** button to update the preview screen with the settings you applied. When you are satisfied with the results, click **OK**.

The Distributed Duplicate Timeline effect allows you to quickly duplicate an object on the Stage, as well as change the scale, color, rotation, and alpha transparency while animating it over a specified number of frames. In this example, each copy of the snowboard outline is offset five pixels horizontally (X) and three pixels vertically (Y) from the previous snowboard outline. The Offset Start Frame specifies the number of frames to play before the next object appears.

Notice that there are now three snowboard outlines on the Stage and on the Timeline. Also, notice that my snowboard layer was renamed Distributed Duplicate 1, reflecting the name of the effect you applied to it. That's all there is to it! Next, you will examine what Flash 8 actually did to the shape.

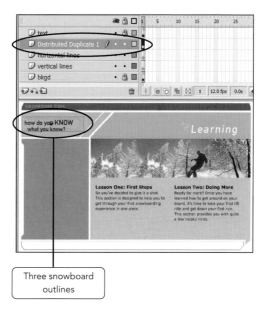

Three snowboard outlines

Note: The number 1 in the Distributed Duplicate layer may be different in your project file. This number represents the order in which the effect is applied out of all effects in your document. What's important to note is that it was renamed with the effect you applied, in this case the Distributed Duplicate Timeline effect.

6 Make sure the **Property Inspector** is open; if it's not, press **Ctrl+F3** (Windows) or **Cmd+F3** (Mac). Select the snowboard outlines on the **Stage**.

Notice it's been converted to a graphic symbol. The Property Inspector also displays the name of the Timeline effect you applied and an Edit button. Clicking the Edit button lets you open the Distributed Duplicate dialog box again with your settings intact, so you can change them if you'd like.

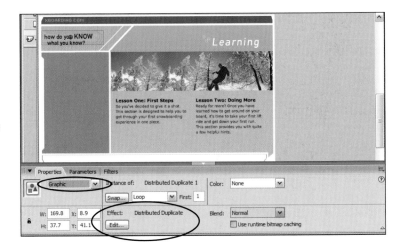

NOTE:

What Happens When I Add a Timeline Effect?

When you add a Timeline effect to an object, Flash 8 creates a layer and transfers the object to the new layer. The object is placed inside the effect graphic symbol, and all tweens and transformations required for the effect reside in the graphic symbol on the newly created layer.

This new layer automatically receives the same name as the effect, appended with a number that represents the order in which the effect is applied, out of all effects in your document.

When you add a Timeline effect, a folder with the effect's name is added to the Library, containing the elements used in creating the effect.

---

7 In the **Library**, notice there is an **Effects** folder. Inside that folder is the original shape. There is also another symbol, **Distributed Duplicate 1**, which contains the snowboard outline with the settings you applied in the **Distributed Duplicate Timeline Effects** dialog box.

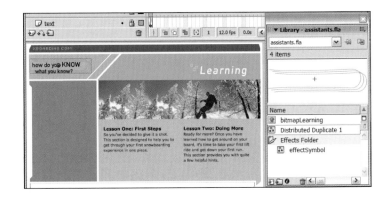

Now that you have an understanding of how Timeline effects work, you'll learn the Copy to Grid Timeline effect in the following steps. This effect is used to copy the selected item in a matrix formation based on the settings you specify. This tool is useful for creating repeating patterns.

TIP:

Editing Timeline Effects

If a symbol on the Stage has a Timeline effect applied to it, you cannot double-click to edit it. You can modify a symbol with a Timeline effect in one of three ways:

- **Property Inspector:** Select the symbol on the **Stage** and click the **Edit** button in the **Property Inspector**.

- **Menu bar:** Select the symbol on the **Stage** and choose **Modify > Timeline Effects > Edit Effect**.

- **Contextual menu:** Select the symbol on the **Stage** and **right-click** (Windows) or **Ctrl+click** (Mac) and choose **Timeline Effects > Edit Effect** from the contextual menu.

Whichever method you use will open the **Edit Effect** dialog box of the Timeline effect.

NOTE:

Editing Symbols That Have Timeline Effects

As noted earlier, when you use a Timeline effect, Flash 8 creates a layer and transfers the object to the new layer. The object is placed inside the effect graphic symbol, and all tweens and transformations required for the effect reside in the graphic symbol on the newly created layer.

When you double-click a symbol with a Timeline effect applied to it, such as the Copy to Grid 1 symbol shown here, you will be presented with an Effect Settings Warning. Basically, the warning lets you know that if you proceed to edit the symbol, you lose the ability to adjust the effect you applied earlier.

---

8 On the **Timeline**, lock the **Distributed Duplicate 1** layer to avoid accidentally changing it. Click the **horizontal lines** layer to select it.

You will draw a horizontal line on the Stage with the Line tool in the following steps.

9 Choose **Window > Color Mixer** to open the Color Mixer panel. Select the **Line** tool from the **toolbar**, and in the **Color Mixer** panel, select **white** for the **Stroke color**. Set the **Alpha** to **50%** and press **Enter** (Windows) or **Return** (Mac).

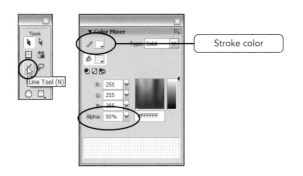

Stroke color

10 On the **Stage**, hold down the **Shift** key to draw a straight horizontal line where the photo meets the solid gray area. After you've drawn the line, select the **Selection** tool from the **toolbar** and click the line to select it. In the **Property Inspector**, set the **Stroke** to **0.25**.

You will add the Copy to Grid Timeline effect next.

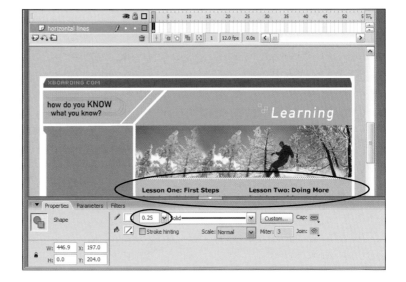

11 With the line still selected on the **Stage**, **right-click** (Windows) or **Ctrl+click** (Mac) and choose **Timeline Effects > Assistants > Copy to Grid** from the contextual menu to open the **Copy to Grid** dialog box.

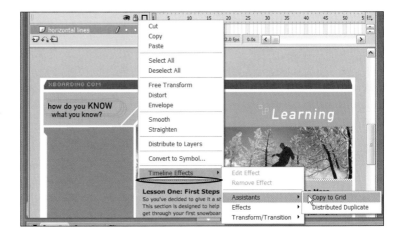

12 In the **Copy To Grid** dialog box, type **24** in the **Grid Size: Rows** field, type **1** in the **Grid Size: Columns** field, type **5** in the **Grid Spacing: Rows** field and type **1** in the **Grid Spacing: Columns** field. These settings create a grid of 24 lines with 1 column. The spacing between each line will be five pixels above and below. Click the **Update Preview** button.

When you click the Update Preview button, you can't see anything in the preview window. That's because the lines you are drawing are white. You will learn how to get around this next.

13 Move the **Copy To Grid** dialog box over so you can see the **Stage**. Notice the **Stage** has been updated with rows of horizontal lines. Back in the **Copy To Grid** dialog box, click **OK** to accept these settings.

Notice the changes on the Timeline and in the Library. On the Timeline, the layer named horizontal lines was renamed Copy to Grid 1. This layer contains the grid of horizontal lines you just created. In the Effects folder in the Library, notice that there are now two graphic symbols, the original snowboard outline and the original horizontal line. Also in the Library is the Copy to Grid 1 graphic symbol, which contains the setting you applied to the horizontal line in the Copy To Grid dialog box in Step 12.

Note: The numbers appended to the symbols in the Library may be different in your project file.

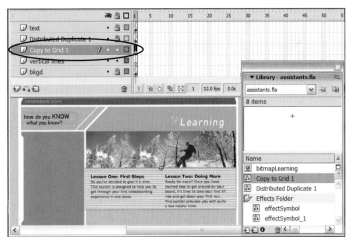

14 On the **Timeline**, lock the **Copy to Grid 1** layer and click the **vertical lines** layer to select it.

---

15 Select the **Line** tool from the **toolbar**. On the **Stage**, draw a vertical line where the photo meets the solid dark gray area. Hold down the **Shift** key and click and drag to draw a straight line.

You will add the Copy to Grid Timeline effect next.

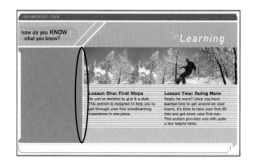

---

16 With the line still selected on the **Stage**, **right-click** (Windows) or **Ctrl+click** (Mac) and choose **Timeline Effects > Assistants > Copy to Grid** from the contextual menu.

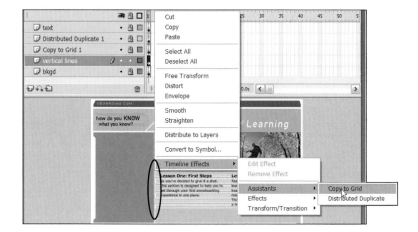

17 In the **Copy To Grid** dialog box, match the settings to the ones shown in the illustration here. These settings will create a grid of 30 vertical lines. The spacing between each line will be five pixels on either side of the line. Click the **Update Preview** button and slide the **Copy To Grid** dialog box out of the way for a moment so that you can view the changes on the **Stage**.

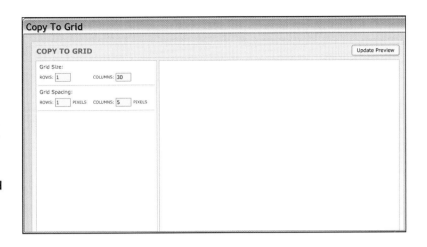

18 When you are satisfied with your settings, click **OK** in the **Copy To Grid** dialog box to accept the settings.

Notice the changes on the Timeline and in the Library. On the Timeline, the vertical lines layer was renamed Copy to Grid 2. This layer contains the grid of vertical lines you just created. In the Effects folder in the Library, notice there are now three graphic symbols, one for each original shape (snowboard outline, horizontal line, and vertical line). Also in the Library is the Copy to Grid 2 graphic symbol, which contains the setting you applied to the vertical line in the Copy To Grid dialog box in Step 17.

Note: The numbers appended to the layer names on the Timeline and to the symbol names in the Library may be different in your project.

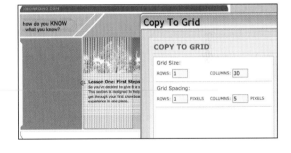

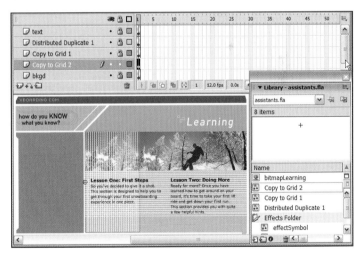

19 Choose **Control > Test Movie** to check out your new interface design.

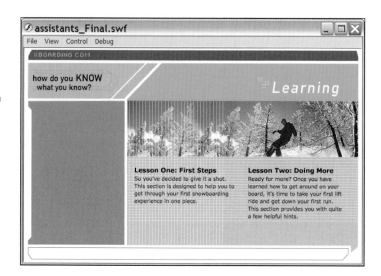

Nice! Instead of doing all the work creating the shape, turning it into a graphic symbol and laying out all the instances on the Stage in a repeating pattern, you used the Copy to Grid and Distributed Duplicate Timeline effect assistants, which saved you the time and energy of doing it all yourself!

Note: If you want to change the stroke color of the lines, double-click the graphic symbol in the **Effects** folder inside the **Library** to open it in **Symbol Editing** mode.

20 When you are done previewing the interface design, close the preview window. Close **assistants.fla**. You don't need to save your changes.

In the next exercise, you will learn how to animate the new Flash 8 filter effects.

8 | Animating with the Blur Filter

In this exercise, you will combine animation techniques you learned in this chapter with the filter techniques you learned in Chapter 7, *"Filters and Blending Modes."* As you will see in this exercise, animating filters is an easy way to create interesting visual effects for your Flash movies.

---

1 Open **blurAnimation.fla** from the **chap_08** folder. If you followed Exercise 3 in Chapter 7, this file will look familiar!

This file has an overlay object with a blending mode and Blur filter applied to produce a colorizing effect. The first animation in this exercise involves changing the properties of the Blur filter over three keyframes and animating these changes over 12 frames.

---

2 In the **Property Inspector**, click the **Filters** tab. On the **Timeline**, select the image in **Frame 1** of the **overlay** layer. In the **Filters** tab, click the small **Lock/Unlock** button to unlock the **Blur X** and **Blur Y** settings. Type **0** in the **Blur X** field but leave the **Blur Y** field set to **20**.

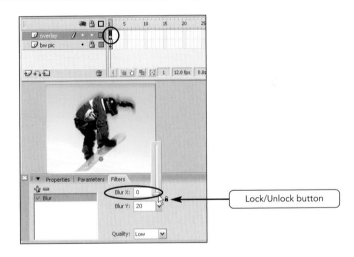

---

3 On the **overlay** layer, select **Frame 6** and press **F6** to add a keyframe. This will copy the contents of **Frame 1**, including the **Blur** filter, to **Frame 6**. Select **Frame 12** on the **bw pic** layer and press **F5** to add frames**.**

4 On the **overlay** layer, select **Frame 6**. Click the **Stage** with the **Selection** tool to select the overlay image. In the **Filters** tab of the **Property Inspector**, match the **Blur** settings to the ones shown in the illustration here.

Now that you have two keyframes with different filter settings, you can set up the first tween, which you'll do next.

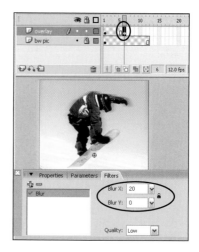

5 On the **overlay** layer, click anywhere between **Frame 1** and **Frame 6** to select a frame. In the **Property Inspector**, click the **Properties** tab and choose **Motion** from the **Tween** drop-down menu. This will create the first motion tween of the animation. To see the results of the tween, scrub the **playhead** back and forth between **Frame 1** and **Frame 6**. The blur around the boarder shrinks inwards.

Next, you will set up the third keyframe and create the second tween animation.

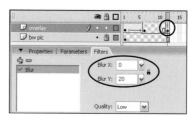

6 Click **Frame 12** of the **overlay** layer and press **F6** to add a keyframe. This adds a copy of the **overlay** image from **Frame 6** into **Frame 12**. Click the **Stage** with the **Selection** tool to select the **overlay** image. In the **Filters** tab of the **Property Inspector**, match the **Blur** settings to the ones shown in the illustration here.

7 On the **Timeline**, click anywhere between **Frame 6** and **Frame 12** in the **overlay** layer to select a frame. In the **Property Inspector**, click the **Properties** tab and choose **Motion** from the **Tween** drop-down menu to add the second filter tween.

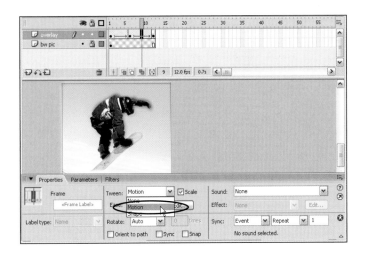

8 Move the **playhead** to **Frame1** and press **Enter** (Windows) or **Return** (Mac) to view the motion tween.

The blur around the boarder shrinks and grows out from the center. Tweening the filter settings of two or more keyframes is a simple, yet effective, way to add visual interest and polish to Flash projects.

Next, you'll work through another example to get a better appreciation for the potential and power of animating with the new filters in Flash 8.

9 Close **blurAnimation.fla**. You don't need to save your changes.

9 | Animating with the Drop Shadow Filter

In this exercise, you'll learn how to animate the Drop Shadow filter, continuing to combine animation techniques you learned in this chapter with the filter techniques you learned in Chapter 7 "Filters and Blending Modes."

---

1 Open **jumpshadow_final.fla** from the **chap_08** folder. Choose **Control > Test Movie** to preview the final animation.

Notice the boarder's shadow changes in strength and location depending on the position of the boarder image. The Drop Shadow filter is perhaps the most important and popular filter; you will learn how to work with its various properties and settings as you re-create this animation.

---

2 When you are finished previewing the animation, close the preview window and **jumpshadow_final.fla**. Open **jumpshadow.fla** from the **chap_8** folder. Scrub the **playhead** back and forth between **Frame 1** and **Frame 48**.

Notice the Timeline animation sequence is composed of seven keyframes and six motion tweens. To create the drop shadow animation, you will add a Drop Shadow filter and modify its settings in each of the first six keyframes.

---

3 Position the **playhead** at **Frame 1**. Select the **Selection** tool from the **toolbar** and click the boarder image on the **Stage**. In the **Property Inspector**, click the **Filters** tab and click the **Add Filter** button (**+**). Choose **Drop Shadow** from the list of filters.

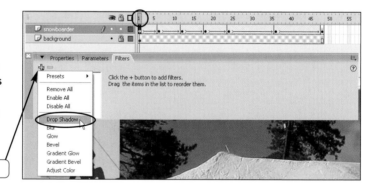

Add Filter button

4 Match the settings in the **Filters** tab to the ones shown in the illustration here. Make sure the **Color** is set to **black** and the **Knockout**, **Inner shadow**, and **Hide object** options are all deselected.

The Distance and Angle settings establish how far and at what angle the shadow will be positioned from the object. The Blur settings establish how diffuse or sharp the edges of the shadow will be.

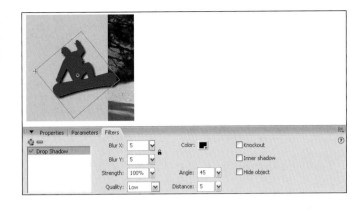

The Drop Shadow filter offers a number of different options that let you carefully customize your drop shadows. For more information about the options for customizing drop shadows, refer to the note at the end of this exercise.

5 Move the **playhead** to **Frame 6**. On the **Stage**, click the boarder to select it.

Flash 8 has already added a Drop Shadow filter to this keyframe because of the tween animation on the Timeline in Frame 1. If you apply a filter and motion tween to one frame, the ending keyframe of the tween will automatically receive the same filter treatment (although the filter settings may be different, as is the case here).

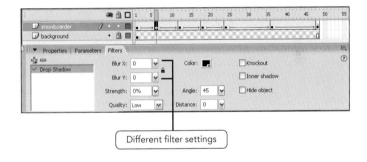

Different filter settings

6 Match the settings in the **Filters** tab to the ones shown in the illustration here.

Notice the drop shadow is now much farther from the boarder graphic and is much more blurry. This is a result of the larger Distance and Blur settings.

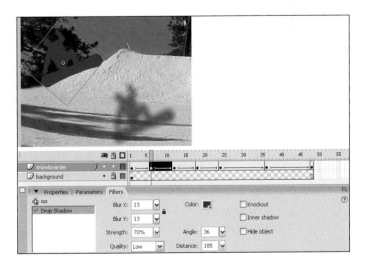

7 Move the playhead to **Frame 12** and select the boarder on the **Stage**. Match the settings in the **Filters** tab to the ones shown in the illustration here.

Notice the Drop Shadow is farther away and even more blurry and unclear. The higher Blur settings and the lower Strength setting creates this effect.

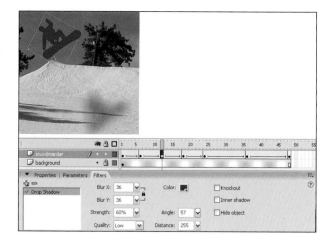

8 Change the drop shadow settings for the keyframes on **Frames 18**, **24**, and **36**. The keyframe on **Frame 48** is off the **Stage** so it does not need a drop shadow. Use the information in the following illustration for the filter settings for each keyframe.

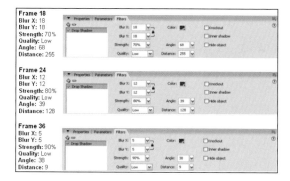

9 After you set the properties for each of the keyframes, press **Enter** (Windows) or **Return** (Mac) to preview your work. You can also scrub the **playhead** back and forth along the **Timeline** to see the results.

Notice the drop shadow moving along with, but also changing shape and distance from, the boarder. This is a great way to add more interest and visual appeal to a simple motion tween animation. Experiment with the various Drop Shadow filter settings to refine and change the animation.

10 When you are finished experimenting, close **jumpshadow.fla**. You don't need to save your changes.

Animating filters, as demonstrated in the exercises in this chapter, is a fast and easy way to add more interest, polish, or realism to your standard motion tweens. Once you become adept at creating motion tween

animations and are familiar with the new filter effects in Flash, you can then combine the two techniques to create more effective and impressive animations.

VIDEO:

jumpShdow.mov

To make this animation more realistic, you could create a secondary movie clip that is flipped horizontally and use the Hide Object feature to create a more realistic shadow for your original movie clip. To learn how to do this, check out **jumpShdow.mov** located in the **videos** folder on the **HOT CD-ROM**.

NOTE:

Understanding the Drop Shadow Settings

Drop Shadow Settings	
Blur X and Y	Sets the width and height of the drop shadow.
Distance	Sets the distance of the shadow from the object.
Color	Sets the shadow color.
Strength	Sets the darkness of the shadow. The higher the numerical value, the darker the shadow.
Angle	Sets the angle of the shadow.
Quality	Sets the quality level of the drop shadow. A high setting approximates a Gaussian blur. A low setting maximizes playback performance.
Knockout	Knocks out (or visually hides) the source object and displays only the drop shadow on the knockout image.
Inner shadow	Applies the shadow within the boundaries of the object.
Hide object	Hides the object and displays only its shadow, creating a more realistic shadow.

Congratulations! You have finished a very important chapter. In this chapter, you learned how to create motion tween animations with symbols, how to use Timeline effects to automate certain animation tasks, and how to animate with the new filters in Flash 8. The knowledge you gained will give you an excellent starting point for experimenting with your own animations. When you are ready, turn the page to learn how to work with bitmap images.

Working with Bitmaps

So far, even though you have used bitmaps as background images in several of the exercise files, you've mostly worked with vector-based graphics. Although many people think of Flash 8 as simply a vector-editing and animation program, you will soon learn it has some pretty impressive bitmap-editing features as well. This chapter concentrates on editing bitmap images, specifically examining how Flash 8 treats them differently from vectors-based graphics. You will learn how to import and optimize bitmaps, how to create a static and animated mask of a bitmap, and how to create interesting animation effects after converting bitmap images to vector-based graphics.

Understanding the Benefits of Bitmaps

Vector graphics are best known for their crisp appearance, small file size, and flexibility in scaling. Their efficient file size helps movies download and play faster. However, vector graphics have a few negative aspects. Complex vector artwork made up of many individual vector objects can generate large files, making them harder for the computer to process and play back. Also, a photographic look is hard to achieve with vector graphics. As a result, a common complaint is that many Flash projects look very similar.

Bitmap images (also known as raster graphics) are stored in the computer as a series of pixel values, with each pixel taking a set amount of memory. Because each pixel is defined individually, this format is great for photographic images with complex details. However, bitmaps lose their image sharpness when you drastically increase or decrease their size.

To counter this problem, Flash 8 now includes an enhancement—bitmap smoothing—to improve the image quality at these severely enlarged or reduced sizes, as shown in the illustration here. To apply bitmap smoothing, double-click the bitmap image in the **Library** to open the **Bitmap Properties** dialog box, and then select the **Allow smoothing** option.

In addition, the appearance of bitmaps in the Flash 8 authoring program and in the Flash Player is now more consistent. Conveniently, Flash 8 lets you import bitmap graphics in many different formats, including JPEG, GIF, and TIFF. If you have QuickTime 4 or later installed on your machine, the list of files available for import increases even further. The following chart lists the bitmap file formats you can import into Flash 8. For a chart describing the vector file types supported by Flash 8, see Chapter 19, "*Integration.*"

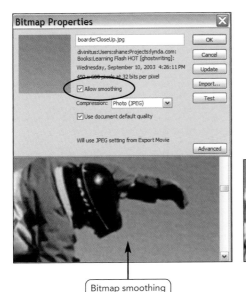

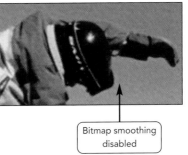

Bitmap smoothing
enabled

Bitmap smoothing

Bitmap File Types				
File Type	Extension	Windows	Mac	QuickTime 4 or Later Needed?
Bitmap	.bmp	X	X	No with Windows; Yes with Mac
GIF and animated GIF	.gif	X	X	No
JPEG	.jpg	X	X	No
PICT	.pct, .pict, .pic	X	X	Yes with Windows; No with Mac
PNG	.png	X	X	No
MacPaint	.pntg	X	X	Yes
Photoshop	.psd	X	X	Yes
QuickTime images	.qtf	X	X	Yes
Silicon Graphics	.sai	X	X	Yes
TGA	.tgf	X	X	Yes
TIFF	.tif, .tiff	X	X	Yes

Note: Flash 8 honors the transparency settings of graphic file formats that support transparency, such as GIF, PNG, and PICT files.

Compression in Flash 8

When you export a movie, Flash 8 automatically applies its own compression settings to bitmaps. You can change the graphics compression settings in two ways. You can set a single compression method and amount for every graphic in the project using the global Publish settings, which you'll learn about in Chapter 17, "*Publishing and Exporting*," or you can use the Bitmap Properties dialog box to set and preview compression settings for each individual file. Any changes you make in the Bitmap Properties dialog box will affect the image in the Library and all the instances of it within the project file.

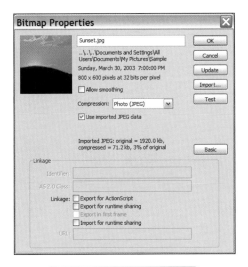

Lossy (JPEG) compression

Lossless (PNG/GIF) compression

In the following exercise, you will learn how to compress bitmap images by changing the compression settings in the Bitmap Properties dialog box. There are two choices for compression: Photo (JPEG), also known as lossy; or Lossless (PNG/GIF). Generally, a photographic image will compress better with lossy (JPEG) compression, and images with a lot of solid colors will compress

better as lossless (PNG/GIF). What's nice is that you'll be able to see a preview within this dialog box to determine which choice produces images that look better.

When Flash 8 outputs your finished movie, it takes this individual image compression into account and overrides the default compression settings.

1 | Importing and Compressing Bitmaps

This exercise demonstrates how to import a bitmap and adjust its compression settings.

---

1 Copy the **chap_09** folder from the **HOT CD-ROM** to your **Desktop**. Open a new document in Flash 8. Save the file (**File > Save As**) in the **chap_09** folder as **import.fla.**

---

2 Choose **File > Import > Import to Stage**, or press **Ctrl+R** (Windows) or **Cmd+R** (Mac) to open the **Import** dialog box. Browse to the **import1.jpg** file located inside the **chap_09 folder**. Select the file and click **Open**.

When you import a file using the Import to Stage command, you might wonder where the file goes. Flash 8 automatically places the file in three locations: on the Stage, in the Library, and in the Bitmap Fill section of the Color Mixer panel.

Note: import1.jpg may or may not have the .jpg extension, depending on which platform you are using (Windows or Mac) and whether you have the extensions turned on or off. Either way is fine, since the file name, import1, is what's required to locate this file. For more information about hiding and revealing file extensions, refer to the Introduction.

---

3 Press **Ctrl+L** (Windows) or **Cmd+L** (Mac) to open the **Library** panel.

---

4 In the **Library**, select the **import1** image. Click the **Properties** button to open the **Bitmap Properties** dialog box.

Properties

TIP :

Additional Ways to Access the Bitmap Properties

In addition to the Properties button in the Library panel, there are three additional ways to access the Bitmap Properties dialog box.

1. Double-click the thumbnail preview in the **Library**.

2. Double-click the icon next to the image name in the **Library**.

3. In the upper-right corner of the **Library**, click the **Options** button and choose **Properties** from the pop-up menu.

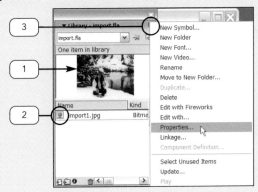

5 In the **Bitmap Properties** dialog box, position the pointer over the preview window. Notice the pointer changes to a hand. Click and drag the image in the preview window until you see the girl.

Since the girl is the focus of the image, you want to make sure the compression settings will give you a much better view of the compression changes you are about to make.

6 Choose **Lossless (PNG/GIF)** from the **Compression** pop-up menu and click **Test** to update the preview image and the compression information at the base of the window.

Notice the new compression information appears at the bottom of the dialog box. You just changed the compression settings for the import1 image. The new compressed image size is 580.4 KB, 57 percent of the original, which was 1006.7 KB. If you click OK, this setting will alter the bitmap in the Library and the instance on the Stage. Don't click OK just yet—you're going to make a couple more changes.

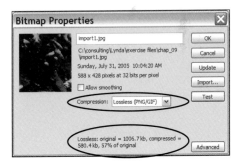

Why Is File Size Important?

As you build project files in Flash 8, you may have to keep your total SWF file size below a certain threshold, to make playback optimal for all users viewing the Web site, including those using dial-up connections. With this in mind, you need to find a good balance between image quality (check the preview window after you click the Test button) and file size. You may have to experiment with several settings, but the file-size savings will be well worth the time spent!

---

7 In the **Bitmap Properties** dialog box, choose **Photo (JPEG)** from the **Compression** pop-up menu. Deselect the **Use imported JPEG data** check box, and add your own quality setting by typing **80** (100 is best; 0 is worst) in the **Quality** box. Click the **Test** button again.

Notice the new compression information appears at the bottom of the dialog box. The new compressed image size is 57.1 KB, significantly smaller than the size obtained using loss-less PNG/GIF compression, which at 580 KB was more than 10 times the size. Additionally, the image still looks great in the preview window. A good rule of thumb is that most photographic content compresses best with the Photo (JPEG) setting, and graphical content with solid colors, graphic shapes, text, and so on, compresses best with the Lossless (PNG/GIF) setting.

---

8 Click **OK**. When the Flash file is published, this bitmap will be compressed using the last settings you applied.

---

9 Close **import.fla**. You don't need to save your changes.

Understanding the Bitmap Properties Dialog Box

There are a number of options in the Bitmap Properties dialog box. This handy table will help you understand the options:

Bitmap Properties Dialog Box

Option	Description
Preview window	Shows the current bitmap properties so you can see how the settings you choose affect the image.
Filename	Displays the bitmap's Library item name. Clicking in the File Name field and typing a new name will change the bitmap's name.

continues on next page

Bitmap Properties Dialog Box *continued*

Option	Description
Image path	Displays the path for the image.
File information	Shows the date the bitmap was last modified, the file's dimensions, and the color depth.
Allow smoothing	Smoothes or dithers the image when selected. If this box is deselected, the image will appear aliased or jagged.
Compression	Lets you choose between Photo (JPEG) or Lossless (PNG/GIF) compression. Photo compression (JPEG) is best for complex bitmaps with many colors or gradations. Lossless compression (PNG/GIF) is best for bitmaps with fewer colors and simple shapes filled with single colors.
Use imported JPEG data	Lets you use the original compression settings and avoid double compression when selected. If this box is deselected, you can enter your own values—between 1 and 100—for the Quality of the image.
Update button	Lets you update the bitmap image if it has been changed outside of Flash 8. It uses the image path to track the original image's location and updates the image selected in the Library with the file located in the original location.
Import button	Lets you change the bitmap in the Library by specifying the path to another image. If a new path is specified, a new image will appear in the Library, and all instances in the project file automatically update with the new bitmap.
Test button	Lets you see the changes you make to the settings of the Bitmap Properties dialog box in the preview window and displays the new compression information at the bottom of the dialog box.
Advanced/Basic	Opens and closes the Linkage properties options.
Linkage	Allows you to add bitmaps to a document at runtime or to share them with other Flash projects. To do this, specify a name for the bitmap in the linkage identifier field and then choose the Export options desired.

2 | Importing Bitmap Sequences

One way to create a "mock" video effect in Flash 8 is to use a sequence of photographs in which each image is just slightly different from the previous image. When these images are placed in keyframes, one right after another, and you test the movie, it will appear as if the camera is rolling! The following exercise demonstrates how to create frame-by-frame animations (or mock video) by importing a series of bitmap graphics all at once.

---

1 Open **bitmapSequence_Final.fla** from the **chap_09** folder.

You'll see a series of images in Frames 1 through 14.

---

2 Press **Enter** (Windows) or **Return** (Mac) to preview the movie.

Although it's just a series of still photographs, it appears as though you are watching a video of a snowboarder making a jump. As you can see, you can effectively simulate video footage by using still images in Flash 8. You'll learn how to create this animation sequence next.

---

3 Close **bitmapSequence_Final.fla**.

---

4 Open **bitmapSequence.fla** from the **chap_09** folder.

This is a blank file with a black background. Next, you'll import the series of images you want to use.

---

5 Choose **File > Import > Import to Stage**, or press **Ctrl+R** (Windows) or **Cmd+R** (Mac). In the **chap_09** folder, double-click to open the **sequence** folder.

Notice there are 14 numbered files in the sequence folder named bigair—xx.

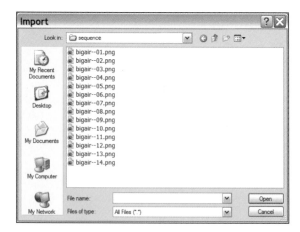

6 Select the **bigair--01.png** file and click **Open**. Flash 8 automatically detects the image you are trying to import as part of a sequence of images. In the warning message that appears, click **Yes** to import the whole series of images.

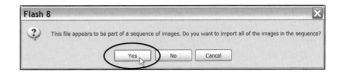

If you ever want to import a sequence of images as successive frames and have Flash recognize it as a sequence, be sure to number the images in the order you want the sequence to appear, such as image01, image02, and so on. Whenever Flash 8 sees sequentially numbered images in the same folder, it will ask you whether the images should all be imported as a sequence.

When you clicked Yes in the last step, Flash 8 imported all 14 files in the sequence, placed them on the Stage, and created a new keyframe for each one on the Timeline. Notice the imported images are not centered on the Stage. Why? By default, Flash 8 places the imported sequence in the upper-left corner of the Stage. You'll change this in the next steps.

7 In the status bar on the **Timeline**, click the **Edit Multiple Frames** button. Make sure the **Edit Multiple Frames** markers span all 14 frames. If they don't, drag the handles so they cover all 14 frames. Click the layer name to select all the frames on the layer. Click and drag the bitmap image into the center of the **Stage**. When finished, turn off **Edit Multiple Frames** by clicking the button again.

Although it may seem complicated, using the Edit Multiple Frames feature lets you reposition all the frames at once.

Edit Multiple Frames markers span all frames.

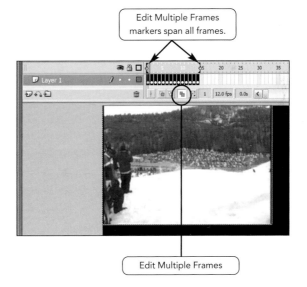

Edit Multiple Frames

8 Choose **Control > Test Movie** to test the movie. When you are finished, close the preview window.

Even though each frame contains a separate image, when you test the movie, it appears as if you're watching video footage!

Note: Next, you'll change the movie frame rate to make it look more realistic.

---

9 Select the **Selection** tool from the **toolbar**. Click anywhere outside the image on the **Stage** to deselect it. In the **Property Inspector**, type **16** in the **Frame rate** field to speed up the movie and make the bitmap sequence animation appear more realistic. Choose **Control > Test Movie** to preview the movie.

The bitmap images will be displayed on the Stage much quicker, better simulating video playback, which usually displays 15 to 30 pictures, or frames, per second.

---

10 When you're finished previewing the movie, close the preview window. Type **6** in the **Frame rate** field in the **Property Inspector**. Choose **Control > Test Movie** to preview the movie.

Depending on the effect you're looking for, you may need a few tries to determine the perfect frame rate.

---

11 When you're finished, close the preview window, save your changes, and keep **bitmapSequence.fla** open for the next exercise.

---

3 | Converting Bitmaps to Vectors

When you import bitmaps, you are not limited to using the files as they exist in their original form. You can convert imported bitmap images to vector graphics using the **Trace Bitmap** feature in Flash 8. This feature traces the shapes of a bitmap graphic and creates a new set of vector shapes simulating the appearance of the original bitmap image. Using the Trace Bitmap feature is not an exact science; it requires a little experimentation to get the best results. This exercise demonstrates how to use the Trace Bitmap feature to turn a bitmap image into a vector graphic.

---

1 If you just completed Exercise 2, **bitmapSequence.fla** file should still be open. If it's not, go back and complete Exercise 2. Turn off the **Edit Multiple Frames** button.

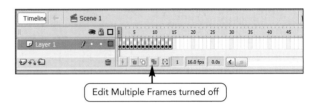

Edit Multiple Frames turned off

---

2 With **Frame 1** selected on the **Timeline** and the **Selection** tool selected in the **toolbar**, select the image on the **Stage** and choose **Modify > Bitmap > Trace Bitmap** to open the **Trace Bitmap** dialog box.

Using the settings in the Trace Bitmap dialog box, you'll transform the bitmap on the Stage into a vector graphic.

NOTE:

What Is Trace Bitmap?

The Trace Bitmap feature lets you convert imported bitmaps into vector art. You might want to do this to create an interesting animation effect, reduce the file size of a photographic image, or zoom into a photographic image during an animation. The Trace Bitmap feature traces the outlines and internal shapes of a bitmap graphic and simulates the appearance of the bitmap file by creating a new set of vector shapes. You can use the settings in the Trace Bitmap dialog box to control how closely the new vector shapes match the original image.

3 In the **Trace Bitmap** dialog box, type **80** in the **Color threshold** field and type **5** in the **Minimum area** field. Choose **Very Tight** from the **Curve fit** pop-up menu and choose **Many corners** from the **Corner Threshold** pop-up menu to create a vector shape with sharp edges that more closely matches the original bitmap. Click **OK**.

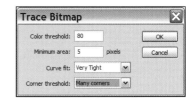

This combination of settings will produce a vector graphic that closely resembles the original bitmap because it will reproduce more detail from the original bitmap. Be aware that the more detail a bitmap contains, and the lower your settings in the Trace Bitmap dialog box, the longer it will take to convert the bitmap to a vector and the larger your movie's file size will be. A reference chart describing all the settings in the Trace Bitmap dialog box is provided at the end of this exercise.

---

4 When the conversion process completes, click anywhere outside of the image to deselect it.

Notice the traced bitmap closely resembles the original.

Note: When you use the Trace Bitmap function, the changes will affect only the selected

Original bitmap

Vector image after using Trace Bitmap

image on the Stage. The bitmap in the Library will remain unchanged. When you publish your movie, the new vector image will appear instead of the original image.

---

5 Move the **playhead** to **Frame 14**. On the **Stage**, select the bitmap on **Frame 14** and choose **Modify > Bitmap > Trace Bitmap** to open the **Trace Bitmap** dialog box.

You will modify the last image in the sequence next.

---

6 In the **Trace Bitmap** dialog box, type **200** in the **Color threshold** field and type **10** in the **Minimum area** field. Choose **Very Smooth** from the **Curve fit** pop-up menu and choose **Few Corners** from the **Corner threshold** pop-up menu. Click **OK**.

As you can see, this combination of settings creates a vector graphic that is more abstract and does not resemble the original image as closely as the settings you used on the Frame 1 image. Fewer corners, and corners that are smoother and less defined, were reproduced from the original bitmap, resulting in a vector image with a lot less detail and definition.

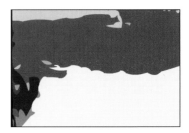

7 Repeat Steps 5 and 6 to convert the remaining 12 bitmap images on the **Stage** to vector graphics. Experiment with different settings for each image to see how the original image changes.

Tip: By using undo—**Ctrl+Z** (Windows) or **Cmd+Z** (Mac)—you can always return the vector art to the original bitmap version and try it again if you don't like how the new image turned out.

---

8 Choose **Control > Test Movie** to preview the animation.

You have produced a stylized version of the video containing vector graphics. This technique is often used for aesthetic reasons. If you scale vector graphics, they keep crisp edges, whereas if you scale a bitmap, it becomes blurry and jagged.

Note: Tracing works best on bitmaps with few colors and gradients. Tracing a bitmap with many colors will not only tax the computer's resources, but can also result in a vector graphic that is larger in file size than the original bitmap. To achieve the best results, experiment with different settings and take note of the file sizes.

---

9 Close **bitmapSequence.fla**. You don't need to save your changes.

NOTE:

Understanding the Trace Bitmap Options

There are a number of options in the Trace Bitmap dialog box. This handy table will help you understand the options:

	Trace Bitmap Dialog Box	
Option	**Description**	
Color threshold	Sets the amount by which the color of each pixel can vary before it is considered a different color. As the threshold value increases, the number of colors in the image decreases, and the resulting traced bitmap image will have fewer colors than the original. The color threshold range is 1 to 500.	
Minimum area	Determines the number of surrounding pixels to consider when determining the color of a pixel. The lower the number, the more the pixel color will resemble the pixels nearby. The higher the number, the less the color will resemble adjacent pixels. The area range is 1 to 1000.	
Curve fit	Determines how smooth (Smooth or Very Smooth) the outlines in the traced shape are drawn or how closely they match the original image (Tight or Very Tight).	
Corner threshold	Determines whether to use sharp edges (Many Corners) or smoother edges (Few Corners).	

Choosing the appropriate options in the Trace Bitmap dialog box can be confusing. Here are a few key tips:

If you want to conserve file size or create a more abstract image, choose a higher color threshold, a higher minimum area, smooth curve fit, and few corners.

If you want to match the original image as closely as possible, choose a lower color threshold, a lower minimum area, very smooth curve fit, and many corners.

4 | Using Basic Masking

Masking is a technique that lets you hide and reveal areas of a layer. The mask layer is a special layer that defines what is visible on the layer beneath it. Only layers that are beneath the shapes in the mask layer will be visible. This technique is useful when you want to fill text with a photograph or hide (mask) a portion of the background of a photo. In this exercise, you will create a mask with text so the image on the layer below appears inside the text.

---

1 Open **mask.fla** from the **chap_09** folder. Make sure the **Library** is visible. If it's not, choose **Window > Library**.

This file has a blue background and contains one symbol in the Library.

---

2 Choose **File > Import > Import to Stage**. In the **chap_09** folder, double-click the **sideMountain.jpg** file to open and automatically place the bitmap on the **Stage**.

---

3 On the **Timeline**, double-click **Layer 1** and rename it **mountain**. Press **Enter** (Windows) or **Return** (Mac).

In the next few steps, you'll mask this layer.

---

4 Lock the **mountain** layer by clicking the dot under the **Lock** icon for the layer.

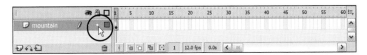

Locking layers prevents you from accidentally moving or selecting the bitmap on the mountain layer.

---

5 Click the **Insert Layer** button to add a new layer. Double-click the newly created layer, rename it **xboarding**, and press **Enter** (Windows) or **Return** (Mac). Make sure the stacking order of the layers matches order shown in the illustration here. If it doesn't, click and drag to reposition the layers so the **xboarding** layer is above the **mountain** layer.

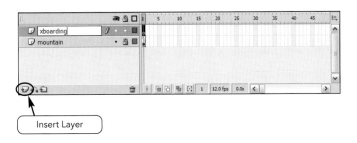

Insert Layer

6 Take a look at the contents of the **Library**. Notice the **siteName** symbol. I have included this graphic symbol in the **mask.fla** file to help you with this exercise. Drag an instance of the **siteName** symbol onto the **Stage** and position the **X** over the snowboarder in the bitmap image.

The symbol instance of the xboarding.com name is going to end up as the mask for the bitmap. You can think of the text inside the symbol instance as a cookie cutter that will let you see only what you cut out of the mountain image.

Tip: To better see where the snowboarder is in relation to the xboarding graphic, click the **View Outlines** icon for the **xboarding** layer.

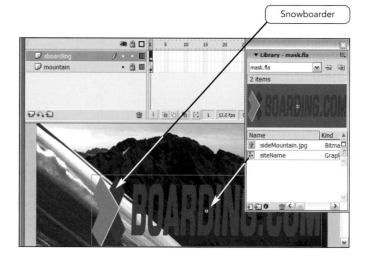

Snowboarder

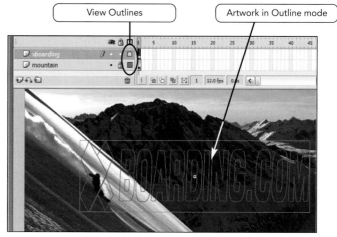

View Outlines

Artwork in Outline mode

7 With the **xboarding** layer selected, choose **Modify > Timeline > Layer Properties** to open the **Layer Properties** dialog box. Select **Type: Mask** and click **OK** to convert the **xboarding** layer into a mask layer.

Note: When converting a layer to a mask layer, you can choose to bypass the Layer Properties dialog box by **right-clicking** (Windows) or **Ctrl+clicking** (Mac) the layer name and choosing **Mask** from the contextual menu.

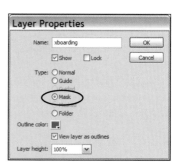

In this step, you created a mask layer (the xboarding layer), which has a defined mask area based on the siteName symbol. Next, you need to create the masked layer—the layer beneath that will show through the mask layer. In this example, you'll create a masked layer using the mountain layer.

8 To make the **mountain** layer become masked by the **xboarding** mask layer, double-click the **mountain** layer icon to open the **Layer Properties** dialog box. Select **Type: Masked** and click **OK**.

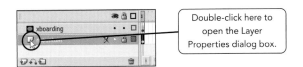

Double-click here to open the Layer Properties dialog box.

Notice that the icon and position of the mountain layer has changed.

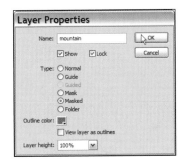

9 Click the dot under the **Lock** icon for the **xboarding** layer so both layers are locked.

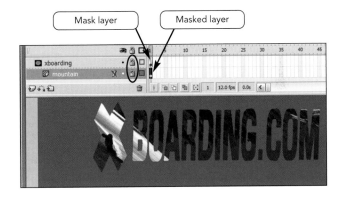

Mask layer

Masked layer

The bitmap now shows through the text shapes!

Tip: In order to see the mask, you must have both the mask layer and the masked layer locked. To lock the layer, you can either click the Lock column in the layers or **right-click** (Windows) or **Ctrl+click** (Mac) the layer's name and choose **Show Masking** from the contextual menu.

You have just created your first mask! As you can see, you can create some really interesting effects using mask and masked layers in Flash 8. Next, you will animate the mask.

10 Save your changes and keep **mask.fla** open for the next exercise.

5 | Using Animated Masks

In the last exercise, you learned how to create a basic mask using text. But masks don't have to be static! This exercise demonstrates how to create a text mask that moves over a bitmap background.

1 If you just completed Exercise 4, **mask.fla** should still be open. If it's not, go back and complete Exercise 4.

2 On the **xboarding** layer, click **Frame 20** to select it and choose **Insert > Timeline > Keyframe** to add a keyframe.

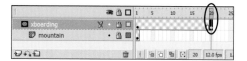

3 On the **mountain** layer, click **Frame 20** to select it and press **F5** to add frames.

4 Unlock the **xboarding** layer by clicking the **Lock** icon. Click the first keyframe to select it and click and drag to move the **xboarding** instance off the **Stage** to the left.

5 With the **xboarding** instance still selected in **Frame 1**, choose **Modify > Transform > Flip Vertical** to flip the **xboarding** instance upside down.

This position will serve as the beginning of the animation.

6 On the **Timeline**, select one of the frames in the **xboarding** layer between **Frame 1** and **Frame 20**. In the **Property Inspector**, choose **Motion** from the **Tween** pop-up menu to add a motion tween to the mask.

7 Click the dot under the **Lock** icon to lock the **xboarding** layer.

Notice you can immediately see the masked image on the Stage.

8 Press **Enter** (Windows) or **Return** (Mac) to test the animation. The **xboarding** text flips and rotates with the mountain picture peeking through the letters.

Great job! In just a few steps, you changed the basic mask from the previous exercise to an animated mask.

9 Close **mask.fla**. You don't need to save your changes.

6 | Animating Bitmaps

When you are working with bitmaps, you can make them fade in from invisible to visible or vice versa. This handy technique can be accomplished by converting the bitmap to a symbol and creating a motion tween of the symbol's alpha setting. You will learn how to do this in the following steps.

1 Open **effectsFinal.fla** from the **chap_09** folder.

This is a finished version of the project you will complete in this exercise.

2 Choose **Control > Test Movie** to preview the SWF file.

You will see a pencil outline being drawn, the outline being filled with a bitmap that fades into view, and then a background image fading into view. In this exercise, you will complete the last part of the animation—fading the bitmaps from invisible to visible.

3 Close **effectsFinal.fla**.

4 Open **bitmapEffects.fla** from the **chap_09** folder.

This file contains the first part of the animation demonstrated in the **bitmapEffects.mov** video. The file contains two layers: the boarder layer contains a bitmap of a jumping boarder; the stroke layer contains a pencil outline animation around the boarder and is locked, so you don't accidentally modify it. You'll be working with the boarder layer in this exercise.

The first thing you'll do is create a motion tween of the boarder changing from invisible to visible.

5 On the **boarder** layer, click the keyframe on **Frame 1** to select it. Click and drag the keyframe from **Frame 1** to **Frame 6** to move the keyframe.

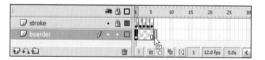

As you can see, you can easily move keyframes on the Timeline by clicking and dragging.

6 With the **Selection** tool selected in the **toolbar**, click the **boarder** on the **Stage** to select it and press **F8** to open the **Convert to Symbol** dialog box. Type **boarder** in the **Name** field, and select **Behavior: Graphic**. Click **OK**.

This will be the starting point of the tween animation.

Wondering why you converted the board to a symbol? In the next few steps, you will be using alpha to create the fade effect, and you can't apply an alpha effect to an object that is not a graphic symbol or movie clip symbol.

---

7 On the **boarder** layer, select **Frame 20** and choose **Insert > Timeline > Keyframe** to add a keyframe to **Frame 20**.

This will be the end of the tween animation.

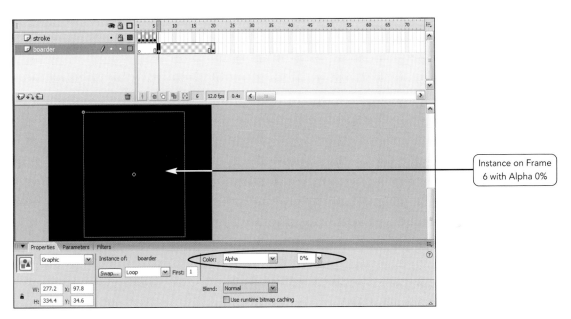

Instance on Frame 6 with Alpha 0%

8 Move the **playhead** back to **Frame 6** and click to select the **boarder** symbol instance on the **Stage**. (Be careful to select the instance on the **Stage** and not the frame so that the **Property Inspector** shows you the correct attributes.) In the **Property Inspector**, choose **Alpha** from the **Color** pop-up menu and set the value to **0%**.

---

9 Click anywhere between **Frames 6** and **20** to select one of the frames. In the **Property Inspector**, choose **Motion** from the **Tween** pop-up menu.

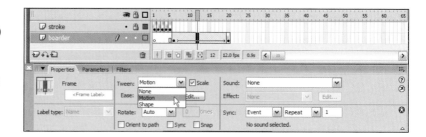

10 In the **stroke** layer, select **Frame 20** and press **F5** to add frames to match the number of frames on the **boarder** layer.

Once the outline animates around the boarder, this step keeps the outline visible on the Stage during the following tween animation.

11 Press **Enter** (Windows) or **Return** (Mac) to preview the animation. The outline will draw itself, and then the **boarder** layer will fade from invisible to full color.

You have one more tween animation to create.

12 On the **Timeline**, lock the **boarder** layer and click the **Insert Layer** button to add a new layer. Rename the new layer **background**. Click and drag to position it below the **boarder** layer so it is the bottom layer on the **Timeline**.

13 Select **Frame 20** and press **F7** to add a blank keyframe to **Frame 20** of the **background** layer. Hide the **stroke** and **boarder** layers so you can see only the **background** layer for the next few steps.

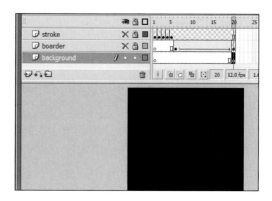

14 Press **Ctrl+L** (Windows) or **Cmd+L** (Mac) to open the **Library**. Drag an instance of the **boarderCloseUp** bitmap graphic onto the **Stage**.

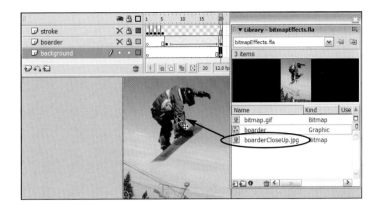

15 Choose **Ctrl+K** (Windows) or **Cmd+K** (Mac) to display the **Align** panel. Click the **To Stage** button and then click the **Align vertical center** and **Align horizontal center** buttons to center the image.

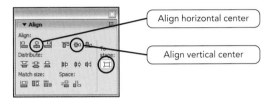

Note: The Align panel lets you position selected objects relative to the Stage (if the To Stage button is selected) or relative to one another (if several objects are selected).

16 With the snowboarder bitmap still selected on the **Stage**, press **F8** to convert the bitmap to a symbol. In the **Convert to Symbol** dialog box, type **origImage** in the **Name** field and select **Behavior: Graphic** to convert the bitmap to a symbol so you can create a motion tween in the following steps.

17 Select **Frame 35** on the **background** layer and choose **Insert > Timeline > Keyframe** to add a keyframe to **Frame 35**.

This will be the end of the tween animation.

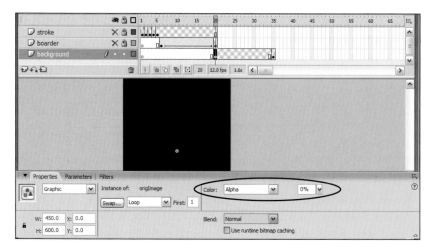

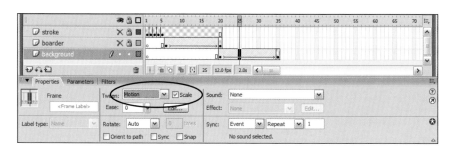

18 Move the **playhead** back to **Frame 20** and select the **origImage** symbol instance on the **Stage**. (Be careful to select the instance on the **Stage** and not the frame so the **Property Inspector** shows you the right attributes.) In the **Property Inspector**, choose **Alpha** from the **Color** pop-up menu and set the value to **0%**.

This will be the beginning of the animation on the background layer.

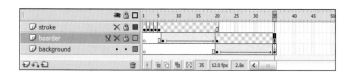

19 Click anywhere between **Frames 20** and **35** to select one of the frames. In the **Property Inspector**, choose **Motion** from the **Tween** pop-up menu.

20 In the **boarder** layer, click **Frame 35** to select it and press **F5** to add frames to match the number of frames on the **background** layer.

This will make the boarder layer remain visible on the Stage during the background tween animation.

21 Shift+click **Frame 45** of both the **boarder** and **background** layers to select **Frame 45** of both layers. Press **F5** to add frames up to **Frame 45**.

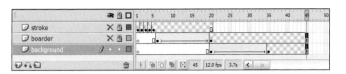

This will add frames so once the background fades in, it will remain for 10 more frames before the animation starts over again.

---

22 Choose **Control > Test Movie** to preview the final animation. The outline will draw itself, the **boarder** layer will fade from invisible to full color, and then the background will fade in. Great work!

Note: When you press **Enter** (Windows) or **Return** (Mac), you see only a preview of the animation inside the editing environment, which may not play exactly as the SWF file will in the Flash Player. To see a more realistic test of the animation, choose **Control > Test Movie**, which will play back the actual SWF inside the Flash Player. In Chapter 17, *"Publishing and Exporting,"* you will learn an even more reliable way to see how the file will look in a browser: using the Publish command.

---

23 When you are finished, close **bitmapEffects.fla**. You don't need to save your changes.

VIDEO: | **bitmapEffects.mov**
To learn more about animating bitmaps, check out **bitmapEffects.mov** in the **videos** folder on the **HOT CD-ROM**.

That's it—you've finished another chapter! Get ready to learn about buttons next.

10

Buttons

There are three types of symbols in Flash 8: graphic symbols, button symbols, and movie clip symbols. You learned about graphic symbols in Chapter 6, *"Symbols and Instances,"* and you'll learn about movie clip symbols in Chapter 11, *"Movie Clips."* You'll learn about button symbols in this chapter.

Buttons are a very useful type of symbol. They can contain rollover states and animated rollover states, or even be made invisible. What you might not realize is that there's more to making buttons than creating the artwork for them. You can also program buttons to accept "actions" written in ActionScript (covered in Chapter 12, *"ActionScript Basics and Behaviors"*). Through actions, you can make buttons play, stop, rewind, fast forward, change artwork, and do numerous other things in your Flash movies! Before programming your buttons, however, you need to learn how to create them. Learning Flash 8 involves putting a lot of puzzle pieces together, and button symbols are an extremely important part of the puzzle. You will find a use for them in all of your Flash projects. In this chapter, you will build a solid foundation for working with buttons, including how to create, add sound to, test, and preview them.

Button States

Just as with graphic and movie clip symbols, button symbols have their own Timelines. The difference with a button symbol's Timeline is that it displays four prelabeled, premade frames: Up, Over, Down, and Hit. The first three frames of the button Timeline determine the appearance of the button during three different kinds of mouse interactions. The fourth frame, Hit, determines the clickable area of the button. The terms *Up*, *Over*, *Down*, and *Hit* are also called states, which are described in the following table. As you know from previous chapters, the Timeline must contain keyframes in order to contain changing content. Button Timelines have slots for the Up, Over,

Down, and Hit states, but they start out empty. You must insert keyframes in these slots, where you can then place content that constitutes the button in the various states of interaction.

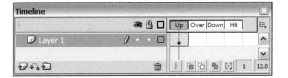

When you create a button symbol, Flash 8 automatically adds a blank keyframe in the first frame—the Up state—of the button.

Button States	
State	**Description**
Up	The Up keyframe contains artwork defining the button appearance before the user's mouse interacts with the button.
Over	The Over keyframe defines the button appearance when the user moves the mouse over the Hit area of the button. This is also referred to as the rollover state of the button.
Down	The Down keyframe defines the button appearance when it's clicked. The user sees this state for only a split second (or longer if he or she holds down the mouse).
Hit	The Hit keyframe defines the actual, active area of the button. It is also referred to as the hot area of the button. The contents of the Hit frame are always invisible to the user.

Button Types

Fundamentally, all button symbols are constructed alike. However, you can significantly change their appearance and behavior by altering the frames you use and the content of the four keyframes. The possibilities are nearly endless, but they will generally fall into the following four categories:

Button Types	
Type	**Description**
Basic	A basic button has the same content in the Up, Over, and Down states. Users can click it, and it can contain actions, but it does not change appearance or provide visual feedback during the user's interaction with it.
Rollover	A rollover button changes appearance when the user rolls over it, providing visual feedback about the user's mouse position. This is accomplished by inserting different content in the Over state than in the Up state.
Animated	An animated rollover button is similar to a rollover button, but one or more of its keyframes (usually the Over state) contains an animation within a movie clip instance. Whenever that keyframe is displayed, a movie clip animates. You will learn how to make animated rollover buttons and movie clips in the next chapter.
Invisible	Invisible buttons contain a blank keyframe in the Up state and a keyframe in the Hit state. They can also contain artwork in the Over or Down state, although they never contain artwork in the Up state. Because there is no artwork in the Up state, the button is invisible to users until they mouse over it. You will learn how to make an invisible button in Exercise 5.

1 | Creating Rollover Buttons

This exercise teaches you how to create, test, and preview a basic rollover button. You will learn how the button's Timeline is different from the main Timeline, and about the four different states of buttons.

---

1 Copy the **chap_10** folder from the **HOT CD-ROM** to your **Desktop**. Open **rollOverButton.fla** from the **chap_10** folder.

This is a blank file with a gray background. You'll use this file to create buttons.

---

2 Choose **Insert > New Symbol** to create a new button symbol and to open the **Create New Symbol** dialog box. Type **btnRollo** in the **Name** field and select **Behavior: Button**. Click **OK**.

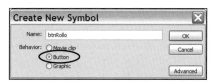

As soon as you click OK, you will enter the button's Timeline. Each button symbol has its own independent Timeline. Even though the button contains multiple button states, it will occupy only one frame in the main Timeline. Note the four frames of the button Timeline: Up, Over, Down, and Hit. Buttons do not automatically "play" as the main Timeline does or as animated graphic symbols do. Rather, the button's Timeline remains paused on the Up state keyframe, displaying only the content in this keyframe, until the user's mouse pointer comes into contact with the button. The other keyframes in the button symbol (Over and Down) are shown only in reaction to the mouse pointer position.

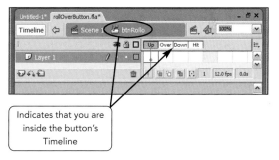

Indicates that you are inside the button's Timeline

NOTE: | **Button Naming Conventions**

When developing Flash content, use symbol names that include an abbreviation indicating which type of symbol it is. For example, use *btnRollo* or *rollo_btn*. If you start the name with the symbol abbreviation, you can sort symbols alphabetically in the Library with the buttons grouped together, all the graphic symbols grouped together, and all the movie clip symbols grouped together.

---

3 Choose **View > Grid > Show Grid** to cover the **Stage** with a grid.

The grid is visible only in the Flash 8 editing environment and will not be exported with your movie.

---

4 Select the **Line** tool from the **toolbar**. Make sure the **Stroke Color** is set to **black** and **Object Drawing** is deselected. Draw a small triangle that spans about two grid boxes in height. The right point of the triangle should be on the center crosshair on the **Stage** (which is actually the **registration point** of the button), as shown in the illustration here.

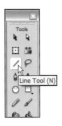

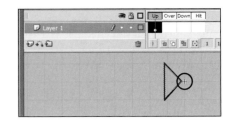

Placing the triangle on the center crosshair ensures the triangle is set to pivot on this point. If you choose to rotate, scale, transform, or position the triangle button, it will always pivot from the registration point, as you learned to do in Chapter 4, "*Animation Basics.*"

The triangle you created in this step will serve as the Up state for the button, the default button image the user sees before interacting with it.

Tip: To make it easier to draw the triangle, change the view to **200%** in the edit bar.

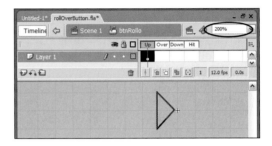

5 Select the **Paint Bucket** tool from the **toolbar**. Set the **Fill Color** to the fourth color down in the first column of the **Fill Color** palette (value **#999999**). Click once inside the triangle to fill the triangle with gray.

Why do you have to choose that specific gray? The next three exercises will build on one another, and it is important to use the right color in this first exercise so that by the time you get to Exercise 3, the colors will match the interface you will be working with.

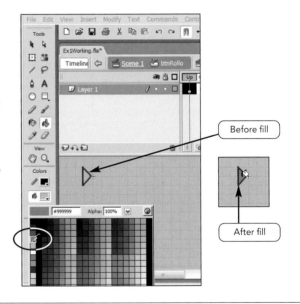

Before fill

After fill

6 Select the **Selection** tool from the **toolbar** and move the pointer over the black stroke of the triangle. Double-click it to select all three line segments. (You can also **Shift+click** each line segment if double-clicking does not select all three segments.) Press **Delete** on the keyboard to delete the black stroke.

You now have a solid gray triangle without a stroke around it.

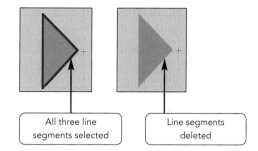

All three line segments selected

Line segments deleted

---

7 Press **F6** to add a keyframe to the **Over** frame of the button and to copy the content—the triangle—from the last keyframe into the **Over** frame.

---

8 Select the **Paint Bucket** tool from the **toolbar**, and choose **white** for the **Fill Color**. Click once inside the triangle to fill the triangle with white.

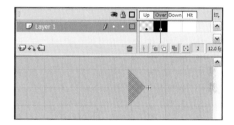

---

9 Press **F6** to add a keyframe to the **Down** state of the button. Set the **Fill Color** to the same color you used in Step 5: **#999999**. Click once inside the triangle to fill it with gray.

---

10 Scrub the **playhead** to see the different states of the button. The **Up** state triangle should be gray, the **Over** state triangle should be white, and the **Down** state triangle should be gray again.

To complete the button symbol, you need to define the Hit state of the button, which you'll do next.

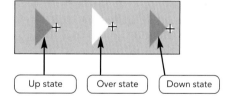

Up state

Over state

Down state

---

11 Press **F6** to add a keyframe to the **Hit** frame of the button.

The Hit frame defines the "hot" area of the button, or the area that will react to the mouse interaction. In this case, this area will be the exact same shape as the button.

The Hit state is invisible to the user, so it does not matter what color the content in the Hit keyframe is. The Hit state defines the Stage area that will be used to activate the button rollover.

Hit Me!

The Hit state of the button has one objective: to define an active area when the mouse pointer comes into contact with it. Because the Hit keyframe defines the area of the button that is reactive to the mouse, the Hit area must cover the entire active area of the button. If the button is tiny and the Hit area is small or smaller, users may have diffi-culty interacting with the button at all. For tiny buttons or text-only buttons, use a solid shape that is slightly larger than the button's Up or Over states. If you leave the Hit keyframe blank, its content will default to the graphic content in the last filled keyframe.

12 In the edit bar, click **Scene 1** to return to **Scene 1** of the main **Timeline**.

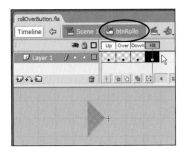

You are located in the Button symbol's Timeline.

You are located in Scene 1 of the main Timeline.

Where's the Button?

When you choose Insert > New Symbol (as you did back in Step 2), Flash 8 automati-cally places the new button symbol in the Library, so you will not see the button on the Stage of the main Timeline. If you want to use the new button in your movie, you must drag an instance of the button onto the Stage. In order to test the button, you have three options: you can test it in the Library, on the Stage, or by using Control > Test Movie. You will try each option next.

13 Press **Ctrl+L** (Windows) or **Cmd+L** (Mac) to open the **Library**. Click the **btnRollo** symbol in the **Library**. In the preview window, click the **Play** button to preview the button in the **Library**.

The button will play one frame right after the next (Up, Over, Down, and Hit). This quick preview, however, may not be very realistic. The following steps show you how to preview the button on the Stage.

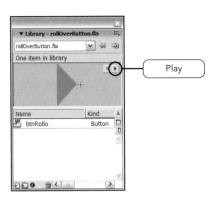

Play

14 Choose **View > Grid > Show Grid** to hide the grid on the **Stage**. Drag an instance of the button you created onto the **Stage**.

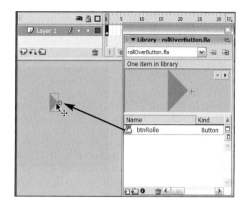

---

15 Choose **Control > Enable Simple Buttons**, which will let you to test the button right on the **Stage**.

---

16 Move your mouse over the button to see the **Over** state. Click the button to see the **Down** state.

---

17 Choose **Control > Enable Simple Buttons** to deselect this option. The button will no longer be active on the **Stage**.

---

18 Choose **Control > Test Movie** to produce a SWF file (you'll learn more about this in Chapter 17, "*Publishing and Exporting*"), which lets you test buttons in yet another way.

This method of testing will yield the same visual results as choosing Enable Simple Buttons; it's just another way to accomplish the same thing.

---

19 Move the mouse over the button to trigger the **Over** state. When you are finished, close the SWF file to return to the editing environment.

---

20 Save your changes and keep **rollOverButton.fla** open for the next exercise.

2 | Creating Rollover Buttons with Text

In the previous exercise, you learned how to create and test a button. This exercise shows you how to alter that button by altering its Hit state and adding text.

---

1 If you just completed Exercise 1, **rollOverButton.fla** should still be open. If it's not, go back and complete Exercise 1.

---

2 In the **Library**, double-click the button symbol icon to open the button's **Timeline**.

---

3 Inside the button symbol's **Timeline**, double-click **Layer 1** and rename it **triangle**. Lock the **triangle** layer.

---

4 Click the **Insert Layer** button to add a new layer to the button's **Timeline**. Rename the layer **text**.

---

5 Select the **Text** tool from the toolbar. In the **Property Inspector**, choose **Verdana** from the **Font** pop-up menu and **16** from the **Font Size** pop-up menu. Choose **white** from the **Text Color** box.

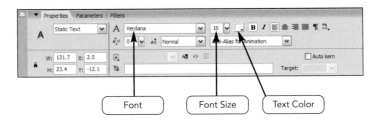

Font   Font Size   Text Color

---

6 On the **Stage**, click to the right of the triangle and type the word **BACKGROUND** in capital letters.

When you add the text, it automatically adds frames to the Timeline so the word *BACKGROUND* appears across each of the Up, Over, Down, and Hit states.

---

7 In the Timeline, select the **Over** state of the button on the **text** layer. Press **F6** to add a keyframe to the **Over** frame.

---

8 Select the **Selection** tool from the **toolbar** and click the text block on the **Stage** in the **Over** frame. In the **Property Inspector**, click the **Text Color** box and choose a **dark gray** color, **#666666**, to change the text color for the text in the **Over** frame.

---

9 Choose **Control > Test Movie** to test the button.

NOTE:

Using Text in the Hit State

Button not activated   Button activated   Button not activated

You may have noticed the button may or may not work depending on where you click. Because you used text in the Hit state, the button will not be active until the mouse passes directly over the actual text itself (not in-between the characters), which can be confusing, because the button will not work unless the user places the mouse pointer directly over a solid part of a letter. A hole in an *O* or even the space between letters can cause the button to flicker on and off, which is why you shouldn't use text to define the Hit state of your buttons. You will learn how to use a solid shape to define the Hit state next.

---

10 When you test a movie, it opens the results in a separate preview window. Close the preview window to return to the editing environment. Move the **playhead** to the **Hit** frame.

To trigger the button, the mouse must move over the area defined as the Hit state. In this case, the Hit frame is defined by the content inside it, which consists of the triangle and the text, *BACKGROUND*. The current Hit state causes the button to be triggered only when the mouse rolls exactly over the text or the arrow. This is not the correct way to create a Hit state, so you need to modify it.

11 In the button's **Timeline**, **Shift+click** both layers in the **Hit** frame to select both layers. **Right-click** (Windows) or **Ctrl+click** (Mac) the selected layers and choose **Remove Frames** from the contextual menu to remove both keyframes in the **Hit** state.

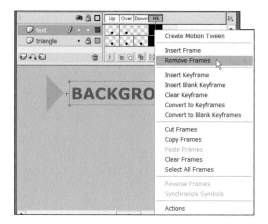

You will be adding new content to define the Hit area in the next few steps.

12 Lock the **text** layer and click the **Insert Layer** button to add a new layer to the button's **Timeline**. Position the new layer below the **triangle** layer and rename it **hit**.

13 On the **hit** layer, click the **Hit** frame and press **F7** to add a blank keyframe to the **Hit** button state.

14 Unlock all the layers and click the **Onion Skin** button. Make sure the onion skin markers span all four states of the button.

You will be creating the new Hit state next, and you need to be able to see the artwork in the other frames.

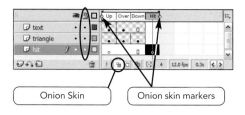

Onion Skin   Onion skin markers

15 Select the **Rectangle** tool from the **toolbar**. On the **Stage**, draw a rectangle covering both the triangle and the text.

By creating the Hit area this way, the mouse will only need to move over the rectangle in order for the button to be triggered.

16 Click the **Onion Skin** button to turn off onion skinning.

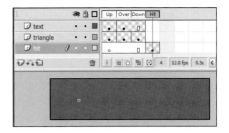

After you draw the rectangle, you end up with a solid shape that will define the new Hit area of the button. It doesn't matter what color the Hit state is or if it contains a stroke and a fill. Just make sure it covers the appropriate area.

---

17 In the edit bar, click **Scene 1** to leave the button symbol's **Timeline** and return to the main **Timeline**.

Notice the button instance you placed on the Stage in the previous exercise. Since you modified the actual symbol itself in this exercise, the button instance on the Stage will automatically be updated with the text and the new Hit state.

---

18 Choose **Control > Enable Simple Buttons** to test the button on the **Stage**. Move your mouse over the button to see the **Over** state. Click the button to preview the **Down** state.

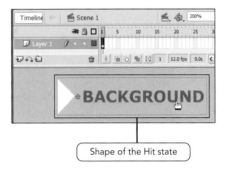

Shape of the Hit state

Now that you've defined the Hit state as a solid shape covering the entire Up state of the button (the arrow and the text), it's much easier to interact with. As soon as the mouse pointer reaches the edge of the invisible rectangle shape (the Hit state), the Over state is triggered and the image in the Over keyframe is displayed.

---

19 Choose **Control > Enable Simple Buttons** to deselect this option. The button will not be active on the **Stage** anymore.

---

20 Save **rollOverButton.fla** as **textButton.fla** in preparation for the next exercise. Close the file.

NOTE:

Understanding the Hit State

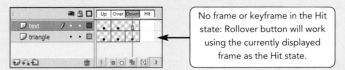

No frame or keyframe in the Hit state: Rollover button will work using the currently displayed frame as the Hit state.

If there is no frame or keyframe in the specified Hit state, the Hit shape of the button is set by the currently displayed keyframe. Therefore, if the Up and Over keyframes contain different shapes, the Hit state will change when the user rolls over the button. This is not an ideal way to create buttons.

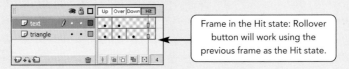

Frame in the Hit state: Rollover button will work using the previous frame as the Hit state.

If a frame is specified in the Hit state, it will use the contents of the last set keyframe.

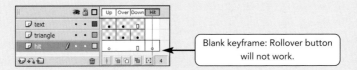

Blank keyframe: Rollover button will not work.

Setting a blank keyframe in the Hit state will disable the rollover—a Hit state is required to trigger the Over and Down states. If the shape for the button is large enough for the Hit state, you don't have to create a keyframe or new artwork in that frame. In this exercise, however, the text was not an adequate shape or size for the user to trigger the rollover consistently. The best method is to test your rollovers first, to ensure that the Hit state is an adequate shape for the job.

Remember, the Hit state should cover the entire area you want to designate as reactive to the mouse.

In the last two exercises, you learned how to create buttons and preview the results, and you learned why the Hit state is important. Another handy skill is making duplicate copies of buttons. For example, you can quickly create a navigation bar for a Web site by copying buttons and changing the text in each copy. This exercise shows you how to duplicate buttons in the Library and how to align them on the Stage. You'll also learn how to use Library items from other movie projects. This exercise demonstrates a practical workflow for reusing and modifying an existing button design.

1 Open **duplicateAlign.fla** from the **chap_10** folder.

This file contains one layer with a background image.

2 Press **Ctrl+L** (Windows) or **Cmd+L** (Mac) to open the **Library**.

Notice there are three items in the Library: the interface graphic symbol and two bitmaps.

3 Choose **File > Import > Open External Library** and select **textButton.fla** from the **chap_10** folder. This will open just the **Library**, including the button symbol you created in the exercise, of the **textButton.fla** file.

You will be using the button from the **textButton.fla** library in the following steps.

Notice there are now two Libraries open. One is the Library from the duplicateAlign movie you are currently working on; the other is the Library from the textButton movie.

The Open External Library technique comes in handy when you need to use assets from another project without having to open up the project file (FLA). This technique will save you time, keep your computer screen less cluttered, and help you avoid the headache of managing several open projects at the same time.

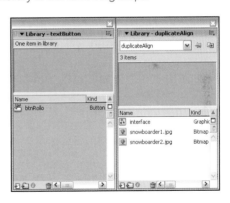

4 In the main **Timeline**, insert a new layer and rename it **buttons**. Make sure the **buttons** layer is positioned above the **background** layer.

5 In the **textButton Library**, drag an instance of the **btnRollo** symbol onto the **Stage**, and place it over the gray box on the left side of the **Stage**.

Notice after you place the instance on the Stage, the btnRollo symbol is now located in both libraries. You added the symbol from the textButton movie to the duplicateAlign movie, and Flash 8 automatically adds the symbol to the Library for you.

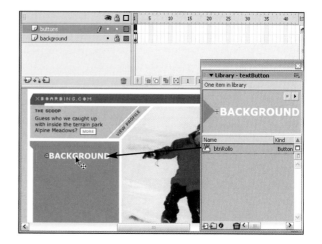

6 In the **duplicateAlign Library**, right-click (Windows) or **Ctrl+click** (Mac) the **btnRollo** symbol and choose **Duplicate** from the contextual menu to make a copy of the button symbol and to open the **Duplicate Symbol** dialog box.

7 In the **Duplicate Symbol** dialog box, type **btnSafety** in the **Name** field and make sure **Behavior: Button** is selected. Click **OK**.

You have just made an exact duplicate of the button you previously created. Notice the new btnSafety symbol in the Library.

---

8 In the **Library**, double-click the **btnSafety** button to open its **Timeline**. Lock the **triangle** and **hit** layers so you don't accidentally edit anything on those layers.

Notice the Timeline looks identical to the original button you created. You'll be changing the text of this button next.

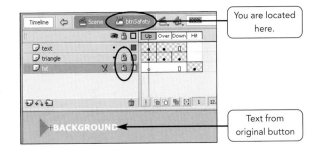

You are located here.

Text from original button

---

9 On the **text** layer, click in **Frame 1** (the **Up** state of the button). Double-click the text block on the **Stage** to highlight the text, and type the word **SAFETY** to replace the existing text.

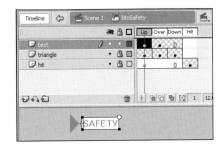

---

10 On the **text** layer, click **Frame 2** (the **Over** state of the button). Double-click the text block on the **Stage** and type the word **SAFETY** in capital letters.

---

11 In the edit bar, click **Scene 1** to leave the button symbol's **Timeline** and return to the main **Timeline**.

12 Drag an instance of the new button, **btnSafety**, from the **Library** onto the **Stage**, just below the **background** button. Choose **Control > Enable Simple Buttons** to test the button. When you are finished testing, choose **Control > Enable Simple Buttons** to deselect this feature.

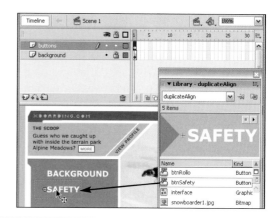

13 Repeat Steps 6 through 10 to create three more duplicate buttons. Name them **btnLearning**, **btnGear**, and **btnWhatsNew**, respectively. Inside each button, name the text **LEARNING**, **GEAR**, and **WHAT'S NEW**.

14 In the edit bar, click **Scene 1** to return to the main **Timeline**.

15 Drag down diagonally the right corner of the **duplicateAlign Library** panel to resize the entire panel so you can see all the buttons you created. If your **textButton Library** is stacked below the **duplicateAlign Library**, collapse this **Library** first by clicking the collapse arrow.

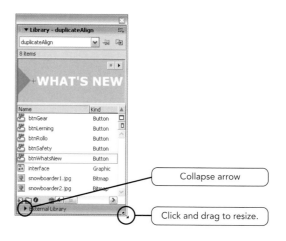

Collapse arrow

Click and drag to resize.

16 Drag the **btnLearning**, **btnGear**, and **btnWhatsNew** buttons onto the **Stage** below the other two buttons.

17 Press **Ctrl+A** (Windows) or **Cmd+A** (Mac) to select all five buttons on the **Stage**. Choose **Window > Align** to open the **Align** panel. Make sure the **To Stage** button is turned off. Click the **Align left edge** and **Distribute vertical center** buttons to align all the buttons on the **Stage** to the left and to space them apart equally.

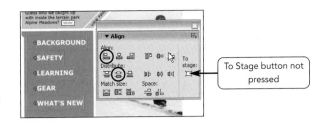

To Stage button not pressed

18 Make sure the buttons are still selected. Using the **arrow** keys on the keyboard, nudge the buttons to the left or right so that the left side of each button is flush with the white border, as shown in the illustration here. To aid in this placement, choose **Control > Enable Simple Buttons** and mouse over the buttons. The white triangle in the button **Over** state should line up with the white interface border.

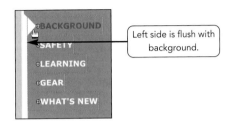

Left side is flush with background.

19 Choose **Control > Test Movie** to test the rollover buttons.

You streamlined the creation of this navigation system by creating the artwork for only one button, duplicating it four times, and changing only the text inside each button.

20 Leave **duplicateAlign.fla** open for the next exercise.

NOTE:

Duplicate vs. Instance

In the last exercise, you could not have just dragged the button from the Library to the Stage three times because the original symbol contains text. To change the text, you would have to go into the symbol itself to modify it. You can change the shape, size, rotation, skew, and color of any instance, but cannot change actual artwork or text without changing the original symbol. To get around this problem, you instead duplicated the Library item of one button, and created four new buttons based on the original.

4 | Adding Sound to Buttons

Each button state can hold a different sound to give feedback to the user. This exercise shows you how to add a simple sound to a button.

1 If you just completed Exercise 3, **duplicateAlign.fla** should still be open. If it's not, go back and complete Exercise 3.

2 Choose **File > Import > Open External Library** and select the **buttonSounds.fla** file from the **chap_10** folder.

This command opens only the Library of the **buttonSounds.fla** file. In this exercise, you will be using the sound files in this Library.

3 In the **duplicateAlign Library**, double-click the **btnGear** button to open its **Timeline**. Click the **Insert Layer** button to add a new layer. Rename the layer **sound**, and make sure it is the top-most layer.

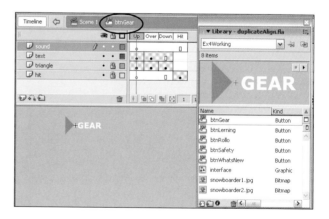

4 Select the **Selection** tool from the **toolbar**. On the **sound** layer, click the **Over** frame and press **F7** to add a blank keyframe.

You will be adding a sound to this frame next.

---

5 In the **buttonSounds Library**, select any of the sound files and click the **Play** button in the **Library** preview window to preview the sound.

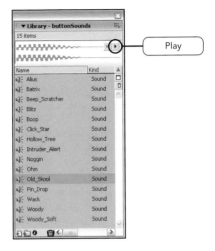

---

6 With the **Over** frame selected in the **sound** layer, drag an instance of the **Intruder_Alert** sound from the **buttonSounds Library** onto the **Stage**.

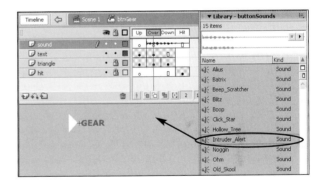

That's all there is to it! You have just added a sound to the button.

Note: You will not see a visual representation of the sound on the Stage. Instead, you will see sound waves in the Over frame of the Timeline. It's okay if the sound extends into the Hit frame in the button's Timeline. Having a sound in the Hit frame will have no effect on the button because the Hit state is determined by artwork on the Stage, not sound in the Timeline.

---

7 In the edit bar, click **Scene 1** to return to the main **Timeline**.

Since you modified the button in the Library, all of the btnGear instances on the Stage will be updated. You will test this next.

---

8 Choose **Control > Enable Simple Buttons** to test the button on the **Stage**. When you are finished testing it, choose **Control > Enable Simple Buttons**.

You should hear the sound play when you move the mouse over the btnGear button, because you added the sound to the Over state of that button. You will add a sound to the Down state of the What's New button next.

Tip: This is a very brief introduction to working with sound. You'll learn more about Flash's sound capabilities, including which sound formats Flash 8 supports, in Chapter 14, "*Sound.*"

---

9 In the **duplicateAlign Library**, double-click the **btnWhatsNew** button to open its **Timeline**.

---

10 Lock the **text** layer. Click the **Insert Layer** button to add a new layer. Rename this layer **sound**, and make sure it's the top-most layer.

---

11 With the **Selection** tool selected in the **toolbar**, click the **Down** frame in the **sound** layer and press **F7** to add a blank keyframe.

---

12 With the **Down** frame selected in the **sound** layer, drag an instance of the **Blitz** sound from the **buttonSounds Library** onto the **Stage**.

Notice the sound wave appears in the Down frame of the Timeline.

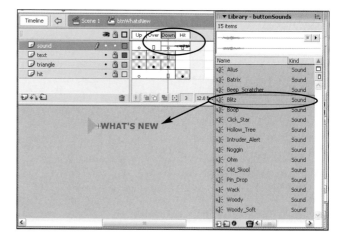

---

13 Choose **Control > Test Movie** to test your buttons.

Notice the sound in the Gear button plays when the mouse rolls over the button and the sound in the What's New button plays when you click the button (because you placed the sound in the Down state).

Tip: You can also choose **Control > Enable Simple Buttons** in the editing environment to hear the button sounds on the Stage.

Notice the sounds you added to the Gear and What's New buttons are now in the duplicateAlign Library.

---

14 Repeat Steps 9 through 12 to add sounds of your choice to the remaining buttons: **btnSafety**, **btnLearning**, and **btnRollo** (the **Background** button).

---

15 Close **duplicateAlign.fla**. You don't need to save your changes.

---

5 | Creating Invisible Buttons

You learned about the importance of the Hit state for rollover buttons in previous exercises. You can also use the Hit state to create invisible buttons. This kind of button comes as an unexpected surprise to users, because there's no visible display of the button object until the user passes the mouse over an invisible region. In this exercise, you will learn how to change regular buttons into invisible buttons.

1 Open **invisButton_Final.fla** from the **chap_10** folder.

This is the finished version of the movie you are going to create in this exercise.

2 Choose **Control > Test Movie** to preview this movie. Move your pointer over the lodges in the picture.

Notice how the descriptions pop up from the image. You will be creating this same effect next.

3 When you are finished looking at this movie, close the file.

4 Open **invisible.fla** from the **chap_10** folder. We created this file ahead of time to get you started.

Notice the file contains two layers—one with a background image on it and the other with three buttons on it.

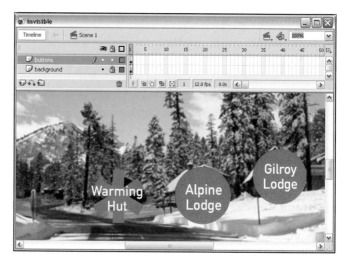

5 Choose **Control >Test Movie** to preview the buttons. Move your mouse over the buttons and notice they are not invisible.

They behave just like normal rollover buttons, with the text changing color when you roll over them with the mouse. You will turn them into invisible buttons to create a surprise rollover effect next.

6 Close the preview window. Back in the project file, open the **Library**. Double-click the **alpine** button's icon to open its **Timeline**. Notice the button has three layers. Scrub the **playhead** to preview the **Up**, **Over**, **Down**, and **Hit** states of the button.

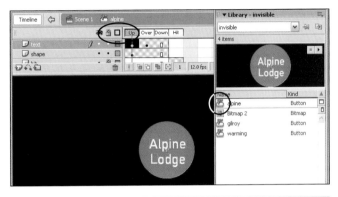

7 Click a blank area of the **Stage** to make sure you have nothing selected. In one motion, click and drag to select the first two frames in the **text** and **shape** layers. Drag the four selected frames one frame to the right and release the mouse.

Why did you move the frames out of the Up state? When you create an invisible button, the Up state must be empty so users won't know that a button even exists until the mouse moves over the area defined in the Hit frame You will test the button next.

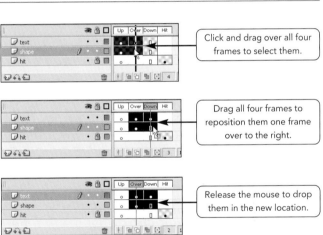

Click and drag over all four frames to select them.

Drag all four frames to reposition them one frame over to the right.

Release the mouse to drop them in the new location.

8 In the edit bar, click **Scene 1** to return to the main **Timeline**.

Notice the alpine button looks different. Because you modified the button in the Library, any instance on the Stage will be updated. The button has no Up state, so Flash 8 displays the shape of the Hit frame in a transparent blue color, providing a visual hint of the button's location.

Why not just use a shape with a transparent fill for the Up state when you create a button? That would certainly work as an invisible button, but you would have a difficult time seeing the instances of the button in your work area. An invisible button containing a Hit state is represented by a translucent blue, letting you to easily position and work with the button in the work area.

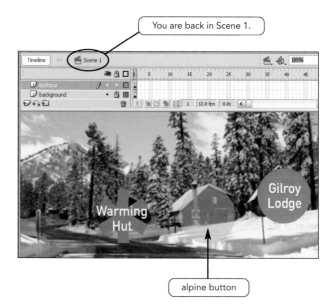

You are back in Scene 1.

alpine button

---

9 Choose **Control > Test Movie** to test the invisible button you just created.

Notice the three different states of the button. Since you moved the frames to the right by one frame in Step 7, the old Up state of the button (white text, graphic background) is now the Over state, and the

| Up state = invisible | Over state = white text | Down state = black text |

old Over state (black text, graphic background) is now the Down state. Test the Gilroy Lodge button and the Warming Hut button to see the difference between the invisible button and the normal buttons.

You will change the other two buttons into invisible buttons next.

---

10 Repeat Step 7 for the other two buttons in the **Library**: the **gilroy** and **warming** buttons.

---

11 Choose **Control > Test Movie** to test all three buttons. Neat!

---

12 When you are finished, close **invisible.fla**. You do not need to save the changes.

VIDEO: | **buttonFilters.mov**

You can transform even plain and simple buttons with the application of one or more of the new filter effects in Flash 8. You can use the Drop Shadow, Blur, Glow, and Bevel filters individually or in various combinations to produce interesting and attractive Flash buttons. Here are some examples:

Home

The Home button here uses the Bevel and Drop Shadow filters to make the button look more three-dimensional.

HOME

This button uses a drop shadow applied to the inside of the text label to give it quite a different three-dimensional look.

To learn more about applying filter effects to buttons, check out **buttonFilters.mov** in the **videos** folder on the **HOT CD-ROM**.

That's it! This chapter gave you a solid foundation for working with and understanding Flash button symbols. You learned about the different button states and the different kinds of buttons you can create in Flash, how to add sound to your buttons, and even how to duplicate and align buttons to quickly create menus. The next chapter will introduce you to movie clips—another very important topic in your Flash education.

11

Movie Clips

Understanding movie clip symbols is key to producing interactive Flash 8 movies. This understanding is the last step in building a foundation that will prepare you for Chapter 12, "*ActionScript Basics and Behaviors.*" As you will see, ActionScripting often requires a movie clip symbol, so don't underestimate the importance of the information contained in this chapter.

Up to this point in the book, you've learned how to create both graphic and button symbols. At last, you will be introduced to movie clip symbols and gain a solid understanding of how to create and use them effectively.

What Is a Movie Clip?

Movie clips are the most versatile, powerful, and useful symbols in Flash 8. However, they are also the most difficult to understand and use. Before you get started with the hands-on exercise, take some time to learn some of the key terms and concepts:

Movie Clip Vocabulary	
Term	**Definition**
Main Timeline	The main Timeline, introduced in Chapter 6, "*Symbols and Instances*," is the Timeline of the scene (or scenes) in your project file. If you have more than one scene, Flash 8 will consider them part of the same main Timeline and will add together the number of frames inside each scene to make up one main Timeline. For example, if Scene 1 contains 35 frames, and Scene 2 contains 20 frames, Flash will consider the main Timeline to span 55 frames. You will learn more about managing and naming scenes in Chapter 12, "*ActionScript Basics and Behaviors*." As you've seen, graphic symbols are closely related to the main Timeline. For example, if your graphic symbol contains 10 frames of animation, the main Timeline must also contain 10 frames for the graphic symbol to play.
Timeline	Unlike graphic symbols, button and movie clip symbols do not have a direct relationship to the main Timeline. They are referred to as "Timeline independent" since they can function (play animation, sounds, and so on) regardless of how many frames the main Timeline contains. For example, if you have a movie clip that contains a 10-frame animation of a chairlift moving up a hill, and you place this on the Stage inside the main Timeline, the chairlift will continue to move up the hill even if the Timeline contains only a single frame. This ability to have different animations and actions occur independently of the main Timeline is what makes movie clips so useful and powerful.
Movie clips	Movie clip symbols can contain multiple layers, graphic symbols, button symbols, and even other movie clip symbols, as well as animations, sounds, and ActionScripting. Movie clips operate independently of the main Timeline. They can continue to play even if the main Timeline has stopped, and they require only a single keyframe on the main Timeline to play, regardless of how long its own Timeline is. This is an important concept when you start to work with ActionScript. Think of movie clips as movies nested in the main Timeline.

Although movie clips are extremely powerful and flexible, you can't preview them by pressing **Enter** (Windows) or **Return** (Mac), as you can with button and graphic symbol instances. Preview movie clips in the **Library** (out of context of the main movie) by choosing **Control > Test Movie**, or by publishing the final movie. (You'll learn about this in Chapter 17, "*Publishing and Exporting*.")

1 | Creating a Movie Clip

This exercise starts you off by showing how to make a movie clip.

---

1 Copy the **chap_11** folder from the **HOT CD-ROM** to your **Desktop**. Open **movieClip_Final.fla** from the **chap_11** folder.

Notice there is only one keyframe in the main Timeline.

---

2 Choose **Control > Test Movie** to preview the movie clip. When you are finished previewing this movie, close the file.

The fill of the movie clip fades in and out repeatedly. This is the xboarding logo you are going to animate and convert into a movie clip in the following steps.

---

3 Open **movieClip.fla** from the **chap_11** folder.

I created this file to help you get you started. It has two layers: one named outline, which contains the outline of the X, and the other named text, which contains the *boarding.com* letters. You are going to create a simple motion tween next.

---

4 Click the **Insert Layer** button to add a new layer to the **Timeline**. Double-click the layer. When the bounding box appears, type **fillTween** and press **Enter** (Windows) or **Return** (Mac) to rename the layer.

---

5 Press **Ctrl+L** (Windows) or **Cmd+L** (Mac) to open the **Library**. Drag an instance of the **gfxFill** graphic symbol onto the **Stage** in the **fillTween** layer. Using the arrow keys on the keyboard, position the **gfxFill** instance so it covers the *X* outline exactly.

In the next few steps, you will be creating an animation of this outline filling in with color, so make sure the gfxFill symbol is positioned directly on top of the outline artwork on the Stage.

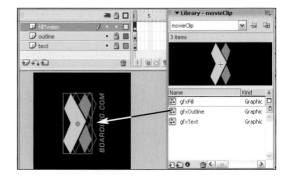

Tip: You may want to change the magnification in the edit bar to **200%** so you can better see the placement of your artwork.

6 In the **fillTween** layer, add keyframes to **Frame 20** and **Frame 40** by selecting each frame and choosing **Insert > Timeline > Keyframe**.

In the following steps, you will be creating a motion tween in which the gfxFill instance starts off invisible in Frame 1, becomes completely visible in Frame 20, and fades to invisible again in Frame 40.

7 Move the **playhead** to **Frame 40** and select the instance on the **Stage**. In the **Property Inspector**, set the **Color** option to **Alpha** and **0%**.

8 Move the **playhead** to **Frame 1** and select the instance on the **Stage**. In the **Property Inspector**, set the **Color** option to **Alpha** and **0%**.

9 Click the **fillTween** layer to select all the frames on the layer. In the **Property Inspector**, choose **Tween: Motion** to add a motion tween across all of the frames.

10 In the **outline** layer, click **Frame 40** and Shift+click **Frame 40** of the **text** layer to select **Frame 40** in both layers. Press **F5** to add frames up to **Frame 40**.

The artwork on the outline and text layers will now be visible throughout the motion tween on the fillTween layer.

11 Press **Enter** (Windows) or **Return** (Mac) to test the animation.

The *X* outline fills in with color, and then the fill fades away.

Next you will create a movie clip using this animation.

12 Click the **text** layer to select all the frames on that layer. **Shift+click** the **outline** and **fillTween** layers to select all the frames on both of those layers as well. Choose **Edit > Timeline > Cut Frames** to cut the selected frames from the main **Timeline**.

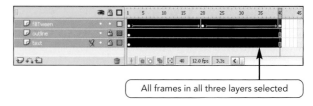

All frames in all three layers selected

Note: Make sure you choose Cut Frames, and not Cut. Cut Frames lets you cut multiple frames and layers, but a simple Cut command doesn't.

---

13 Choose **Insert > New Symbol** and type **mcOutlineFill** in the **Name** field. Make sure **Behavior: Movie clip** is selected. Click **OK** to create a movie clip symbol and open the movie clip symbol's **Timeline**.

---

14 Select the first keyframe and choose **Edit > Timeline > Paste Frames**, which will paste all the frames and all the layers right inside the movie clip, maintaining the layers and layer names just as you they were in the main **Timeline**.

You just created your first movie clip! You will be able to test it in the next steps.

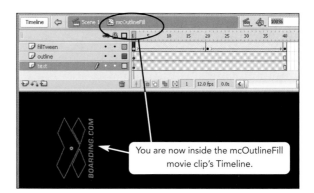

You are now inside the mcOutlineFill movie clip's Timeline.

---

15 In the edit bar, click the **Scene 1** button to return to the main **Timeline**.

In the main Timeline, notice the three layers you originally had are still there, although they have no content on them because you cut the frames and pasted them into the movie clip symbol.

---

16 You no longer need the **text** or **outline** layers, so select each one and click the **Delete Layer** button to delete them.

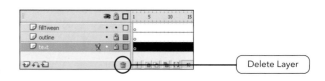

Delete Layer

You may be thinking, "What's with all this cutting, pasting and copying? Wouldn't it be easier just creating the content inside the movie clip in the first place?" Although it would be easier, it may not always be the workflow you actually use. Often, you create artwork on the main Timeline first and later decide to turn it into a movie clip. Because creating artwork inside a movie clip is the easier of the two workflows, practice the harder method, which is to copy and paste artwork from the main Timeline into a movie clip symbol's Timeline.

---

17 Double-click the **fillTween** layer name and rename it **movieClip**. On the **Timeline**, click **Frame 42** and drag backward to **Frame 2** to select **Frames 2** through **40**. **Right-click** (Windows) or **Ctrl+click** (Mac) the selected frame. Choose **Remove Frames** from the contextual menu to remove all the selected frames.

Because there are no frames on Frame 41 or 42, only the frames up to Frame 40 will be selected. However, this method of "overselecting" ensures you don't miss any.

Note: The Cut Frames command cuts the content of the layers and frames, but the Timeline still contains the frames. The only way to remove the frames is to use the Remove Frames command.

---

18 Press **Ctrl+L** (Windows) or **Cmd+L** (Mac) to open the **Library**, and drag an instance of the **mcOutlineFill** movie clip symbol onto the **Stage**.

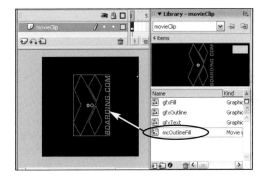

---

19 Choose **Control > Test Movie** to preview the movie clip you just made.

Note the movie clip plays even though there is only one frame in the main Timeline—the movie clip's Timeline is independent from the main Timeline.

---

20 Save your changes and keep **movieClip.fla** open for the next exercise.

TIP: | **Modifying Movie Clip Instances**

Not only do movie clips have a Timeline that is independent from the main movie, but, as you've learned in previous chapters, you can apply Timeline effects, filters, and blend modes to movie clip instances as well. Create the movie clip just once, and then change the attributes (such as scale, alpha, skew, and rotation) of each instance on the Stage to achieve different visual effects. By adding transformations, filters, or blends to the instances on the Stage, you can change the appearance of the movie clip with just a few mouse clicks. The original movie clip, however, will remain unchanged in the Library.

Animated Graphic Symbols vs. Movie Clip Symbols

In this exercise, you'll learn the differences between animated graphic symbols and movie clip symbols. As you'll see, the animated graphic symbol requires multiple frames in the main Timeline whereas a movie clip does not. You'll learn firsthand why I have placed so much emphasis on the Timeline independence of movie clips.

---

1 If you just completed Exercise 1, **movieClip.fla** should still be open. If it's not, go back and complete Exercise 1. Choose **File > Save As** to save another version of this file. Name the new file **mcVsGfx.fla** and save it in the **chap_11** folder.

---

2 Click the **Stage**. In the **Property Inspector**, click the **Size** button to open the **Document Properties** dialog box. Type **400 px** in the **Dimensions: width** field and click **OK** to change the width of the **Stage** to 400 pixels, which will give you a little more room to work.

The best way to learn the difference between an animated graphic symbol and a movie clip symbol is to have one of each symbol type in your project file. You created a movie clip symbol in the last exercise, so in the steps that follow, you will duplicate this symbol and convert the copy to an animated graphic symbol.

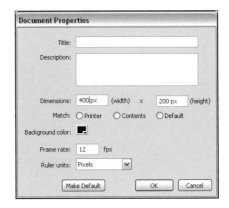

---

3 Press **Ctrl+L** (Windows) or **Cmd+L** (Mac) to open the **Library** if it isn't already open. **Right-click** (Windows) or **Ctrl+click** (Mac) the **mcOutlineFill** movie clip symbol in the **Library**. Choose **Duplicate** from the contextual menu to make a copy of the symbol and to open the **Duplicate Symbol** dialog box.

---

4 Type **gfxOutlineFill** in the **Name** field and select **Behavior: Graphic**. Click **OK** to make an exact copy of the movie clip symbol.

Setting the Behavior option to Graphic changes the way the new symbol functions. Because it contains animation (the fill tween), this kind of symbol is referred to as an *animated graphic symbol*.

---

5 In the **Library**, select the **gfxOutlineFill** symbol and click the **Play** button in the preview window to test the graphic symbol. In the **Library**, select the **mcOutlineFill** symbol and click the **Play** button to test this movie clip symbol.

Both animations appear to be exactly the same.

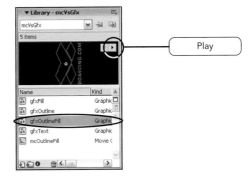

Play

---

6 On the **Timeline**, lock the **movieClip** layer. Add a new layer by clicking the **Insert Layer** button. Rename the new layer **animGfx**.

This layer will hold the animated graphic symbol.

Insert Layer

---

7 Drag an instance of the **gfxOutlineFill** symbol onto the **Stage**, and position it to the right of the **mcOutlineFill** movie clip symbol to add the animated graphic symbol to the main **Timeline**.

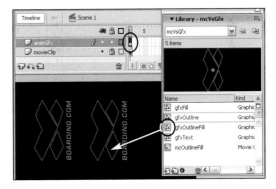

8 Select the **Text** tool from the **toolbar**. Below the **gfxOutlineFill** instance, click the **Stage** and type the text label **Animated Graphic Symbol**. Lock the **animGfx** layer, and unlock the **movieClip** layer. Click the **Stage** and type the text label **Movie Clip Symbol** below the **mcOutlineFill** instance.

As you test the movie in the following steps, the text labels will help you remember which instance is which.

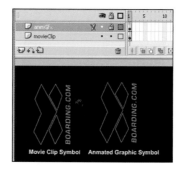

---

9 Press **Enter** (Windows) or **Return** (Mac) to test the movie.

Nothing happens, because pressing Enter (Windows) or Return (Mac) moves the playhead across all the frames in the main Timeline of the movie. But in this movie, you have only one frame, so the playhead has nowhere to go. Therefore, you will see both symbols in their static states only.

---

10 Choose **Control > Test Movie** to preview the movie.

Notice the movie clip symbol plays, and the animated graphic symbol does not. Why?

The main difference between an animated graphic symbol and a movie clip symbol is that the movie clip's Timeline is completely independent of the main movie's Timeline. A movie clip's Timeline can play regardless of

how many frames the main Timeline contains. Animated graphic symbols, on the other hand, play in sync with the main Timeline. The Timeline of an animated graphic symbol is tied to the main Timeline, and therefore at least the same number of frames in the graphic symbol's Timeline must exist in the main Timeline in order for the graphic symbol to play.

---

11 Close the preview window and return to the project file. Back on the main **Timeline**, **Shift+click Frame 40** of both layers and press **F5** to add frames up to **Frame 40**.

Why 40 frames? This is the same number of frames that exist in both the graphic symbol's Timeline and the movie clip's Timeline.

---

12 Press **Enter** (Windows) or **Return** (Mac) to test the movie.

This time, the animated graphic symbol plays, but the movie clip does not. There are now enough frames in the main Timeline so that the animated graphic symbol can play. However, as you learned in Exercise 1, you cannot preview movie clips on the Stage. You must view them either in the **Library** or by using **Control > Test Movie**. This is one of the "rules" of movie clips. They don't preview in the editing environment.

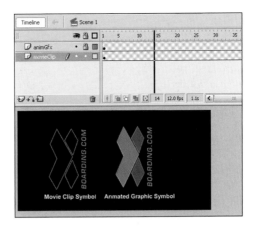

---

13 Choose **Control > Test Movie**.

Now, both symbols animate. To summarize, the animated graphic symbol will play if there are enough frames in the main Timeline, but the movie clip will play in the preview window regardless of how many frames are on the Timeline.

---

14 Save your changes and keep **mcVsGfx.fla** open for the next exercise.

NOTE:

Why Is Timeline Independence Important?

The Timeline independence of movie clips is extremely important when programming interactive presentations. ActionScripting, which you'll learn about in the next chapter, can refer to movie clips because they have the capacity to be "named" and referenced in scripts, whereas graphic symbols do not.

3 | Creating an Animated Rollover Button

This exercise demonstrates how to turn a normal rollover button into an animated rollover button by nesting a movie clip in the Over state of a button symbol. If you've been wondering why Timeline independence is important, this example will drive the point home.

1 If you just completed Exercise 2, **mcVsGfx.fla** should still be open. If it's not, go back and complete Exercise 2. Choose **File > Save As** and save a copy of the file as **animRolloBtn.fla** in the **chap_11** folder.

2 In the **Property Inspector**, click the **Settings** button to open the **Document Properties** dialog box. Type **600 px** in the **Dimensions: width** field and click **OK** to change the width of the **Stage** to 600 pixels, which will give you more room to work with this exercise.

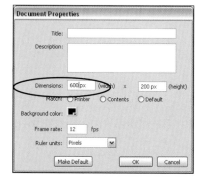

After changing the document dimensions, your Stage should match the illustration here.

3 In the **Library**, click the **New Symbol** button to open the **Create New Symbol** dialog box.

You will be creating an animated button symbol in the following steps.

4 In the **Create New Symbol** dialog box, type **btnAnim** in the **Name** field, and select **Behavior: Button**. Click **OK**.

You are now inside the editing environment for the button symbol's Timeline.

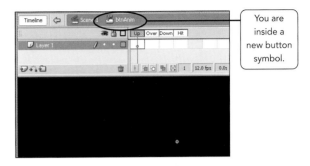

You are inside a new button symbol.

5 Rename **Layer 1** to **outline**. Drag an instance of the **gfxOutline** symbol onto the **Stage**.

This symbol is static and contains only the outline of the X.

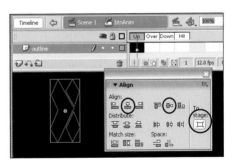

6 With the **gfxOutline** instance still selected on the **Stage**, choose **Window > Align** to open the **Align** panel. Click the **To stage** button, and then click the **Align vertical center** and **Align horizontal center** buttons to perfectly align the instance in the center of the **Stage**.

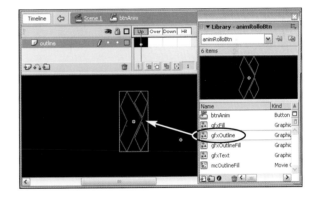

7 In the **Library**, drag an instance of the **gxfText** symbol onto the **Stage**, just to the right of the *X* outline. This symbol is static and contains the word *boarding.com* on only one frame. The **Align** panel should still be open. If it is not, press **Ctrl+K** (Windows) or **Cmd+K** (Mac). Make sure the **To Stage** button is selected, and click **Align vertical center** in the **Align** panel. You have now created the **Up** state of the button.

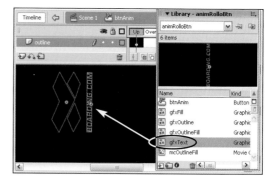

---

8 In the **Down** frame, press **F5** to add frames in both the **Over** and **Down** states of the button. Lock this layer so you don't accidentally select anything on it. You will be adding a movie clip symbol to the button in the following steps.

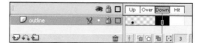

---

9 Click the **Insert Layer** button to add a new layer. Rename it **movieClip**.

---

10 In the **Library**, **right-click** (Windows) or **Ctrl+click** (Mac) the **mcOutlineFill** movie clip symbol. Choose **Duplicate** from the contextual menu to make a copy of the symbol and to open the **Duplicate Symbol** dialog box.

11 Type **mcOverAnim** in the **Name** field and select **Behavior: Movie clip**. Click **OK** to make an exact copy of the symbol.

This movie clip will be used for the Over state of the button, but first you have to make a modification to the mcOverAnim symbol, which you'll do next.

12 In the **Library**, double-click the **mcOverAnim** movie clip icon, which will take you into the movie clip's **Timeline**.

Notice that it looks exactly like the Timeline for the mcOutlineFill movie clip symbol you created in Exercise 1. You will modify this movie clip next.

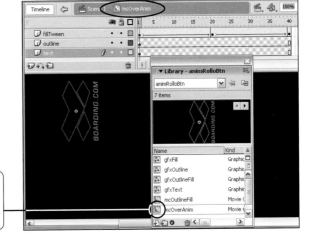

Double-click here to view the movie clip's Timeline.

13 Select the **text** layer and click the **Delete Layer** button to delete the **text** layer. Repeat this step to delete the **outline** layer.

The **Timeline** for the **mcOverAnim** movie clip should now have only one layer with the fill tween on it.

You deleted these extra layers because you need only the X artwork for the animated Over state you are creating for the button.

14 Scrub the **playhead** to see the motion tween animation. This movie clip will serve as the **Over** state of the button (once you add it to the button's **Timeline**).

Tip: You can also preview the motion tween inside the movie clip by pressing **Enter** (Windows) or **Return** (Mac) or by selecting **mcOverAnim** in the **Library** and clicking the **Play** button in the **Library** preview window.

15 In the **Library**, double-click the **btnAnim** icon to open the button symbol's **Timeline**. On the **movieClip** layer, choose **Insert > Timeline > Keyframe** in the **Over** frame and again in the **Down** frame to add blank keyframes to both the **Over** and **Down** states of the button.

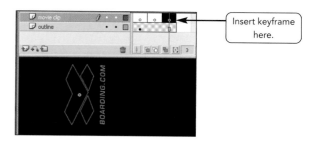

Insert keyframe here.

16 With the **Over** state of the button selected, drag an instance of the **mcOverAnim** movie clip onto the **Stage**. Use the **Align** panel to center the movie clip in the middle of the **Stage**, just as you did in Step 6. When you are finished, lock the **movieClip** layer.

You have just added the movie clip to the Over state of the button. You will add the Hit state to the button next to complete the exercise.

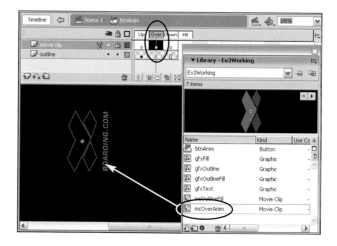

17 Click the **Insert Layer** button to add a new layer to the button symbol's **Timeline**. Rename the new layer **hit** and place it at the bottom of the **Timeline**.

18 On the **hit** layer, choose **Insert > Timeline > Keyframe** in the **Hit** frame to add a blank keyframe. In the **toolbar**, select the **Rectangle** tool and draw a rectangle that covers the *X* outline and the **boarding.com** text. You may want to unlock the outline layer and click the **Onion Skin Outlines** button to turn on onion skinning outlines to make sure the rectangle covers the *X* outline and the **boarding.com** text. Turn the onion skin outlines off when you are done positioning these elements.

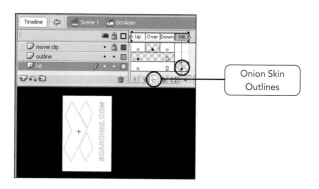

Onion Skin Outlines

The rectangle will serve as the Hit state of the button, so when the user's mouse touches any part of the rectangle, the Over state will be triggered.

19 You are finished with the button. Click **Scene 1** to return to the main **Timeline**.

20 In the main **Timeline**, lock both the **animGfx** and **movieClip** layers. Click the **Insert Layer** button to add a new layer, and rename the layer **animBtn**. You will be placing the button you just created on this layer next.

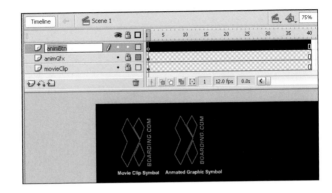

21 Select the **Selection** tool from the **toolbar** and drag an instance of the **btnAnim** button symbol onto the **Stage**, to the right of the animated graphic symbol. In the **toolbar**, select the **Text** tool. Below the **btnAnim** instance, click the **Stage** and type the text label **Animated Button Symbol**.

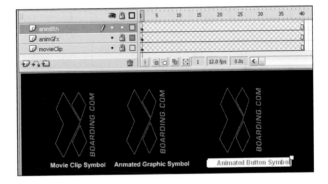

22 Choose **Control > Test Movie** to preview and test all of the symbols.

The movie clip and animated graphic symbol continue to animate, while the button symbol animates only when you move the mouse over it.

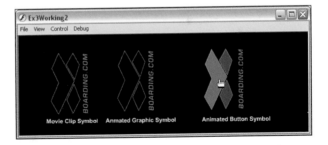

23 Save your changes and keep **animRolloBtn.fla** open for the next exercise.

Putting an Animated Rollover Button into Action

In the previous exercise, you learned how to use a movie clip in a button's Over state to create an animated rollover button. In this exercise, you'll learn how to use that same button in a different project file and place it in a Web page interface.

1 If you just completed Exercise 3, **animRolloBtn.fla** should still be open. If it's not, go back and complete Exercise 3. Press **Ctrl+L** (Windows) or **Cmd+L** (Mac) to open the **Library** if it is not already open.

Notice the top of the Library reads **Library:animRolloBtn.fla**. Next, you will be taking the animated button symbol you made in the last exercise and using it in another file.

2 Open the **animBtnLive.fla** from the **chap_11** folder.

This file is similar to one you worked on in the last chapter, but in this file, the logo is missing from the interface. You will add the logo in a few steps. Notice the top of the Library has changed to **Library: animBtnLive.fla**. By default, the Library window displays the currently active project file.

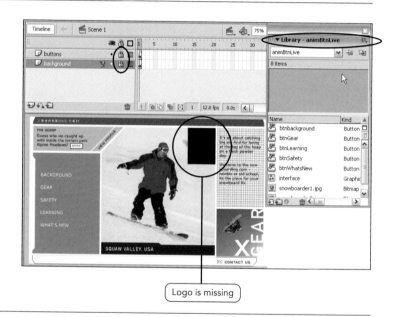

Logo is missing

3 Choose **animRolloBtn** from the **Library Selection** drop-down menu. In the **Library** panel, click the **New Library** button to open an additional **Library** window. Choose **animBtnLive** from the **Library Selection** drop-down menu.

Now, libraries from both open project files are visible at the same time, and you will be able to share assets from one project

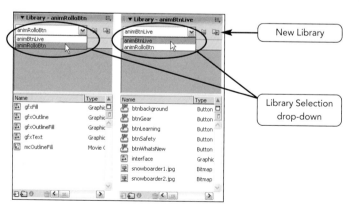

New Library

Library Selection drop-down

to the other. In addition to the **File > Open As Library** workflow you learned in Chapter 10, "*Buttons*," this is another way you can use assets such as symbols from one project in another project. You will add the movie clip symbol from the animRolloBtn movie to the animBtnLive movie next.

4 In the main **Timeline** of the **animBtnLive**, insert a new layer and rename it **logo**.

5 From the **animRolloBtn Library**, drag an instance of **btnAnim** onto the **Stage** and place it over the black box, as shown in the illustration here.

After you place the instance on the Stage, the btnAnim symbol is copied automatically to the animBtnLive Library. When you added the symbol from the animRolloBtn movie to the animBtnLive movie, Flash 8 automatically added the symbol to the Library for you.

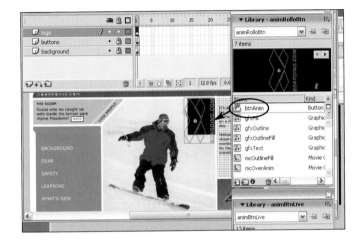

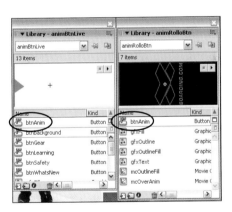

6 Choose **Window > Transform** to open the **Transform** panel. With the instance still selected, make sure the **Constrain** box is selected, and type **75.0%** in either the **width** or **height** field to change the size of the instance so it fits in the box in the interface. If needed, use the arrow keys on your keyboard to move the instance over the center of the black background.

7 Choose **Control > Test Movie** and roll the mouse over the logo to test the animation.

8 When you are finished, close **animRolloBtn.fla** and **animBtnLive.fla**. You don't need to save your changes.

Congratulations! You have made it through an essential chapter. You have learned how to create, modify, and nest movie clips inside buttons. In the next chapter—one of the most challenging chapters in the book—you will use movie clips in more advanced ways. When you're ready, turn the page and get started.

12

ActionScript Basics and Behaviors

So far, you've learned how to draw, mask, animate, and create symbols. The creation of fully interactive presentations, however, requires the application of ActionScript, the internal programming language within Flash 8. It's similar, but not identical, to JavaScript. However, you do not have to know JavaScript or be a programmer to include ActionScript in your movies. The new Script Assist mode, which reinstates the Normal scripting mode in earlier versions of Flash, assists with writing scripts, so that it's not necessary to write all the code from scratch. Using behaviors is even easier. Behaviors are prepackaged modules of working code for accomplishing simple and repetitive tasks, such as navigation controls.

ActionScript is important because you can't accomplish many basic Flash activities—such as stopping and restarting a movie, or controlling audio volumes—without it. ActionScript also extends the power and flexibility of your project by letting you navigate the main Timeline, control movie clips, link to other URLs on the Internet, load other movies into a Flash 8 movie, and much, much more. By the time you are finished with this chapter, you will have a solid understanding of how to add ActionScript to objects and frames and why you would choose one over the other. You will also learn most of the "must-know" ActionScripts required for your own Flash projects.

Working with ActionScript code is one of the most technically challenging aspects of Flash 8. This chapter will not teach you everything there is to know about ActionScript, but it does cover the basics and will give you a solid foundation to build on.

The Behaviors Panel

The Behaviors panel lets you add specific functionality to movies quickly and easily, without the need to write any code on your own. There are several categories of behaviors: Data, Embedded Video, Media, Movie Clip, Sound, and Web. Each provides menu options for adding scripts that will perform specific tasks. For example, the Web > Go to Web Page behavior creates a script that tells a button to open up another Web page when clicked. Because this is such a common need in a Flash project, the Go to Web Page behavior can save you the time and needed expertise from writing the script yourself.

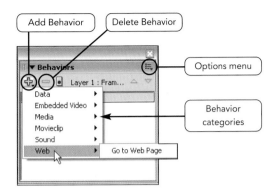

To use the Behaviors panel to create a script, simply locate the menu option you want in the panel, click it, and then fill out the options in the resulting dialog box. You'll see examples of this later on in the chapter.

Where Can I Place ActionScript?

ActionScript can only be attached to a button instance, a movie clip instance, or a keyframe on the Timeline. ActionScript cannot be attached to an instance of a graphic symbol or to nonsymbol shapes on the stage. This chapter shows you how to attach ActionScript to each of these elements using both the Actions panel and the Behaviors panel.

The Actions Panel Defined

In Flash 8, you use the Actions panel to build ActionScripts that can control your movie. The Actions panel is where you create and edit object actions or frame actions, which you'll learn about in great detail later in this chapter.

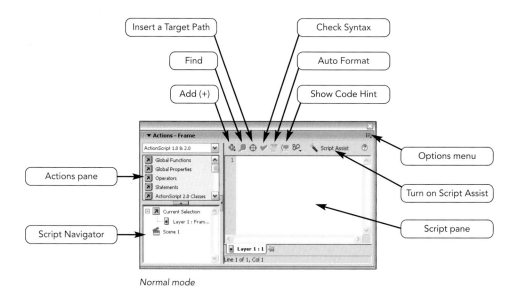

Normal mode

Script Assist mode

The Actions panel works in two modes, displaying a slightly different interface for each mode. Normal mode, the topmost view, lets you create ActionScript by choosing from the list of code found within the Actions pane, by using the Add (+) button, or by typing code manually into the Script pane. It requires that you write the correct syntax and any additional parameters required by the action statements.

Script Assist mode, the bottom view, lets you build scripts the same way but assists with syntax and action parameters by letting you choose from options available in text boxes and pop-up menus above the Script pane. When adding ActionScript from the Actions pane, Flash 8 prompts you to fill in the required parameters (arguments), and in some cases, even provides the correct parameter selections in the area above the Script pane. Little or no actual scripting is involved in Script Assist mode, instead you simply select from the various options for each chosen action.

When you're in Script Assist mode, the Actions panel changes in the following ways:

- The Add (+) button functions differently in Script Assist mode. When the focus is on the ActionScript window, it adds the selection after the currently selected text block. If the focus is in the edit pane, the selection is added to that field.

- The Remove (–) button appears, which lets you remove the current selection in the scrolling text area.

- Up and down arrow icons appear, which let you move the current selection in the scrolling text area forward or backward within the code.

- The Check Syntax, Auto Format, Show Code Hint and Debug Options buttons and menus, disappear. (They don't apply in Script Assist mode.)

- The Insert Target button is disabled, unless you're editing a field. Using Insert Target places the resulting code in the current edit field.

In both modes, the Actions pane separates items into categories such as Functions, Properties, and Statements, and also provides an Index category that lists all items alphabetically. When you click an item once, its description appears at the upper right of the panel. When you double-click an item, it appears on the right side of the panel, in the Script pane.

You can also keep a script available when you click off of the frame or object by using the Pin Current Script button. In the exercises of this chapter, you will have a chance to work with many of these features.

Because this book is targeted at beginners, hand-coding ActionScript in Normal mode will be introduced, but kept to a minimum since you cannot write some types of scripts in Script Assist mode. Once you're finished with this book, you'll have a solid understanding of ActionScript basics, and will be better prepared to go deeper into ActionScripting.

1 | Controlling the Timeline

In Flash 8, once a movie starts, it plays in its entirety (or it reaches the last frame of the Timeline) unless instructed otherwise. Fortunately, you can control how Flash 8 plays movies by using actions in the Actions panel. This exercise teaches you how to assign **stop** and **play** actions to button instances in order to control an animation on the main Timeline. You will also learn how to apply actions to frames on the main Timeline to further control the movie.

---

1 Copy the **chap_12** folder from the **HOT CD-ROM** to your **Desktop**. Open **stopAndPlay_Final.fla** from the **chap_12** folder.

This is the finished version of the project you'll be building in this exercise.

---

2 Choose **Control > Test Movie** to preview the movie. In the SWF file, click the **Play** button to set the boarder in motion, moving down the mountain. Click the **Stop** button to stop the boarder. When you are finished stopping and playing this movie, close the preview window and this file.

You will learn how to add the same functionality to this movie in the following steps.

---

3 Open **stopAndPlay.fla** file from the **chap_12** folder. Choose **Control > Test Movie** to preview the movie. Click the **Stop** and **Play** buttons.

This is an unfinished version of the movie you just previewed. It contains everything except the ActionScript, which you will add in this exercise. Notice how nothing happens when you click the Stop button—the movie continues to play. Why? Because no actions have been added to these buttons yet, and therefore the buttons do not control the movie. You will learn to do this next.

---

4 Close the preview window and return to the project file. On the **Stage**, click the **Stop** button instance to select it.

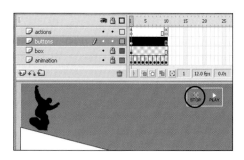

Adding Object or Frame Action Instruction

To add an action to an object, you must select the object and then add the action. **Note:** When you add actions to an object, the object must either be a movie clip symbol or a button symbol. To add an action to a frame in a Timeline, you must place an action in a keyframe. You will have a chance to do this later in the exercise.

5 Choose **Window > Actions**, or press **F9** (Windows) or **Option+F9** (Mac), to open the **Actions** panel.

Notice the top of the Actions panel reads *Actions – Button*. Because you have selected the button instance, Flash 8 knows you will be adding actions to the button instance on the Stage.

6 In the **Actions** panel, click the **Script Assist** button to switch to **Script Assist** mode.

7 In the **Actions** pane, click the **Global Functions** category to access a list of all the actions that fall under that category. Click **Movie Clip Control** to expand that category. Double-click the **on** action to add it to the **Script** pane. Select the **Event: Release** option.

This line of script instructs Flash 8 to execute the next line of code when the user presses and then releases the mouse over the Stop button.

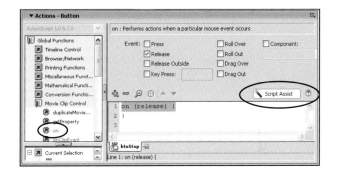

8 With the first line of script still selected, in the **Actions** pane, select **Global Functions > Timeline Control** and double-click the **stop** action to add it to the **Script** pane.

You have just added your first action to the project. The Stop button instance now has the power to stop the Timeline when you test the movie, which you will do shortly!

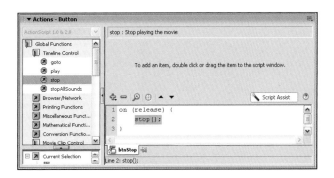

Tip: You can also add an action to the list by dragging it from the Actions pane to the Script pane, or by clicking the Add (+) button and choosing the action from the pop-up menus.

When you double-clicked the **stop** action in the Actions pane, ActionScript appeared in the Script pane, which holds the ActionScript statements and displays all the code for the actions applied to an object.

The **stop** action has no parameters, so in this case the area above the Script pane was empty.

A tab below the Script pane displays the name of the object or frame the code is attached to. This helps ensure you are adding the ActionScript to the right item.

In this case, you have applied the script to an instance of the btnStop button on the Stage, and since you have not named the instance (which is not necessary in this exercise, but always a good idea), the script tab states the name of the symbol itself. If you had named the instance in the Property Inspector, the instance name would appear here instead. You name instances so you can use ActionScripting to directly refer to ("communicate with") that instance. In later exercises in this chapter, you will name an instance in order to get the ActionScripting working.

---

9 Choose **Control > Test Movie** and try out the **stop** action you just added. When you click the **Stop** button, the movie will stop! When you are finished, close the preview window.

Once you stop a movie, you must explicitly instruct it to start again. You will do this next with the **play** action.

---

10 On the **Stage**, click the **Play** button instance to select it. In the **Actions** pane, select **Global Functions > Movie Clip Control** and double-click the **on** action to add it to the **Script** pane. Select the **Event: Release** option.

This line of script instructs Flash 8 to execute the next line of code when the user presses and then releases the mouse over the Stop button.

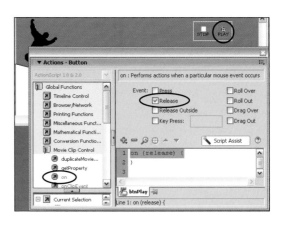

---

11 With the first line of the ActionScript still selected, select **Global Functions > Timeline Control** and double-click the **play** action to add it to the **Script** pane.

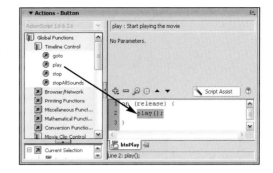

You have just added a **play** action to the button instance on the Stage.

12 Choose **Control > Test Movie** to test the movie again. Click the **Stop** button to stop the movie. Click the **Play** button to make the movie play again! When you are finished, close the preview window.

Notice the movie immediately plays as soon as the preview window opens. You'll learn to change this using frame actions next.

13 Back in the **main Timeline**, click the **Insert Layer** button to add a new layer to the **Timeline**. Make sure this layer is the topmost layer. Double-click the layer and rename it **actions**. Press **Enter** (Windows) or **Return** (Mac).

By default, the main Timeline in the movie will automatically begin to play unless you tell it otherwise. You can keep a movie from playing automatically by adding an action to the Timeline telling the movie to stop before it begins playing. The movie will then begin in a stopped position, and will not play until the user clicks the Play button.

14 In the main **Timeline**, select **Frame 1** of the **actions** layer, which contains a blank keyframe. In the **Actions** pane, select **Global Functions > Timeline Control** and double-click the **stop** action to add it to the **Script** pane.

There is an action in this frame.

Notice the Actions panel no longer reads *Actions – Button*, but instead *Actions – Frame*. This gives you immediate feedback as to where the action is located and whether you are applying the action to an object, such as a button or movie clip, or to a keyframe. Also, the Timeline will display a small *a* inside the frame as further feedback that there is an action in the keyframe.

NOTE: | **Adding a Layer for the Frame Action**

Throughout the rest of this book, I model good practice by having you create a separate layer to hold frame actions. It will always be located on top of all the other layers and be labeled *actions*. As the movies you create become more and more complex, troubleshooting and debugging a movie will be significantly easier if you know you can always find the frame actions in the same place: on the first layer of the movie, on the layer named *actions*.

15 Choose **Control > Test Movie** to test the movie again. The movie will now begin in a static state, waiting for the user to click the **Play** button. Click the **Stop** and **Play** buttons to control the animation.

Notice when the boarder reaches the bottom of the slope it stops. You added a **stop** action to the first keyframe, so the movie will begin in a stopped state. When a user clicks the Play button, it sets the playhead in motion. The playhead will play through all the frames and will automatically loop by default, stopping at the first frame, where it encounters that **stop** action again. You can choose to bypass the **stop** action in the first frame; you will do this next.

16 Close the preview window. In the main **Timeline**, select **Frame 10** of the **actions** layer and press **F6** to add a keyframe. In the **Actions** pane, select **Global Functions > Timeline Control** and double-click the **goto** action to add it to the **Script** pane. In the Script Assist area, select the **Go to and play** radio button and type the number **2** in the **Frame** field.

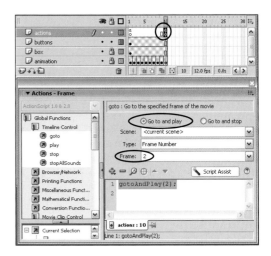

Notice the script **gotoAndPlay(2);** appears in the Script pane. This script tells Flash 8 to send the playhead to Frame 2 and play the movie when the playhead reaches Frame 10, creating a small loop. Each time the playhead reaches Frame 10, it will go to Frame 2, play the rest of the frames, and then return to Frame 2, bypassing Frame 1, and its **stop** action.

17 Choose **Control > Test Movie** and test the movie again.

The movie begins in a stopped state. As soon as you click the Play button, the movie plays and continues to play over and over, without stopping, until you click the Stop button.

18 When you are finished, close **stopAndPlay.fla**. You don't need to save your changes.

stop_play_actions.mov

To learn more about the concepts presented in this exercise, check out **stop_play_actions.mov** located in the **videos** folder on the **HOT CD-ROM**.

Interactivity and Actions: Events and Event Handlers

When you play a movie, certain actions, such as pressing a key on the keyboard or pressing the mouse button, are considered events in Flash 8. Flash events fall into one of the following categories: mouse events, movie clip events, keyboard events, and Timeline events. For every event, there must be an event handler that manages the event. The four types of basic events are described in the following sections.

When you add an action to a button symbol or a movie clip symbol, you must introduce an event. The script you added to the Stop and Play buttons in the last exercise, **on (release)**, was the event, which means the **play** action was triggered when the user clicked and released the mouse. The event handler was the **on** action, which handled button events.

Mouse Events

Mouse events occur when users interact with a button instance. When an action (such as a **stop** action) is added to a button instance, an **on** event handler is automatically added, as you saw in Exercise 1. The default **on** event is **release**.

The following table defines each possible mouse event:

Mouse Events Defined	
Event	**When It Occurs**
press	When the mouse pointer is moved over the Hit area of the button, and the mouse is pressed
release	When the mouse pointer is moved over the Hit area of the button, and the mouse is pressed and then released
releaseOutside	When a press occurs on the Hit area of a button, then the mouse pointer is moved outside of the Hit area and released

continues on next page

Mouse Events Defined *continued*	
Event	**When It Occurs**
`rollOver`	When the mouse pointer moves over the Hit area of a button
`rollOut`	When the mouse pointer moves off the Hit area of a button
`dragOver`	When the mouse is pressed on the Hit area of a button, then rolls out of the Hit area, and reenters the Hit area with the mouse still pressed
`dragOut`	When the mouse is pressed on the Hit area of a button, then the mouse pointer rolls out of the Hit area with the mouse still pressed
`keyPress`	When the specified key is pressed on the keyboard

Keyboard Events

Keyboard events are similar to mouse events, but they occur when users press a key on the keyboard, rather than interacting with the mouse. One application of this event is a slideshow that moves forward and backward by pressing the arrow keys on the keyboard. In Normal mode, to change the mouse event to a keyboard event, click the **Code Hint** button to open the **Code Hint** menu and double-click a keyboard event to add it to the **Script** pane. In Script Assist mode, select the **Event: Key Press** option and press **Enter** (Windows) or **Return** (Mac). In this example, Flash 8 will execute the script when the user presses **Enter** (Windows) or **Return** (Mac).

Note: Use caution when assigning keyboard events to a movie that will be displayed on the Web. Keypresses will not be executed in a browser unless the user has already clicked inside the movie at some point. In addition, your users might not intuitively know to use their keyboards unless they are instructed to do so.

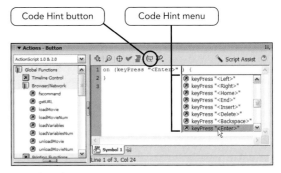

Normal mode

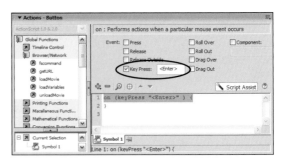

Script Assist mode

Movie Clip Events

Movie clip events occur when something happens with a movie clip instance. When you add an action (such as **play**) to a movie clip instance, you need to add an **onClipEvent** event handler. The default **onClipEvent** is **load**.

Note: You can also create a movie clip that receives button events; this will automatically have the **on** (rather than the **onClipEvent**) event handler.

The following table defines the available movie clip events:

Movie Clip Events Defined	
Event	**When It Occurs**
load	When the movie clip is inserted and appears on the Timeline
unload	When the movie clip is removed from the Timeline
onEnterFrame	When the playhead hits a frame, the action is triggered continually at the frame rate of the movie
mouseDown	When the mouse button is pressed
mouseMove	Every time the mouse is moved
mouseUp	When the mouse button is released
mouseDown	When the mouse button is pressed
keyDown	When a key is pressed
keyUp	When a key is released
data	When data is received in a **loadVariables** or **loadMovie** action

Timeline Events

Unlike mouse, keyboard, and movie clip events, Timeline events occur when the playhead reaches a keyframe containing actions on the Timeline.

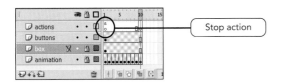

Stop action

In the last exercise, you added a Timeline event by adding the **stop** frame action to the first keyframe in the project file. When the movie begins, the playhead will encounter the **stop** frame action located on Frame 1 and stop there. Timeline events can exist on the main Timeline or in any graphic or movie clip instance's Timeline.

2 | Controlling Movie Clips

In the last exercise, you attached the **stop** and **play** actions to button instances to control an animation on the main Timeline. You can also use the **stop** and **play** actions to control the Timeline of any movie clip. In order to control a movie clip, you must give it an instance name, and it must be present on the Timeline. This exercise shows you how.

1 Open **stopAndPlayMC.fla** from the **chap_12** folder.

This project file looks very similar to the original project file from Exercise 1, with two exceptions: In the **stopAndPlayMC** project file, there is a movie clip rather than an animation layer in the main Timeline, and there is only one frame in the main Timeline. This exercise shows you how to use actions to control a movie clip rather than the main Timeline.

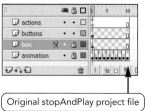

Original stopAndPlay project file

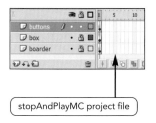

stopAndPlayMC project file

2 Choose **Control > Test Movie** to preview the movie. Click the **Stop** and **Play** buttons. When you are finished previewing the movie, close the preview window.

Notice nothing happens, and the movie continues to play. Because you haven't added actions to these buttons yet, the buttons do not control the movie. You will add actions to control the movie clip in the steps that follow.

NOTE:

The Power of Movie Clip Symbols

Many exercises in this chapter use movie clip symbols. Movie clip symbols are addressed differently in ActionScript than other kinds of symbols. As you learned in Chapter 11, "*Movie Clips*," movie clip symbols are the most powerful and flexible of all symbols since they can contain multiple layers, graphic symbols, button symbols, even other movie clip symbols, as well as animations, sounds, and ActionScript. Because movie clip symbols can contain all of these things and can be represented on the Timeline in just one keyframe, your Timeline will be more organized and less cluttered. And, don't forget that movie clip symbols are Timeline-independent, meaning that the movie clip will continue to play even though the playhead in the main Timeline has stopped.

Although movie clip symbols are more complex to learn, with practice you will find that they actually make creating your Flash projects easier! In the following steps, you will learn how to control a movie clip symbol by giving it an instance name so that you can refer to it in ActionScript.

3 On the **Timeline**, unlock the **boarder** layer. On the **Stage**, click the snow to select the movie clip instance. In the **Property Inspector**, type **boarder** in the **Instance Name** field to assign an instance name to the movie clip on the **Stage**.

In Exercise 1, the **stop** and **play** actions you added to the buttons automatically controlled the main Timeline. Conversely, in order to control a movie clip, you have to refer to the movie clip by its instance name when you apply actions to the buttons in the next steps.

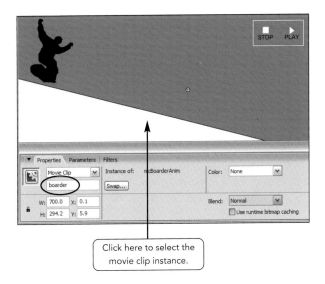

Click here to select the movie clip instance.

---

4 On the **Stage**, select the **Stop** button instance to select it.

---

5 Press **F9** (Windows) or **Option+F9** (Mac) to open the **Actions** panel. Click the **Script Assist** button to enable **Script Assist** mode. In the **Actions** pane, select **Global Functions > Movie Clip Control** and double-click the **on** action to add it to the **Script** pane. Select the (default) **Event: Release** option.

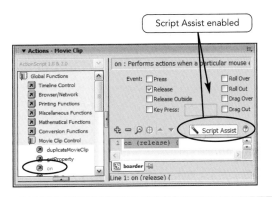

Script Assist enabled

---

6 In the **Actions** pane, with the first line still selected, select **Global Functions > Timeline Control** and double-click the **stop** action to add it to the **Script** pane.

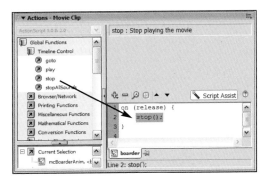

---

7 Click the **Script Assist** button to exit **Script Assist** mode and enter **Normal** mode. Place your cursor before the **stop** script.

You need to add the instance name of the movie clip by hand to tell it to stop playing next, which you can do only in Normal mode.

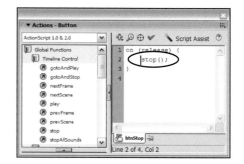

8 Type **boarder.** before the **stop** script. (Be sure to include the period after the word **boarder**.)

This tells the movie clip boarder, which you named in Step 3, to stop playing when the user clicks the Stop button. This is slightly different than choosing the **stop** action, as you did in Exercise 1, because this time, you want to use an action that controls a movie clip, rather than the main Timeline.

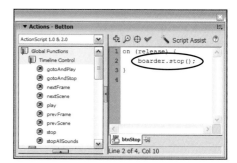

NOTE: | **Controlling Movie Clips**

In Flash 8, movie clips are controlled with either actions or methods. Methods are functions that are assigned to an object. For example, to make a movie clip stop, you need the instance name, a period, and then the method, such as **boarder.stop();**, as you typed in the last step. In this example, the **stop** method halts the playhead in the boarder movie clip instance.

---

9 Choose **Control > Test Movie** to try out the **stop** action you just added to the button instance. When you are finished previewing, close the preview window.

When you click Stop, the boarder movie clip will stop in its tracks! Next, you will add the ActionScript to play the boarder movie clip.

---

10 On the **Stage**, click the **Play** button to select it.

---

11 In the **Actions** pane, select **Global Functions > Movie Clip Control** and double-click the **on** action to add it to the **Script** pane. From the **Code Hint** menu, choose **release** for the mouse event.

This is the identical command you added to the Stop button, but since you switched to Normal mode, you are applying it using a different method.

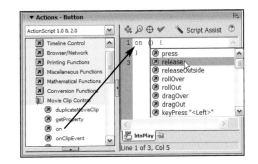

12 In the **Script** pane, place your cursor after the open curly brace and press **Enter** (Windows) or **Return** (Mac) to bring the cursor down to the second line.

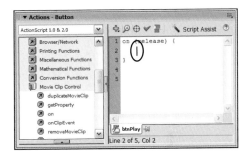

13 In the **Actions** pane, select **Global Functions > Timeline Control** and double-click the **play** action to add it to the **Script** pane.

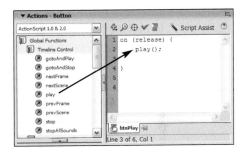

14 Place your cursor before the **play** script and type a period (.). Then place the cursor before the period.

You will add the instance name of the movie clip by inserting a target path next.

15 Click the **Insert a target path** button.

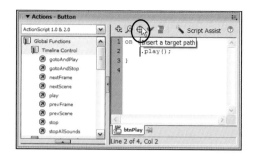

16 In the **Insert Target Path** dialog box, select **boarder** and click **OK**.

Wondering what a target path is? Check out the note on the next page for more information.

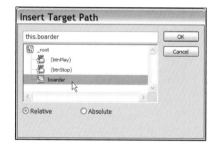

17 In the **Script** pane, notice the ActionScript now reads `this.boarder.play();`. This tells the **boarder** movie clip to begin playing when the user clicks the **Play** button.

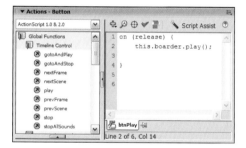

18 Choose **Control > Test Movie** and try out the **Stop** and **Play** buttons. Click the **Stop** button, and the **boarder** movie clip stops in its tracks. Click the **Play** button, and the **boarder** movie clip begins playing from where it stopped. When you are finished previewing, close the preview window.

Next, you will add a frame action to the main Timeline to start the movie in a stopped state.

NOTE:

Understanding Target Paths

Target paths are hierarchical addresses that display movie clip instance names, variables, and objects inside your movie. After you name a movie clip instance in the Property Inspector, as you did in Step 3, you can use the **Insert a target path** button to find all the movie clip instance names in the movie (you have only one movie clip instance name in this exercise) and select the one you want to direct the action to. Using the **Insert a target path** button to find the boarder instance name is the same as typing the boarder name in the Script pane, as you did in Step 8 for the Stop button. Target paths help you locate movie clip instances if you forget exactly where they are or how they are spelled.

19 Click the **Insert Layer** button to add a new layer to the **Timeline**. Name it **actions**. If it is not already the top of the **Timeline**, click and drag the **actions** layer above all the other layers.

20 Select **Frame 1** of the **actions** layer. In the **Actions** pane, select **Global Functions > Timeline Control** and double-click the **stop** action to add it to the **Script** pane.

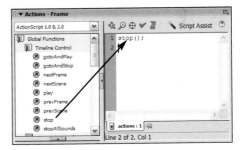

21 In the **Script** pane, type **boarder.** before the **stop** action.

This script, although in the main Timeline, tells the Timeline of the boarder movie clip instance to stop, so the boarder clip begins in a stopped state.

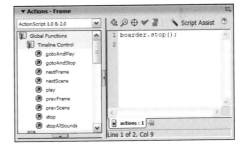

22 Choose **Control > Test Movie**.

Notice the movie begins playing in a stopped position. Go ahead and click the buttons to make your movie play and stop.

23 When you are finished, close **stopAndPlayMC.fla**. You don't need to save your changes.

VIDEO: | **controlMC.mov**

To learn more about the concepts presented in this exercise, check out
controlMC.mov in the **videos** folder on the **HOT CD-ROM**.

What Is Dot Syntax?

In the last exercise, you added a period, or dot (.),
between the instance name and the **stop** and **play**
methods: **boarder.stop();**. In ActionScripting, the
period indicates properties or methods that relate
to a movie clip or other objects. This is part of the
ActionScript syntax, also referred to as **dot syntax**.

In Flash 8, dot syntax simply refers to the formatting convention used to create ActionScripting.
Dot syntax is used to construct statements that
consist of objects, properties, methods, and variables. Each dot syntax statement begins with the
name of the object followed by a period (.) and

ends with the property, method, or variable you
want to identify. For example, in the statement
this.boarder.play ( );, *this* is the main Timeline,
the object is the movie clip named *boarder*, and
the method is *play*. The parentheses hold the
parameters (called **arguments**) that apply to an
action; in this case, no parameters are required.
With the action **gotoAndPlay();**, the argument
would go between the parentheses and would be
the frame number you want to go to. The semicolon (;) marks the end of a statement (just as a
period marks the end of a sentence).

EXERCISE

3 | Using the goto Action

In addition to the **stop** and **play** actions, Flash also has more specific actions that tell the playhead exactly where to start and stop on the Timeline. This exercise demonstrates how you can use ActionScript to create a Flash 8 movie you can navigate one frame at a time, similar to a slideshow. You will use the **goto** action to send the playhead to any frame you specify.

1 Open **slideShow_Final.fla** from the **chap_12** folder. This is the finished version of the slideshow you are going to create. Choose **Control > Test Movie** to preview the movie. Click the **Next** button to advance the slideshow forward. Click the **Back** button to display the previous slide. When you are finished, close the preview window and **slideShow_Final.fla** file.

2 Open the **slideShow.fla** file from the **chap_12** folder.

This is an unfinished version of the movie you just previewed, containing only the slideshow images. You will add new layers, buttons, and the necessary ActionScripting in this exercise.

3 Choose **Control > Test Movie** to preview the movie. Close the preview window when you are finished.

Notice the frames go by very fast, one after another. By default, the movie will automatically play through the frames unless you tell it otherwise. You will add a **stop** action to Frame 1 so that the movie starts in a stopped state.

4 In the main **Timeline**, click the **Insert Layer** button to add a new layer to the **Timeline**. Rename the new layer **actions**. Make sure the new layer is above the **images** layer. If it is not, click the layer name and drag it above the **images** layer.

5 On the **actions** layer, select **Frame 1**.

6 In the **Actions** panel, click the **Script Assist** button to switch to **Script Assist** mode. In the **Actions** pane, select **Global Functions > Timeline Control** and double-click **stop** to add a **stop** action to the **Script** pane.

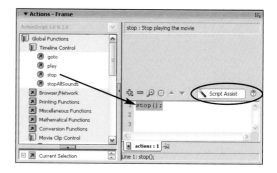

Adding the **stop** action to the main Timeline causes the movie to begin in a stopped position.

7 Choose **Control > Test Movie** to preview your movie.

Notice the movie begins in a stopped position. Close the preview window and return to the project file. You will add the buttons to your movie in the following steps.

8 Click the **Insert Layer** button to add another new layer to the **Timeline**. Rename the new layer **controls**. Drag the **controls** layer below the other two layers. Lock the **actions** and **images** layers so that you don't accidentally select anything in either of those layers.

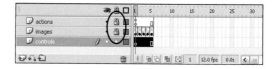

9 Select **Frame 1** of the **controls** layer. Press **Ctrl+L** (Windows) or **Cmd+L** (Mac) to open the **Library**. Drag an instance of **btnNext** and **btnBack** onto the **Stage**. Position them side by side. Select both of the button instances using **Ctrl+A** (Windows) or **Cmd+A** (Mac), then press **Ctrl+K** (Windows) or **Cmd+K** (Mac) to open the **Align** panel. Click the **Align bottom edge** button to align the bottom edge of the buttons.

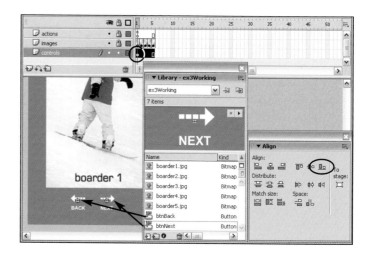

10 Click the **btnNext** instance to select it.

You will be adding actions to the button instance Next. (You may have to click off the Stage to deselect both buttons and then click the btnNext instance to select only that instance.)

11 In the **Actions** pane, select **Global Functions > Movie Clip Control** and double-click the **on** action to add it to the **Script** pane. Select the **Event: Release** option.

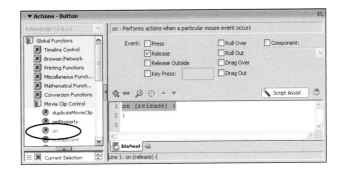

12 Click the **Script Assist** button to switch to **Normal** mode. In the **Script** pane, place your cursor after the open curly brace and press **Enter** (Window) or **Return** (Mac) to bring the cursor down to the second line.

13 In the **Actions** pane, select **Global Functions > Timeline Control** and double-click **nextFrame** to insert it into the **Script** pane.

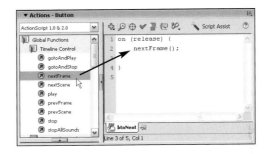

You have just added ActionScript to the Next button. Now when the user clicks the Next button and releases the mouse, the playhead will advance to the next frame and stop. Part of the description in the **nextFrame** action will send the playhead to the next frame and automatically stop, so you do not need to add an additional **stop** action.

Tip: You switched from Script Assist mode into Normal mode because the **nextFrame** action is only available in Normal mode. You will often switch in and out of Script Assist mode, since some things are easier or only available in Normal mode.

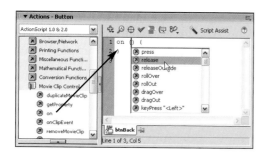
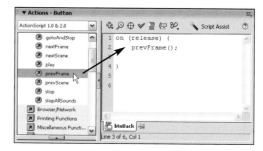

14 On the **Stage**, click the **Back** button instance to select it. In the **Actions** pane, select **Global Functions > Movie Clip Control** and double-click the **on** action to add it to the **Script** pane. In the **Code Hint** menu, choose **release** from the list. Place the cursor after the opening curly brace and press **Enter** (Window) or **Return** (Mac) to insert a new line. Select **Global Functions > Timeline Control**, and double-click the **prevFrame** action.

You have added a very similar ActionScript to the Back button, this time using Normal mode. Now when you click the button, the playhead will move to the previous frame and stop.

---

15 Choose **Control > Test Movie** to test your movie. Click the **Next** arrow button several times to advance the slideshow to the next picture and click the **Back** arrow button to reveal the previous picture.

Great! Notice when you continue to click the Next arrow, the slideshow stops at boarder 5 (the last frame) and never starts over at Frame 1. Likewise, notice when you continue to click the Back arrow, the slideshow stops at boarder 1 (the first frame) and never loops to Frame 5. You can fix this to make the slideshow loop back to the beginning or to the end by adding a few keyframes and changing some of the ActionScript, which you will do next.

---

16 On the **controls** layer, click **Frame 2** to select it and press **F6** to add a keyframe. On the **controls** layer, click **Frame 5** to select it and press **F6** to add a keyframe.

Adding a keyframe will copy all the contents of Frame 1, including the actions attached to the buttons, to Frames 2 and 5.

---

17 Position the playhead over **Frame 1**. On the **Stage**, select the **Back** button instance. (You may have to click off the **Stage** to deselect both buttons first and then select the **Back** button.)

You are going to change the ActionScript in this button next.

18 In the **Actions** panel, highlight the line in the Script pane that reads **prevFrame ();**. Select **Global Functions > Timeline Control** and double-click the **gotoAndStop** action to add it to the **Script** pane. Type **5** between the parentheses. This new line directs the **playhead** to the last frame of the slideshow, **Frame 5**. Choose **Control > Test Movie** to preview the movie again. Click the **Back** button. Picture 5 appears (**Frame 5**). The movie is no longer stuck on picture 1.

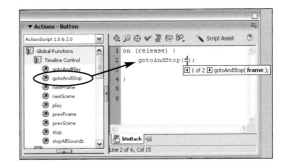

Instead of the script telling the playhead to go to the previous frame (which it can't do because this is Frame 1, the first frame), you have now changed the script to tell Flash 8 to go to Frame 5 and stop there when you release the mouse.

---

19 Position the **playhead** over **Frame 5**. On the **Stage**, select the **btnNext** instance.

Next you will change the ActionScript in this button so that it is no longer stuck on picture 5.

---

20 In the **Actions** panel, highlight the line in the Script pane that reads **nextFrame ();**. Select **Global Functions > Timeline Control** and double-click the **gotoAndStop** action to add it to the **Script** pane. Type **1** between the parentheses.

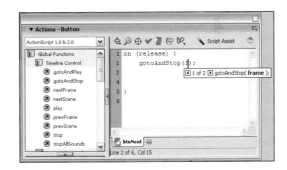

When you release the mouse on this button instance, instead of telling the playhead to go to the next frame (which it can't do because this is Frame 5, the last frame), the ActionScript instructs the playhead to just go to Frame 1 and stop there.

---

21 Choose **Control > Test Movie** to preview the movie again.

Now the movie should loop when it reaches either the first or last frame.

---

22 When you are finished testing the movie, close **slideShow.fla**. You don't need to save your changes.

4 | Using the Go to Web Page Behavior

You can open other Web sites from within a Flash 8 movie. This exercise introduces the Behaviors panel and the Go to Web Page behavior, which is used to create links to other documents on the Web. The following steps demonstrate how to use the Go to Web Page behavior to link to an external Web site and to generate a pre-addressed email message.

---

1 Open **getURL.fla** from the **chap_12** folder.

We created this file to get you started.

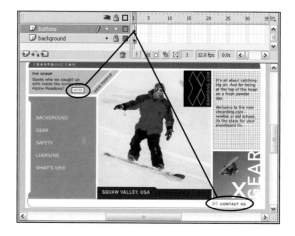

There are two button instances on the Stage: More and Contact Us. You'll add the Go to Web Page behavior, which will open up an HTML page in a new browser window, to the More button. Then, you will use the same behavior with the Contact Us button to create an email message.

---

2 Choose **Window > Behaviors** to open the **Behaviors** panel. On the **Stage**, select the **More** button to add a behavior to it. In the **Behaviors** panel, click the **Add Behavior** button and choose **Web > Go to Web Page**.

---

3 In the **Go to URL** dialog box, type **thescoop.html** in the **URL** field and choose **"_blank"** from the **Open in** pop-up menu.

When a user clicks the More button, the HTML file **thescoop.html** will open in a Web browser. Additionally, the "_blank" setting tells Flash 8 to open the link in a new browser window.

You can control the window or frame displaying the linked file by changing the parameters in the Open in pop-up menu. The following chart explains each of the four options:

Understanding the Go to URL Window Parameter Options

The following table outlines the Go to URL window parameter options:

Go to URL Window Parameter Options	
Option	**Description**
_blank	Opens the link in a new browser window
_self	Opens the link in the same browser window that is occupied by the current Flash 8 movie
_parent	Opens the link in the parent window of the current window
_top	Opens the link in the same browser window and removes any existing framesets

Note: The **thescoop.html** file is located in the **chap_12** folder. If you want to keep your HTML files in another directory, separate from the project file, simply define the directory it is in followed by a forward slash (/), like so: newdirectory/thescoop.html.

4 Choose **Control > Test Movie** and click the **More** button to test the link you just created. The **Go to Web Page** behavior will launch your default browser and load the HTML Web page you specified into a new window. When finished, close the browser window and the preview window.

You can use the Go to Web Page behavior as an email link by adding *mailto* to an email address (like you can with an **HREF** tag in HTML). In the steps that follow, you will add the Go To Web Page behavior to the second button to create an email link that will produce a preaddressed email message: **mailto:fl8hot@lynda.com**.

5 Back in the project file, select the **Contact Us** button on the **Stage**. In the **Behaviors** panel, choose the **Go to Web Page** behavior again.

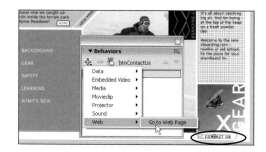

6 In the **Go to URL** dialog box, type **mailto:fl8hot@lynda.com** in the **URL** field and choose **"_blank"** from the **Open in** pop-up menu.

These settings will pre-address the email message to fl8hot@lynda.com when you click the Contact Us button and open the email message in a new window.

7 Choose **File > Publish Preview > HTML** to open the SWF file in a browser window so you can test the email link. When the browser window opens, click the **Contact Us** button to test the link.

A new email message window should open when you click the button!

8 When you are finished testing the movie, close your browser window and **getUrl.fla**. You don't need to save your changes.

Up to this point in the book, you have been working with one scene, Scene 1, in the main Timeline. In the following exercise, you will learn how to create additional scenes, as well as how to rename, duplicate, and target them using ActionScript.

---

1 Open **gotoScene_Final.fla** from the **chap_12** folder.

This is the finished version of the file you are going to create.

NOTE: | **Missing Fonts**

When you open **gotoScene_Final.fla**, you may see a dialog box that reads "One or more of the fonts used by this movie are not available. Substitute fonts will be used for display and export. They will not be saved to the Macromedia Flash authoring document." This simply means your computer does not have some of the fonts that were used to create the artwork in this file. Go ahead and click **Use Default** so your computer will pick a default font to replace the unrecognizable fonts in the movie.

---

2 Choose **Control > Test Movie** to preview the movie. Click each of the navigation buttons to view a different section of the Web site. When you are finished previewing the movie, close the preview window and then close the project file.

When you click the buttons, behind the scenes (pun intended), the playhead is moving to the appropriate scene in the movie. You will learn how to re-create this Web site next.

NOTE: | **What Are Scenes?**

In Flash 8, you're not limited to only the frames on the Timeline of the main movie. You can have several Timelines, which play one right after another. Flash 8 calls these multiple Timelines scenes. Scenes let you break up large projects into smaller, more manageable pieces, similar to the way in which many Web sites are broken up into individual Web pages. If no ActionScript is present in the main Timeline to stop the movie, the playhead will play Scene 1, then Scene 2 and all remaining scenes, in order, until the end is reached or a **stop** action is encountered. You can use scenes to break up a Web site into different sections, to structure a project where many smaller movies get loaded on demand, or even as a way to organize different stages of a project.

3 Open **gotoScene.fla** file from the **chap_12** folder. Choose **Control > Test Movie** to preview the movie. When you are finished previewing the movie, close the preview window.

The navigation buttons don't go anywhere when you click them, because there are no actions on the buttons telling them where to go. You will be adding ActionScript to the buttons in the steps that follow.

4 In the main **Timeline**, choose **Window > Other Panels > Scene** to open the **Scene** panel. The **Scene** panel displays a list of the scenes in this movie. At this point, you have only one scene named **Scene 1**, by default. In the **Scene** panel, double-click the **Scene 1** name and rename the scene **main**. When you press **Enter** (Windows) or **Return** (Mac), the name will change to **main** in the **Scene** panel and also in the edit bar of the project window.

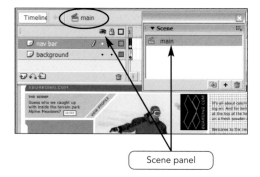

Scene panel

5 In the **Scene** panel, click the **Duplicate Scene** button five times to duplicate the **main** scene five times. Next, double-click each of the duplicate scenes in the **Scene** panel and rename them to match the navigation buttons on the **Stage**: **background, gear, safety, learning**, and **what's new**.

Note: When you name the scenes in a movie, try to keep the names short and descriptive, since you will be using ActionScripting to target the scenes.

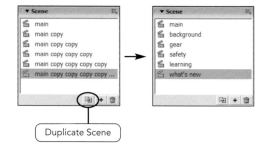

Duplicate Scene

You have just added five new scenes to the movie, although they will all look exactly the same because you just duplicated the main scene. You will change the content inside each scene next. You'll soon realize the value of duplicating scenes as you learn to align new artwork from scene to scene.

6 On the right side of the edit bar, click the **Edit Scene** button. A menu will appear with the list of scenes you just created in this project. From the menu, select the **background** scene, which will take you into the **Timeline** of that scene. When you are finished, close the **Scene** panel.

Notice the scene name changed in the edit bar, the background scene is highlighted in the Scene panel, and there is a checkmark

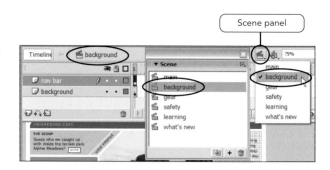

Scene panel

next to the background scene in the Edit Scene button pop-up menu. These cues tell you which scene you are currently inside within the project.

Note: The Edit Scene button is useful to move quickly from scene to scene. The Scene panel can also be used to jump from scene to scene, but additionally, this is where you can add, delete, name, and copy scenes in your movie.

---

7 Click anywhere on the **Stage** to select the artwork. In the **Property Inspector**, notice it says *Instance of: mcMain*, which means the artwork on the **Stage** is contained in an instance of the **mcMain** movie clip. Because

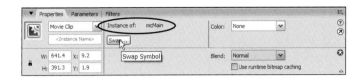

you are now located in the background scene, you need to change the artwork to reflect the correct scene; you can do this easily. Make sure the **mcMain** instance is still selected, and in the **Property Inspector**, click the **Swap Symbol** button.

---

8 In the **Swap Symbol** dialog box, select the **mcBackground** movie clip and click **OK** to swap (or change) the **mcMain** movie clip with the **mcBackground** movie clip.

Tip: In the Swap Symbol dialog box, you can also double-click the symbol you want to swap rather than selecting it and clicking OK. By swapping a symbol, you keep it in perfect alignment with the symbol that was there before. Keep in mind that this is true only if both symbols have the same dimensions, which is the case in this exercise.

As soon as you click OK, the artwork changes in the background scene. This artwork was created ahead of time and saved as a movie clip. It is the same size as the main scene movie clip; the difference is in the colors, the photo, and the text. This technique helps keep all the artwork registered in the same place. It's not easy to register artwork from scene to scene any other way, because you don't have onion skinning between scenes, only between frames on the Timeline.

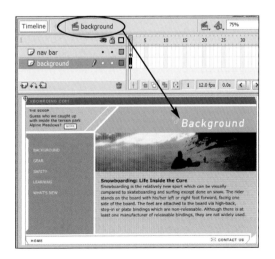

9 Click the **Edit Scene** button and choose the scene named **gear** to open the **gear** scene's **Timeline**.

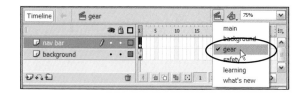

10 Select the artwork on the **Stage**, and in the **Property Inspector**, click the **Swap Symbol** button. In the **Swap Symbol** dialog box, double-click the **mcGear** movie clip.

After you double-click the mcGear movie clip, the Stage should match the illustration here. Notice the Property Inspector reflects the name of the new movie clip you chose.

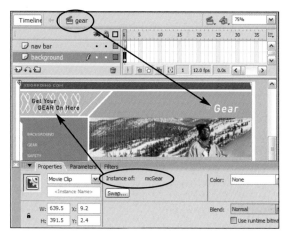

11 Repeat Steps 9 and 10 for the remaining scenes: in **safety**, swap the **mcSafety** movie clip; in **learning**, swap the **mcLearning** movie clip; in **whatsNew**, swap the **mcWhatsNew** movie clip. When you are finished, use the **Edit Scene** button to quickly check each scene and make sure the scene name in the edit bar matches the artwork.

Next, you will add the ActionScripting to the buttons to tell Flash 8 to go to a specific scene when the user clicks a button.

12 In the edit bar, click the **Edit Scene** button and choose **main** to open the **main** scene's **Timeline**.

You will add ActionScript to the buttons in the following steps.

13 On the **Stage**, select the **Background** button. Press **F9** (Windows) or **Option+F9** (Mac) to open the **Actions** panel, and click the **Script Assist** button to switch to **Script Assist** mode. In the **Actions** pane, select **Global Functions > Movie Clip Control** and double-click the **on** action to add it to the **Script** pane. Select **Event: Release**.

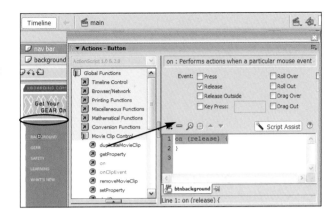

14 In the **Actions** pane, select **Global Functions > Timeline Control** and double-click the **goto** action to add it to the **Script** pane. Click the **Go to and stop** radio button and choose **background** from the **Scene** pop-up menu.

This ActionScript tells Flash 8 that as soon as the user releases the mouse on the Background button it should go to the scene named background and stop at Frame 1.

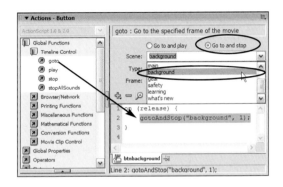

15 Repeat Steps 12, 13, and 14 for the **Gear**, **Safety**, **Learning**, and **What's New** buttons on the **Main** scene. Choose **gear** from the **Scene** pop-up menu for the **Gear** button; **safety** for the **Safety** button; **learning** for the **Learning** button; and **whatsNew** for the **What's New** button. When you're finished, choose **Control > Test Movie** to test the movie.

You now have five buttons on the main scene, each with ActionScript that instructs Flash 8 to go to the appropriate scene

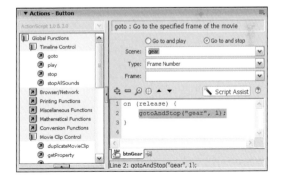

when the user releases the mouse on each button. Next, you will copy the buttons and the ActionScript from the main scene and paste them into each of the other five scenes.

16 Making sure you are still in the **main** scene, select **Frame 1** in the **nav bar** layer to select all the content in **Frame 1**. Choose **Edit > Timeline > Copy Frames**.

17 Click the **Edit Scene** button and choose the **background** scene to open its **Timeline**. Select **Frame 1** in the **nav bar** layer and choose **Edit > Timeline > Paste Frames** to paste the buttons, including all the ActionScript attached to the button, from the **main** scene in **Frame 1** of the **nav bar** layer into **Frame 1** of the **nav bar** layer in the **background** scene, replacing any content that was previously in the frame.

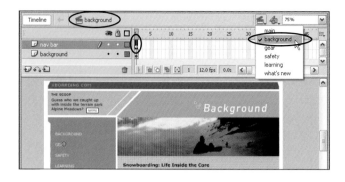

Why I am copying the buttons into a scene that already has buttons? There are many ways to do this, but the idea is to be efficient as possible in your workflow. So rather than recode each button in every scene, copying and pasting frames is a quick and easy way to copy all the buttons with their attached ActionScript into another scene.

---

18 Repeat Step 17 for the remaining scenes: **gear**, **safety**, **learning**, and **whatsNew**.

Be sure to select Frame 1 in the nav bar layer inside each scene before you paste the frames so that you paste the buttons into the right location!

---

19 Choose **Control > Test Movie** to test the movie. When you are finished testing the movie, close the preview window.

Notice all the scenes play, one right after another. By default, the movie will continue to play, one scene after another, unless you tell the playhead to stop by adding a **stop** action to a frame on the Timeline. You will do this next.

---

20 Back in the project file, click the **Edit Scenes** button and choose the **main** scene. Inside the **main** scene's **Timeline**, click the **Insert Layer** button to add a new layer, and rename it **actions**. Make sure the **actions** layer is above all the other layers; if it is not, click the layer name and drag it above all the other layers.

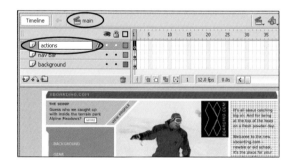

21 Select **Frame 1** in the **actions** layer, and in the **Actions** pane, select **Global Functions > Timeline Control** and double-click the **stop** action to add it to the **Script** pane.

This will cause the movie to stop when the playhead reaches the first frame in the main scene.

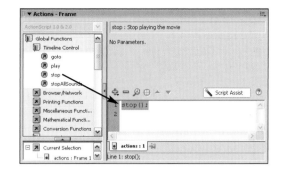

---

22 Repeat Steps 20 and 21 to add a **stop** frame action to **Frame 1** of the **background**, **gear**, **safety**, **learning**, and **whatsNew** scenes.

This will force the playhead to stop as soon as it reaches Frame 1 in each of the scenes.

---

23 Choose **Control > Test Movie** to test the movie. Preview the scenes by clicking each navigation button. When you are finished testing your movie, close the preview window.

Notice after you click a button there is no visual feedback to let you know which scene you are in. You will change this last element of the movie next.

---

24 Back in the project file, click the **Edit Scene** button and choose the **background** scene. On the **Stage**, click the **Background** button to select it.

---

25 In the **Property Inspector**, choose **Graphic** from the **Symbol Behavior** pop-up menu. You may get a warning indicating that converting the symbol will delete the ActionScript. If you do, just click **OK**. This will convert the **Background** button instance in this scene to a graphic symbol. Graphic symbols cannot be clicked on and cannot have actions applied to them. Choose **Tint** from the **Color** pop-up menu, select **white** for the **Tint** color; and type **100%** in the **Alpha** field.

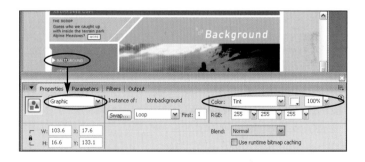

Because the Up state of this button contains a triangle next to the word *Background*, changing the tint to white will turn the triangle white and provide visual feedback to the user regarding where he or she is located. So when you are in the background scene, the Background button will be white, and you will not be able to click it because you are already in the background scene. Cool!

Why Do I Need to Change the Behavior and Color of My Button?

By changing the behavior of the button to a graphic, the button instance (not the original button symbol in the Library) will turn into a graphic symbol, using the button's Up state as the graphic. When the button is a graphic, the user will not be able to click it since it is no longer a button. Further, by also changing the color of the button-turned-graphic, you provide the user with extra visual feedback that he or she is located in a particular section of the Web site.

26 Repeat Steps 24 and 25 for the remaining scenes: **gear**, **safety**, **learning**, and **whatsNew**. Inside the **gear** scene, select the **Gear** button and change its **Symbol Behavior** to **Graphic** and **Tint** to **white** at **100%**. Likewise, inside the **safety** scene, select the **Safety** button; inside the **learning** scene, select the **Learning** button; and inside the **whatsNew** scene, select the **What's New** button. In the **Property Inspector**, make the same changes for each button.

27 Choose **Control > Test Movie** to test the movie one last time! Click each button to go to the appropriate scene. Notice once you are inside a scene, its button shows the white arrow and cannot be clicked.

New graphic symbol indicating current location

28 When you are finished testing the movie, close the preview window and **gotoScene.fla**.

In this exercise, you learned how to use scenes to divide a project file into more manageable sections, and how to link to them via ActionScript. In the next exercise, you will learn how to break down your project file even more by dividing up the Timeline through the use of frame labels.

What Are Frame Labels, and Why Use Them?

Frame labels identify a frame by a name, rather than by a number. When you add and delete frames in the movie, the frame numbers change, causing problems in ActionScript where it refers to frame numbers. At the same time, frame labels do not change when frames are added or deleted, keeping your ActionScript viable and working.

In the next exercise, rather than break up the navigation into separate scenes, you will keep all the work in a movie clip and use frame labels to divide the movie clip's Timeline into sections.

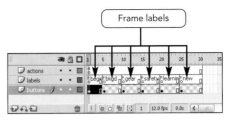

Plus, you'll use ActionScript to direct the playhead to the appropriate frame label within the Timeline. Although you'll be working with frame labels within movie clip Timelines, you can include frame labels in the main Timeline as well.

EXERCISE

6 | Creating a Pop-Up Menu Using Frame Labels

There are many ways to create interactive menus in Flash 8. From scrolling menus to animated menus to draggable menus, all you need is a little creativity and a few bits of ActionScripting to develop a rich variety of navigation systems. This exercise gives you additional practice with the Behaviors panel and starts you on your way to creating interactive navigation schemes by teaching you how to develop a basic pop-up menu using frame labels.

---

1 Open **menu_Final.fla** from the **chap_12** folder. This is the finished version of the menu you are going to create. Choose **Control > Test Movie** to preview the movie. Click the different navigation buttons and notice some of them will reveal a pop-up menu. When you are finished, close the preview window and close **menu_Final.fla**.

---

2 Open **menu.fla** file from the **chap_12** folder.

This is an unfinished version of the movie you just previewed. Notice there is one layer named btns, which contains the same movie clip symbol used in the previous exercise.

In this exercise, you will expand the navigation to include a pop-up menu, using frame labels and behaviors to make this pop-up menu work. In the next exercise, you will build upon what you have learned and take your project a step further by using the same movie clip symbol and adding functionality to the buttons on the menu to load different SWF files into the interface by using the **loadMovieNum** action.

As you may have guessed by now, this movie clip contains buttons symbols and graphic symbols, as well as ActionScript, and it will be used over and over throughout the completed project in this book, which is why a movie clip symbol was used over a button symbol or graphic symbol.

---

3 Double-click the menu on the **Stage** to open the movie clip's **Timeline**. Choose **Control > Test Movie** to preview the menu. When you are finished previewing the menu, close the preview window.

Notice there is one layer with five buttons. As you click each button, you will see that there are no pop-up menus. You will be creating them next.

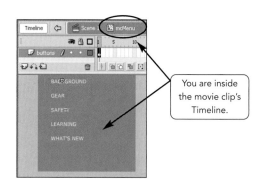

You are inside the movie clip's Timeline.

---

4 Back in the project file, inside the **mcMenu** movie clip, click the **Insert Layer** button to add a new layer to the **Timeline**. Rename this layer **labels**. Make sure this layer is above the **buttons** layer.

5 On the **Timeline**, select **Frame 1** in the **labels** layer. In the **Property Inspector**, type the name **begin** in the **Frame Label** field to add the frame label **begin** to **Frame 1**, where the menu is in the starting position.

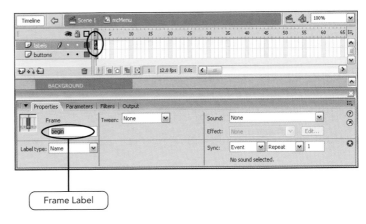

As soon as you add the label name, notice the hollow circle and the flag on the Timeline—visual cues showing you a label exists on this frame. **Note:** You will not be able to see the begin frame label name just yet, because there are not enough frames on the Timeline, but you will see it after the next step.

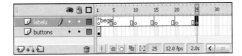

Frame Label

6 On the **labels** layer, select **Frame 5** and press **F7** to add a new blank keyframe. Repeat this step for **Frames 10, 15, 20,** and **25**.

7 Click **Frame 5** of the labels layer. In the **Property Inspector**, type the name **bkgd** in the **Frame Label** field. In **Frames 10, 15, 20,** and **25**, add the names **gear**, **safety**, **learning**, and **new**, respectively. Select **Frame 30** and press **F5** to add frames up to **Frame 30** so you can see the **new** label. When you are finished, your **Timeline** should match the illustration here.

Tip: In order for a frame label to be visible on the Timeline, there must be enough frames to display the entire name; so by pressing F5, you can add frames and see the name. **Note:** Even if you can't see the whole name, the label is still there; you can always tell that by looking for the flag on the frame or by looking at the Frame Label in the Property Inspector.

8 Click the **Insert Layer** button to add another layer to your movie. Rename the new layer **actions**. Make sure the new layer is above the **labels** layer.

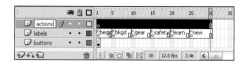

9 Select **Frame 1** in the **actions** layer. Press **F9** (Windows) or **Option+F9** (Mac) to open the **Actions** panel. In the **Actions** pane, select **Global Functions >Timeline Control** and double-click the **stop** action to add it to the **Script** pane.

This action tells the playhead to stop on Frame 1 when the movie begins. You will add behaviors to the buttons in the following steps.

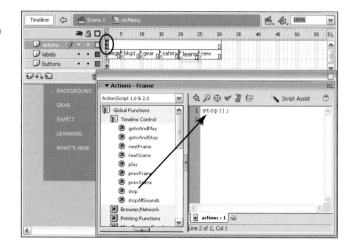

10 Choose **Window > Behaviors** to open the **Behaviors** panel. On the **Timeline**, position the **playhead** to **Frame 1** and select the **Background** button instance on the **Stage**. In the **Behaviors** panel, click the **Add Behavior** button and choose **Movieclip > Goto and Stop at frame or label** from the pop-up menu.

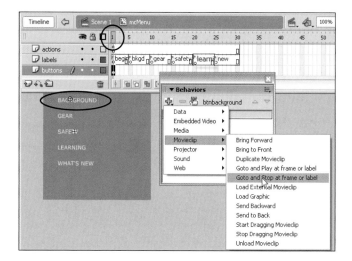

11 In the **Goto and Stop at frame or label** dialog box, make sure **mcMenu** is selected and type **bkgd** in the **Enter the frame number or frame label at which the movie clip should stop playing** field. Click **OK** to close the dialog box.

This behavior tells Flash 8 that as soon as the user releases the mouse on the Background button, go to the frame label bkgd and stop there.

12 Make sure the **playhead** stays on **Frame 1** and repeat Steps 10 and 11 to add behaviors to the four remaining navigation buttons. For the **Gear** button, type **gear** for the frame label; for the **Safety** button, type **safety** for the frame label; for the **Learning** button, type **learning** for the frame label; and for the **What's New** button, type **new**.

Notice these names correspond to the frame labels you added in Step 7.

13 On the **buttons** layer of the **Timeline**, click **Frame 5** to select it and choose **Insert > Timeline > Keyframe** to copy the buttons, including the behaviors, into each frame. Repeat this step for **Frames 10**, **15**, **20**, and **25**. Select **Frame 30** and press **F5** to add frames up to **Frame 30** on the **buttons** layer. When finished, your **Timeline** should match the illustration here.

14 Choose **Control > Test Movie** to test the buttons.

Notice nothing much happens. In the previous step, you copied all the contents of the last keyframe into the next keyframe; although the behaviors send the playhead to a different frame label, nothing changes because the content in each frame is the same. In the steps that follow, you will slightly modify the buttons in each keyframe so that the menu changes at each keyframe.

15 Position the playhead over **Frame 5** and select the **Background** button on the **Stage**. In the **Property Inspector**, choose **Graphic** from the **Symbol Behavior** pop-up menu. You may get a warning indicating that converting the symbol will delete the ActionScript. If you do, just click **OK**. Choose **Tint** from the **Color** pop-up menu, select **white** for the color, and type **100%** in the **Alpha** field.

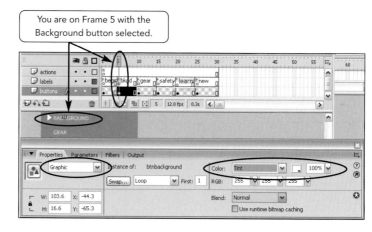

You are on Frame 5 with the Background button selected.

This will change the behavior of the Background button instance in this frame to a graphic symbol. When the playhead reaches the background label, the Background button will be white, and you will not be able to click it.

16 Move the **playhead** to **Frame 10**. Select the **Gear** button on the **Stage**, and in the **Property Inspector**, choose **Graphic** from the **Symbol Behavior** pop-up menu. Choose **Tint** from the **Color** field, select **white** for the color, and type **100%** in the **Alpha** field.

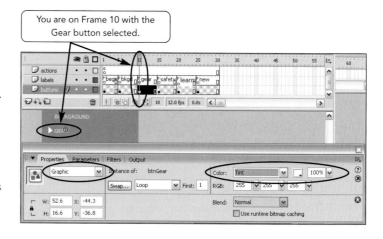

You are on Frame 10 with the Gear button selected.

This will change the behavior of the Gear button instance in this frame. When the playhead reaches the gear label, the Gear button will be white, and you will not be able to click it.

17 Repeat Step 16 to modify the **Safety** button on **Frame 15**, the **Learning** button on **Frame 20**, and the **What's New** button on **Frame 25**.

Make sure you are changing the correct button on the correct frame. Position the playhead to the correct frame, select the appropriate button on the Stage, and then make the changes in the Property Inspector.

18 Choose **Control > Test Movie** to test the movie. Click each of the buttons. When you are finished testing the movie, close the preview window.

Notice the arrow appears, indicating where you are located. All you have left to do is to add the subnavigation menus, which you will do next.

---

19 In the project file, move the **playhead** to **Frame 10**. Press **Ctrl+L** (Windows) or **Cmd+L** (Mac) to open the **Library**. Notice two buttons named **btnGearSub1** and **btnGearSub2**.

These are subnavigation buttons that we created for you.

---

20 On **Frame 10**, hold down the **Shift** key and click the **Safety**, **Learning**, and **What's New** buttons on the **Stage** to multiple-select all three buttons. Use the **down arrow** key on your keyboard to move them down toward the bottom of the **Stage** to make room for two subnavigation buttons, which you will add next.

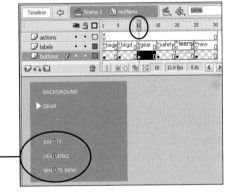

> Move all three buttons down.

---

21 Drag an instance of **btnGearSub1** and **btnGearSub2** from the **Library** onto the **Stage** and position them beneath the **Gear** button.

These will serve as the subnavigation buttons for the Gear section.

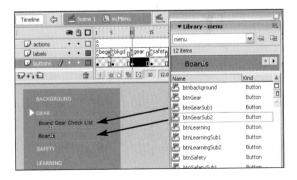

Note: In this example, the two subnavigation buttons are positioned so that the bottom dotted line of one button lines up and overlaps the top dotted line on the other button, so it appears as if there is only one dotted line between the two buttons. Use the Zoom button in the edit bar to get a closer view and make this positioning easier.

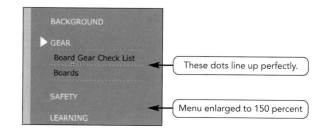

These dots line up perfectly.

Menu enlarged to 150 percent

---

22 Choose **Control > Test Movie**. When you click the **Gear** button, the arrow and the subnavigation buttons appear. When you are finished, close the preview window.

---

23 In the project file, move the **playhead** to **Frame 15**. Hold down the **Shift** key and select the **Learning** and **What's New** buttons on the **Stage**. Use the **down arrow** key on your keyboard to move them down toward the bottom of the **Stage** to make room for two subnavigation buttons, which you will add next.

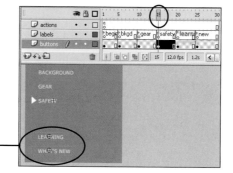

Move both buttons down.

---

24 Drag an instance of **btnSafetySub1** and **btnSafetySub2** from the **Library** onto the **Stage** and position them beneath the **Safety** button.

These will serve as the subnavigation buttons for the Safety section. You have one last subnavigation section to add, which you'll do next.

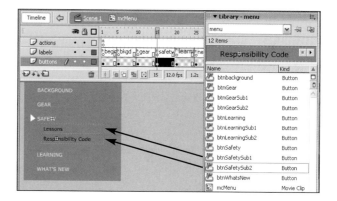

25 Move the **playhead** to **Frame 20**. On the **Stage**, select the **What's New** button. Use the **down arrow** key on your keyboard to move the **What's New** button down toward the bottom of the **Stage** to make room for two sub-navigation buttons. From the **Library**, drag an instance of **btnLearningSub1** and **btnLearningSub2** onto the **Stage** and position them beneath the **Learning** button.

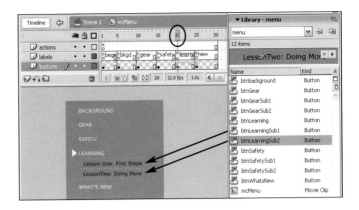

These will serve as the subnavigation buttons for the Learning section.

26 Choose **Control > Test Movie** to test your pop-up menu! Click each of the buttons to make sure they are all working correctly. When you are done testing the menu, close the preview window.

27 When you are finished, close the preview window and **menu.fla**. You do not need to save your changes.

In the next exercise, you will create a menu similar to the one you just created, but instead of using behaviors, you will write the ActionScript yourself using the `loadMovieNum` action.

VIDEO: | **menu.mov**
To learn more about the concepts presented in this exercise, check out **menu.mov** located in the **videos** folder on the **HOT CD-ROM**.

What Is loadMovieNum?

In earlier chapters, you learned the differences between the project file (FLA) and the movie file (SWF). In this chapter, you will learn how a SWF file can load other SWF files into itself. This idea is similar to links on an HTML page, which replace content with other HTML pages when clicked.

Why would you want to do this in Flash 8? Large projects can take a long time to download. You can structure your projects so many smaller movies are loaded on demand, which creates a better user experience. This process is called Load Movie in Flash 8, because it utilizes the `loadMovieNum` action.

As you stack SWF files on top of one another, their arrangement simulates layers, which is called

levels in ActionScripting. The main Timeline (named Scene 1 by default) is always located at Level 0. You can load additional movies into other level numbers, such as 5 or 20. Movies loaded into an occupied level replace the movie in that level. The number of levels is infinite, and as you load movies into different levels, any movies that are currently in different levels will still be visible. Movies loaded into higher levels play in front of movies in lower levels. This stacking order is similar to the stacking order of layers on the Timeline. You will learn how to load movies with the `loadMovieNum` action in the following exercise.

7 | Loading Movies

Loading multiple SWFs into a main SWF using the **loadMovie** action is an efficient way of presenting large Flash 8 documents. The **loadMovie** action loads individual SWF files on demand, eliminating the need to load a large file all at once. This exercise shows you how.

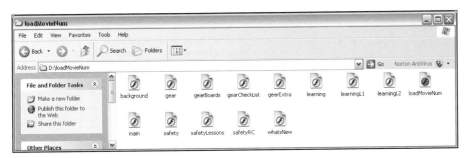

1 Open the **loadMovieNum** folder in the **chap_12** folder. Inside you will see many SWF files and one FLA file. Double-click any of the SWF files to open and preview the artwork inside them. These are the SWF files you will be loading into the main FLA file in the steps that follow. When you are finished, close the SWF files.

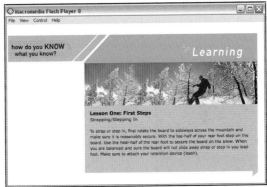

2 Open **loadMovieNum.fla** from the **loadMovieNum** folder. We created this file to get you started. Choose **Control > Test Movie** to preview the movie. When you are finished previewing the movie, close the preview window.

Notice all you see is an empty interface with the navigation menu. This will serve as the main movie file. In the steps that follow, you will use the **loadMovieNum** action to load the external movies you previewed in Step 1 into levels above the main movie.

Note: If you get an error message telling you to check if the file destination is locked, or to check whether the file name is not too long, try removing the **Read-only** option to both **chap_12** and its sub-folder, **loadMovieNum**.

3 In the project file, double-click the menu to open the movie clip's **Timeline**. (This menu is identical to the one you built in the last exercise.) Select **Frame 1** of the **actions** layer on the **Timeline**. Choose **Window > Actions** to open the **Actions** panel. If it is not already enabled, click the **Script Assist** button to enable **Script Assist** mode. In the **Actions** pane, select **Global Functions > Browser/Network** and double-click the **loadMovie** option to add the action, **loadMovieNum**, to the **Script** pane.

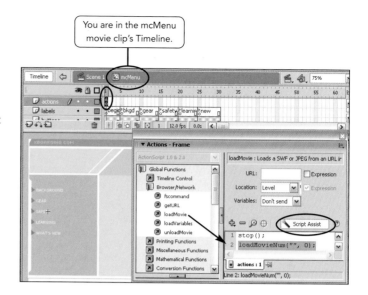

You are in the mcMenu movie clip's Timeline.

TIP: | **Why Add the Actions to a Frame Rather Than an Object?**

You can add the **loadMovieNum** action to either a frame or an object. Which one you choose will largely depend on how you set up your movie. Actions added to a keyframe, as in the previous step, will be executed as soon as the playhead hits the keyframe. In the following steps, you will also add the **loadMovieNum** ActionScript to objects.

---

4 In the **URL** field, type **main.swf**, and type **50** in the **Location: Level** field to instruct Flash 8 to load the SWF file you specified (**main.swf**) into **Level 50**, which is above the main movie.

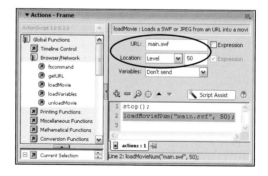

NOTE: | **Movie Levels**

Why Level 50? Since you can load a movie into any level, I choose 50 so you have plenty of other "open" levels under 50 and over 50 to load additional content. Movies in other levels are still visible; those loaded into higher levels will be placed in front of movies in lower levels. Level numbers can only be positive, and the main Timeline is always located at Level 0, so when you load any additional movies they always appear above the main Timeline.

Load Movie and Addressing

When you use the `loadMovieNum` ActionScript, the URL path can be either relative or absolute. Use caution whenever using a relative address. Flash 8 will always look for the files in the same folder as the main project file. In this example, a relative path is used; it is simply **main.swf**. Therefore, all the SWF files must be located in the same folder as the main movie; otherwise, Flash 8 will not know where to find these files.

5 Choose **Control > Test Movie** to test the ActionScript you added. You will now see content inside the interface. When you are finished, close the preview window.

Notice you added the **main.swf** file, but the menu is still visible on the left side. Since you loaded **main.swf** file into Level 50, it is above the original interface located in Level 0. Areas of a level with no artwork will be transparent, allowing the original interface below to show through.

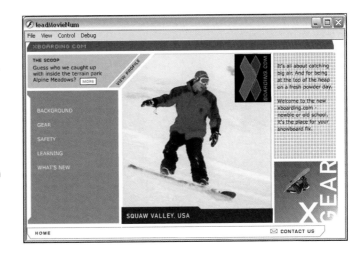

The File Cabinet Analogy

As you begin to stack SWF files on top of one another in levels, their arrangement simulates layers on the Timeline. Imagine a file cabinet. This file cabinet is analogous to the main movie. Inside the cabinet, you have empty drawers, which are similar to levels within the main movie.

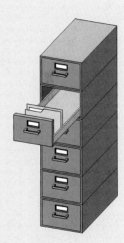

Let's say each drawer can contain only one folder, which is analogous to the SWF file. If you want to place a purple folder (SWF file) into a drawer (Level 4) that already has a green folder (SWF file) in it, you have to first take out the green folder before you can put the purple one in, However, if you have the green folder (SWF file) already in a drawer (Level 4), you can add a blue folder (SWF file) to a drawer above it (Level 5, for example). In Flash 8 terminology, this would translate to the main movie at Level 0, a SWF file loaded into Level 4 above both the main movie, and another SWF file loaded into Level 5, above both the main movie and the SWF file in Level 4.

6 In the project file, select the line containing the `loadMovieNum` action in the **Actions** pane. Click the **Reference** button (Windows) or **Help** button (Mac) to open the **ActionScript Reference Guide** within the **Help** panel. The **Help** panel displays information about all of the ActionScript **Global Functions**. Scroll down to locate the section on the `loadMovieNum` action. If you select an action or a line of code, the **Help** panel will display information about that action.

Tip: You can also access the Help panel by choosing **Help > Help (F1)**.

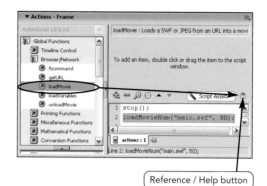
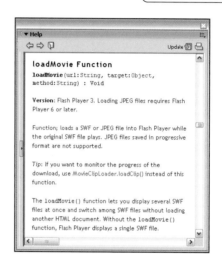

Reference / Help button

7 You should still be inside the menu movie clip's **Timeline**. Select **Frame 5** of the **actions** layer and press **F7** to add a blank keyframe. In the **Actions** pane, select **Global Functions > Timeline Control** and double-click the **stop** action to add it to the **Script** pane.

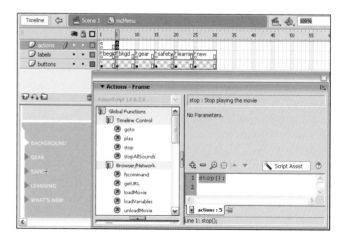

8 In the **Actions** pane, select **Global Functions >
Browser/Network** and double-click `loadMovie`
to add it to the **Script** pane. Type **background.swf**
in the **URL** field and **50** in the **Location: Level**
text field.

This instructs Flash 8 to load the SWF file you
specified (**background.swf**) into Level 50, above
the main movie.

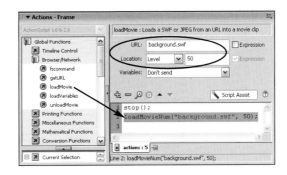

9 Choose **Control > Test Movie** and click the
Background button. The background content
replaces the main content. How did this happen?
Each time you use the `loadMovieNum` command to
load a movie into a level already containing content, the new content will replace the old content.
When you are finished previewing the file, close
the preview window.

TIP: **Loading into an Already Occupied Level**

You don't have to load a movie into the next empty level; you can load a movie to any
level you wish. However, if you load a movie into a level already occupied by another file,
the old file is removed by the new movie.

---

10 Repeat Steps 7 and 8 for **Frames 10, 15, 20,** and **25**. For **Frame 10**, type **gear.swf** and **50** in the
URL and **Location: Level** text fields, respectively; for **Frame 15**, type **safety.swf** and **50**; for **Frame 20**,
type **learning.swf** and **50**; and for **Frame 25**, type **whatsNew.swf** and **50**. This will set the parameters for
each `loadMovie` action so the correct content gets loaded into **Level 50** when the **playhead** hits the
appropriate frame.

11 Choose **Control > Test Movie**. Click each of the top-level navigation buttons to test the movie. When you are finished, close the preview window. You will add ActionScript to the sub-navigation buttons in the steps that follow.

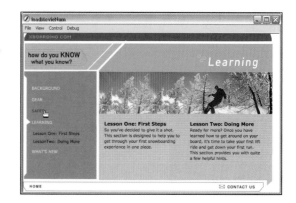

12 Back in the project file, move the **playhead** to **Frame 10**. On the **Stage**, select the **Board Gear Checklist** button. You will be adding the `loadMovieNum` action to this button next.

13 In the **Actions** pane, select **Global Functions > Movie Clip Control** and double-click the **on** action to add it to the **Script** pane. Select **Event: Release**. You will add the `loadMovieNum` action in the following steps.

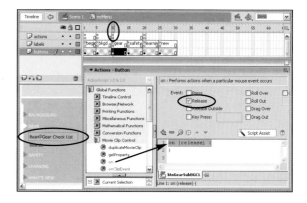

14 In the **Actions** pane, select **Global Functions > Browser/Network** and double-click the **loadMovie** action to add it to the **Script** pane. Type **gearCheckList.swf** in the **URL** field and **50** in the **Location: Level** text field. This instructs Flash 8 to load the **gearCheckList.swf** file into **Level 50** when the user clicks this button.

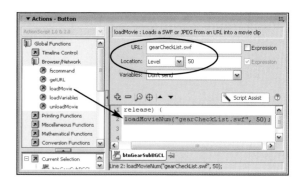

15 On the **Stage**, select the **Boards** button. In the **Actions** pane, select **Global Functions > Movie Clip Control** and double-click the **on** action to add it to the **Script** pane. Select **Event: Release**.

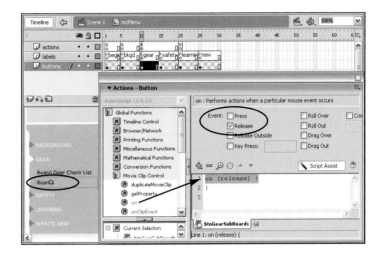

16 In the **Actions** pane, select **Global Functions > Browser/Network** and double-click the **loadMovie** action to add it to the **Script** pane. Type **gearBoards.swf** in the **URL** field and **50** in the **Location: Level** text field.

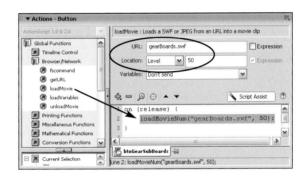

17 Repeat Steps 15 and 16 for the four remaining subnavigation buttons: two buttons on **Frame 15** and two buttons on **Frame 20**. This will add the `loadMovieNum` action to each of the subnavigation buttons.

For each of the buttons, the ActionScript should look like the following:

Frame 15—Lessons button:
```
on (release) {
    loadMovieNum("safetyLessons.swf", 50);
}
```

Frame 15—Responsibility Code button:
```
on (release) {
    loadMovieNum("safetyRC.swf", 50);
}
```

Frame 20—Lesson One: First Steps button:
```
on (release) {
    loadMovieNum("learningL1.swf", 50);
}
```

Frame 20—Lesson Two: Doing More button:
```
on (release) {
    loadMovieNum("learningL2.swf", 50);
}
```

You have one last button to add. In the following steps, you will copy the ActionScript on the Lesson Two: Doing More button and paste it into the Home button on the main Timeline. Since the code will be the same for the two buttons, with the exception of the name of the SWF file you will load, copying and pasting the code is an efficient way of adding ActionScript to your buttons.

---

18 Select the **Lesson Two: Doing More** button. In the **Script** pane, highlight the ActionScript. Press **Ctrl+C** (Windows) or **Cmd+C** (Mac) to copy it.

Next, you'll paste the ActionScript to the Home button on the main Timeline.

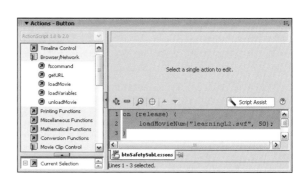

---

19 In the edit bar, click **Scene 1** to return to the **main Timeline**. Unlock the **background** layer and select the **Home** button in the bottom-left corner of the **Stage**. In the **Actions** panel, click the **Script** pane and press **Ctrl+V** (Windows) or **Cmd+V** (Mac) to paste the ActionScript. Next, you will modify the code to load the appropriate movie.

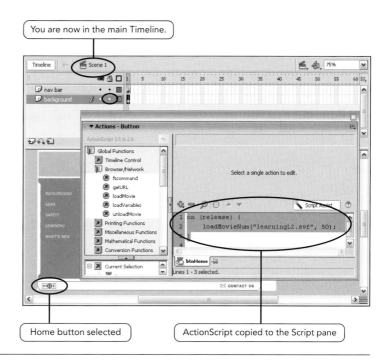

You are now in the main Timeline.

Home button selected

ActionScript copied to the Script pane

20 In the **Script** pane, click the `loadMovieNum` line to select it. Replace **learningL2** with **main** in the **URL** parameter text field.

Once you are familiar with the nuances of ActionScript, copying and pasting the ActionScript rather than navigating through the ActionScript toolbar is one way to speed up your production time.

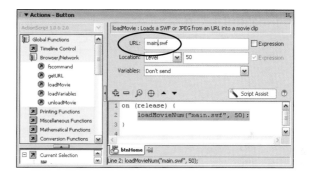

21 Choose **Control > Test Movie** to preview your movie. Try all the buttons, including the subnavigation buttons, to see how they work. When you are finished, close the preview window.

Now that you are familiar with loading movies into the same level, next you'll load a movie into a different level.

22 Open the **loadMovieNum** folder inside the **chap_12** folder. Double-click the **gearExtra.swf** file to preview the file. Notice there is only one small button in the preview window. You will be loading this file in the main movie next. When you are finished, close the SWF file.

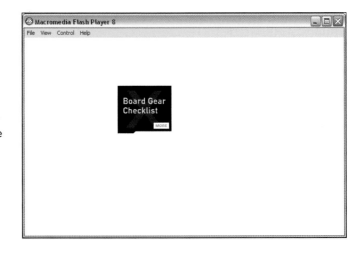

Why is there so much extra space around the button? When you load movies into levels, Flash 8 automatically places the loaded movie flush top left in the Macromedia Flash Player. Up to this point in the exercise, you have loaded movies into levels that all had the same dimensions. If you load a new movie into a level with much smaller dimensions, it will automatically be registered in the upper-left corner and therefore might not be placed where you want it.

There are two ways around this issue. In this case, the button in **gearExtra.swf** has been strategically placed where it should "land" in the interface. Its dimensions match each of the other SWF files you have worked with in this exercise. Because areas with no content in loaded movies are transparent, the button will be positioned correctly when loaded into Flash. Another way to have precise control over movie placement is to load it into a movie clip, rather than a level. In this exercise, you will be working with the level method.

---

23 Back in the project file, double-click the **mcMenu** movie clip on the **Stage** to open the movie clip's **Timeline**. Select **Frame 10** of the **actions** layer on the **Timeline**. Notice the previous frame actions you added in earlier steps are still there. Click the last line of the script to select it. In the **Actions** pane, select **Global Functions > Browser/Network** and double-click the **loadMovie** action to add it to the **Script** pane. Type **gearExtra.swf** in the URL field and **60** in the **Location: Level** text field.

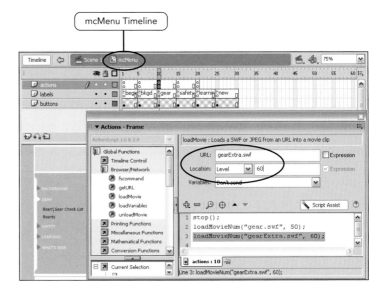

You just added a new script below the **loadMovieNum** script you created earlier. This new script tells Flash 8 to load the SWF file you specified (**gearExtra.swf**) into Level 60, above the main movie (at Level 0) and also above the **gear.swf** file in Level 50.

What is really going on behind the scenes? When the user clicks the Gear button, the playhead will be sent to the gear label inside the menu movie clip's Timeline. (You already programmed this ActionScripting when you built the menu in the last exercise.) When the playhead hits the gear label on the Timeline (which is Frame 10), first it will stop (because you have a **stop** action), then it will load the **gear.swf** file into Level 50, and then load the **gearExtra.swf** file into Level 60.

---

24 Choose **Control > Test Movie** and click the **Gear** button on the menu. Notice the button from **gearExtra.swf** file is there! This is because you loaded the **gear.swf** file into **Level 60**, above any content loaded into **Level 50**. As far as stacking order goes with loaded movies in Flash 8, the higher the level number, the closer to the top of the stacking order; so in this case, the **gearExtra.swf** file is loaded just above the **gear.swf** file. Close the preview window when you are finished.

When you click any of the other buttons on the menu, notice the **gearExtra.swf** file appears, no matter what section you are in. Why? This is because the **gearExtra.swf** file has been loaded into Level 60, and it will stay there (no matter what else is going on in other levels, such as Level 50) until you tell it otherwise.

Note: You may have noticed that if you click the gearExtra button, the Board Gear Checklist page shows up. Why? This is because inside the project file that created the **gearExtra.swf** is a button with the following ActionScript attached to it:

```
on (release) {
loadMovieNum("gearCheckList.swf", 50);
}
```

This means that when a user clicks the button, it will load the **gearCheckList.swf** file into Level 50.

---

25 In the project file, the **playhead** should still be over **Frame 10**. On the **Stage**, select the **Board Gear Checklist** button. In the **Script** pane, select Line 2 (`loadMovieNum ("gearCheckList.swf", 50);`) of the script. In the **Actions** pane, double-click the `unloadMovie` action to add it to the **Script** pane below line 2. Type **60** in the **Location: Level** text field.

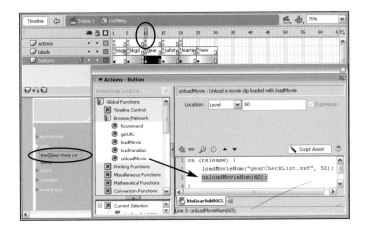

Now, when a user clicks the Board Gear Checklist button, Flash unloads whatever movie is currently in Level 60. (This happens to be **gearExtra.swf**.)

---

26 Choose **Control > Test Movie** and click the **Gear** button on the menu. Notice the button from the **gearExtra.swf** file is there! Click the **Safety** and **Learning** buttons and notice the **gearExtra.swf** content remains in place. Now click the **Board Gear Checklist** button and notice the **gearExtra.swf** content is gone. This is because you set up your movie to unload the **gear.swf** file from **Level 60** when the user clicks and releases the **Board Gear Checklist** button.

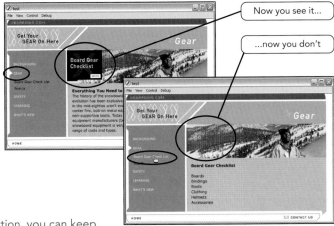

In summary, by using the `loadMovieNum` action, you can keep the main movie small, loading additional movies into levels above the main movie as they are needed.

---

27 When you are finished, close **loadMovieNum.fla**. You do not need to save your changes.

That's a wrap on this chapter. A lot of information was covered in the exercises, and if anything isn't crystal clear, you can always go back and review it. Take a well-deserved break and then get ready for the *"Working with Text"* chapter, which comes next.

13

Working with Text

When working with text, you have many options beyond simply selecting the Text tool and typing text on the Stage. You can create horizontal or vertical text, change the text attributes such as kerning (spacing between characters) and line spacing, apply transformations such as rotation and skew, and much more. As you go through this chapter, you will learn to make text scroll, and you'll create text fields where users can input information. New in Flash 8 is Flash Type—an improved font-rendering technology that renders smaller text sizes more clearly. Flash 8 also includes a spell-check feature and supports Cascading Style Sheets (CSS), which lets you create text styles you can apply to HTML, making design across HTML and Macromedia Flash 8 content more consistent.

Flash 8 lets you create three different types of text elements: static text, dynamic text, and input text. You'll learn about these different types of text elements and try them out with hands-on exercises.

Text Field Types

The Text tool can create three types of text: static text, dynamic text, or input text.

Static text displays information that does not change, such as label buttons, forms, or navigation components. Dynamic text is used to show up-to-date information generated automatically from an external text file or a database. Use dynamic text when you want to automatically show information that gets updated often. Input text is text the user inputs, such as a user name and password, forms, and surveys. As you go through the exercises in this chapter, you will get hands-on experience with each of these text types.

When you add a text field to the Stage, a text block is created with a corner handle to identify the type of text field you are creating. The following table identifies the different types of text fields:

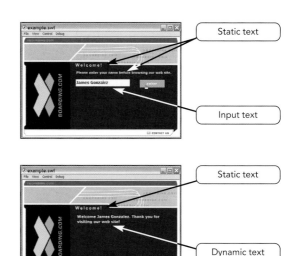

Types of Text Field Boxes					
Text Field	**Orientation**	**Defined or Extending**	**Handle Position**	**Handle Shape**	**Example**
Static	Horizontal	Extending	Upper-right corner	Round	xboarding.com
Static	Horizontal	Defined	Upper-right corner	Square	xboarding.com
Static (right to left)	Vertical	Extending	Lower-left corner	Round	x b o a r d
Static (left to right)	Vertical	Defined	Lower-left corner	Square	x b o a r d

continues on next page

Types of Text Field Boxes *continued*

Text Field	Orientation	Defined or Extending	Handle Position	Handle Shape	Example
Static (left to right)	Vertical	Extending	Lower-right corner	Round	
Static (left to right)	Vertical	Defined	Lower-right corner	Square	
Dynamic or input	Horizontal only	Extending	Lower-right corner	Round	xboarding.com
Dynamic or Input	Horizontal only	Defined	Lower-right corner	Square	xboarding.com

---

TIP: | **Changing the Text Field Box**

You can switch a text field from an extending text field to a defined text field and back again simply by double-clicking the handle.

TIP: | **Fixing a Text Field Box That Extends Too Far**

If, by accident, you create a text field that continues off the Stage, don't worry. Just choose **View > Work Area** (which is selected by default) and reduce the magnification to make the entire line of text visible. You can then force the text to wrap downward by either placing the cursor inside the text block and adding your own line breaks, or by dragging the text field handle to create a defined text field that will fit within the Stage area. When you create a defined text field, the text within that field will wrap to fit the field size.

Creating, Modifying, and Formatting Text

In Flash 8, you have a lot of control over the attributes of type. By using the Property Inspector, you can change, preview, and adjust text with a few clicks. The next section gives you a close look at most of the available settings.

As soon as you select the Text tool, the Property Inspector displays the available text attributes (with the exception of the Width and Height controls, which require a selection first). The table that follows this illustration details each of these items:

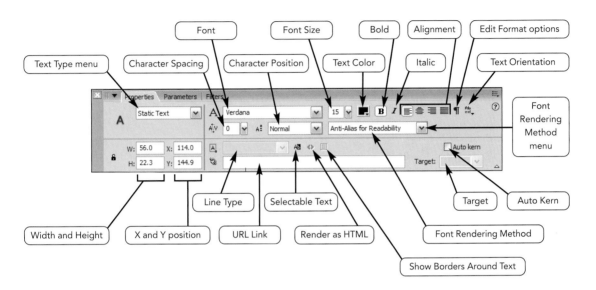

Text Attributes Defined	
Attribute	**Description**
Text Type menu	Lets you choose from one of three text fields (**Static**, **Dynamic**, or **Input Text**). Each text type has its own associated options that will appear in the Property Inspector when that text field type is selected. **Static Text** is the default.
Font	Displays the name of the current font. The menu lists all of the available fonts. As you scroll through the font list, Flash 8 displays a preview of what each font will look like.
Character Spacing	Lets you adjust the space between characters in selected text. Click the arrow next to the Character Spacing field and use the slider to increase or decrease the amount of space between characters.
Character Position	**Normal:** Resets characters to the baseline. **Superscript:** Shifts characters above the baseline. **Subscript:** Shifts characters below the baseline.

continues on next page

Text Attributes Defined *continued*

Attribute	Description
Font Size (Font Height)	Displays the current font size in points. Click the arrow to the right of the Font Size field and use the slider to adjust the size of the font.
Auto Kern	Controls the spacing between pairs of characters. Selecting this option will automatically use the font's built-in kerning information. (See the sidebar following this table for more information on kerning.)
Font Rendering Method	Default text in Flash 8 is anti-aliased, meaning that the edges of the text are smoothed. Five different font rendering options are available from this pop-up menu. **Device Fonts** uses fonts that are currently installed on the user's computer, producing a smaller SWF file. **Bitmap Text (no anti-alias)** produces sharp text edges, without anti-aliasing, resulting in a larger SWF file because font outlines must be included in the SWF file. **Anti-Alias for Animation** produces anti-alias text that animates smoothly, and in some cases, faster. This option also produces a larger SWF file size because font outlines are included in the SWF file. **Anti-Alias for Readability** uses the advanced anti-aliasing engine providing the highest-quality, most legible text. This option produces the largest SWF file size because it includes font outlines and also special anti-aliasing information. **Custom Anti-Alias** is the same as Anti-Alias for Readability, but it provides options for visually manipulating the anti-aliasing to produce the best possible appearance for new or uncommon fonts.
Text Color	Lets you change the color of the type. **Note:** For text blocks, you can use only solid colors, not gradients. If you want to use gradients, you have to break the text apart, which will convert it to a shape.
Bold	Bolds the selected type.
Italic	Italicizes the selected type.
Text Orientation	Changes the direction of the text. You can choose **Horizontal**; **Vertical, Left to Right**; and **Vertical, Right to Left**.
Alignment	Controls how the selected text will be aligned: **Left Justified**, **Center Justified**, **Right Justified**, or **Full Justified**.

continues on next page

	Text Attributes Defined *continued*
Attribute	**Description**
Rotation	Lets you have more control over vertical text and change its rotation. This option is available only for vertical text.
Indent	Accessible from the **Format Options** panel. Controls the distance between the margin of a paragraph and the beginning of the first line of a paragraph.
Line/Column spacing	Accessible from the **Format Options** panel. Line spacing (also referred to as **Leading**) controls the spacing between lines of type (horizontal text) or between vertical columns (vertical text).
Width and Height	Displays the width and height of a selected text field.
X and Y position	Displays the X and Y position of the top left of a selected text box, relative to the Stage. The top left of the Stage is 0, 0.
URL Link	Creates a hyperlink attached to selected text. In effect, this option creates a button that will link to an internal or external HTML file, without the need to create a button symbol. Flash automatically adds a dotted line under the linked text in the FLA file. Note, however, that hyperlinks created using this feature will not carry any visual feedback (such as an underline) in the SWF file, although when previewed in a browser, the hand icon will appear when the user moves the mouse over the linked text. You learned a better way to create a hyperlink in Chapter 12, "*ActionScripting Basics and Behaviors.*"
Line Type	Lets you choose among **Single line** (displaying the text on one line), **Multiline** (displaying the text in multiple lines with word wrap), **Multiline No Wrap** (displaying the text in multiple lines), and **Password**. This option is available only for dynamic and input text.
Selectable Text	Allows a user to select your text and copy it.
Render as HTML	Preserves rich text formatting, including fonts, hyperlinks, and bold with the appropriate HTML tags. You will learn to use this option in Exercise 4.
Show Border Around Text	When selected, displays a white background with a black border for the text field. This option is available only for dynamic and input text fields.
Var (Variable)	For dynamic or input text only, specify a variable name for the selected text.
Target	Used in conjunction with the URL Link feature. When assigning a hyperlink to selected text, you can also specify a target. Choosing a target lets you specify the URL to load in a new window or to a specific Web page layout that utilizes framesets.

To Kern or Not to Kern?

When font sets are created, the individual characters might look great all by them-selves, but some letter combinations may be spaced too close or too far from each other. To solve this problem, many fonts are created with additional instructions about spacing between specific characters. This is known as **kerning** information.

> Background
> Snowboarding is the relatively new sport which can be
> visually compared to skateboarding and surfing except
> done on snow. **The rider stands on the board with his/her**
> left or right foot forward, facing one side of the board.
> The feet are attached to the board via high-back, step-in
> or plate bindings which are non-releasable. **Although**
> there is at least one manufacturer of releasable bindings,
> they are not widely used.

Blue text = Auto kerning

Red text = Auto Kern off

To illustrate this point, we created two text blocks (one blue and one red) and placed them in the exact same position, with the blue text on top of the red text. We selected the Auto Kern feature in the Property Inspector for the blue text, and we left the red text with its default spacing. Notice how the red text shows through in some spots. This indicates that the Auto Kern feature has changed the spacing of the blue text.

When you create horizontal text, kerning sets the horizontal distance between characters. When you create vertical text, kerning sets the vertical distance between characters.

Character Spacing

Working with Static Text and Device Fonts

Static text is best used in situations where the text will not change, such as buttons, labels, forms, and navigation. When you add static text to your movie, by default Flash 8 will embed the font outlines in the SWF file for the font you're using. Depending on the font you choose and the amount of text you use, the font outlines can add to the overall file size of the SWF. If your goal is to keep file sizes as small as possible, use device fonts.

Device fonts are fonts that won't embed themselves in the SWF file. Instead, you choose a device font for the users' machines to display—_serif, _sans, or _typewriter—and the users' machines will display that device font for the static text. Using device fonts reduces the file sizes because the font outlines are not embedded in the SWF file. Device fonts can be sharper and more legible than exported font outlines at sizes below 10 points. However, because device fonts are not embedded, text may look different than expected in user systems that do not have an installed font corresponding to the device font. At the end of this exercise, we discuss the pros and cons of using static text and device fonts, but first you'll begin with learning how to spell-check your projects.

---

1 Copy the **chap_13** folder from the **HOT CD-ROM** to your **Desktop**. Open **staticText.fla** from the **chap_13** folder. Read the copy in the interface.

Notice any misspelled words? Next you'll check your project file for any spelling errors and correct them with the spell-check feature.

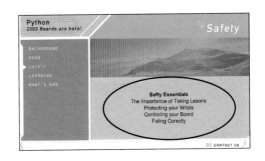

---

2 Choose **Text > Check Spelling** to open the **Check Spelling** dialog box. Click **Change** to correctly spell the words **Safety**, **Lessons**, **Controlling**, **Falling**, and **Correctly**. Click **OK** when you are prompted with the **Flash 8** dialog box.

Note: The spell-check feature works only with editable text. Because it doesn't work with text that has been broken apart (which you learned about in Chapter 5, "Shape Tweening"), be sure to spell-check your movie before you break apart any text.

You can modify the spelling setup by choosing **Text > Spelling Setup** or by clicking **Setup** in the **Check Spelling** dialog box.

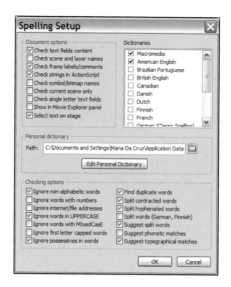

3 Read the copy in the interface again.

Notice all the misspelled words are now spelled correctly! With your movie free of spelling errors, next you will learn about static text and device fonts.

4 Select the **Selection** tool from the **toolbar**. On the **Stage**, select the block of text. Then choose **Window > Properties > Properties** to open the **Property Inspector**.

Note that the Font Rendering Method menu displays Anti-Alias for Animation.

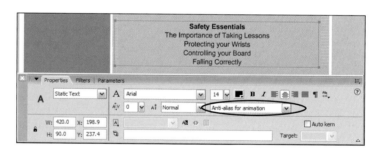

5 Choose **Control > Test Movie** to preview the text. When the preview window opens, choose **View > Bandwidth Profiler**. When you are done viewing the **Bandwidth Profiler**, close the preview window and return to the project file.

The Bandwidth Profiler appears at the top of the preview window and, among other things, tells you the file size of your SWF file. Currently, the file size is 30 KB. This file size accounts for all the graphics and font outlines being used in this movie.

In the following steps, you will modify the text block by using a device font to make the file size smaller.

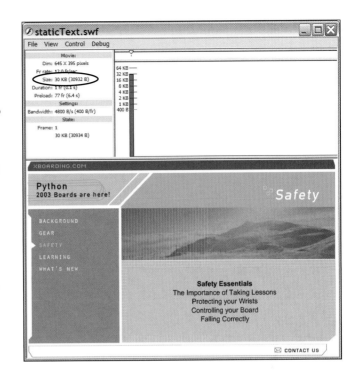

What Is the Bandwidth Profiler?

The Bandwidth Profiler, a feature in the Test Movie environment, shows useful information including movie dimensions, frame rate, size, duration, preload, bandwidth, and frame.

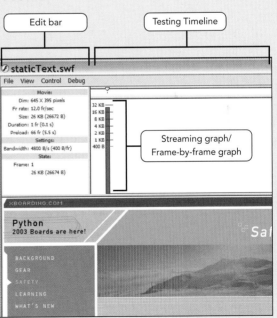

Bandwidth Profiler Information	
Option	What It Shows
Dim	The width and height (dimensions) of the movie.
Fr rate	The speed at which the movie plays based on the frames per second.
Size	The file size, in kilobytes (KB), of the movie or scene you are testing. The number in parentheses represents the size in bytes.
Duration	The total number of frames in your movie or scene. The number in parentheses represents the length of your movie or scene in seconds rather than frames.
Preload	The number of frames that need to be downloaded before the movie begins playing.
Bandwidth	The speed used to simulate an actual download when used with the Simulate Download command.
Frame	The top number shows the current frame position of the playhead. The bottom number shows the file size for the frame where the playhead is positioned. The number in parentheses represents the total file size. You can get individual frame information by moving the playhead in the Bandwidth Profiler Timeline, which is especially helpful for detecting frames that have a lot of content.

6 With the **Selection** tool, click the text block to select it. In the **Property Inspector**, choose **Use Device Fonts** from the **Font Rendering Method** menu.

Flash includes three device fonts, **sans** (similar to Helvetica or Arial), **serif** (similar to Times Roman), and **_typewriter** (similar to Courier). With this selection, during SWF file playback, Flash will select the first device font it locates on the user's system and will render this text using this font. Because device fonts are not embedded, the resulting SWF file should be smaller. Next, you will test the movie again to check for any change in file size.

7 Choose **Control > Test Movie** to preview the text. The **Bandwidth Profiler** should still be visible above the preview window. If it's not, choose **View > Bandwidth Profiler**. Notice the size is now 26 KB, whereas before setting your text to a device font the file size was 30 KB, a savings of 4 KB!

Four kilobytes might not sound like much, but if you're designing a banner ad, and your target file size is a paltry 10 KB, 4 KB is 40 percent of the total!

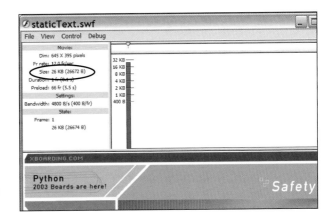

8 Choose **View > Bandwidth Profiler** to hide the **Bandwidth Profiler**, and close the preview window. Close **staticText.fla**; you do not need to save your changes

---

NOTE:

Embedded Fonts vs. Device Fonts

When you select a specific font for a text block in the Property Inspector, Flash 8 automatically takes all the font information (the font's description, kerning, leading, and so on) and embeds it in the exported movie. This is what is known as an **embedded font**. The capability to embed fonts makes Flash 8 a great platform for using unusual fonts in movies because the user doesn't have to have the same fonts installed on their computers to see the results. Flash 8 automatically includes all the necessary information.

The downside to using embedded fonts is that they increase the file size of the SWF. Also, some fonts cannot be exported with the movie because Flash 8 cannot embed the font's outline, which may happen because the font was not installed properly or because the computer has only the screen font. The font may display properly in the production file (FLA) yet falter when the movie is exported (SWF) because the actual font to which the screen font refers cannot be found when the movie is published. To check for this, you can choose **View > Preview Mode > Anti-Alias Text** (which is already enabled by default) to preview the text. Rough or jagged text is an indication that the text will not be exported when the SWF file is published.

Because the font outlines will be embedded in the SWF file when you publish your movie, all the fonts in the Flash 8 document must be installed on your computer. If you receive a FLA from a friend or colleague that uses a font not installed on your computer, an error message informs you that a substitute font will be used in its place. At this point, you have two options. You can allow Flash 8 to replace the font with a default replacement (click the **Use Default** button), or you can replace the font with a font installed on your computer (click the **Choose Substitute** button).

continues on next page

Embedded Fonts vs. Device Fonts *continued*

Device fonts were created as a solution this issue. They are special fonts that will not be embedded in the exported movie, therefore creating smaller SWF files. Rather than using an embedded font, the Flash Player displays the text using the closest match on the user's computer to the device font.

The drawback to device fonts is that if a user doesn't have a similar font installed on his or her system, he or she might see text that bears little resemblance to the text you see on your machine. To combat this concern, Flash 8 includes three built-in device fonts to help produce results closer to what you expect. These fonts are all available under the Type pull-down menu, along with the other fonts:

- **_sans:** Similar to Helvetica or Arial

- **_serif:** Similar to Times Roman

- **_typewriter:** Similar to Courier

Anti-aliasing

Anti-aliasing is a term that refers to blurring of the edges to make the text appear smooth. Most digital artists prefer the way anti-aliased text looks, but at small sizes the blurred edges make the text appear fuzzy and hard to read. For text that is 10 point or smaller, alias text is sharper and easier to read because the edges of the text are not blurred.

Alias Text vs. Anti-Alias Text	
Alias Text	**Anti-Alias Text**
# Xboard	# Xboard
Alias text at large sizes appears jaggy. The edges of the text lack the smoothing effect.	Anti-alias text at large sizes appears smooth because the edges are blurred to smooth the text. Anti-alias text works best with large font sizes.
Xboard	Xboard
Alias text at small sizes is sharper and easier to read. Alias text works best on sizes 10 point or smaller.	Anti-alias text at small sizes is fuzzy and hard to read because the smoothing effect on the edges causes the text to become blurry.

Flash Type

Flash 8 provides improved WYSIWYG text rendering, referred to as Flash Type, which is especially effective in making smaller font sizes appear more clear and readable. Flash Type works in both the Flash authoring application and in Flash Player 8. This improved text-rendering is automatically enabled whenever Flash Player 8 is the selected version of the player.

Warning: Flash Type may cause a slight delay when loading movies with a large number of fonts and may also cause an increase in the Flash Player's memory usage.

2 | Using Small Type and Aliased Text

When working with small type (10 point or smaller), the text might become difficult to read because of the anti-aliasing that is automatically applied to vector shapes, including type, in Flash 8. Anti-aliasing is a blurring, or "smoothing," of the edges of vector shapes and text. In most cases, anti-aliasing improves the appearance of a shape because it gives its edges a smooth appearance. However, the blurring generated by anti-aliasing can make small text hard to read. Anti-aliasing has been improved in this version of Flash for users with Flash Player 7 or later for static, dynamic, and input text, especially for very small text.

---

1 Open the **aliasText.fla** file from the **chap_13** folder. Choose **Control > Test Movie** to preview the text blocks. When you're finished, close the preview window.

Notice the two text blocks side by side. Both text blocks have the same text attributes. Notice that both text blocks look the same and are a little hard to read, which is caused by blurriness generated by the anti-aliasing applied to the text blocks.

---

2 Select the text block on the right. In the **Property Inspector**, choose **Bitmap text (no Anti-Alias)** from the **Font Rendering Method** pop-up menu.

Notice how the text block on the right immediately appears sharper, crisper, and easier to read compared to the text block on the left.

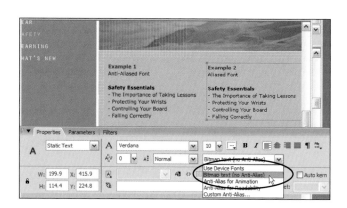

---

3 Test the movie once more by choosing **Control > Test Movie**.

Notice the text block on the right is still much easier to read! You can apply alias text to static, dynamic, and input text fields. However, if a user does not have version 7 or newer of the Flash Player plug-in, only static text will appear aliased. Dynamic or input text fields will still appear anti-aliased.

---

4 Select the text block on the left. In the **Property Inspector**, choose **Anti-Alias for Readability** from the **Font Rendering Method** pop-up menu.

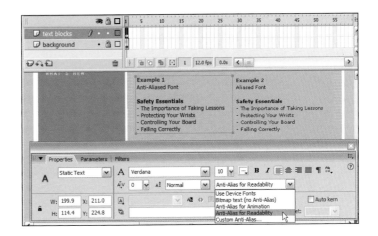

5 Test the movie once more by choosing **Control > Test Movie**.

Notice how the text block on the left appears much sharper, crisper, and easier to read. This is a new anti-alias setting in Flash 8 that is especially useful for making text smaller than 11 point easier to read.

6 Close the preview window and close **aliasText.fla**. You do not need to save your changes

3 | Loading Text into Dynamic Text Fields

Dynamic text is best used for information that needs to be updated often, such as news, weather reports, or company information. You can use a bit of ActionScripting and a dynamic text field to store an external file holding updated text. Flash 8 is a robust program for handling this type of data-driven content coming from a database or an external file. The following exercise takes you through these steps and teach you how to load a text file (TXT) directly into a dynamic text field.

---

1 Open the **textFileLearning.txt** file in the **chap_13** folder.

Notice this is not a Flash 8 file, but a TXT file, that will open in the default text editor on your computer. (You might need to turn on word wrapping so you can see all the text at once.) We created this TXT file to get you started.

---

2 In order for Flash 8 to recognize the information in this file, you need to give it a variable name. Place your cursor at the very beginning of the paragraph and type **content=**. You have now declared that the text within the text file will be assigned to the variable name **content**.

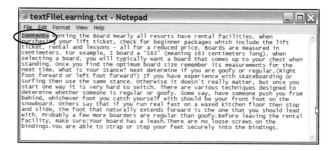

NOTE: | ### What Is a Variable?

A variable is simply a container that holds information, such as a name or number.

For example, in the following ActionScript
author="Gonzalez";

the variable name (or container) is **author**, and everything after the equal sign is the value of the variable, which, in this example, is **"Gonzalez"**.

NOTE: | ### URL-Encoded Text

When you use the **loadVariables** action (which you will do later in this exercise) to load an external text file, the data in the text file must be in a special format called **URL-encoded**. This format requires that each variable travel in a pair with its associated value. The variable and the associated value are separated by the = symbol. In Step 2, the variable name is **content**, and the associated value is all the text that immediately follows the = symbol.

---

3 Save and close the text file. Make sure you save it in the **chap_13** folder, Flash 8 will be looking for it here in later steps.

4 In Flash 8, open the **dynamicText.fla** file from the **chap_13** folder.

Notice this file contains one layer with a background image. You will add the dynamic text box next.

5 In the **Timeline**, add a new layer by clicking the **Insert Layer** button, and rename this layer **holder**.

6 Select the **Text** tool from the **toolbar** and click the **Stage**. In the **Property Inspector**, choose **Dynamic Text**, **Multiline**, and **Show Border Around Text**. Make sure the **Font Color** is set to black and the **Font Type** is set to **Verdana** with a **Point Size** of **10**.

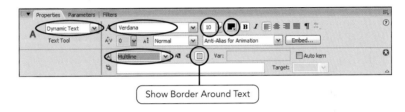

Show Border Around Text

When you draw the text field on the Stage (which you will do next), these settings will create a dynamic text field with a white background and a black border that can support multiple lines of text that will wrap.

7 With the **holder** layer selected, click and drag on the **Stage** to create a text field.

Tip: After you draw the text field, you can drag the handle of the dynamic text field to resize the text field, if necessary.

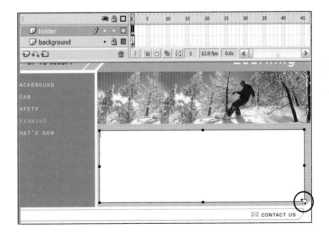

8 In the **Property Inspector**, type **content** in the **Var** (variable) field, which will be the variable name assigned to the text field (the same variable name you assigned to the text inside the TXT file in Step 2).

TIP: | **Loading External Data into a Movie**

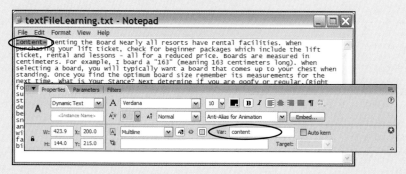

Whenever you load external data into a dynamic text field in Flash 8, you need to perform two important tasks. First, you must give the dynamic text field the same variable name you assign to the text inside the TXT file (as you have just done). Second, you must give Flash 8 the name of the external file (**textFileLearning.txt**) you want to load into your text field and the location where that text field resides within your Flash 8 movie. You will perform this second task next.

---

9 Click the **Insert Layer** button to add a layer. Rename the layer **actions**. Make sure the **actions** layer is above all other layers. In the **actions** layer, select **Frame 1**. Choose **Window > Actions** to open the **Actions** panel.

10 In the **Actions** panel, make sure it reads **Actions – Frame**. In the **Actions** pane, make sure **Script Assist** mode is turned off. Select **Global Functions > Browser/Network** and double-click the `loadVariables` action to add it to the **Script** pane.

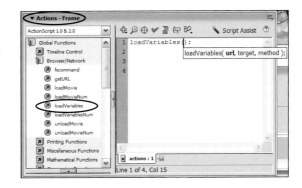

11 Click between the parentheses ( ) and type **"textFileLearning.txt", this**. (Don't forget the quotation marks.)

This ActionScript command tells Flash 8 to look for **textFileLearning.txt** and to load the variables from that file into the current (**Scene 1**) Timeline (**this**). Since the variable name **content** was applied to both the dynamic text field and the text within the **textFileLearning.txt** file, the text field will dynamically generate the text from the TXT file.

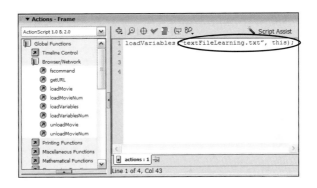

Note: Since the TXT file is in the same folder as the project file (FLA) and the SWF file, you can simply type the name of the file (the relative address) in the URL field. If, however, the TXT file was located in a different folder, you would have to specify the path to that folder (the absolute address) in the URL field, such as: **../projectSnow/learning/textFileLearning.txt**.

12 Choose **Control > Test Movie** to test your movie. Notice how the text is dynamically generated inside the Flash movie (**dynamicText.swf**) without actually typing anything inside the Flash 8 project file (**dynamicText.fla**)! When you're finished, close the preview window, save any changes, and close the **dynamicText.fla** file.

Troubleshooting tips: If you don't see any text when you test the movie, select the dynamic text field back in the project file and make sure the **Font Color** is set to black. On the **actions** layer, click **Frame 1**, and in the **Actions**

panel check the spelling of the TXT filename. Also, make sure you're using the same case (upper- or lowercase) in the ActionScripting as you are using in the TXT filename. One last tip—make sure that you have quotation marks around the name of the TXT file in the `loadVariables` line of code.

Next, you will make changes to the **textFileLearning.txt** file and see that Flash 8 will automatically update the content in the dynamic text field without opening the production file (**dynamicText.fla**). If you want to change the content inside the text file, all you need to do is open the TXT file, make the changes, and open the SWF file again. You will do this in the following steps.

---

13 Open **textFileLearning.txt** from the **chap_13** folder. After the text **Renting the Board**, type **and Other Accessories**. When you are finished, save the file.

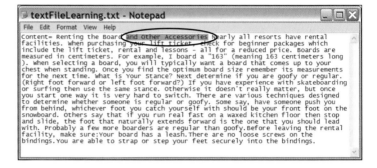

---

14 Hide Flash 8 for a moment and look inside the **chap_13** folder on your **Desktop**. Notice the **dynamicText.swf** file.

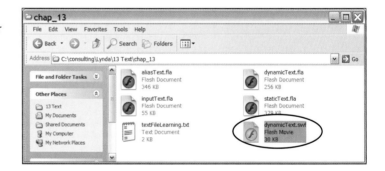

---

15 Double-click the **dynamicText.swf** file to open it in the **Flash Player**.

Notice the changes you made to the TXT file in Step 13 have been updated in the SWF file without opening up the production file (**dynamicText.fla**)!

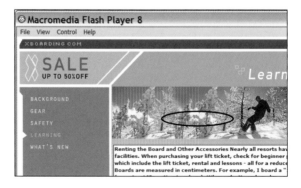

---

16 Back in the **textFileLearning.txt** file, delete the **and Other Accessories** text and save your changes. Open the **dynamicText.swf** file and notice the changes have been updated again without opening the production file.

---

17 Make more changes if you'd like. When you're done, close the **dynamicText.swf** file but keep the **textFileLearning.txt** file open. You'll format this text in the following exercise.

As you can see, the text loaded into the dynamic text field is unformatted (no paragraph breaks, bolding, and so forth). You'll learn how to format the loaded text with HTML next.

> **NOTE:**
>
> ### Changing Character Attributes
>
> The text that loads into the dynamic text field will take on all the character attributes that are applied to the field within the Property Inspector. You can quickly change the way the text is displayed in the SWF file by making modifications to the text properties in the Property Inspector. First, select the dynamic text field. Then change the font name, the font height, and the font color. You can even deselect the Show Border Around Text option to remove the white background from the text. Test the movie again, and you will see a completely different look for your text field!

4 | Working with Dynamic Text and HTML

In the last exercise, you created a dynamic text field that displayed the content of an external text file. In this exercise, you will go one step further by changing the dynamic text field so that Flash 8 recognizes and preserves HTML formatting applied to the content inside the external text file.

1 The **textFileLearning.txt** file should still be open from the last exercise. If it's not, open it from the **chap_13** folder.

NOTE:

Dynamic Text HTML Support

Flash 8 supports the following HTML tags in dynamic and input text fields: **<a>** = anchor, **<b>** = bold, **<font color>** = font color, **<font face>** = typeface, **<font size>** = font size, **<i>** = italic, **<img>** = image, **<li>** = list item, **<p>** = paragraph, **
** = line break, **<u>** = underline, and **<a href="...">** = hyperlinks.

Flash 8 also supports the following HTML attributes in dynamic and input text fields: **leftmargin**, **rightmargin**, **align**, **indent**, and **leading**.

You will add some of these tags in the next few steps.

2 Add bold HTML tags around the words **Renting the Board**, and add one line break tag so it reads: **<b>Renting the Board</b>
**. Save your changes, and keep the file open.

By changing one setting in the Property Inspector of the **dynamicText.fla** file, you will see the HTML-based text file loaded into the same dynamic text box. You will do this next.

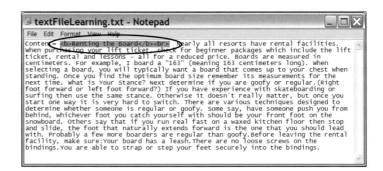

3 Open the **dynamicText.fla** file from the **chap_13** folder. This is the same FLA file you worked with in the last exercise.

4 With the **Selection** tool, select the dynamic text field on the **Stage**. In the **Property Inspector**, click the **Render as HTML** button, which will allow the dynamic text block to interpret the HTML code and dynamically display any of the supported HTML tags within the external text file.

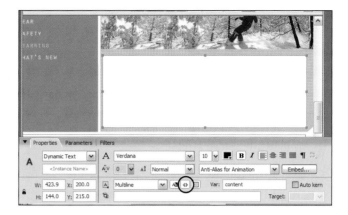

5 Choose **Control > Test Movie** to test your movie. Notice that Flash 8 recognized the HTML formatting you made in the text file. When you are done viewing your changes, close the preview window.

You will add more HTML formatting to the **textfileLearning.txt** file next.

Note: In the last exercise you previewed the changes you made to the **textFileLearning.txt** file by opening the **dynamicText.swf** file. For ease of workflow, you will now preview your

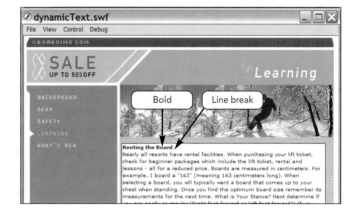

changes using **Control > Test Movie** and creating the SWF file again from the production file (**dynamicText.fla**). This minimizes going back and forth from the Flash 8 application to the Desktop and vice versa.

6 Back in the **textFileLearning.txt** file, add font color HTML tags around the words **lift ticket, rental and lessons** so it reads **<font color="#3399FF">lift ticket, rental and lessons</font>**.

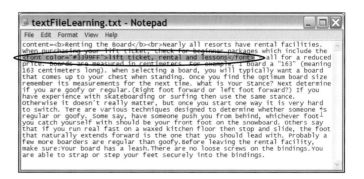

7 Add italic HTML tags around the words **reduced price** so it reads `<i>reduced price</i>`. Save your changes and keep the file open.

You will preview your work next.

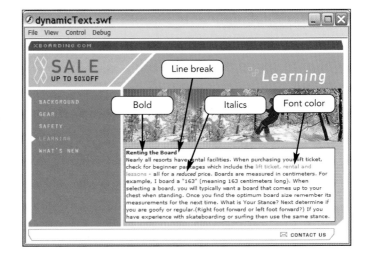

8 Choose **Control > Test Movie** to test your movie again. Notice that Flash 8 recognized the additional HTML formatting you made in the text file. When you're finished, close the preview window.

You will add a bit more HTML formatting to the **textfileLearning.txt** file next.

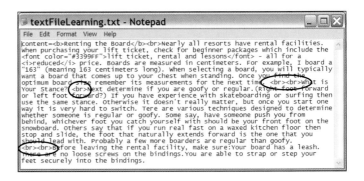

9 To break this large block of text up into smaller, more readable chunks, add five more line breaks (`<br>`)—just as you did in Step 2 after the text **Renting the Board**—to the locations indicated in this illustration.

10 To make the last three sentences of the copy more readable, add list item HTML tags (**<li>**) to the locations indicated in this illustration. Save your changes and close the file.

You will preview your new changes next.

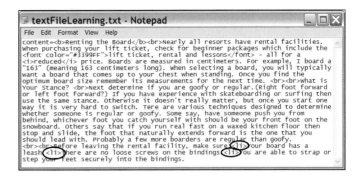

11 Choose **Control > Test Movie** to test your movie.

Notice that Flash 8 recognized all the HTML formatting you made in the text file! There is, however, some missing content below the edge of the text box. See the sidebar below to learn how to get the text to scroll up and down within the dynamic text field.

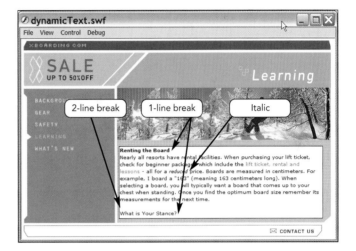

12 Save your changes to **dynamicText.fla**. Keep the file open if you plan to now view the **scrollableText.mov** file and complete the next part of the exercise.

VIDEO: | **scrollableText.mov**

To get the text to scroll up and down within the dynamic text field box, you need to add buttons to the interface and add some ActionScript. To learn how to do this, view the **scrollableText.mov** video in the **videos** folder on the **HOT CD-ROM**.

5 | Working with Input Text

Now that you've worked with static and dynamic text fields, it's time to explore the last remaining text field type: input text. Input text fields, as the name implies, let users input text into them, much like an HTML form. If you've ever purchased a product online, you had to give the vendor your name, address, credit card number, and so forth. You entered that information in an input text field. In this exercise, you will learn how to use an input text field to create an area for visitors to enter their names. Then you will use that name, in combination with some other text, to populate a dynamic text field.

1 Open the **inputText.fla** file from the **chap_13** folder.

Notice this file has one layer with a background image on it.

2 Click the **Insert Layer** button four times to add four new layers above the **background** layer. Starting from the top, name the four new layers **actions**, **enter_btn**, **text**, and **name field**.

You will be adding the input text field, some text, a button, and actions to these layers in the following steps. Below the text *Welcome!*, you will enter in a little bit of text and create an input text field. The input text field is where the visitor to your Web site will enter in his or her name. Later in this same exercise, you will use that name in a dynamic text field by adding some ActionScript.

3 In the **Timeline**, select the **text** layer. From the **toolbar**, select the **Text** tool and click the **Stage**. In the **Property Inspector**, set the **Text Type** to **Static Text**, **Font** to **Arial**, **Font Size** to **14**, and the **Text Color** to **white** and **bold**. Set the **Text Alignment** to **Align left**, and select the **Auto kern** option. Set the **Font Rendering Method** to **Anti-Alias for Animation**.

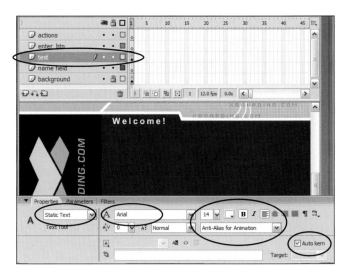

4 Click the **Stage** to create a text block, and type **Please enter your name before browsing our Web site:**. Reposition the text block with the **Selection** tool if you need to.

5 Lock the **text** layer and select the **name field** layer. Select the **Text** tool and click the **Stage**. In the **Property Inspector**, set the **Text Type** to **Input Text**. On the **Stage**, create a text box (by clicking and dragging) below the **Please enter your name before browsing our Web site:** text.

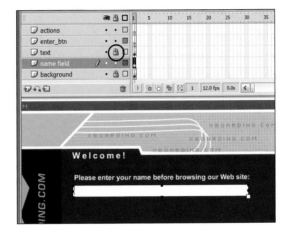

6 With the **Selection** tool, select the input text field you just created on the **Stage**. In the **Property Inspector**, make sure the **Text Type** is set to **Input Text**, **Font** to

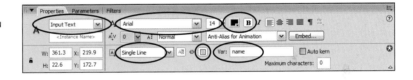

Arial, **Font Size** to **14**, and **Font Color** to **black** and **bold**. Set the **Line Type** to **Single Line**, select the **Show Borders** button, and in the **Var** field, type **name** to name this input text field.

NOTE:

Naming Variables

ActionScript variable names can contain only letters, numbers, and underscores. Variable names should begin with a lowercase letter and cannot begin with numbers or underscores. Additionally, words that are used by ActionScript, such as *scroll*, should not be used as variable names. For more information on ActionScript coding standards, visit **http://www.macromedia.com/devnet/flash/whitepapers/actionscript_standards.pdf**.

Input Text Options

Clicking the Show Border Around Text button creates a border and background around the input text box. If Show Border Around Text is not enabled, a dotted line will surround the text box in the FLA file, although when you publish the movie, there will be no border or background.

The **Maximum characters** setting lets you set the maximum number of characters that a visitor can type in the text box. The default is set to 0, meaning no maximum number of characters.

The **Line Type** option lets you set the text box to either **Single Line** (displaying the text on one line), **Multiline** (displaying the text in multiple lines), **Multiline no wrap** (displaying the text on one line unless a line break [Enter/Return] is used), or **Password** (automatically turns all characters into asterisks as they are typed in the field of either the SWF file or the executable).

The **Var** setting (variable) lets you assign a variable name to the text field.

---

7 In the **Property Inspector**, click the **Embed** button to open the **Character Embedding** dialog box, where you specify the range of the typeface you've chosen (Arial, in this example) to be embedded in the SWF file. In the list box, **Shift+click** to select **Uppercase** and **Lowercase**. Click **OK** to accept these changes.

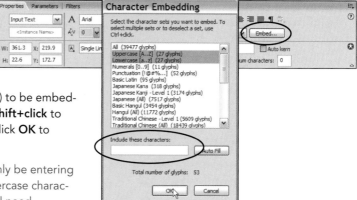

Since visitors to your Web site will only be entering their names, the uppercase and lowercase characters should be the only ones they will need.

Tip: If you want to embed only a few characters, and not an entire range, you can type specific characters into the **Include these characters** field. For example, if you only wanted to embed letters and numbers *a, b, c, d, e, f, 1, 2, 3, 4, 5,* and *6,* you would type those characters into this box, without commas or spaces (unless you want to embed those as well).

Embedding Font Outlines

When using a static text field, as explained earlier, the font outlines for all the text you used will be embedded in the SWF file. Then you're able to use any font you want in your project, and users will see the font you chose whether they have the font installed on their computers or not.

When using a dynamic or input text field, however, Flash 8 does not automatically embed the font outline for the font you've chosen. Instead, you must manually specify in the Property Inspector, as you just did in Step 7, what part of the font face (upper-case characters, lowercase, numerals, and so forth) you want to embed in the SWF file. If you don't do this for *each* dynamic and/or input text field, the viewer's computer will treat the text in that field like a device font. Unless the user has the same font face you've chosen for the text field, a substitute will be chosen that comes closest to the one you've picked. This substitute type will be displayed as aliased (jagged edge) instead of anti-aliased (smooth edge)! So unless you're trying to save file size by not embedding font outlines in your SWF file, make sure you specify your font embedding settings for each dynamic and/or input text field in your project.

Embedding Multiple, Identical Font Outlines

If you have two input text fields, and each text field is using the Arial font, you will still need to specify the font embedding options for *both* input text fields individually. If you embed the upper- and lowercase characters for both input text fields, does that mean the font outlines for Arial upper- and lowercase will be embedded twice, increasing your file size even more? No, thankfully it doesn't; the font outlines will only be loaded once.

---

8 In the **Timeline**, lock the **name field** layer, and select the **enter_btn** layer.

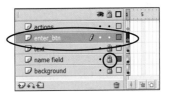

9 Press **Ctrl+L** (Windows) or **Cmd+L** (Mac) to open the **Library**. Drag the **btnEnter** button symbol onto the **Stage** and position it below the lower-right corner of the name field.

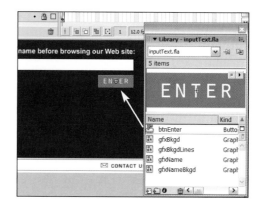

10 Make sure the **btnEnter** button is selected. Press **F9** (Windows) or **Option+F9** (Mac) to open the **Actions** panel. Click the **Script Assist** button to enable **Script Assist** mode. Select **Global Functions > Movie Clip Control** and double-click the **on** action to add it to the **Script** pane. Select the **Event: Release** (the default) and **Event: Key Press** options. Press **Enter** (Windows) or **Return** (Mac) so **<Enter>** is listed as the **Key Press** parameter.

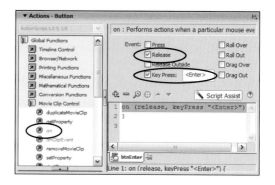

11 With the first line of script still selected in the **Actions** pane, select **Statements > Conditions/Loops** and double-click the **if** action to add it to the **Script** pane.

Later in this exercise, on Frame 2, you will create a dynamic text field where the user's name will be displayed along with some additional text. By entering his or her name and clicking the Enter button, the visitor will successfully go to the next frame. However, if the visitor doesn't enter any information into the name field, he or she won't be allowed to go to the next frame. This **if** action you are about to create will verify that the viewer enters something into the name field.

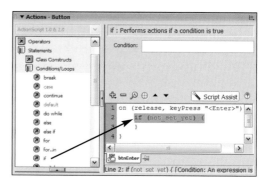

12 In the **Condition** parameter text field, type **name != null**.

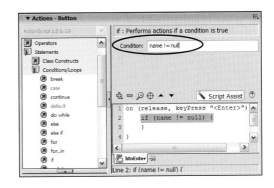

name is the variable name of the input text field where the viewer enters his or her name. **!=** means does not equal, and **null** means no value. So, in plain English, this **if** action essentially says "If the input text field name is not empty (meaning, someone has typed *something* into it), then...".

In the next few steps, you will complete the rest of this statement.

13 With the if statement still selected, select **Global Functions > Timeline Control** and double-click the **goto** action. Select the **Go to and stop** option and from the **Type** pop-up menu, choose **Frame Number**. Type **2** in the **Frame** text field.

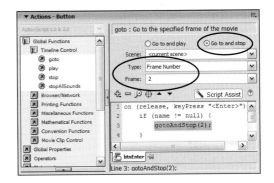

This script instructs Flash 8 to go to the next frame in the Timeline and stop. In plain English, this script means, "When the user clicks the Enter button, or presses Enter/Return on his or her keyboard, AND the name field has some text in it, then go to the next frame in the Timeline." If the viewer has not entered any text into the name field, Flash 8 won't go to the next frame. Next, you will create the message on the next frame, which the viewer will see once he or she enters a name into the name field and clicks the Enter button or presses Enter or Return.

14 Lock the **enter_btn** layer, and click the **Insert Layer** button to create a new layer. Rename the new layer **message**. **Shift+click Frame 2** of the **message** and **actions** layers and press **F7** to create blank keyframes there. On the **background** layer, select **Frame 2** and press **F5** to add a frame there.

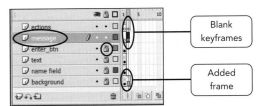

Blank keyframes

Added frame

15 Select **Frame 2** of the **message** layer. From the **toolbar**, select the **Text** tool and click the **Stage**. In the **Property Inspector**, set the **Text Type** to **Dynamic Text**, and then draw a large rectangle below the "**Welcome!**" text.

This rectangle will be the dynamic text field where the message, incorporating the visitor's name, will be displayed. You will set the remaining options in the Property Inspector next.

---

16 With the **Selection** tool, select the dynamic text field you just created on the **Stage**. In the **Property Inspector**, make sure the **Text Type** is still set to **Dynamic Text**. Set the **Font** to **Arial**, **12** point, **white**, and **bold**. Make sure the **Text Alignment** is set to **Center**, **Line Type** is set to **Multiline**,

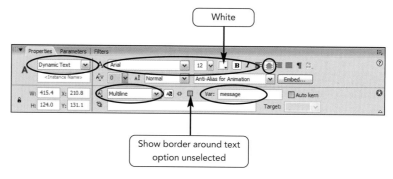

and the **Show border around text** option is deselected. In the **Var** (variable) field, type **message**.

You will set the character options for the dynamic text field next.

---

17 In the **Property Inspector**, click the **Embed** button. In the **Character Embedding** dialog box, select **Uppercase**, then while holding down the **Ctrl** (Windows) or **Cmd** (Mac) key, single-click **Lowercase** and **Punctuation** to select all three options at the same time. Click **OK**.

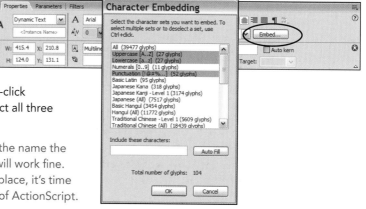

For a simple message that includes the name the visitor entered, these three ranges will work fine. Now that you have all the pieces in place, it's time to put it all together with a little bit of ActionScript.

18 Lock the **message** layer. In the **actions** layer, click **Keyframe 2**. Press **F9** (Windows) or **Option+F9** (Mac) to open the **Actions** panel.

At this point, what you're trying to accomplish with ActionScript is to write a little bit of text that will be combined with the name the visitor entered in the input text field, and then place that name inside a dynamic text field (which you gave a variable name of **message**).

---

19 Click the **Script Assist** button to exit **Script Assist** mode. Click in the **Script** pane and type **message =**. Remember that **message** is the variable name you assigned to the dynamic text field on **Frame 2**.

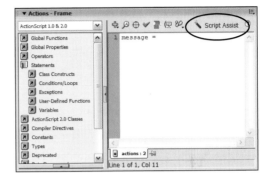

---

20 After **message =**, type **"Welcome, "** + **name** + **". Thank you for visiting our Web site!";**.

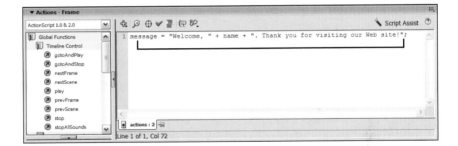

NOTE:

String Literal vs. Expression

In the text you just entered, notice that some is in quotes, and some (like *name*) is not. The text in quotes is called a **string literal**. If you want Flash 8 to display text just as it is typed, put it in quotes. Anything not in quotes (in this case, *name*), will be treated as an **expression**. An expression is a bit of ActionScripting representing a value. You don't *literally* want to put the text *name* in the dynamic text field, you instead want Flash 8 to go get the *value* of the **name** variable (which is whatever the visitor to your site enters in the input text field) and insert it into a sentence. To combine string literals with expressions, use + (the addition operator).

Last, to prevent the movie from initially playing, you need to add a **stop** action to the first keyframe.

21 In the **actions** layer, select **Frame 1.** Press **F9** (Windows) or **Option+F9** (Mac) to open the **Actions** panel. Make sure the **Actions** panel reads **Actions – Frame**. Select **Global Functions > Timeline Control** and double-click the **stop** action to add it to the **Script** pane.

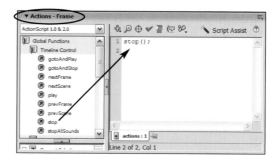

Congratulations! You're done! Now it's time to test your handiwork, so cross your fingers.... ;-)

---

22 Choose **Control > Test Movie**. When the preview window appears, type your name in the name field and click **Enter**.

You should now see a simple block of text that incorporates your name into it! Little does the visitor to your site realize the hard work you put into making that block of text seem so simple.

---

23 When you are finished, close **inputText.fla**. You do not need to save your changes.

Troubleshooting tip: If you don't see your name in the dynamic text field when you test the movie, go back to the project file and in the **message** layer, select the dynamic text field in **Frame 2** and make sure the **Show Border Around Text** button is deselected; otherwise, you won't be able to see the white text. Also click **Frame 2** of the **actions** layer and in the **Actions** panel check the ActionScript to make sure you have correctly inserted the code for the frame action. Refer to Steps 19 and 20.

You have successfully made it through the text chapter! Time to take a quick break and get amped up (pun intended) for the sound chapter next!

14

Sound

One of Flash's hidden strengths is that it can consistently and reliably play back sound across a wide variety computer platforms and environments. In fact, this capability may be the best reason to use Flash for projects in which sound is an important component. For example, if you need accurate and consistent sound playback on a Web site, Flash 8 is an ideal tool for the job.

In Flash 8, you can use sound for many purposes—including narration, background soundtracks, rollover noises, and sound effects that complement animation. Flash works with a variety of sound formats, including WAV, AIFF, and MP3 files. Under most circumstances, MP3 is the best format because it produces smaller files while maintaining excellent sound quality.

This chapter gives you a solid understanding of how to work with sounds in Flash 8, including how to import, compress, and control various properties of a sound file. You will learn how to change the format of sound using MP3 compression settings, how to create background sounds, and how to control sound using buttons. The last three exercises are also designed to provide real workflow scenarios where you will learn how to synchronize voice sound clips with an animation and how to control the volume of your sounds.

1 | Importing Sounds

In this exercise, you will learn how to import sound files into Flash 8. You'll also learn about the types of sound files you can import into Flash 8 and where they go when you import them.

---

1 Copy the **chap_14** folder from the **HOT CD-ROM** to your **Desktop**. Open a new file and save it as **basicSound.fla** in the **chap_14** folder.

---

2 Choose **File > Import > Import to Library**. Navigate to the **sounds** folder (also inside the **chap_14 folder**) and browse to the **soundsPC** folder if you are using a Windows machine or the **soundsMac** folder if you are using a Macintosh.

Note: If you choose File > Import > Import to Stage, the sound files will not be imported to the Stage but instead, will be imported into the Library.

TIP:	**I Don't See Any Files!**
	If you don't see any sounds in the list, make sure you select **Files of Type: All Files** in the **Import** dialog box rather than **Files of Type: All Formats**.

---

3 To import the sound files from inside the **soundsPC/soundsMac** folder:

Windows users:
Ctrl+click Free.wav, Lektropolis.wav, and **Space_Jam.wav** to select them, and click **Open** to import the sounds into Flash 8.

Mac users:
Cmd+click Free.aif, Lektropolis.aif, and **Space_Jam.aif** to select them, and click **Import** to import the sounds into Flash 8.

NOTE:	**What Kinds of Sounds Can I Import?**
	You can import a variety of sound files into Flash 8, depending on which platform you use and whether you have QuickTime 4 or later installed on your machine. If you have QuickTime 4 or later installed on your system, you can import additional sound file formats. The table that follows lists the types of sound file formats you can import into Flash 8.

Sound File Types Supported by Flash 8		
File Format	Windows	Mac
WAV	Yes	Yes, with QuickTime 4 or later installed
AIIF	Yes, with QuickTime 4 or later installed	Yes
MP3	Yes	Yes
Sound Designer II	No	Yes, with QuickTime 4 or later installed
Sound-only QuickTime movies	Yes, with QuickTime 4 or later installed	Yes, with QuickTime 4 or later installed
Sun Au	Yes, with QuickTime 4 or later installed	Yes, with QuickTime 4 or later installed
System 7 sounds	No	Yes, with QuickTime 4 or later installed

TIP: | **Where Did the Sounds Go?**

When you import an image, you will see the image on the Stage as soon as you click File > Import > Import to Stage. When you import a sound with this same command, however, it is not visible on the Stage. Instead, you must open the Library to view the sound files. You will do this next.

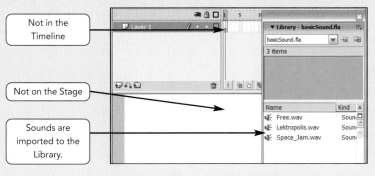

4 Press **Ctrl+L** (Windows) or **Cmd+L** (Mac) to open the **Library**. You will see the three sounds you just imported. Select each sound, one at a time, and click the **Play** button to listen to each one.

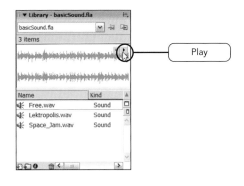

That's all there is to it! Importing sounds is easy. Working with them on the Timeline can be a bit more challenging. By the end of this chapter, you will get experience working with sounds on the Timeline, modifying and compressing sounds, and controlling sound volume with some simple ActionScript.

---

5 Save this file and keep it open for the next exercise. You will learn how to compress sounds inside of Macromedia Flash 8 next.

Now that you know how to import sounds into Flash 8, the next step is to learn how to compress them. Compressing sounds is especially important for keeping your file sizes as small as possible. Uncompressed sounds increase file sizes drastically, which can lead to a variety of playback problems. In this exercise, you will learn how to compress sound by using the MP3 compression setting in the Sound Properties dialog box.

1 If you just completed Exercise 1, **basicSound.fla** should still be open. If it's not, go back and complete Exercise 1.

2 In the **Library**, click the **Free.wav** (**Free.aif** on the Mac) sound to select it. Click the **Properties** button to open the **Sound Properties** dialog box. (You can also open the **Sound Properties** dialog box by double-clicking a file's sound icon in the **Library**.)

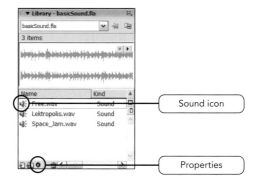

NOTE:

Sound Compression: Movie-wide or Individual?

In Flash 8, you have two general options for sound compression: You can set compression settings for all sounds in the movie in the Publish Settings dialog box, or you can set the compression settings for each sound file individually in the Library. You will learn next how to set sound compression in the Library. You will learn about the Publish settings in Chapter 17, "*Publishing and Exporting.*" Whenever possible, I recommend setting compression settings individually for each sound. The individual method usually takes more time and effort, but it produces better results because not all sounds are the same.

3 Notice the sound is large at its default compression setting: **2506.8 kB**. Choose **MP3** from the **Compression** pop-up menu

The MP3 compression setting offers the best compression rates and sound fidelity. Users with the Macromedia Flash 4 and later players can hear MP3 sounds.

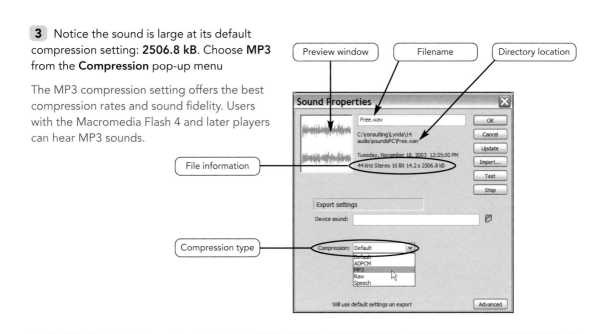

Sound Compression Defined

Option	Description
Default	This option uses the global compression settings in the Publish Settings dialog box. You will learn about the Publish settings in Chapter 17, "*Publishing and Exporting.*"
ADPCM	This compression model is an older method of compression from Macromedia Flash 3. It sets compression for 8-bit and 16-bit sound data. You may want to consider using this format if you need to author back to the Flash 3 Player.
MP3	Compatible with the Macromedia Flash 4 and later Players. It offers the best combination of high compression rates with good sound fidelity.
Raw	This format will resample the file at the specified rate but will not perform any compression.
Speech	This option uses a compression method designed specifically for speech sound files. You will work with this compression type in Exercise 5 of this chapter.

4 Choose **Bit Rate: 8 kbps**. Click the **Test** button to hear the sound with the new compression applied. Notice the file does not sound very good, but its file size has drastically decreased from the original **2506.8 kB** to **14.2 kB**.

Note: The lower the bit rate, the lower the sound quality and the lower the file size; the higher the bit rate, the higher the sound quality and the larger the file size.

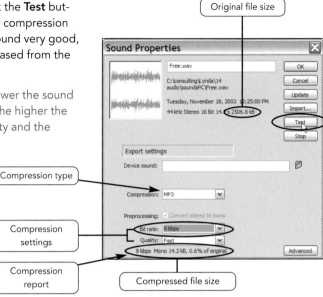

Original file size

Compression type

Compression settings

Compression report

Compressed file size

5 Choose **Bit Rate: 160 kbps** and deselect the **Preprocessing: Convert stereo to mono** option. Click the **Test** button to hear the sound again. Notice how much better the sound quality is at **160 kbps**. However, look at the file size: It has increased to **284.2 kB**. Although this is smaller than the original **2506.8 kB**, it is more than 20 times the size of the file at the **8 kbps** bit rate.

Note: The Preprocessing option is available only for bit rates of 20 kbps or higher. This feature, when selected, converts mixed stereo sounds to mono.

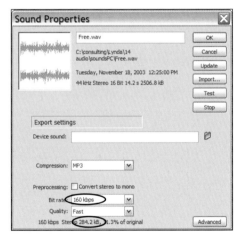

6 Choose **Bit Rate: 24 kbps** and make sure the **Preprocessing: Convert stereo to mono** option is deselected. Click the **Test** button to preview the sound. Notice the sound quality is not as good as before, but it's still acceptable. The file size has dropped to **42.6 kB**.

When you are working with sound files in Flash 8, you will want to test several bit-rate settings to determine which one offers the lowest file size without sacrificing sound quality. The best procedure is to start at a high or medium setting and to reduce settings until the sound quality is no longer acceptable for the purpose at hand. Once you reach the point where the sound quality is no longer acceptable, go back one step to the last acceptable setting and leave it there. You're done. This technique ensures you always achieve the best possible audio quality at the smallest possible file size.

7 Choose **Quality: Best**. Click the **Test** button. This takes a bit longer to convert the file to the MP3 format but the file will sound better and the file size will be the same. The only trade-off is that it will take longer to convert the file inside Flash 8. However, this is a small price to pay for much improved sound.

Note: Since the file size is the same (between Best and Fast), you will notice no difference in download time, although the Best sound will sound better.

8 When you are finished, click **OK** to accept the settings and close the **Sound Properties** dialog box.

To summarize, remember that the name of the game is to get the best possible sound at the smallest possible file size. Start with larger, better sounding files and keep reducing them until you finish with smaller files that still contain acceptable sound quality. Also, use the MP3 compression setting whenever possible because of its superior compression capabilities. With MP3 compression you have the best of both worlds with no extra effort: small file size with good sound quality.

9 Save your changes and close **basicSound.fla**.

You just learned how to import and compress sounds in Macromedia Flash 8. In the next exercise, you will learn how to work with background sound and sound effects.

Note: Once you produce the SWF file, users on both Windows and Mac machines will be able to hear the sound in your Flash 8 movie, and the sound's original format won't matter. The sound is compressed as ADPCM, MP3, Raw, or Speech when you create the SWF file, and these options are platform-independent.

3 | Creating Background Sound with Sound Effects

As you develop projects in Flash 8, you will find that some projects really come to life with the addition of some background audio. This exercise shows you how to add background sound, including how to use one of the sound effects in the Property Inspector. You will also be introduced to the Edit Envelope dialog box, which is a handy tool for customizing effects applied to your sound files.

---

1 Open **bkgdSound.fla** from the **chap_14** folder. Choose **View > Magnification > Show All** to see the whole image on the **Stage**.

Notice it contains one layer with a background image.

---

2 Press **Ctrl+L** (Windows) or **Cmd+L** (Mac) to open the **Library**.

Notice there are bitmaps, a graphic symbol, and some buttons but no sounds... yet.

---

3 On the main **Timeline**, click the **Insert Layer** button to add a new layer. Rename this new layer **sound** and make sure it is above the **background** layer.

TIP:	**Why Am I Making a New Layer for the Sound?**
	It is good practice to place sound files, like frame actions, on their own separate layer. This will separate the sound from other artwork and animation, letting you view the waveform (the picture of the sound) better and to work with the sound more easily.

4 Choose **File > Import > Import to Library**. Browse to the **mp3** folder inside the **sounds** folder inside the **chap_14** folder and select the **Hype.mp3** file. Click **Open** (Windows) or **Import** (Mac) to import the MP3 sound file.

Yet another great thing about MP3 files is that they work on both Macintosh and Windows machines.

---

5 After you import the sound, notice it gets added directly to the **Library**. Click the **Play** button to test the sound.

You will be adding this sound to the Timeline next.

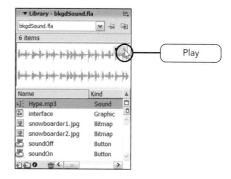

NOTE:

Audio in the Movie vs. Audio in the Library

Although the sound file has been successfully imported into the Flash 8 project file, it does not actually exist in the movie yet—it exists only in the Library. In order for the sound to be a part of the movie, you must add it to a keyframe on the Timeline.

6 With the first frame in the **sound** layer selected, drag the **Hype.mp3** sound out of the **Library** and drop it anywhere on the **Stage**. After you drop the sound, you will not see a representation of that sound anywhere on the **Stage**. However, the sound will appear on the **Timeline** in the form of a blue waveform, providing visual feedback that the sound is located there.

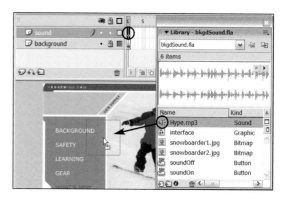

NOTE:

Adding Sounds to Keyframes

Sounds can only be added to keyframes. The best way to do this is to first create a blank keyframe in the Timeline where you want your sound to start playing. Select this keyframe and drag the sound from the Library and drop it anywhere on the Stage. Without first creating a keyframe, the sound will not go where you want it, but instead will attach itself to the last keyframe before the current location of the playhead.

7 Choose **Control > Test Movie** to preview the movie with the new sound added. You will hear the sound play once and stop. When you are finished, close the preview window.

---

8 In the **sound** layer, click **Frame 1** to select the sound. In the **Property Inspector**, notice the name of the sound displayed in the **Sound** pop-up menu and that the **Sync** option is set to **Event**.

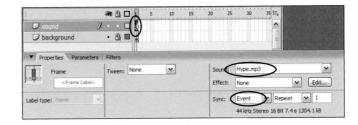

The Sync: Event setting causes the sound to start playing when the play-head reaches the frame that contains it. The sound will continue to play all the way to the end, independently of whatever is happening on the main Timeline—even if the main Timeline stops or is only one frame in length.

---

9 In the **Property Inspector**, choose **Stream** from the **Sync** pop-up menu.

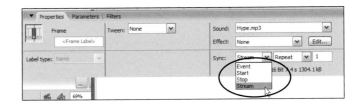

---

10 Choose **Control > Test Movie** to preview the movie.

This time you will not hear the sound at all. Why? Unlike the Event setting, the Stream setting stops the sound when the movie stops. So if you have only one frame in your movie, and you apply a Stream setting to a sound in the main Timeline, the sound will not play. Unlike Event sounds, Stream sounds play only within the frames they occupy.

---

11 Close the preview window when you are done previewing your movie.

Stream sounds have many benefits. These will be discussed in the table at the end of this exercise and again in Exercise 6, where you will synchronize Stream sounds to animation.

---

12 In the **Property Inspector**, choose **Sync: Start**.

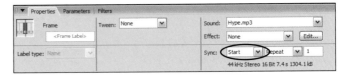

This setting is most often used for background sounds and is very similar to the Event setting. It causes the sound to begin playing as soon as the keyframe holding it is reached, and the sound will play to the end, independently of the main Timeline, just as an Event sound will. The difference is that if a Start sound is already playing, no new instance of the sound can be played, so only one version of the sound will play at a time.

With the Event setting, if an instance of the sound is playing and another instance is triggered, another version of the sound will start playing, resulting in the two sounds playing over each other.

The Start sound setting is useful when you have a layer with a sound that is already playing, and you don't want the new sound to begin until the currently playing sound has stopped. The Start setting prevents the sound from playing over itself. For a more detailed explanation of all the sound settings, see the "Modifying Sound Settings" section following this exercise.

13 Choose **Control > Test Movie** to preview the movie. With the **Start** sound setting, the sound will play just as it did with the **Event** setting. When you are finished, close the preview window. You will add basic sound effects in the following steps.

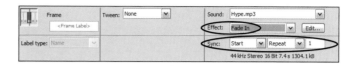

NOTE:

Testing Sounds

You can test all sounds using **Control > Test Movie**. You can also test sounds in the editing environment by pressing **Enter** (Windows) or **Return** (Mac), but this method has its limitations, since certain conditions must be met in order for the sound to play:

- When the main Timeline has only one frame, you cannot test sounds using Enter/Return.

- When the main Timeline has more than one frame, you can test Event and Start sounds using Enter (Windows) or Return (Mac), and they will play in their entirety (even if there are just two frames on the Timeline, but the sound takes 100 frames to play). You will learn more about Event, Start, and Stream sounds in the next steps of the exercise.

- When the main Timeline has more than one frame, you can test Stream sounds using Enter/Return. Use caution, however, because if there are not enough frames on the main Timeline to play the entire sound, or if another keyframe is encountered before the sound finishes, the sound will stop and be cut short. Stream sounds are tied directly to the main Timeline.

14 In the **Property Inspector**, choose **Effect: Fade In**. This will make the sound start out soft and gradually become louder. For the **Sync** setting, make sure **Start** is selected. Choose **Repeat** and enter **1** for the number of times the sound will repeat.

15 Choose **Control > Test Movie** to preview the sound settings you applied. Notice the sound fades in. Keep listening—the sound will repeat once and then stop. When the sound has stopped playing, close the preview window.

16 In the **Property Inspector**, choose **Loop** instead of **Repeat**.

This setting will make the sound play over and over continuously throughout the movie. The Start setting will not affect the overall file size, since the file is downloaded only once.

---

17 Choose **Control > Test Movie** to listen to the sound settings you applied. Notice the sound fades in, and continues to play over and over again (**Loop**) for as long as you have the preview window open. When you are done previewing the sound, close the preview window.

---

18 In the **Property Inspector**, click the **Edit** button to open the **Edit Envelope** dialog box.

In the Edit Envelope dialog box, you can edit your sound. Notice the Effect option is set to Fade In. This effect was created when you chose it from the pop-up list in the Sound panel of the Property Inspector.

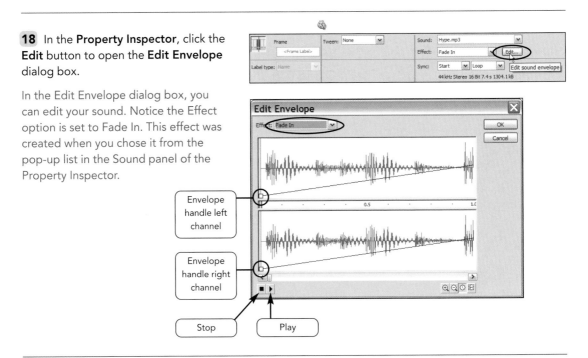

---

19 In the **Edit Envelope** dialog box, click the **Play** button to test the sound. Notice the sound starts out softly and gradually becomes louder. Click the **Stop** button. Experiment with moving the right and left envelope handles, which will change the way the sound fades into the right and left speakers. Click the **Play** button again to test it.

---

20 In the **Edit Envelope** dialog box, drag the **Time In** control to change the start point of the sound. Click the **Play** button again to test it. When you are happy with the way your adjustments sound, click **OK** to accept the settings.

Note that the **Effect:** setting changed from **Fade In** to **Custom** when you moved the **Time In** control.

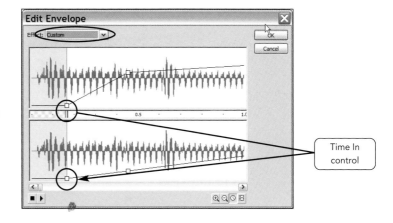

21 Choose **Control > Test Movie** to preview the movie again. You will hear the sound with your custom effects applied to it.

Tip: If you don't like the custom effects you created, rather than clicking **OK** in the **Edit Envelope** dialog box, you can either click **Cancel** or you can choose an **Effect** option other than **Custom** in the **Property Inspector**. This will reset the sound to the effect you choose.

22 Save **bkgdSound.fla** and keep it open for the next exercise.

You will learn how to control the sound with On and Off buttons in the next exercise.

Modifying Sound Settings

After you place an instance of a sound on the Timeline, you can use the settings in the Property Inspector to control the behavior of the sound, as you learned in this exercise. The following sections provide an in-depth look at the sound settings options.

Effect Option

The Effect option in the Property Inspector lets you choose preset effects you can apply to your sound. Choosing the Custom setting lets you create your own sound effects.

Sync Option

The Sync option in the Property Inspector lets you set the synchronization of the sound file in the movie. Each option controls the behavior of the sound on the Timeline.

Effect Options Explained

Option	Description
Left Channel	Plays only the left channel of a stereo sound
Right Channel	Plays only the right channel of a stereo sound
Fade Left to Right	Creates a panning effect by playing a stereo sound from the left channel to the right channel (or left speaker to right speaker)
Fade Right to Left	Creates a panning effect by playing a stereo sound from the right channel to the left channel (or right speaker to left speaker)
Fade In	Makes the sound gradually become louder as it begins to play
Fade Out	Makes the sound gradually become softer as it nears the end
Custom	Lets you create your own effects for the sound

Sync Options Explained

Option	Description
Event	Begins playing the sound when the playhead reaches the frame that holds the sound on the Timeline. Event sounds will continue to play independently, even if the Timeline stops. If a different instance of the same sound is started, the sounds will overlap. This option is good for short sounds, such as buttons clicks or quick sound effects.
Start	Behaves similarly to an Event sound, except that a second instance of the sound cannot be started until any currently playing instances have finished, which prevents the sound from overlapping itself. This option is good for background sound.
Stop	Stops the indicated sound. Use this feature if you have a sound in the main Timeline that spans 50 frames, for example, and is set to Start. The sound will play from start to finish, no matter what happens in the main Timeline. If you need the sound to stop at Frame 30, add the same sound to a keyframe in Frame 30 and set its sync to Stop. This will stop the Start sound (or an Event sound) from playing.
Stream	Forces the movie to keep pace with the sound. If the movie cannot download its frames fast enough to keep pace, the Flash Player forces it to skip frames. Stream sounds stop when the Timeline stops or when another keyframe is encountered on the same layer. One advantage to Stream sounds is that they begin to play before the entire sound file is downloaded, which is not the case for Event and Start sounds. Stream sounds are ideal for narration and animation.

Repeat/Loop Option

The Repeat option in the Property Inspector sets the number of times the sound will repeat. The Loop option sets the sound to play continuously. Repeating or looping Event or Start sounds has no effect on file size. However, use caution when you choose Sync: Stream because repeating or looping a Stream sound will cause Flash 8 to add frames for each loop, thereby increasing the file size significantly.

Edit Button

Clicking the Edit button in the Property Inspector opens the Edit Envelope dialog box, where you can edit your sound.

The Edit Envelope dialog box

In the Edit Envelope dialog box, you can change the effect of the sound, change the start and end points of a sound, modify the envelope handles to change the volume of the sound, test the sound, view the sound using seconds or frames, and zoom in and out to see more or less of the sound wave.

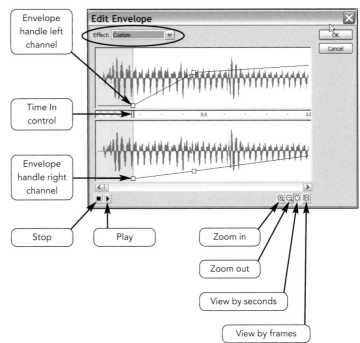

4 | Controlling Sound with On/Off Buttons

Even though you like the audio you've chosen for the background sound of your movie, certain users may not want to listen to it. It's always good practice to enable users as much playback control as possible. This exercise teaches you how to add sound controls to your movie so users can stop and play the sound. Later, you will learn how to add additional controls for letting users adjust the volume of your sound elements.

1 Open **soundOnOff_Final.fla** from the **chap_14** folder.

2 Choose **Control >Test Movie** to preview the movie. Click the **sound off** button to stop the sound. Click the **sound on** button to start it again. Cool! You will be creating this movie in the steps that follow. When you are finished, close the preview window and **soundOnOff_Final.fla**.

3 Open **bkgdSound.fla** from the **chap_14** folder (it it's not still open from the last exercise). Save the file as **soundOnOff.fla** inside the **chap_14** folder.

4 Select the **sound** layer on the **Timeline**. In the **Property Inspector**, make sure **Sync** is set to **Start**, choose **Repeat**, and type **5**.

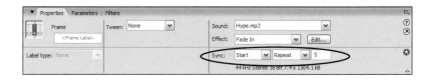

These settings will make the sound fade in, play independently of the Timeline, and repeat five times.

Tip: If you want the sound to play continuously, looping over and over, select **Loop** instead of **Repeat**.

5 On the **Timeline**, click the **Insert Layer** button to add a new layer and rename it **buttons**. Click and drag the **buttons** layer below the **sound** layer.

6 Open the **Library** and notice there are two buttons inside: one named **soundOn** and one named **soundOff**. These are basic rollover buttons that we created ahead of time for you. Select **Frame 1** of the **buttons** layer and drag an instance of each button to the location on the **Stage** shown here.

Now that you have added the buttons to the movie, you will add ActionScript and behaviors to the buttons that make the sound stop playing or begin playing.

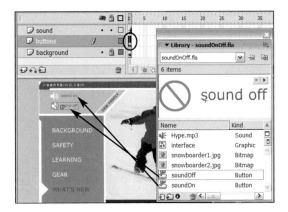

7 Choose **Window > Behaviors** to open the **Behaviors** panel. Select the **sound off** button on the **Stage**. In the **Behaviors** panel, click the **Add Behavior** button and choose **Sound > Stop All Sounds** to open the **Stop All Sounds** dialog box.

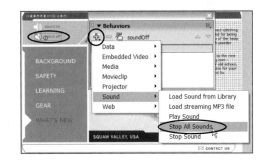

8 In the **Stop All Sounds** dialog box, click **OK** to accept that this behavior will stop all sounds from playing.

This behavior will stop any sounds that are currently playing on the Timeline.

9 Choose **Control > Test Movie** to test the **sound off** button. Notice the sound stops playing after you click the **sound off** button. Nice! Close the preview window when you are finished previewing your movie.

Now that the sound off button is working, next you'll get the sound on button working. Since there is no playAllSounds behavior, getting the sound to play again is a little trickier, but the following steps will get your sound on button working in no time!

Testing Behaviors and Scripts

It's always good practice to test your movie immediately after adding a new behavior or line of ActionScript.

10 On the **Timeline**, add a new layer and name it **actions**. Make sure the **actions** layer is above all the other layers. You are going to add a **stop** action to the **Timeline**, but first you will add frames to the **Timeline**.

11 On the **Timeline**, click **Frame 2** of the **actions** layer, then **Shift+click Frame 2** of the **background** layer to select **Frame 2** of all the layers at once. Press **F5** to add a frame to each layer. You need to have a least two frames on the **Timeline** for the next technique to work.

12 Select **Frame 2** of the **actions** layer and press **F7** to add a blank keyframe. Press **F9** (Windows) or **Option+F9** (Mac) to open the **Actions** panel. Click the **Script Assist** button to switch to **Script Assist** mode. Select **Global Functions > Timeline Control** and double-click the **stop** action to add it to the **Script** pane. This action tells the **playhead** to stop when it gets to **Frame 2**.

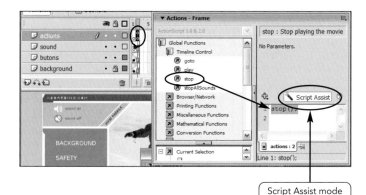

Script Assist mode enabled

Why add the **stop** action on the Timeline? Even though you have added ActionScript to stop all sounds, the main Timeline is still going to loop by default. To prevent it from doing this, you added a **stop** action to Frame 2. Keep in mind that the sound file will not stop, since event and start sounds are independent of the main Timeline. So even though you stop the Timeline at Frame 2, the sound will keep playing until you click the sound off button. You will add the necessary ActionScript to the Play button next.

13 On the **Stage**, click the **sound on** button to select it. In the **Actions** panel, select **Global Functions > Movie Clip Control** and double-click the **on** action to add it to the **Script** pane. Select **Event: Release**.

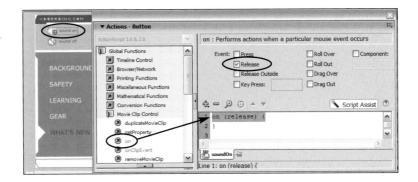

14 With the previous line of script still selected in the **Script** pane, select **Global Functions > Timeline Control** and double-click the **play** action to add it to the **Script** pane. This action tells the **playhead** to move to the next frame, which is **Frame 1**, causing the sound to begin to playing again.

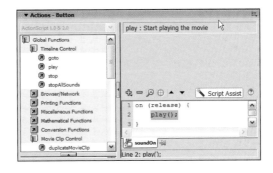

When the movie begins, the sound also starts playing because the sound starts on Frame 1. The play-head moves on to Frame 2 and encounters a **stop** frame action, which tells the playhead to stop. Since the Sync is set to Start, the sound will continue to play although the Timeline has stopped at Frame 2. When you click the sound off button, the sound will stop playing. When you click the sound on button, the ActionScript instructs the playhead to play. The playhead will move on to the next frame, in this case to Frame 1, and play the sound again. This is why you needed to add frames in Step 11.

15 Choose **Control > Test Movie** to preview the movie again. Click the **sound off** button and then click the **sound on** button.

Notice how the sound immediately stops when you click the sound off button and starts over again when you click the sound on button. You have successfully added a background sound to your movie with stop and play controls!

16 Close the preview window and close **soundOnOff.fla**. You do not need to save your changes.

5 | Compression Settings for Narration

You can control sound in Flash 8 so that it synchronizes with animation, such as narration or a sound effect that matches a character's movement. This exercise shows you how to import and compress sounds using speech compression and how to set the Stream Sync option so that voice sound files synchronize with animation. You will also learn how to modify the Timeline for easier editing.

---

1 Open **soundSync_Final.fla** from the **chap_14** folder. This is a finished version of the file you will create in the next two exercises. Choose **Control > Test Movie** to preview the movie.

Notice the narration voice is synchronized perfectly with the animation. You will create this same effect in the following steps.

---

2 When you are finished previewing the movie, close this file.

---

3 Open the **soundSync.fla** file from the **chap_14** folder.

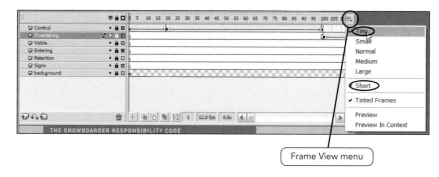

Frame View menu

We created this file to get you started. Notice the seven layers in the main Timeline. The top six layers hold different parts of the animation, and the bottom layer holds a background image. Scrub (click and drag) the playhead back and forth to see the letters animate. In a few steps, you will be adding the voice sound clips to the Timeline and deciding where each sound should begin.

Tip: Since there are a lot of frames in the main Timeline, you can change the frame view temporarily by clicking the **Frame View** menu and choosing **Tiny** and **Short**, which will let you see more frames at once on the Timeline.

You can also expand/contract the Timeline by clicking and dragging the bottom of the Timeline.

Click and drag to expand the Timeline.

4 On the main **Timeline**, click the **Insert Layer** button to add a new layer. Rename the layer **sounds**. Drag the **sounds** layer so that it is on top of all the other layers.

You will import the sound files next.

5 Choose **File > Import > Import to Library**. Open the **chap_14** folder. Inside the **sounds** folder, open the **codeSounds** folder. **Shift+click** to select all the sounds and click **Open** to import them.

6 Press **Ctrl+L** (Windows) or **Cmd+L** (Mac) to open the **Library**. Click **Kind** (Windows) or **Type** (Mac) to organize the **Library** assets by type instead of by alphabetical order. Notice the six sounds are now in the **Library**. Select the **control** sound and click the **Play** button to test it. Select the other sounds in the **Library** and click the **Play** button to test those as well.

You will change the compression setting of the sounds next.

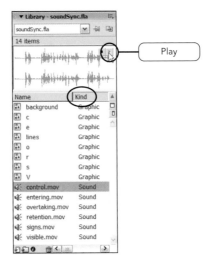

7 Select the **control** sound and click the **Properties** button at the bottom of the screen to open the **Sound Properties** dialog box.

Tip: You can also double-click a file's sound icon to open the Sound Properties dialog box.

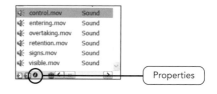

Properties

---

8 Notice the sound is large at its default compression setting: **1517.0 K**. From the **Compression** pop-up menu, choose **Speech**. From the **Sample rate** pop-up menu, choose **22kHz**. Click the **Test** button to test the sound.

Notice the sound quality is pretty good. However, you may be able to squeeze more audio information out of this file without adversely affecting its sound quality. In the next steps, you'll keep reducing the sample rate until the audio quality is no longer acceptable, and then undo the last reduction.

Original file size uncompressed

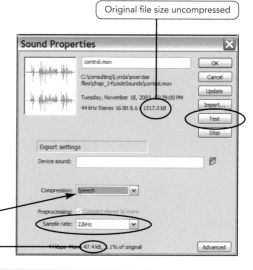

Compression type

Compressed file size

---

9 Choose **Sample rate: 11kHz** and click the **Test** button. Notice the file size has been reduced to only **23.7 kB** and that the sound quality is still pretty good. Let's keep reducing.

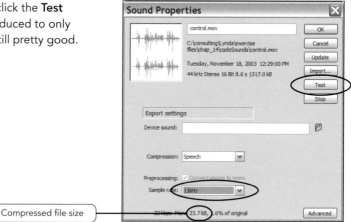

Compressed file size

---

10 Choose **Sample rate: 5kHz** and click the **Test** button. Notice although the file size has been reduced to only **11.9 K**, the sound quality is so bad, it is no longer acceptable. You have gone too far and need to set it back to the last acceptable setting, which was **11kHz**.

You have managed to reduce the file to 23.7 kB from an original size of 1500 kB, which is a substantial savings.

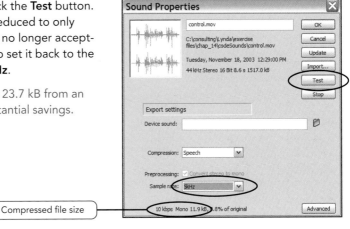

Compressed file size

---

11 Set the **Sample rate** back to **11kHz**.

As you heard for yourself, 11kHz is the recommended sample rate for speech, providing the best combination of small file size and acceptable sound quality.

Speech compression is specifically adapted to speech sounds. The sample rate controls sound fidelity and file size; the lower the sample rate, the smaller the file size and the lower the sound quality.

---

12 In the **Library**, change each of the remaining five sound's compression settings in the **Sound Properties** dialog box. For each sound, choose **Compression: Speech** and **Sample rate: 11kHz**. Click **OK**.

---

13 Save **soundSync.fla** and keep it open for the next exercise.

---

6 | Synchronizing Sound to Narration Cues

In the previous exercise, you learned how to compress sounds using the speech compression setting. This exercise shows you how to use the stream sync option and how to work with the main Timeline so that voice sound files synchronize with animation.

1 If you just completed Exercise 5, **soundSync.fla** should still be open. If it's not, go back and complete Exercise 5. On the **Timeline**, select **Frame 1** on the **sounds** layer. From the **Library**, drag an instance of the **control** sound onto the **Stage**. Notice the waveform on the **Timeline**.

Next, you will adjust the height of the sounds layer to make it easier to work with.

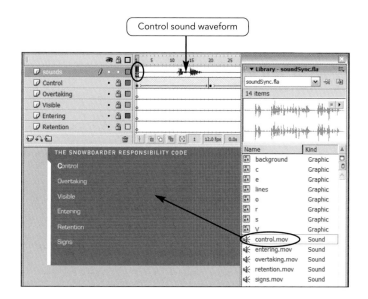

Control sound waveform

2 Double-click the **layer** icon next to the **sounds** layer name to open the **Layer Properties** dialog box.

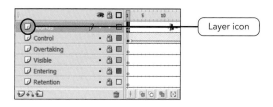

Layer icon

3 In the **Layer Properties** dialog box, choose **200%** from the **Layer height** pop-up menu, and click **OK**. This will make the **sounds** layer taller than all the rest of the layers on the **Timeline,** making it easier to see the waveform.

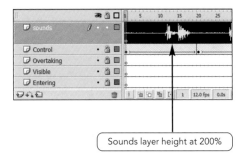

Sounds layer height at 200%

Tip: You can also access the Layer Properties dialog box by choosing **Modify > Timeline > Layer Properties**.

---

4 Select **Frame 1** on the **sounds** layer. In the **Property Inspector**, choose **Sync: Stream** and **Repeat: 0**.

The Stream setting forces the movie to keep pace with the sound. If the movie cannot download its frames fast enough to keep pace, Flash forces it to skip frames.

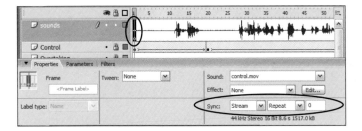

---

5 Choose **Control > Test Movie** to test the sound and the animation.

The sound will play in synchronization with the animation. You will add the remaining sounds to the Timeline in the following steps, but first you'll learn how to change the appearance of the Timeline to see more layers.

TIP: | **Streaming and Looping**

Be careful about setting your sound's Sync to Stream and adding loops. Unlike the Event and Start settings, Stream causes the file size to increase for each loop you specify. If you can avoid it, try not to loop sounds that are set to the Stream setting.

6 On the **Timeline**, click the **Frame View** menu and choose **Normal** and **Short** so you can see more of the layers on the **Timeline**.

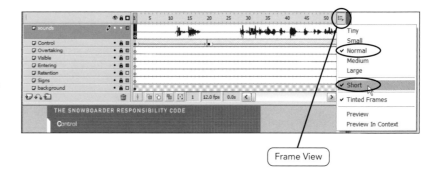

Frame View

---

7 Scrub the playhead back and forth to identify where the *O* animation begins on the **Overtaking** layer. Notice this happens at about **Frame 101**.

You want the overtaking sound clip to start where the *O* animation begins. You will do this next.

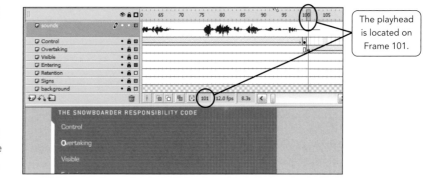

The playhead is located on Frame 101.

---

8 On the **sounds** layer, select **Frame 101** and press **F7** to add a blank keyframe.

You will add the overtaking sound next.

---

9 In the **Property Inspector**, choose **overtaking.mov** from the **Sound** pop-up menu. This will add the **overtaking** sound to **Frame 101**. Choose **Sync: Stream**, **Repeat**, and **0**.

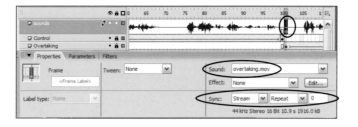

Flash 8 lets you conveniently access sounds inside the movie's Library from the Sound pop-up list in the Property Inspector, which lets you quickly access all the sounds in your Library. You can even switch the sound located in a keyframe by selecting a different sound from the pop-up list.

Adding Sound to the Timeline

In this chapter, you have learned two ways to add sounds to the Timeline. You can drag an instance of the sound onto the Stage, or you can select the frame on the Timeline and then choose a sound from the pop-up Sound list in the Property Inspector. Both workflow methods yield the same result—decide which works best for you.

10 Repeat Steps 7 and 8 to add blank keyframes on the **sounds** layer where each new letter animation begins.

Hint: Each animation is 100 frames long, so place a blank keyframe at the beginning of each new animation: **Frames 201, 301, 401,** and **501.**

---

11 Repeat Step 9 for each of the blank keyframes you just added to attach the appropriate sound.

Hint: Frame 201 (**visible** sound), Frame 301 (**entering** sound), Frame 401 (**retention** sound), and Frame 501 (**signs** sound).

---

12 Test the movie again. Notice some of the sounds are cut short when a new animation begins. Why? This is because some sound files are longer than others. As you can hear, **Stream** sounds will stop as soon as another keyframe or blank keyframe is encountered in the same layer.

In the following steps, you will fix the sound files so they don't get cut short. Now here's where real workflow issues come in to play. Depending on how you plan out your project, you can either lay out the animation on the Timeline first (as this file has been prepared), or you can lay out the sound on the Timeline first. Either way, you will still have to figure out just where the animations should start and finish according to the sounds. So, from this point forward, not only will you become more acquainted with sounds and their settings, but you will be much more comfortable moving frames around on the Timeline.

---

13 On the **sounds** layer, click and drag **Frame 201** (with the **visible** sound) to the right to **Frame 240.** Notice as you do, the sound wave in the previous frame (the **overtaking** sound) continues until **Frame 231.** This means that the **overtaking** sound

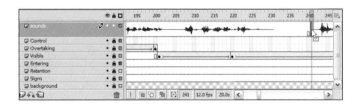

is not 100 frames long, as the animation is. Instead, it is 131 frames long. Therefore, in order for the animation and the sound file to span the same duration, you need to make them match. You will do this next by moving the frames on the **Timeline.**

Note: As you learned in Exercise 3, Stream sounds play only within the frames they occupy. So, in order to hear the sound in its entirety, you will extend the Timeline for each sound.

---

14 Click and drag **Frame 240** back to **Frame 232**, just after the **overtaking** sound wave ends on the **Timeline**, which will start the next sound (**visible**) after the **overtaking** sound ends, without cutting it off.

Note: As soon as the playhead encounters another Stream sound on the Timeline, the previous Stream sound will stop, and the new Stream sound will play.

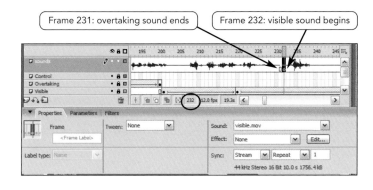

Frame 231: overtaking sound ends

Frame 232: visible sound begins

You will move the frames in the overtaking layer so the animation and sound are in sync next.

---

15 Click and drag the last keyframe in the **Overtaking** layer to **Frame 231**, which will make the **Overtaking** animation and the sound narration end together.

You will synchronize the visible animation to the visible sound in the following steps.

Note: You can move the frames in the Overtaking layer while it is locked, but you cannot move its artwork on the Stage.

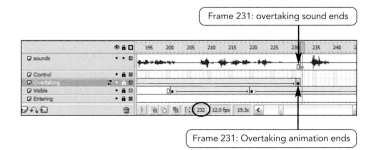

Frame 231: overtaking sound ends

Frame 231: Overtaking animation ends

---

16 Notice the **visible** sound begins on **Frame 232**. Click the **Visible** layer to select all the frames on that layer. Click and drag all the frames to the right at once, so that the tween now begins on **Frame 232**, at the same point the **visible** sound begins.

You will move the last keyframe in the Visible layer so that the animation and sound end together next.

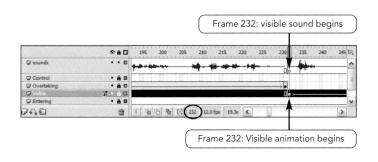

Frame 232: visible sound begins

Frame 232: Visible animation begins

---

17 Notice the **visible** sound ends on **Frame 351**. Click the last keyframe in the **Visible** layer and drag it to **Frame 351**, which will make the **Visible** animation and **visible** sound end together.

You will synchronize the entering animation to the entering sound in the following steps.

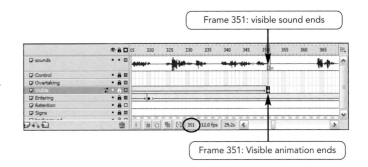

Frame 351: visible sound ends

Frame 351: Visible animation ends

18 Notice the **entering** sound begins on **Frame 352**. Click the **Entering** layer to select all the frames on that layer. Click and drag all the frames to the right at once, so the tween now begins on **Frame 352**.

You will move the last keyframe in the Entering layer so that the animation and sound end together next.

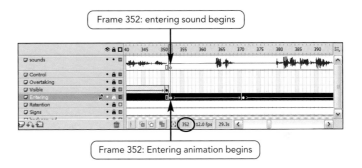

Frame 352: entering sound begins

Frame 352: Entering animation begins

19 Notice the **entering** sound ends on **Frame 451**. Click the last keyframe in the **Entering** layer and drag it to **Frame 451**, at the same point that the **entering** sound ends, which will make the **Entering** animation and **entering** sound end together.

You will synchronize the retention animation to the retention sound in the following steps, but first you'll test your movie.

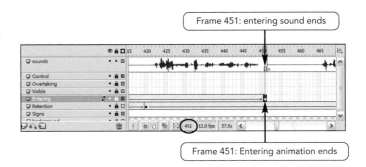

Frame 451: entering sound ends

Frame 451: Entering animation ends

20 Choose **Control > Test Movie**. Notice the sounds and the animations to the first few letters are now synchronized, and the sounds are not cut short!

You will complete the rest of the movie in the following steps.

21 Notice the **retention** sound begins on **Frame 452**. Click the **Retention** layer to select all the frames on that layer. Click and drag all the frames to the right at once, so that the tween now begins on **Frame 452**.

You will move the last keyframe in the Retention layer so that the animation and sound end together next.

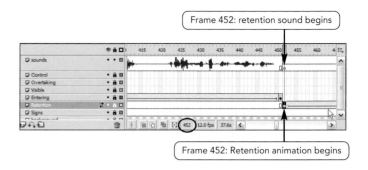

Frame 452: retention sound begins

Frame 452: Retention animation begins

22 Notice the **retention** sound ends on **Frame 581**. Click the last keyframe in the **Retention** layer and drag it to **Frame 581**, which will make the **Retention** animation and **retention** sound end together.

You will synchronize the Signs animation to the signs sound in the following steps.

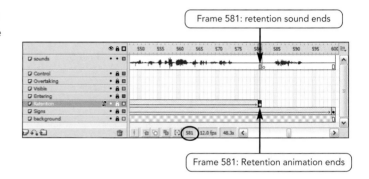

Frame 581: retention sound ends

Frame 581: Retention animation ends

23 Notice the **signs** sound begins on **Frame 582**. Click the **Signs** layer to select all the frames on that layer. Click and drag all the frames to the right at once, so that the tween now begins on **Frame 582**.

Next, you will move the last keyframe in the Signs layer so that the animation and sound end together.

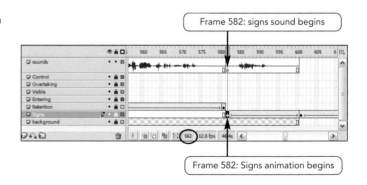

Frame 582: signs sound begins

Frame 582: Signs animation begins

24 Notice the **signs** sound ends on **Frame 630**. Click the last keyframe in the **Signs** layer and drag it to **Frame 630**, which will make the **Signs** animation and **signs** sound end together.

You will clean up the Timeline next. When you are done, you will have a movie with perfectly synchronized narration and animation!

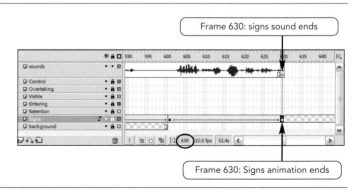

Frame 630: signs sound ends

Frame 630: Signs animation ends

25 On the **background** layer, select **Frame 630** and press **F5** to add frames, which will make the **background** layer visible throughout the entire movie.

You will delete the extra frames in the Signs layer next.

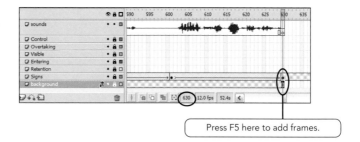

Press F5 here to add frames.

26 In the **Signs** layer, click and drag to select all the remaining frames after **Frame 630**. **Right-click** (Windows) or **Ctrl+click** (Mac) and choose **Remove Frames** from the contextual menu, which will clean up the **Timeline** by removing all the selected frames.

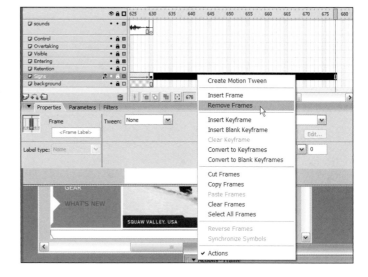

27 Choose **Control > Test Movie** again to preview the movie and double-check that all the animations and sounds are synced together.

28 When you are finished, save **soundSync.fla** and keep it open for one more exercise.

7 | Controlling Animation and Sound with Stop and Play Buttons

In the previous exercise, you learned how to sync the sound with the animation. This exercise takes the project file one step further. You will add Stop and Play buttons from the Common Libraries that ship with Flash 8, and make the animation and the sound stop at the same time.

---

1 If you just completed Exercise 6, **soundSync.fla** should still be open. If it's not, go back and complete Exercise 6. Choose **File > Save As** to rename the file as **SoundAnimCtrl.fla** in the **chap_14** folder

---

2 In the main **Timeline**, click the **Insert Layer** button to add a new layer. Rename the new layer **buttons** and place it below the **sounds** layer.

You will add Stop and Play buttons to the Stage from the Common Libraries in the following steps.

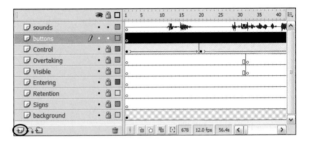

---

3 Choose **Window > Common Libraries > Buttons** to open the **Buttons Library**. Double-click the **Playback** folder to expand it.

Note: In the Common Libraries that ship with Flash 8, you will find premade buttons and sounds you can quickly add to your Flash movies.

---

4 Select **Frame 1** in the **buttons** layer. Drag an instance of the **playback – stop** and **playback – play** buttons from the **Buttons Library** to the **Stage**.

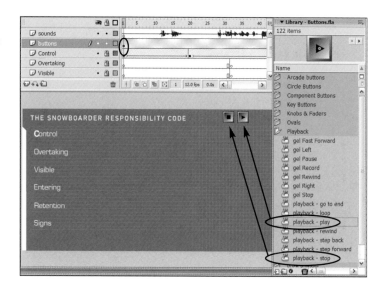

5 Press **Ctrl+L** (Windows) or **Cmd+L** (Mac) to open the **Library**. Notice the two buttons you just added from the **Buttons Library** are now in the **Library** of your project file.

You will add the ActionScript to the **Stop** button on the **Stage** next.

6 On the **Stage**, click the **Stop** button instance to select it. Press **F9** (Windows) or **Option+F9** (Mac) to open the **Actions** panel. Click the **Script Assist** button to enable **Script Assist** mode. Select **Global Functions > Movie Clip Control** and double-click the **on** action to add it to the **Script** pane. Select **Event: Release**.

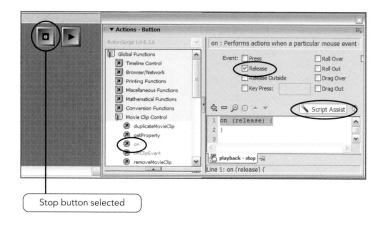

Stop button selected

7 With the first line of the script still selected in the **Script** pane, select **Global Functions > Timeline Control** and double-click the **stop** action to add it to the **Script** pane. This script tells the **playhead** to stop when the user clicks the **Stop** button.

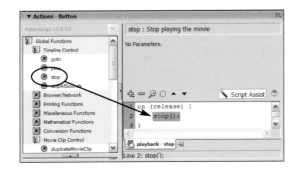

8 Choose **Control > Test Movie** to test the **Stop** button.

Notice when you click the Stop button, the sound and the animation stop at the same time. Cool! You will add the ActionScript to the Play button next.

9 With the **Stop** button still selected on the **Stage**, select all three lines of ActionScript for the **Stop** button in the **Script** pane. **Right-click** (Windows) or **Ctrl+click** (Mac) and choose **Copy** from the contextual menu.

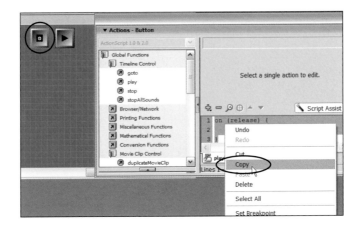

10 Select the **Play** button on the **Stage**. In the **Actions** panel, **right-click** (Windows) or **Ctrl+click** (Mac) in the **Script** pane and choose **Paste** from the contextual menu.

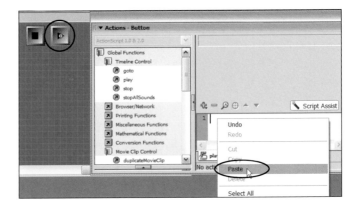

11 In the **Actions** window, click the **Script Assist** button to exit **Script Assist** mode. In the **Script** pane, change **stop** to **play**.

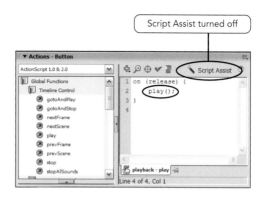

Script Assist turned off

12 Choose **Control > Test Movie** to test the movie again. Click the **Stop** button and notice the sound and animation stop at the same time. Click the **Play** button and notice the sound and animation begin playing at the same time and pick up where they last ended.

The ActionScript you added to the buttons in this exercise instructs the playhead to either stop or play, and since the sound Sync is set to Stream, the sounds will stop anytime the playhead stops. Stream sounds are dependent on the Timeline.

13 When you are finished, close the preview window and close **SoundAnimCtrl.fla**. You do not need to save your changes.

Now that you have learned how to import audio files into Flash and compress them, sync them up to animations on the Timeline and start and stop them, it is now time to learn how to control the volume of these sounds. You will learn how to do this in the next exercise.

8 | Adding Volume Control

Now that you know how to add sound to your Flash 8 movies and how to stop and play them, you will expand your Flash 8 skills by learning how to add volume control through ActionScript. Controls are an important component for any project containing sound so users can adjust their own volume settings.

---

1 Open **volumeCntrl_Final.fla** file inside the **chap_14** folder. This is the finished version of the movie you are going to script.

---

2 Choose **Control > Test Movie** to preview the movie. Notice the **Hi**, **Med**, and **Low** volume buttons at the top of the interface. Click the buttons to adjust the volume of the background sound up and down. To stop the sound from playing, click the red **sound off** button. To play the sound again, click the **sound on** button. Cool! When you are finished, close the preview window.

---

3 Open **volumeCntrl.fla** inside the **chap_14** folder. This file looks the same as the final version you just closed, but does not contain any of the ActionScripting required to get the volume buttons working. You will add the needed scripting in this exercise. Notice the volume button in the **Library** and a layer labeled **volButns**, where three instances of this button have been placed.

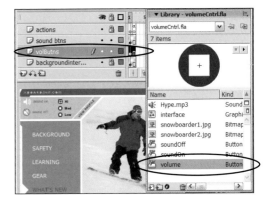

The first thing you need to do to set up volume control of a sound is to create a global sound object using ActionScripting. Once you've created and named a sound object, you associate, or link, a sound file to it in the Library. After you've named and linked the sound object, it is ready to be controlled with ActionScript. You can use ActionScript to play, stop, pan and control a variety of other sound properties, but you will restrict its use in this exercise to just controlling sound volume.

---

4 In the **actions** layer, select **Frame 2**. Press **F9** (Windows) or **Option+F9** (Mac) to open the **Actions** panel. Make sure the **Script Assist** mode is off. In the **Script** pane, place the cursor after the semicolon in the first line and press **Enter** (Windows) or **Return** (Mac) to bring the cursor down to the second line.

Script Assist is off.

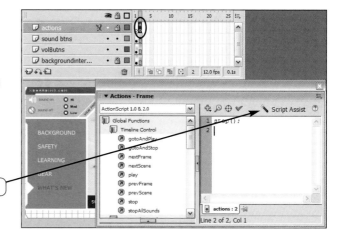

5 Type **soundObject1** as the name for you new sound object followed by an equals sign (**=**).

You can use any name here, but it is good practice to use a short, descriptive name that will help you understand this script later, after you have forgotten its details. In this case, I used a simple name followed by a number, since I can create as many sound objects as I need.

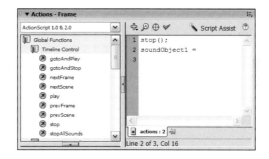

6 In the **Actions** pane, select **Action Script 2.0 Classes > Media > Sound** and double-click the **new Sound** action to add it to the **Script** pane. Place your cursor after the closing parenthesis and add a semicolon (**;**). Press **Enter** (Windows) or **Return** (Mac) to bring the cursor down to the next line.

The **new Sound** action can accept an optional parameter, the name of a movie

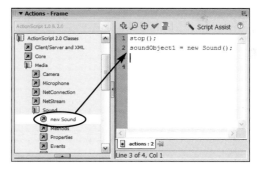

clip, between the parentheses, so Flash will place the cursor here waiting for you to add the movie clip name. By not specifying a movie clip at this time, you create a sound object that controls all sounds on the Timeline. This is just the situation you want, so leave the parameter blank. Next, you will attach a sound from the Library to your new sound object.

7 In the **Library**, select the **Hype.mp3** sound file. From the **Options** pop-up menu, choose **Linkage** to open up the **Linkage Properties** dialog box.

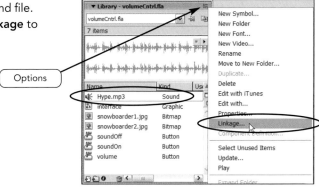

8 In the **Identifier** field, type the name **linkSound** to identify your linked sound. In the **Linkage** section, make sure the **Export for ActionScript** and **Export in first frame** options (the default) are selected. Click **OK**.

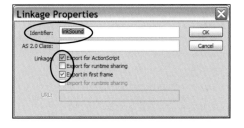

Again, you can enter any unique Identifier name here, but it's best to use a short, descriptive label to help you identify this name in your scripts. The Export for ActionScript option commands Flash to export the selected sound in the SWF file using your unique identifier name so it's available when called by the sound object. Next, you will use this label to attach the sound object to a Library sound.

NOTE:

More About Sound Objects

Flash sound objects are a bit abstract, but they are such useful and powerful tools that they deserve a bit more explanation here.

The first thing you need to know is that a sound object is not the actual sound used in the Flash file, but it is simply a reference to the sound resources you will be using. Think of it as a translator between a sound's properties, such as volume, balance, or duration, and the actual sound in the Library. ActionScript attaches the sound resource to the Flash movie at runtime. Sound objects make it possible to dynamically play sounds anytime, anywhere because they eliminate the restriction of placing sounds in keyframes on a Timeline.

A sound object is composed of three elements:

- A sound file from the Library.

- The sound instance created with the **new Sound ()** script (referred to as a *constructor function*).

- A **MovieClip** object or Timeline that stores the attached sound file.

continues on next page

More About Sound Objects *continued*

You may recall that in step 6 of this exercise, you left off the **MovieClip** parameter in the constructor function. If you are controlling only one sound with ActionScript in your movie, like you do in this exercise, eliminating the movie clip reference will not cause any problems. However, if you need to control multiple sound objects, you will need to store all your attached sound files in **MovieClip** objects.

For more information on this topic, see Appendix B, in particular the books listed about ActionScripting.

9 If it is not already selected, select the second frame of the **actions** layer. In the **Actions Panel**, place your cursor in the **Script** pane on the third line of the script. In the **Actions** pane, select **ActionScript 2.0 Classes > Media > Sound > Methods** and double-click the **attachSound** action to add it to the **Script** pane. Change **not_set_yet** to **soundObject1** (the name of your sound object). With your cursor between the parentheses, type the unique identifier name,

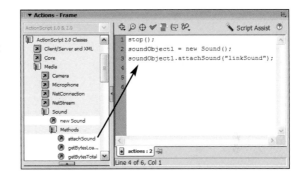

linkSound, within the quotation marks. After the closing parenthesis, type a semicolon (;) and bring the cursor to the next line. Your script pane should now match the one here.

It is critical that you enter the identifier name within quotation marks so Flash understands that you are referring to the literal name of the identifier and not an ActionScript expression. Now that you have a sound object attached to a sound in the Library, you can control it with some simple ActionScript! In the next step, you will start by writing a line of script to play the sound file.

10 In the **Actions** pane, select **ActionScript 2.0 Classes > Media > Sound > Methods** and double-click the **start** action to add it to the **Script** pane. Change **not_set_yet** to **soundObject1**. Between the parentheses after **start**, type **0, 999**. After the closing parenthesis, type a semicolon (**;**) and bring the cursor to the next line. Your script pane should now match the illustration here.

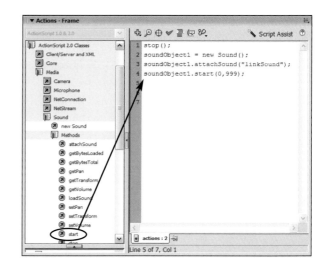

The **start()** method takes two parameters. The first, **soundOffset**, establishes how many seconds, from its beginning, the sound will start playing. You set the sound to play from the very beginning (0 seconds). The **Loops** parameter will loop the sound playback 999 times, essentially playing it indefinitely. Let's now test the scripts you have written so far.

11 Choose **Control > Test Movie** to preview the movie. The background music starts playing automatically and loops repeatedly. When you are done testing the movie, close the preview window.

Now that you have the background sound playing via the sound object, you can add the scripts to control its volume, which you will do in the next several steps.

TIP: | **Test After Each New Line of Script**

Normally, you would test a script after each new line of script. With this particular script however, there is not much to check after adding the two lines beyond the **stop** action. The sound **start** line, however, is a convenient point to check the progress of your script. If the sound plays, all is well. If not, take this opportunity, while the script is still short and simple, to go back to the start of the exercise and double-check your work.

---

12 On the **Stage**, click the **Hi** button to select it (not the label, but the button itself). In the **Property Inspector**, type **hiVolume_btn** in the **Instance Name** field, which assigns a unique instance name to the button so you can reference it with ActionScript.

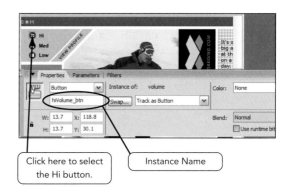

Click here to select the Hi button.

Instance Name

13 Repeat Step 12 to assign the instance names **medVolume_btn** and **lowVolume_btn** to the **Med** and **Low** volume button instances, respectively.

You are now ready to add ActionScript to control the sound object volume, which you will do in the next step.

Tip: Buttons (and movie clips) need to be individually identified before you can reference them with ActionScript. Establishing instance names is the only way to accomplish this, so it is critical that you give the buttons unique instance names at this point in your workflow. In fact, it's good practice to always name button and movie clip instances immediately after creating them.

---

14 In the **actions** layer, select **Frame 2**. In the **Actions** panel, place your cursor in the **Script** pane below the last line and press **Enter** (Windows) or **Return** (Mac) to add an extra line in the script. In the **Actions** pane, select **ActionScript 2.0 Classes > Movie > Movie Clip > Events** (**Event Handlers** on the Mac) and double-click the **onRelease** action to add it to the **Script** pane.

15 Change **not_set_yet** to the name of the button instance, **hiVolume_btn**. Place the cursor at the end of the line (after the opening curly brace) and press Enter (Windows) or **Return** (Mac) to move the cursor down to the next line. The cursor should be automatically indented and your **Script** pane should now match the illustration here.

Cursor is indented.

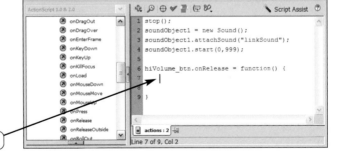

16 In the **Actions** pane, select **ActionScript 2.0 Classes > Media > Sound > Methods** and double-click the **setVolume** action to add it to the **Script** pane. Change **not_set_yet** to **soundObject1**. Between the parentheses after **setVolume**, type **0** (zero). After the closing parenthesis, type a semicolon (;).

This line should stay indented.

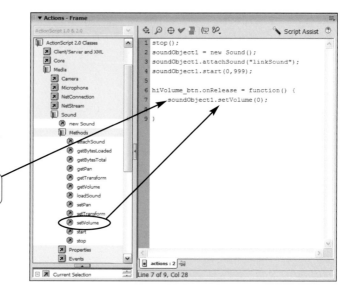

17 Choose **Control > Test Movie** to preview the movie and test this last line of script. The background music starts playing. Click the **Hi** volume button. If you no longer hear the music after clicking the button, the script is working! If Flash gives you an error or you hear no change in the sound volume, check your scripts carefully against the ones here, making any needed corrections, and test the movie again. When finished previewing the movie, close the preview window.

The music stops when you click the Hi volume button because, in the last line of the script, you set the sound objects' volume to zero, which represents no volume. You did this to make it easier to test that the script was working. Next, you will reset the volume parameter to 100 (highest volume) and copy the working script twice for use with the other two volume buttons.

18 In the **Script** pane, place your cursor between the parentheses after **setVolume** and change the value from **0** to **100**. Place the cursor after the last curly brace and type a semicolon (;). Highlight the last three lines of your script and press **Ctrl+C** (Windows) or **Cmd+C** (Mac) to copy the ActionScript.

In the following steps, you will twice paste this copied ActionScript back into the Action panel and change the button names and volume parameters to complete the script.

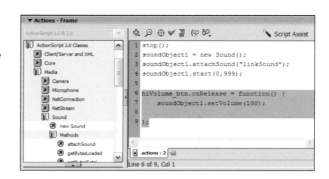

19 In the **Script** pane, place your cursor at the end of the last line of the script and press **Enter** (Windows) or **Return** (Mac) to add a new line. Press **Ctrl+V** (Windows) or **Cmd+V** (Mac) to paste the ActionScript. In the pasted script, change **hiVolume_btn** to **medVolume_btn** and the **setVolume** parameter from **100** to **50**. Your **Script** pane should match the illustration here.

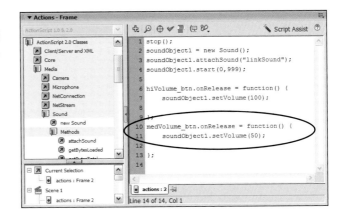

20 In the **Script** pane, place your cursor at the end of the last line of the script and press **Enter** (Windows) or **Return** (Mac) to add a new line. Press **Ctrl+V** (Windows) or **Cmd+V** (Mac) to paste the ActionScript again into the **Script** pane. In the pasted script, change **hiVolume_btn** to **lowVolume_btn** and the volume parameter from **100** to **10**. Remove the semicolon (**;**) at the end of the final line.

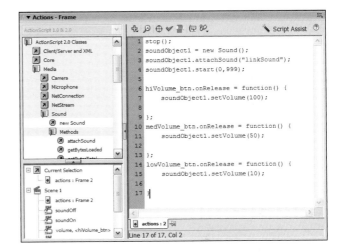

21 Choose **Control > Test Movie** and click each of the volume buttons. Notice the volume of the background sound changes as you click each button.

The **start()** method used in this script to start playing the background sound will play the attached sound each time it is called, even if the sound is already playing. Because of this, you may hear multiple versions of the background sound overlapping itself when you click the sound on button. To correct this, click the sound off button to turn off all the sounds, then click the sound on button only one time.

22 When you are finished testing the buttons, close the preview window and close **volumeCntrl.fla**. You do not need to save your changes.

Congratulations! That completes another chapter. A lot of information was covered here, but you should now feel comfortable working with sound in Flash 8. If you feel like you need more practice, you can always review the exercises again. Working with components and forms is next!

15

Components and Forms

Components help you automate complex tasks, which can be time-consuming and repetitive. For example, rather than building from scratch a scrollable list box offering users choices that are highlighted when the mouse rolls over them, you can drag and drop the List component onto the Stage and presto—you have a scrollable list box! All you have to do is add the words you want to appear in the list. This chapter introduces you to working with components to create a form. In the following exercises, you will add components to a project file, configure them to display the correct information for the user, and then modify them so that they match the interface design.

What Are Components?

Components are like movie clip symbols on steroids—they are a special type of prebuilt movie clip with parameters that let you modify their appearance and behavior. A component can be a simple user interface control, such as a check box

or radio button, or it can be a complicated control element, such as a media controller or a scroll pane. Flash 8 ships with five categories of components: Data, FLV Custom User Interface, FLV Playback, Media Players, and User Interface (UI). The User Interface components include a check box, combo box, menu bar, list box, button, radio button, scroll pane, and several others. You can use the components individually or together to create user interface elements such as forms or surveys. In addition, you can modify the appearance of each component by changing such aspects as the theme color, font, font size, and font color. A table listing a sampling of Flash 8 components follows. For a complete list of Flash 8 components, visit the "Types of Components" section of Flash Help.

Component Examples

Type	Description
Button	Accepts standard mouse and keyboard interactions. You can program this component to carry out a specific command when the user clicks it or presses Enter/Return.
CheckBox	Lets users select or deselect this check box.
ComboBox	Displays a single choice with a pop-up menu revealing additional choices.
Label	Lets you quickly create a label, similar to using a text field with an instance name assigned to it.
List	Offers a list of all choices in a scrollable menu.
Loader	Loads other movies or JPEGs.
Numeric Stepper	Lets users step through an ordered set of numbers.
ProgressBar	Displays the loading progress while a user waits for content to load.
RadioButton	Lets you add several instances of the radio button to your project file and prevents more than one choice in a group of radio buttons.

continues on next page

Type	Description
Component Examples *continued*	
ScrollPane	Lets the user view movie clips, JPEGs, and SWF files through a scrollable window.
TextArea	Displays text or lets users type text.
TextInput	Lets users insert text (for a username or password, for example).
Window	Displays content that includes a title bar and Close button.
UIScrollBar	Lets the user add a scroll bar to a text field.
MediaDisplay	Enables the streaming of media into Flash content without a supporting user interface (Flash Professional only).
MediaController	Provides standard user interface controls (Play, Pause, and so on) for media playback (Flash Professional only).
MediaPlayback	Provides methods for streaming media content (Flash Professional only).

Working with Components

There are four general phases when working with components:

- Adding the components to your project file

- Configuring components

- Modifying the component themes to change their appearances

- Writing ActionScript to gather and submit the data for the form

This chapter concentrates on just the first three phases because phase four involves more complicated ActionScripting and custom server configurations—both subjects that fall outside the scope of this book.

1 | Creating a Form

The first step in working with components is to add them to your Flash 8 project file. This exercise shows you how to do just that by creating a form.

---

1 Copy the **chap_15** folder from the **HOT CD-ROM** to your **Desktop**. Open **orderForm_Final.fla** from the **chap_15** folder. Choose **Control > Test Movie** to preview the file. This is the finished version of the form you'll be creating throughout the exercises of this chapter. Test out the different form elements to see how they work. When you are finished, close the preview window and **orderForm_Final.fla**.

Note: If you click the **Submit** button, nothing happens because this form is not set up to submit the data to a server.

---

2 Open **orderForm.fla** from the **chap_15** folder.

---

3 In the main **Timeline**, click the **Insert Layer** button to add a new layer. Rename the new layer **components** and make sure it is on top, above the other two layers.

Tip: You can choose **View > Magnification > Show All** to see all of the **Stage** at one time.

---

4 Choose **Window > Components** to open the **Components** panel, which is where all the components are stored. Click the **+** (Windows) or **triangle** (Mac) button to expand the **User Interface** category. Drag an instance of the **ComboBox** component onto the **Stage**, to the right of the **How many boards would you like to order?** text.

You have just added the first component to your movie! The ComboBox is a component that will display a single choice with a pop-up menu revealing additional choices. You will configure the ComboBox choices in the next exercise.

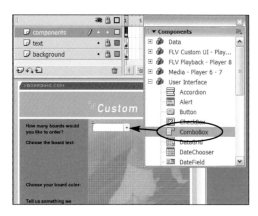

Tip: You can also double-click a component in the Components panel to add it to your project file. However, doing so adds the component to the center of the Stage; you then have to drag it to the desired position

5 Press **Ctrl+L** (Windows) or **Cmd+L** (Mac) to open the **Library**.

Notice the Library now contains the ComboBox component and a folder called **background**, which we created for you ahead of time; it contains all the files that make up the interface of this project file. For each component you add to your project, Flash 8 will add the component to the Library.

6 From the **Components** panel, drag an instance of the **List** component onto the **Stage**, to the right of the **Choose the board text** text.

The List component offers a list of all choices in a scrollable menu.

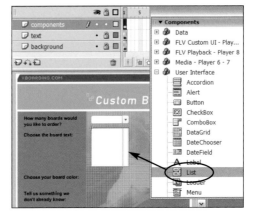

7 From the **Components** panel, drag an instance of the **RadioButton** component onto the **Stage**, to the right of the **Choose your board color** text.

The RadioButton component lets you add several instances of the radio button to your project file (which you will do in the next step) and prevents users from selecting more than one choice in a group of radio buttons.

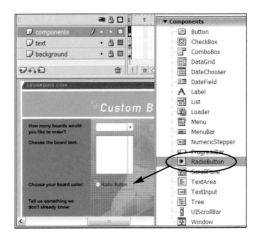

8 From the **Library**, drag three more instances of the **RadioButton** onto the **Stage** and position them as shown in the illustration here. Don't worry about aligning them precisely; you will do this shortly.

Note: Why did you add more radio buttons from the Library? Once you add a component to your project file, the component is added to the Library. From then on, it is easy and convenient to drag additional instances of the component onto the stage from the Library (just as you would for any other Library element).

9 From the **Components** panel, drag an instance of the **TextArea** component onto the **Stage**, to the right of the **Tell us something we don't already know** text. With the **TextArea** component still selected, select the **Free Transform** tool from the **toolbar** and click and drag to resize the **TextArea** component so it matches the illustration here.

The TextArea component lets users add comments along with the form submission. It automatically displays a scroll bar if the message becomes longer than the box.

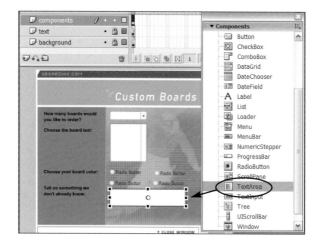

10 From the **Components** panel, drag an instance of the **Button** component onto the **Stage**, just below the **TextArea** component.

The Button component accepts standard mouse and keyboard interactions, and you can program it to carry out a specific command when the user clicks on it or presses Enter/Return.

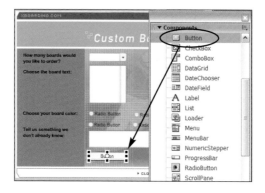

After you add the Button component, take another look at the Library. Notice each of the components you have placed on the Stage is now also located in the Library. You can add additional instances of each of these components by dragging them onto the Stage from the Library.

11 Choose **Window > Align** to open the **Align** panel. With the **Selection** tool, **Shift+click** all the components that are nearest the white vertical interface line to select each. In the **Align** panel, click the **Align left edge** button to align the selected components vertically. (Make sure the **To stage** option is disabled.)

Note: Because of the Snap Align functionality, the components may already be aligned. The Align panel is very helpful for aligning multiple elements at the same time or for distributing elements evenly across the Stage.

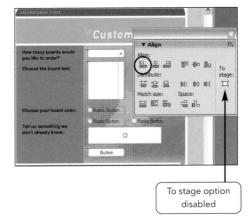

To stage option disabled

12 Click off the **Stage** to deselect everything. **Shift+click** the two rightmost **RadioButtons**. In the **Align** panel, click the **Align right edge** button to align the two components.

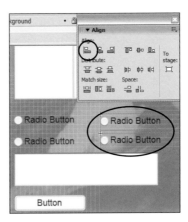

13 Click off the **Stage** to deselect everything. **Shift+click** the top two **RadioButton** components. In the **Align** panel, click the **Align top edge** button to align the top of the **RadioButton** components to each other. Click off the **Stage** to deselect everything again. **Shift+click** the bottom two **RadioButton** components. In the **Align** panel, click the **Align bottom edge** button to align the bottom of the **RadioButton** components to each other.

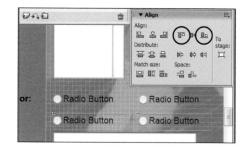

14 When you are finished, save **orderForm.fla** and keep it open for the next exercise.

2 | Configuring Components

Now that you have the components in place, you need to make some adjustments so they display the correct information to the user. This exercise shows you how to do this by setting the parameters for each component.

1 If you just completed Exercise 1, **orderForm.fla** should still be open. If it's not, go back and complete Exercise 1. On the **Stage**, click the **ComboBox** component to select it. Choose **Window > Properties > Properties** to open the **Property Inspector**. Click the **Parameters** tab.

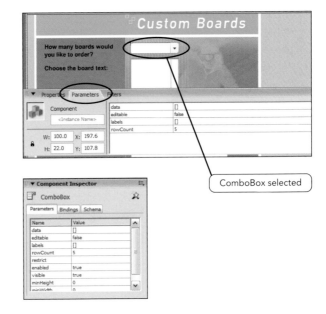

Notice the Property Inspector looks a little different than normal; this is part of the built-in functionality of the component.

Note: In addition to using the Property Inspector, you can also view the parameters for a component by using the Component Inspector panel. To do this, choose **Window > Component Inspector** to open the panel. Select a component instance on the Stage to view the parameters associated with that component. Using the Component Inspector panel will give you the same information as choosing the Parameters tab in the Property Inspector; choose whichever workflow works better for you. In this exercise, you will be using the Property Inspector to modify the component parameters.

2 In the **Property Inspector**, click inside the **Instance Name** text box and type **quantityCB**, which gives the **ComboBox** an instance name so that you can reference it with ActionScript.

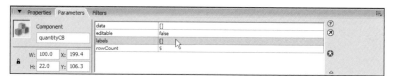

3 Double-click the **labels** parameter to open up the **Values** dialog box, where you will enter the values users can select from a scrollable pop-up menu.

4 In the **Values** dialog box, click the plus (**+**) button to enter a new value. Click in the default field and type **1**. Click the plus (**+**) button again to enter the next value. Click in the default field and type **2**. Repeat this step to add **3**, **4**, and **5** to the list. When you are finished, click **OK**.

5 Choose **Control > Test Movie** to test out your **ComboBox** component. The numbers you entered will appear in a pop-up list, making the configuration for this component complete. When you are finished, close the preview window.

Note: You may have noticed the highlight color when you roll over an option in the ComboBox is light green. This is the result of the Halo theme built into Flash 8 components. In an upcoming exercise, you'll change the color to match the green in the interface design of **orderForm.fla**.

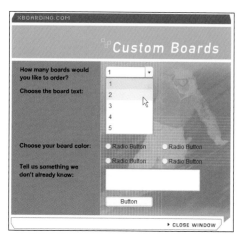

6 Click the **List** component to select it. In the **Property Inspector**, click inside the **Instance Name** text box and type **textLB**, which gives the **List** component an instance name so you can refer to it with ActionScript. Double-click the **labels** parameter to open up the **Values** dialog box. Here again, you will enter the values users can select from a scroll-able pop-up menu.

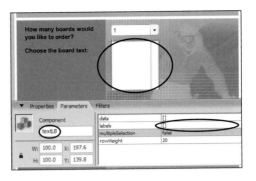

7 In the **Values** dialog box, click the plus (**+**) button to enter a new value. Click in the default field and type **boardThis**. Click the plus (**+**) button again to enter the next value. Click in the default field and type **gone boarding**. Repeat this step six more times to add the rest of the text options to match the illustration shown here. When you are fin-ished, click **OK**.

Tip: If you want to move any of your entries higher or lower in the list, you can select the value and use the up or down arrows at the top of the Values dialog box to move them where you want them.

8 Choose **Control > Test Movie** to test out the **List** component. Use the scroll bar inside the **List** to see all the options you created for the user. Notice, however, the longer text is cut off. You will change this next. When you are finished, close the preview window.

9 In the **toolbar**, select the **Free Transform** tool. On the **Stage**, click the **List** component to select it. Click the **right-middle handle** on the bounding box and drag to the right to resize the **List** component, making all text entries visible.

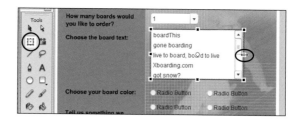

Note: You can modify the width and height of List components in your project file by using the Free Transform tool. However, you can modify only the width of ComboBox components with the Free Transform tool; the height of the ComboBox component is set by the font size of the menu choices and the Row Count parameter that determines the number of choices visible in the pop-up menu at one time.

---

10 Select the **Selection** tool from the **toolbar**. On the **Stage**, select the upper-left **RadioButton**. In the **Property Inspector**, type **redRB** for the **Instance Name**. Select the **groupName** parameter and type **colorGroup**. Select the **label** parameter and type **firecracker red**. Set the **selected** parameter to **true**. Leave the **labelPlacement** parameter set to **right** (the default value).

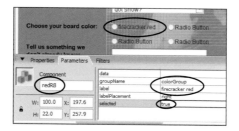

The groupName parameter you set makes this RadioButton part of a group of RadioButtons called colorGroup. The label parameter sets the label that will appear to the right of the RadioButton. A value of true for the selected parameter will make the RadioButton selected by default. (Only one radio button in a group can have the selected state as true.) The labelPlacement parameter sets the location of the RadioButton label text to either the right or the left of the RadioButton.

---

11 On the **Stage**, select the upper-right **RadioButton**. In the **Property Inspector**, type **greyRB** for the **Instance Name**. Select the **groupName** parameter and type **colorGroup**. Select the **label** parameter and type **gunmetal grey**. Make sure the **selected** parameter is set to **false**.

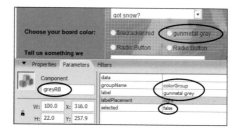

---

12 On the **Stage**, select the lower-left **RadioButton**. In the **Property Inspector**, type **blackRB** for the **Instance Name**. Select the **groupName** parameter and type **colorGroup**. Select the **label** parameter and type **lights out black**. Make sure the **selected** parameter is set to **false**.

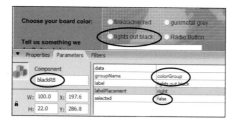

You need to set the parameters for just one more button.

---

13 Select the lower-right **RadioButton**. In the **Property Inspector**, type **blueRB** for the **Instance Name**. Select the **groupName** parameter and type **colorGroup**. Select the **label** parameter and type **midnight blue**. Make sure the **selected** parameter is set to **false**.

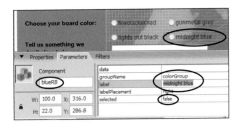

14 Choose **Control > Test Movie** to test out the **RadioButton** components.

Notice the firecracker red RadioButton is selected by default. Although you can click to select any of the other RadioButton components, notice you can select only one at a time. This is an example of components at their finest—all of the behind-the-scenes work has been done for you. You just placed them where you needed them and set their desired parameters. You now have a fully functional group of RadioButton components. Sweet! When you are finished, close the preview window.

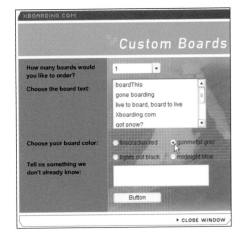

15 On the **Stage**, click the **TextArea** component to select it. In the **Property Inspector**, type **messageTxt** for the **Instance Name**. Make sure the **wordWrap** parameter is set to **true** and the **html** parameter is set to **false**. Leave the **text** parameter empty. Before you test the movie, select the **Free Transform** tool from the **toolbar** and resize the **TextArea** component, if needed, so it matches the illustration here.

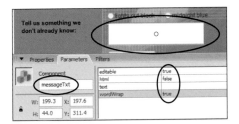

16 Choose **Control > Test Movie** to test the scrolling input text box. Try typing a large amount of text; notice a scroll bar will automatically appear and resize as you type. Cool! When you are finished, close the preview window.

You have one last component to configure next.

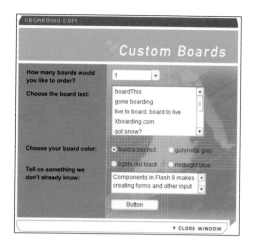

17 On the **Stage**, click the **Button** component to select it. In the **Property Inspector**, type **submitBtn** for the **Instance Name**. For the **label** parameter, type **Submit**, which will be the label that appears on the **Button** component.

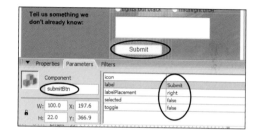

18 Choose **Control > Test Movie** to preview your **Button** component. Notice the label of the button now reads *Submit* instead of *Button*.

Note: In order to test the functionality of the Submit button, including collecting all the data entered on the form and actually sending it to a server, you need to add more ActionScript to the movie. You would also need access to a Web server and middleware such as ColdFusion Server or Microsoft Active Server Pages (ASP). All of this is beyond the scope of this book. You can, however, visit the Macromedia Flash Support Center at **http://www.macromedia.com/support/flash/applications_building.html** to find articles and resources that will teach you how to use ActionScripting to gather and submit data entered into a form like the one you have created here.

19 When you are finished, save **orderForm.fla** and keep it open for the next exercise.

For more information about each of the Flash 8 components, choose **Help > Help**. In the **Help** panel, choose **Using Components**.

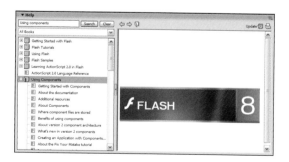

3 | Modifying Component Themes

In the previous exercises you learned how to add components to your project and create a form. You may have noticed the light-green tint that appears when you roll over an item or make a selection. Fortunately, you are not stuck with this tint, called a Halo theme, used in the components. You can modify the Halo of the component as well as the font, font size, and font color with just a few short lines of ActionScript. This exercise shows you how to use ActionScript to change the appearance of components.

1 The **orderForm.fla** file should still be open from the last exercise. If it's not, open it from the **chap_15** folder. Choose **Control > Test Movie** to preview the form you have created up to this point. Notice the highlight color for all the components is light green. You will change this in the following steps. When you are finished, close the preview window.

Green Halo theme

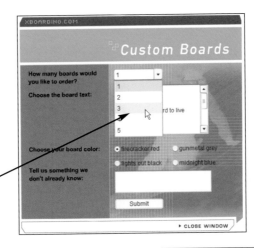

NOTE:

What Is a Halo Theme?

The Halo theme is a built-in style for all of the Flash 8 components used to set the highlight color of buttons and text when you roll over them with your mouse or make a selection. There are three colors to choose from: blue, green, and orange. To change the Halo theme, you will add a few lines of ActionScript. When you get more comfortable with ActionScript, you can create new themes and graphics for components, but these techniques are beyond the scope of this book, so for now you'll keep it simple and stick to blue, green, or orange.

2 Click the **Insert Layer** button to add a layer to the **Timeline**. Rename the new layer **theme** and make sure it is above all other layers.

You will add ActionScript to set the color of the Halo theme next.

3 Select **Frame 1** of the **theme** layer. Press **F9** (Windows) or **Option+F9** (Mac) to open the **Actions** panel. Make sure **Script Assist** mode is off. In the **Script** pane, type the following line of code:

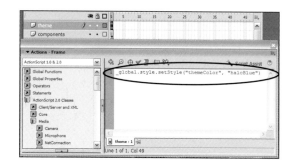

```
_global.style.setStyle("themeColor", "haloBlue")
```

The **_global** action applies the Halo theme to every component in the movie. The **setStyle** command simply tells the components you are setting a specific Halo theme (done with the **"themeColor"** parameter) and that the theme you want is **haloBlue**.

---

4 Choose **Control > Test Movie** to see how the theme has changed from the default color of green to blue. When you're done, close the preview window.

---

5 In the **Script** pane, change **haloBlue** to **haloOrange**.

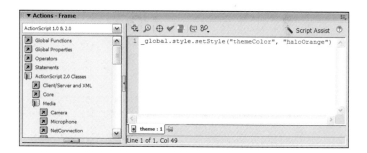

6 Choose **Control > Test Movie** to preview the theme. Notice the highlight color is now orange instead of blue. Close the preview window when you are finished.

Tip: If you don't want to use any of the prebuilt Halo themes for your components, you can simply enter the hexadecimal value for any other color in place of **haloOrange**. For example, changing **haloOrange** to **0xC1CE0F** will make the highlight color for the components match the green used in the interface very nicely. You will do this next.

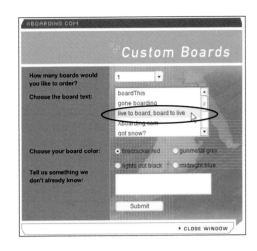

---

7 In the **Script** pane, change **haloOrange** to **0xC1CE0F**.

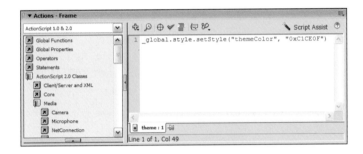

---

8 Choose **Control > Test Movie** to preview your change. Notice the highlight color now matches the color used in the interface design. Close the preview window when you are finished.

Next, you're going to change the font used in the components so that it will be a little easier to read against the background, particularly for the RadioButton text.

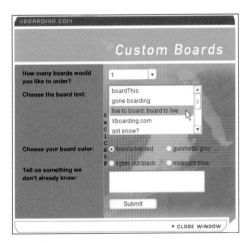

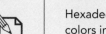

NOTE:

What Is a Hexadecimal Value?

Hexadecimal values are six-digit number/letter combinations used to identify specific colors in ActionScript and many other programming languages. For a quick glance at which hexadecimal values belong to what colors, you can use the Eyedropper tool to sample a color used in the interface or a color swatch in the Color Mixer. The hexadecimal value will generate in the Hexadecimal Value field.

If you're familiar with HTML, you may be more familiar with hexadecimal values in the format *#FFFFFF* instead of *0x000000*. The *0x* in front of the Hex colors is short for "hexadecimal."

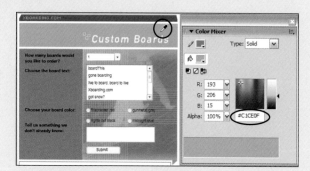

---

9 In the **Script** pane, type the following ActionScript to set the font:

```
_global.style.setStyle("fontFamily"
, "verdana");
```

The **_global** action applies the font to all of the components. The **setStyle** command sets the font family for all of the components to Verdana.

---

10 Choose **Control > Test Movie** to preview the font. Notice the font is now in Verdana, but that the radio button labels are cut off. You will fix this next. When you are finished previewing, close the preview window.

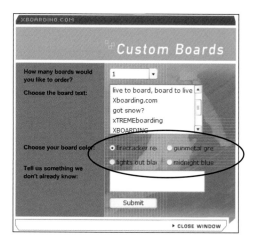

11 Select the **Selection** tool from the **toolbar** and **Shift+click** to select both the **gunmetal grey** and **midnight blue** radio buttons. Move them to the right.

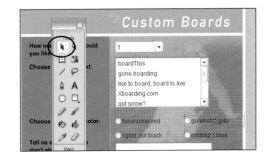

12 Select the **Free Transform** tool from the **tool-bar**. Select the **firecracker red** radio button and click the right-middle handle on the bounding box and drag to the right to resize the **RadioButton** component so that you can read the entire label. Do this for the remaining three radio buttons. Resize the **List** component as well if you could not see all the text entries in Step 10.

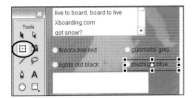

13 Choose **Control > Test Movie** again to pre-view your changes. Notice you can now read the labels of the radio buttons. Close the preview win-dow when you are done.

You're going to change the font size next.

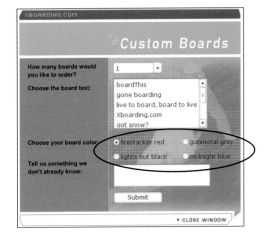

14 In the **Script** pane, add the following ActionScript to set the font size:

```
_global.style.setStyle("fontSize",14);
```

As you may have guessed, you're applying the font size to all of the components using the **_global** action and then setting the font size to 14. You have only one more line of code to go!

15 In the **Script** pane, add the following ActionScript to set the font color for all of the components to solid black:

`_global.style.setStyle("color", 0x000000);`

The **setStyle** command sets the color to the hexadecimal value for black, which is #000000. To set the color to something other than black, use the hexadecimal value for that color in place of the **000000** in the code.

16 Choose **Control > Test Movie** to see the results of your hard work. Notice the font is **Verdana**, **14 point**, and **black** for all of the components, and the Halo theme is now the same color used in the interface design, which helps to unite the color scheme used in the interface. Close the preview window when you are done viewing your changes.

17 Close **orderForm.fla**; you do not need to save your changes.

Using the Macromedia Flash Exchange

Now that you're more familiar with components and how beneficial it can be to use them in your movies, take a look at the Macromedia Exchange. This is a special section of the Macromedia Web site that lets users post components and other extensions to a searchable forum. Many of these components were created by Macromedia or third-party developers. You can download hundreds of reusable components to build projects, templates for designing Flash content, reusable ActionScript code snippets, additional symbol libraries, and more.

To download these extensions, simply go to **http://www.macromedia.com/exchange/flash** and search through the various categories to find extensions you find useful or interesting.

Note: In order to download content from the Macromedia Exchange, you must have a Macromedia account. If you don't already have one, sign up now so you can continue with the download process.

The Categories pop-up menu organizes the extensions into a variety of topics for easy access. You can also check out the Flash Top Ten pop-up menu for the Highest Rated, Newest, and Most Downloaded extensions.

If you select a category from the Categories pop-up menu, you'll get a listing of components and other resources. This page gives you useful information about each extension, such as the author, availability, number of downloads, rating, product compatibility, and date created.

Note: At the time of this writing, few extensions were available for Flash 8. Be sure to check for an update of available extensions.

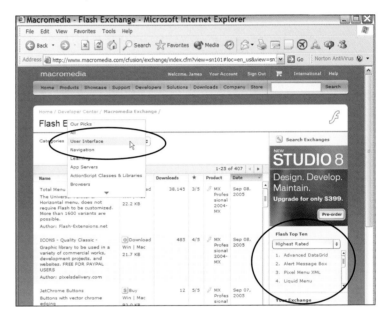

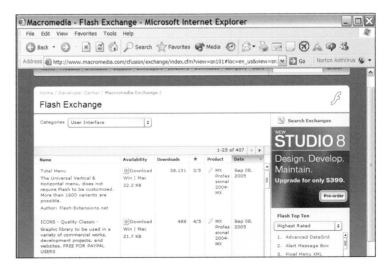

In the Exchange Search, you can search by keyword, category, and several other categories to quickly find what you're looking for.

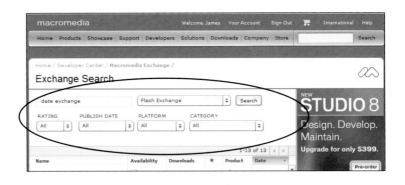

To install an extension, download it to your computer and install following the on-screen instructions provided by the **Macromedia Extension Manager.** (For more information, search on Flash Exchange in Flash Help.)

After installing a Component extension, you'll see the extension in the Components panel. You can use the downloaded components the same way you would any other components in the Components panel—by dragging the component onto the Stage.

That's a wrap on this chapter. Great work! Now that you are more familiar with components, take a quick break and get ready for the next action-packed (pun intended) chapter: *"Video."*

16

Video

The capability to include video inside a SWF file was introduced with the release of Macromedia Flash MX. This feature opened up many opportunities for Flash developers. Video clips imported into Macromedia Flash 8 can be controlled using behaviors and very basic ActionScript, can be targeted to let users jump from point to point in the clip, can have alpha transparency effects applied to them, or can be published from within Flash as a QuickTime file. In this latest version of Flash, Macromedia has added more video compression options, a stand-alone video encoding application for batch processing multiple files, and the capability to trim and edit video clips and apply color correction. It also includes more options for importing video into Flash projects. The exercises in this chapter lay the groundwork for working with Flash Video.

Importing Video into Flash 8

Flash 8 can import video in the most popular file formats. If you have QuickTime 4 or later (Windows or Macintosh) or DirectX 7 or later (Windows only) installed on your system, you can import embedded video clips in a variety of file formats, including MOV, AVI, and MPG/MPEG.

If you attempt to import a file format not supported on your system, a warning message lets you know the operation cannot be completed.

In some cases, Flash might import the video but not the audio. For example, audio is not supported in MPG/MPEG files imported with QuickTime 4. In such cases, Flash displays a warning indicating that the audio portion of the file cannot be imported. You can still import the video without sound.

Flash documents with embedded video can be published as SWF files. Flash documents with linked video must be published in the QuickTime format.

Supported Video Formats with QuickTime 4 or Later (Windows and Macintosh)

File Type	Extension
Audio Video Interleaved	.avi
Digital video	.dv
QuickTime video	.mov
Motion Picture Experts Group	.mpg, .mpeg

Supported Video Formats with DirectX 7 or Later (Windows Only)

File Type	Extension
Audio Video Interleaved	.avi
Windows Media File	.wmv, .asf
Motion Picture Experts Group	.mpg, .mpeg

On2 VP6 and Sorenson Spark Video Compression

By default, Flash Video Encoder exports encoded video using the new **On2 VP6** video codec for use with Flash Player 8, and the **Sorenson Spark** codec for use with Flash Player 7. A **codec** is an algorithm that controls the way video files are compressed and decompressed during import and export.

The On2 video codec is the preferred video codec to use when creating Flash content that uses video. On2 provides the best combination of video quality while maintaining a small file size.

If your Flash content dynamically loads Flash Video (using either progressive download or Flash Communication Server), you can use On2 VP6 video without having to republish your SWF for Flash Player 8, as long as users use Flash Player 8 to view your content. Only Flash Player 8 supports both publish and playback of On2 VP6 video.

Codecs Supported by Flash Versions		
Codec	Published Version (SWF File)	Flash Player Version Required for Playback (Flash Player)
Sorenson Spark	6	6, 7, 8
	7	7, 8
On2 VP6	6	8
	7	8
	8	8

Flash Professional 8 Video Features

Flash Professional 8 offers a variety of additional video features not included in Flash Basic 8. The following chart outlines the most important video features found only in Flash Professional 8:

Flash Professional 8 Video Features	
Media components	Quickly integrate video into your project with streaming media components—such as a seek bar, control buttons, volume settings bar, and more—which you can easily click and drag onto the Stage.
Improved video workflow	Macromedia improved the Video Import wizard to help you deploy video content for embedded, progressively downloaded, and streaming video delivery. You can import video stored locally on your computer, or video already deployed to a Web server or Flash Communication Server.
Stand-alone video encoder	A new stand-alone video encoder application, Flash 8 Video Encoder, is included with Flash Professional 8. This encoder is a separate application that will significantly improve your video production workflow by providing an easy way to convert video files into the Flash Video (FLV) format. It also can perform batch processing of video files.
8-bit alpha support	Flash 8 now supports 8-bit alpha channels at video runtime, which lets you overlay video composited with a transparent or semi-transparent alpha channel over other Flash content.

Macromedia Flash Video (FLV)

The Macromedia FLV file format lets you import or export a static video stream with encoded audio. This format is intended for use with communications applications, such as video conferencing, and files that contain screen share encoded data exported from the Flash Communication Server.

When you export video clips with streaming audio in FLV format, the audio is compressed using the Streaming Audio settings in the Publish Settings dialog box. The video content in the FLV file is compressed with the Sorenson codec.

1 | Importing Video

The first step in working with video is importing it into Flash 8. This exercise shows you how to import a video clip into Flash 8 as an embedded video. Flash Basic 8 users will need to encode using one of the Flash 7 options, or skip Steps 8 through 11.

1 Copy the **chap_16** folder from the **HOT CD-ROM** to your **Desktop**. Open **importVideo_Final.fla** from the **chap_16** folder. This is the finished version of the project you'll be building in the next two exercises. Choose **Control > Test Movie** to preview the movie. Notice the movie begins in a stopped position. Click the **Play** button to start the video clip, and click the **Stop** button to stop the video clip.

You will add the functionality to the buttons, but first you will learn how to import and embed the video clip into Flash 8.

2 When you are finished previewing this movie, close the preview window and close **importVideo_Final.fla**.

3 Open **importVideo.fla** from the **chap_16** folder. We created this file to get you started. Click the **Insert Layer** button to add a new layer to the **Timeline**. Rename the layer **video** and make sure it is at the top of the layer stack.

4 Choose **File > Import > Import to Stage** and select the **jumps.mov** file from the **chap_16** folder. Click **Open** (Windows) or **Import** (Mac).

Note: This is a QuickTime video clip.

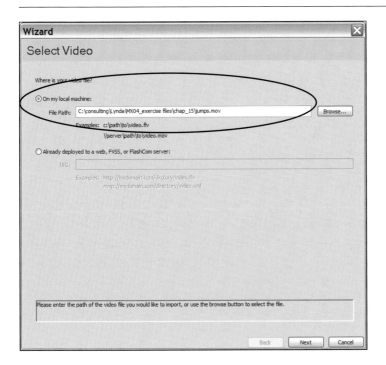

5 In the **Select Video** screen of the **Import Video** wizard window, make sure the **On my local machine** (Windows) or the **On your computer** (Mac) option is selected. Click **Next** (Windows) or **Continue** (Mac).

Flash 8 gives you the option to import video from a local file on your computer or from a remote Web site or FlashCom server.

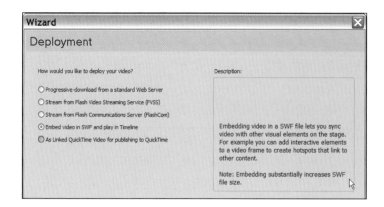

6 In the **Deployment** screen, select the **Embed video in SWF and play in Timeline** option and click **Next** (Windows) or **Continue** (Mac).

Note: You will be given a variety of options for deploying your video, including as a progressive download, streamed from a FVSS or FlashCom server, or as a linked QuickTime movie.

NOTE: | **To Stream or Embed or Link?**

When you import a QuickTime video clip, you can choose to stream it, embed it, or link it. If you choose to embed a video clip, the video becomes part of the movie, just as a bitmap does when imported into Flash 8. The embedded video clip will then play in the SWF file inside the Flash Player. This is helpful because users do not need any special player to view the video—they just need the Flash 6 (or higher) Player installed on their browsers.

Streaming video requires a server running the Flash Communication Server software providing video delivery to each user. With streaming, each user opens a unique connection to the Flash Communication Server, which enables you to provide different content for users based on their ability to access and download content. For example, a user with a dial-up modem can access your streaming content requiring much less bandwidth.

You can also choose to link to an external video file. In this case, the video will not be stored inside the Flash 8 document, and when you export the file from Flash 8, you can not export it as a SWF file—instead, you have to export it as a QuickTime file (MOV). The resulting file will not play in the Flash player, but it will play in the QuickTime player. The next few exercises concentrate on embedded video.

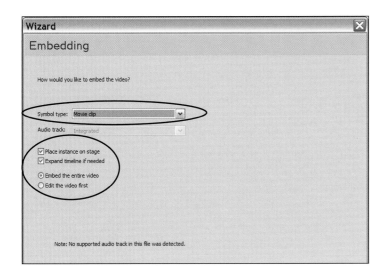

7 In the **Embedding** screen, choose **Movie clip** from the **Symbol type** pop-up menu, select the **Place instance on stage** and **Expand timeline if needed** options, and make sure the **Embed the entire video** option is selected. Click **Next** (Windows) or **Continue** (Mac).

With the Embedding options, you can choose whether to place the video inside a movie clip, place an instance on the Stage, import the entire video, or edit the video first. You will be learning, later in this chapter, how to use the editing capabilities of the Video Import wizard.

Note: The Movie clip option will keep your Timeline less cluttered because all the frames needed to play the video will be nicely self-contained within a movie clip. Also, you may have noticed the audio note at the bottom of the Video Import wizard window. This note will appear if either the audio codec used in the audio track is not supported on your system or if there is no audio attached to the video file, which is the case in this exercise.

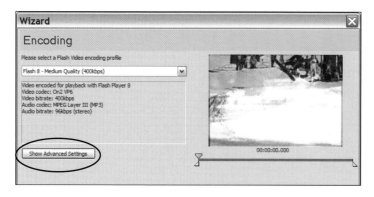

8 In the **Encoding** screen, click the **Show Advanced Settings** button.

Note: This step applies to Flash Professional 8 only. If you have Flash Basic 8, you should encode with one of the Flash 7 options or skip to Step 12.

From the Compression profile pop-up menu, you can specify a bandwidth to target. Selecting Flash 8 - modem quality, for instance, will compress your video so that a visitor to your Web site on a 56K modem should be able to watch the video—uninterrupted—while it is being downloaded (streamed) to the computer. If you want more control over how the video is going to be compressed, you can set additional options, including video codec, frame rate, keyframe placement, and more, in the Advanced Settings section.

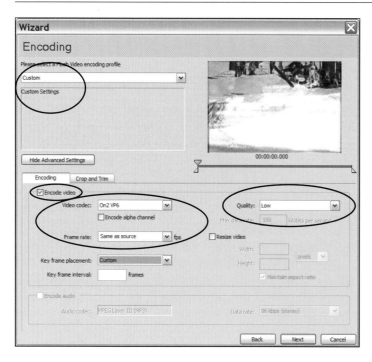

9 In the **Encoding** tab, make sure the **Encode video** option is selected. Set the **Video codec** to **On2 VP6**, **Quality** to **Low**, and the **Frame rate** to **Same as source**.

When you choose to set your own Encoding options, the Video Encoding profile at the top of the wizard displays Custom. A table at the end of the exercise breaks down the compression options you can specify. As you can see, there are quite a few settings in the Advanced Settings pane.

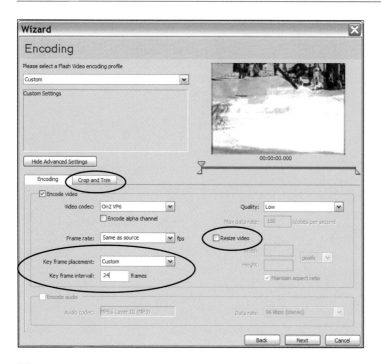

10 Choose **Custom** from the **Key frame placement** pop-up menu. In the **Key frame interval** field, type **24** to create keyframes inside the video every 24 frames. Make sure the **Resize video** option is turned off. Click the **Crop and Trim** tab to preview more sizing options.

The Resize video option lets you change the width and height of the imported video.

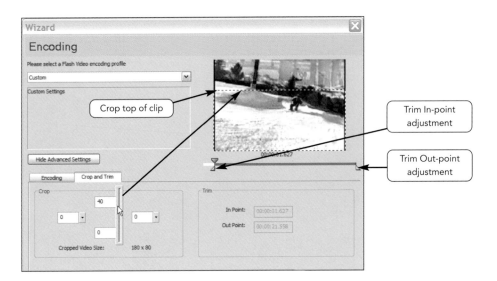

11 The settings in the **Crop** section let you crop the left, top, right, and bottom edges of the video. The **Trim** sliders, which are located directly below the thumbnail preview, let you trim out footage at the beginning (In point) or end (Out point) of the video. Experiment with changing these settings. When you are finished experimenting, set the **Crop** and **Trim** values back to their original settings (0), and click **Next** (Windows) or **Continue** (Mac).

Notice the results of your adjustments are displayed in the preview window in the wizard.

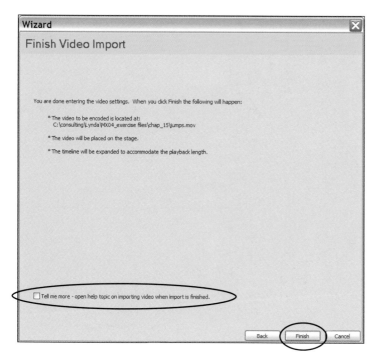

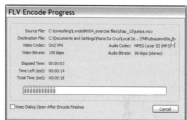

12 In the **Finish Video Import** screen, click **Finish**.

This screen summarizes the settings you specified.

Note: If you select the Tell me more option, you'll open the "Importing Video" section of the Flash 8 Online Help.

When you click the Finish button, the FLV Encode Progress (Flash Video Encoding Progress on the Mac) dialog box appears, providing information about the video clip being imported, including its source file, destination, video codec, video bitrate, audio codec, audio bit rate, and the import progress.

13 When the video import process finishes, the video clip appears on the **Stage**. Click the video clip to select it and move it slightly higher so it is centered inside the background window.

When you imported the video clip into your project, Flash places the video in the Library, creates a movie clip symbol, places the video (and all of the frames needed to display that video) in the movie clip symbol (because in Step 7 you instructed the Video Import wizard to import your video into a movie clip instance), and places an instance of that movie clip in the center of the Stage.

14 Press **Ctrl+L** (Windows) or **Cmd+L** (Mac) to open the **Library**. Notice the **jumps.mov** file, which is the video clip you just imported. Flash 8 has automatically placed it in the **Library**. Select the **jumps.mov** file in the **Library**. Click the **Properties** button to open the **Video Properties** window, which shows the dimensions, duration in seconds, and size in kilobytes of video data. Click **OK** when you are finished.

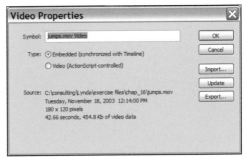

15 Choose **Control > Test Movie** to see your movie in action in the SWF file!

Note: The buttons will not work yet—you will add ActionScript to them in the next exercise.

16 When you are finished, close the preview window. Save **importVideo.fla** and keep it open for the next exercise.

Compression Settings

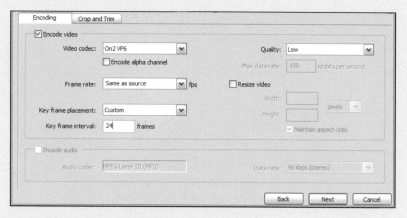

The following table breaks down the compression options you can specify in the Encoding screen of the Video Import wizard:

Compression Settings	
Option	**Description**
Video codec	Encodes the imported video file with either the On2 VP6 (default for Flash 8 player) or Sorenson Spark (default for Flash 7 player) codec.
Frame rate	Sets the number of frames that display for every second of playback.
Key frame placement	Specifies a custom keyframe interval or lets Flash determine the interval based on the source file.
Key frame interval	Specifies the number of keyframes per frame of your actual movie. The more keyframes you have in a video clip (the higher the number), the faster the viewers can fast-forward or rewind through a clip (if you give them that capability). But before you start thinking that's a good thing and adding a bunch of keyframes to your video clip, keep in mind the more keyframes you add to your movie, the larger it will become. For more information about keyframes, see the sidebar following this table.
Quality	Specifies the quality of all the frames in the video. A lower quality value will lower the quality of the video, but results in a video clip with a smaller file size. The opposite is true for a higher quality value.

Video Keyframes

Video keyframes are different than the Timeline keyframes you've learned about. When you set video keyframes, you are determining how often a full, high-quality frame will be captured and stored in the final file. For example, a keyframe setting of 24 instructs Flash to import in full, every 24th frame. If the computer's processor is too slow to play all the frames, the playback will skip frames until it reaches a keyframe. If the computer can keep up with all the frames, it will play them all.

The lower the keyframe value, the more keyframes there will be in the compressed movie. The frames between keyframes (called interframes) will only update based on what has changed in the previous keyframe, thereby reducing file size.

You will not see the video keyframes in the main Timeline inside Flash 8. Instead, the video keyframes are part of the compression settings that compress the actual video file itself. Video keyframes are invisible in the project file; they simply affect the playback quality of the embedded video.

2 | Controlling Video with stop and go Actions

Now that you know how to import video, you need to learn how to control the video playback. This exercise shows you how to control video on the main Timeline by adding ActionScript to buttons to control the video clip.

---

1 If you just completed Exercise 1, **importVideo.fla** should still be open. If it's not, go back and complete Exercise 1.

---

2 On the **Stage**, click the video clip to select it. In the **Property Inspector**, type **jumps** in the **Instance Name** field.

Later in this exercise, you will use the instance name to pass ActionScript to the movie clip.

---

3 On the **Timeline**, lock the **video** layer and unlock the **buttons** layer. On the **Stage**, click the **Play** button to select it. Press **F9** (Windows) or **Option+F9** (Mac) to open the **Actions** panel.

4 In the **Actions** panel, click the **Script Assist** button to switch to **Script Assist** mode. Select **Global Functions > Movie Clip Control** and double-click the **on** action to add it to the **Script** pane. Select the **Release** option.

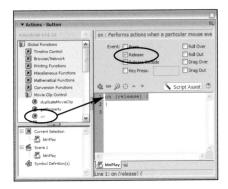

5 With the first line of script still selected, select **Global Functions > Timeline Control** and double-click the **Play** action. Click the **Script Assist** button to exit **Script Assist** mode. Type **jumps.** (don't forget the period) before the **play** command so the script reads: **jumps.play();**.

This tells the movie clip instance named **jumps** to play when the user clicks the Play button.

6 On the **Stage**, click the **Stop** button to select it. Repeat Steps 4 and 5, but instead of **jumps.play();**, type **jumps.stop();**.

7 Choose **Control > Test Movie** to preview the video. Click the **Stop** button to stop the video, and click the **Play** button to play the video again. Cool! When you are finished, close the preview window.

When you test the movie, it begins to play automatically. Next, you will add one more ActionScripting so the movie starts in a stopped position.

8 Click the **Insert Layer** button to add a new layer to the **Timeline**. Rename it **actions**, and make sure it is at the top of the layer stack.

9 On the **actions** layer, select **Frame 1**. In the **Actions** panel, select **Global Functions > Timeline Control** and double-click the **stop** action to add it to the **Script** pane.

The function will not work yet, because you are telling the main Timeline to stop, and you want the movie clip instance labeled *jumps* to stop instead. You will add the instance name of the movie clip to the **stop** action next.

10 In the **Script** pane, type **jumps.** (don't forget the period) before the **stop** command.

11 Choose **Control > Test Movie** to preview the video again.

Notice that the video is stopped.

12 Click the **Play** button to set the video in motion and click the **Stop** button to stop the video again. By adding a few basic actions, you give the user complete control over your video. When you are finished, close the preview window.

13 Close **importVideo.fla**. You do not need to save your changes.

VIDEO: | **controllingVideo.mov**

To learn more about controlling the playback of Flash videos, check out **controllingVideo.mov** in the **videos** folder on the **HOT CD-ROM**.

3 | Controlling Video by Targeting Frame Labels

Not only can you start and stop a video by using ActionScript, you can also target specific points in the video using behaviors. This exercise shows you how to use the **Goto and Play at frame or label** behavior to target different frames within the video sequence. Additionally, you will learn how to use named anchors to navigate through the video.

1 Open **targetVideo.fla** from the **chap_16** folder. Click the **Insert Layer** button to add a new layer to the **Timeline**. Rename the layer **video** and make sure it is at the top of the layer stack.

2 Choose **File > Import > Import to Stage** and select the **catchingAir.mov** file from the **chap_16** folder. Click **Open** (Windows) or **Import** (Mac) to open the **Video Import** wizard.

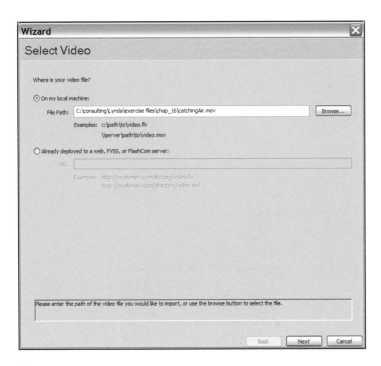

3 In the **Select Video** screen, select **On my local machine** (Windows) or **On your computer** (Mac) to tell Flash where the video file is located. Click **Next** (Windows) or **Continue** (Mac).

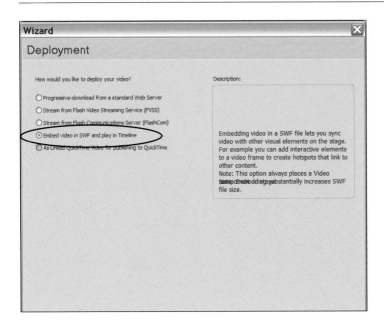

4 In the **Deployment** screen, make sure the **Embed video in SWF and play in Timeline** option is selected. Click **Next** (Windows) or **Continue** (Mac).

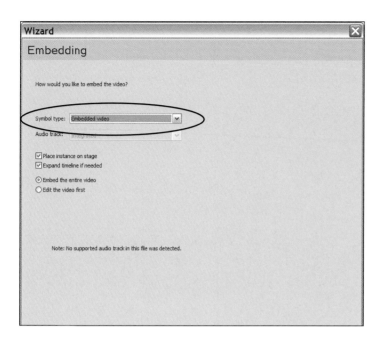

5 In the **Embedding** screen, choose **Embedded video** from the **Symbol type** pop-up menu. Select the **Place instance onstage** and **Expand timeline if needed** options. Make sure the **Embed the entire video** option is selected. Click **Next** (Windows) or **Continue** (Mac).

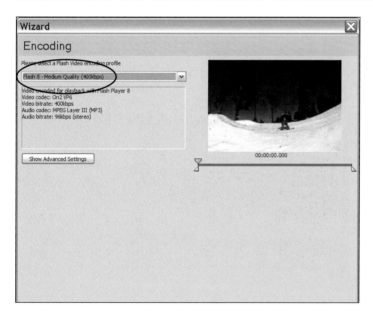

6 In the **Encoding** screen, choose **Flash 8- Medium Quality (400kbps)** from the **encoding profile** pop-up menu to encode the video using the ON2 VP6 codec at medium quality and with the keyframe value set to the same as the original video (Flash Professional 8 only). Click **Next** (Windows) or **Continue** (Mac).

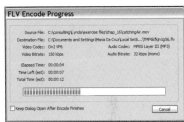

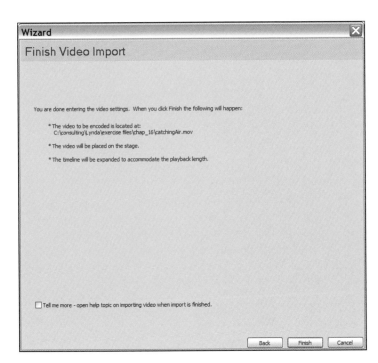

7 In the **Finish Video Import** screen, review your settings and click **Finish**.

The FLV Encode Progress (Windows) or Flash Video Encoding Progress (Mac) window appears. When the import process is complete, the video clip will be placed on the Stage.

8 Click the video clip to select it, and move it so it is centered inside the background window.

Notice the video now occupies 469 frames on the Timeline.

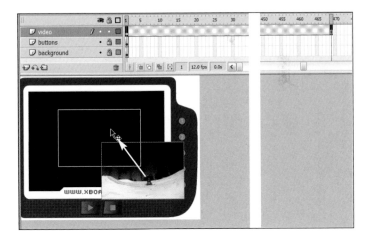

9 On the **Timeline**, move the **playhead** to **Frame 465**. Scrub the **playhead** between **Frame 465** and where the video frames stop at **Frame 469**. Notice how the video fades out at about **Frame 465**. The rest of the frames from 465 to 469 are not necessary because the video has faded to black. Click and drag on the **Timeline** to select **Frames 465** through **469**. **Right-click** (Windows) or **Ctrl+click** (Mac) the selected frames and choose **Remove frames** from the contextual menu to remove them from the **Timeline**.

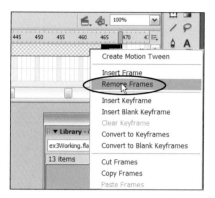

Why remove the frames? In Flash 8, video on the Timeline is treated just like stream sound is treated on the Timeline. Only the frames that exist on the Timeline will be exported with the Macromedia Flash movie (SWF file). To reduce the SWF file size, you can remove unneeded frames from the Timeline. In this example, the SWF file will be reduced from 949 KB to 944 KB by removing those five frames.

Note: Although you deleted frames from the video clip on the main Timeline, the original full video clip is still in the Library.

---

10 On the **buttons** layer, click **Frame 464**. **Shift+click Frame 464** of the **background** layer to select **Frame 464** of both layers. Press **F5** to add frames up to **Frame 464** so you can see the background and the buttons throughout the video.

---

11 Move the **playhead** back to **Frame 1** and click the **Insert Layer** button to add a new layer to the **Timeline**. Rename this layer **labels** and make sure it is positioned at the top of the layer stack.

---

12 On the **labels** layer, select **Frame 1**. In the **Property Inspector**, type **boarder1** in the **Frame Label** field to mark the place where the first snowboarder appears.

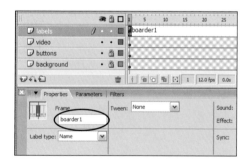

13 Scrub the **playhead** forward to see where a transition occurs and a new snowboarder appears in the video. Notice a new snowboarder appears at **Frame 89**. On the **labels** layer, click **Frame 89** and press **F7** to add a blank keyframe. In the **Property Inspector**, type **boarder2** in the **Frame Label** field to mark the place where the second snowboarder appears.

14 Repeat Step 13 to add blank keyframes and frame labels for three more snowboarders.

Hint: boarder3 = Frame 288, boarder4 = Frame 364, and boarder5 = Frame 412.

In the following steps, you will add behaviors to the buttons to target these frame labels.

15 Choose **Window > Behaviors** to open the **Behaviors** panel.

16 Position the **playhead** at **Frame 1** on the **Timeline**. Unlock the **buttons** layer and click **button 1** on the **Stage** to select it.

You will add behaviors to the buttons in the following steps.

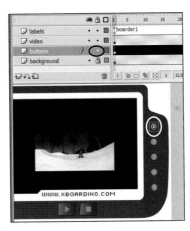

17 Click the **Add Behavior** button and choose **Movieclip > Goto and Play at frame or label** to open the **Goto and Play at frame or label** dialog box.

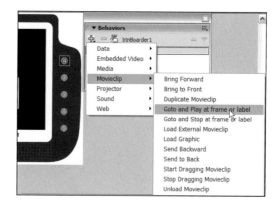

18 Make sure **_root** is selected. In the **Frame Number/Label** field, type **boarder1**. Press **Enter** (Windows) or **Return** (Mac) to accept the new setting and to instruct the **playhead** to go to the frame label named **boarder1** on the main **Timeline** (**_root**) when the user clicks **button 1**.

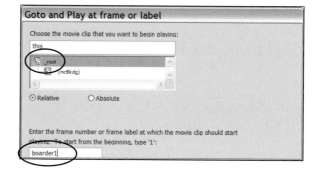

19 Repeat steps 16, 17, and 18 for the remaining four buttons. In the **Frame Number/Label** field, for **button 2**, type **boarder2**; for **button 3**, type **boarder3**; for **button 4**, type **boarder4**; and for **button 5**, type **boarder5**.

20 Choose **Control > Test Movie** and click each of the buttons to the right of the video clip to test the buttons. Each button will play a different snowboarder segment of the video. When you are finished, close the preview window.

You will learn to add anchors to your movie next.

Note: You may have noticed the Stop and Play buttons worked as well! These were programmed for you using the exact same ActionScript you applied in Exercise 2.

21 In the **labels** layer, click the **boarder1** frame label on the Timeline to select that frame (**Frame 1**). In the **Property Inspector**, choose **Anchor** from the **Label type** pop-up menu.

Notice the icon next to the frame label on the Timeline changes. This is an indication that a named anchor is attached to that frame.

NOTE:

What Is a Named Anchor?

In Flash 8, you can create movies that work with the Forward and Back buttons in a browser. This feature is called a **named anchor**, which is a special frame label that resides on the main Timeline and has a unique anchor icon. Once the named anchor is played in a browser window, it is registered in a browser's history. Then, when a user clicks on the Back button in the browser window, the browser will play the previous named anchor position on the Timeline.

The Named Anchor feature will work in the Macromedia Flash 6 Player (or higher) on browsers that support the **FSCommand** with JavaScript, including Internet Explorer or Netscape 3 and above. Named anchors do not work on browsers running on the Macintosh operating system.

22 Repeat Step 21 by selecting each of the remaining four frame labels (**boarder2**, **boarder3**, **boarder4**, and **boarder5**) and then choosing **Anchor** from the **Label type** pull-down menu in the **Property Inspector**.

23 Click the **Insert Layer** button to add a new layer to the **Timeline**. Rename it **actions**, and make sure it is at the top of the layer stack.

24 On the **actions** layer, select **Frame 464** and press **F7** to add a blank keyframe.

You will add a **stop** frame action to this frame next.

25 In the **Actions** panel, select **Global Functions > Timeline Control** and double-click the **stop** action to add it to the **Script** pane.

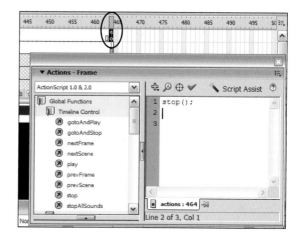

This action will stop the playhead at Frame 464, which is the end of the snowboard movie.

26 Choose **File > Publish Settings** to open the **Publish Settings** dialog box. Click the **HTML** tab, and in the **Template** pop-up menu, choose **Flash with Named Anchors**. Leave the rest of the settings at their defaults, and click **OK** to add JavaScript into the HTML document that will catch the named anchors as they play in the browser.

Note: You will learn all about the Publish settings in detail in Chapter 17, "*Publishing and Exporting.*"

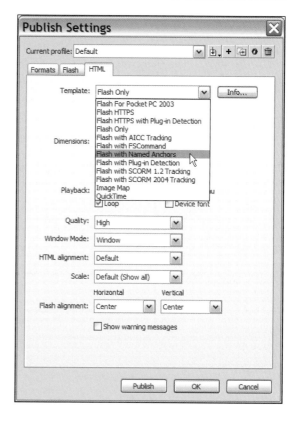

27 Press **F12** to publish your Flash 8 movie and preview it in a browser, where you'll be able to test the named anchors. As the video plays, notice the end of the URL in the browser window: it changes to reflect the named anchor that is currently playing. When the movie reaches the end and stops, test the **Back** button in the browser; it will jump back one anchor to **boarder4**. Click it again and it will jump back to **boarder3**. In the browser, click the **Forward** button, and the movie will advance forward to the next named anchor. Neat! When you are finished, close the browser window.

Tip: You can use named anchors with video or with any content on the main Timeline. Because many users will not be accustomed to using the Forward and Back buttons with Flash movies, you may have to add some text to your movie, instructing the users that they can navigate using the browser Forward and Back buttons.

Note: You will learn more about the Publish Preview options in Chapter 17, "*Publishing and Exporting.*"

NOTE:

Other Uses for Named Anchors

In the past, Flash movies could never utilize the Back button of a browser, which created a usability problem because many people built entire Web sites using the SWF file format. The named anchors technique lets you build browser functionality into any Flash 8 Web site. You learned from this exercise how easy it is to add this feature, so consider this technique for any complete Web site you build in the future. Just make sure the named anchors exist on the main Timeline or in the main Timeline of other scenes. They have to be placed there in order to work correctly.

---

28 When you are finished, close **targetVideo.fla**. You do not need to save your changes.

---

4 | Editing Video

The editing feature in the Video Import wizard lets you choose which portions of the video you want to import into your Flash 8 movie. This is a very useful tool if you don't have the budget to purchase a separate video editing program, such as Apple Final Cut Pro or Adobe Premiere Pro. Instead of opening a separate video-editing program to simply extract a few clips from a larger video clip, you can now streamline your workflow by performing the process right inside of Flash 8. In this exercise, you will learn how to select a video file, extract a few clips from that video, and then import *only* those clips into your Flash movie.

1 Open **importClips.fla** from the **chap_16** folder.

2 Click the **Insert Layer** button to add a new layer to the **Timeline**. Rename it **video**, and make sure it is at the top of the layer stack. Make sure the **video** layer is selected.

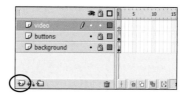

3 Choose **File > Import > Import to Stage** and select the **jumps.mov** file from the **chap_16** folder. Click **Open** (Windows) or **Import** (Mac) to open the **Video Import** wizard.

NOTE:

Importing Video

There are two ways to import video into Flash 8. The first way is to choose **File > Import > Import to Stage**, as you have done up to this point in the chapter. This menu option will import the video clip into the Library and add an instance of it to the Stage. The second way is to choose **File > Import > Import to Library**, which will import the video clip directly into the Library without placing an instance on the Stage. These two techniques will work for any media being imported into Flash 8 as well, including bitmaps, sounds, symbols, and artwork from other programs.

4 In the **Select Video** screen, select **On my local machine** (Windows) or **On your computer** (Mac) and click **Next** (Windows) or **Continue** (Mac). In the **Deployment** screen, make sure the **Embed video in SWF and play in Timeline** option is selected. Click **Next** (Windows) or **Continue** (Mac).

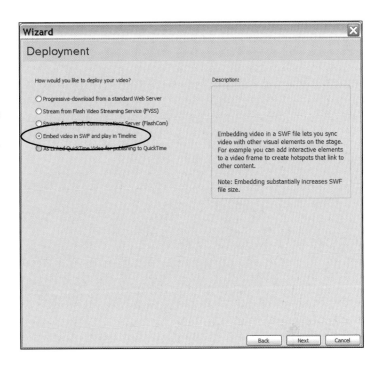

5 On the **Embedding** screen, select **Movie clip** from the **Symbol type** pop-up menu, select the **Place instance on stage** and **Expand timeline if needed** options and make sure the **Edit the video first** radio button is selected. Click **Next** (Windows) or **Continue** (Mac).

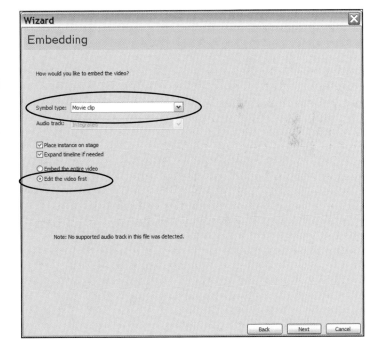

The Customized Editing Screen in the Video Import Wizard

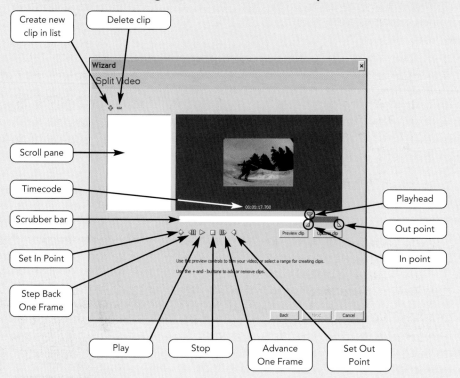

Create new clip in list

Delete clip

Scroll pane

Timecode

Scrubber bar

Set In Point

Step Back One Frame

Playhead

Out point

In point

Play

Stop

Advance One Frame

Set Out Point

The Split Video screen lets you trim the length of your video clips and create multiple clips, simplifying the video editing process and streamlining your workflow. With this editor, it is easy to select exactly which parts of the video to create clips from. You will do this in the following steps.

6 In the **Split Video** screen, drag the **play-head** until the timecode reads **00:00:05.546**.

This is the first frame of one of the jumps in this video. You will mark this as the first frame of your soon-to-be clip next.

7 Click the **Set In Point** button to move the **In** point (the beginning marker of your new clip) to the current position of the **playhead**.

8 Position the **playhead** to timecode **00:00:07.820** (the last frame of this jump clip). If needed, use the left and right arrow keys on your keyboard to fine-tune the time-code setting. Click the **Set Out Point** button to set the **Out** point to the current position of the **playhead**.

9 Click the **Preview clip** button to review the trimmed clip. Click the **Create new clip in list** button to add a new clip to the scroll pane. Rename the new clip **jump1**.

Next, you're going to define one more clip, and then import both clips into your Flash project.

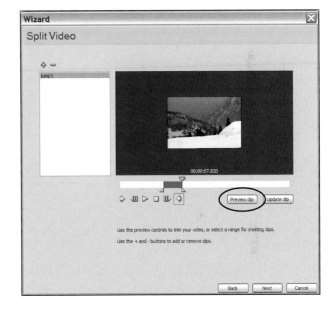

10 Drag the **Out Point** slider all the way to the end of the video.

11 Drag the **playhead** to timecode
00:00:16.855 (the last frame of this jump
clip). If needed, use the left and right
arrow keys on your keyboard to fine-tune
the timecode setting. Click the **Set In
Point** button to define the beginning
point of this clip.

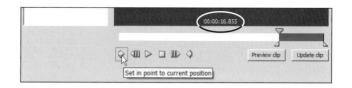

The Out point of this clip is the very last frame of the video, which you already set in Step 10.

12 Click the **Preview clip** button to
review the trimmed clip. Click the **Create
new clip in list** button to add a new clip
to the scroll pane. Rename the new clip
jump2. Click **Next** (Windows) or
Continue (Mac).

You've selected a video clip on your hard
drive and selected two small clips from
the larger video. Next, you're going to
import both clips into your Flash 8 project.

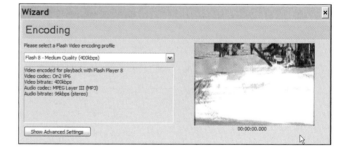

13 In the **Encoding** screen, choose
Flash 8- Medium Quality (400kbps)
from the **encoding profile** pop-up menu.
Click **Next** (Windows) or **Continue** (Mac).
In the **Finish Video Import** screen,
review your settings and click **Finish**.

14 When the import is complete, Flash places both video clips in the **Library** and one (**jump2**) on the **Stage**. Drag the video clip onto the **Stage** so that it is centered inside the background window.

Tip: If you want to include the second video clip (jump1) in the project, drag it from the Library onto the Stage.

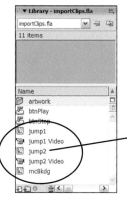

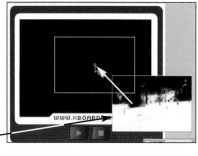

---

15 On the **Stage**, click the video clip. In the **Instance Name** field of the **Property Inspector**, type **jumps**.

This is now the instance name of the jump2 video clip. This name is also incorporated into the ActionScript that has already been added to the Stop and Play buttons at the bottom of the Stage.

---

16 Choose **Control > Test Movie** to preview your new video clip.

As you can see, now instead of the video playing the whole way through, it is playing only the jump2 clip you defined in the Video Import wizard!

This is a fast, easy way to trim away unwanted portions of a video clip. In addition, trimming your video clips also decreases the size of the final SWF file.

---

17 When you are finished, close **importClips.fla**. You do not need to save your changes.

As handy as the Flash 8 Video Import wizard is, it has limitations. You can encode only one video clip at a time, which can make the process of encoding multiple video clips very time-intensive. If you work extensively with video-based content, Flash Professional 8 includes the Flash 8 Video Encoder, a stand-alone video encoding application you can install on a dedicated computer and use to batch process video clips. Batch processing can speed up your workflow by freeing up your production computer and letting you encode multiple clips at a time.

In this exercise, you will get an introduction to Flash 8 Video Encoder by adding several video clips to the encoder, setting encoding options for each clip, and batch encoding all the clips in one process.

1 Locate the Flash 8 Video Encoder application on your computer. By default, it is installed in a **Flash 8 Video Encoder** folder in the **Macromedia** folder in the **Program Files** (Windows) or **Applications** (Macintosh) folder.

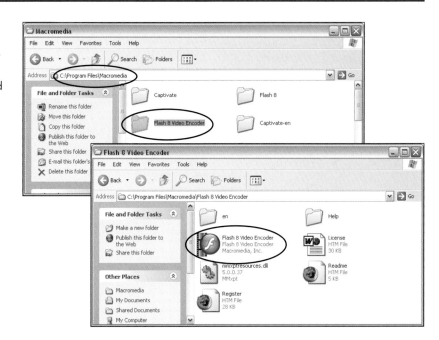

2 Double-click the **Flash 8 Video Encoder** application file to launch the application.

3 Click the **Add** button to open the **Open** dialog box. Browse to the **chap_16** folder. Hold down the **Ctrl** (Windows) or **Command** (Mac) key and click the **catchingAir.mov**, **jumps.mov**, **linking.mov**, and **shortJump.mov** video clips to multiple-select all four movies. Click **Open**.

Notice the four video clips are displayed and selected in the video encoder list in the Flash 8 Video Encoder dialog box, and the encoding Status reads *Waiting*. The Settings values are all set to the current default setting (Flash 8 – Medium Quality). The Encoder is waiting for you to set the encoding settings for each video clip. You can adjust settings for each clip individually or for multiple clips at the same time. You will do each in the next several steps.

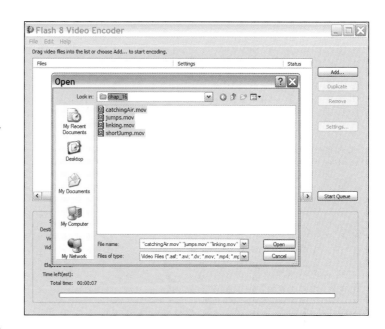

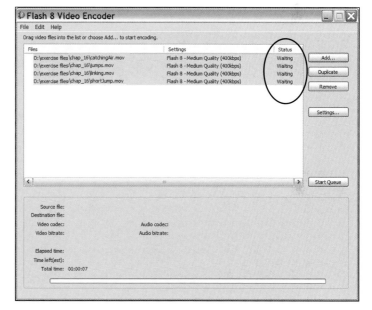

4 Click the **catchingAir** clip to select it. Click the **Settings** button.

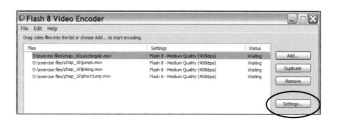

5 In the **Flash Video Encoding Settings** dialog box, click the **Advanced Settings** button so the settings match those shown here.

In the Advanced Settings area you can set the encoding options, establish cue points, and crop and trim the video clip.

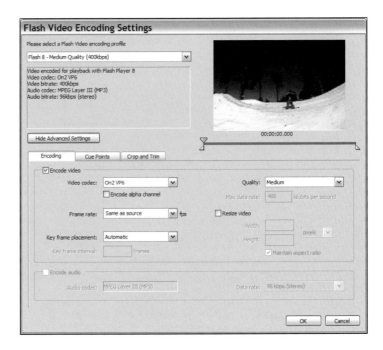

6 Click the **Cue Points** tab.

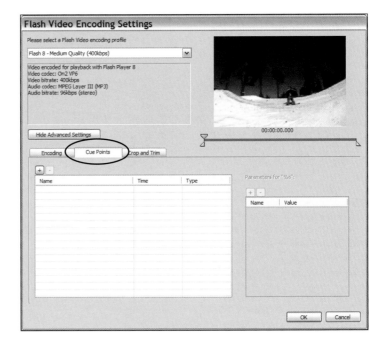

Cue Points

Cue points are established points, or markers, in the video clip that you can use to trigger other actions during playback of the clip. For example, you can create a Flash presentation that has video playing in one area of the screen while text and

graphics appear in another area. Cue points placed in the video trigger updates to the text and graphic, keeping them in sync and current with the video.

You can create cue points in either the Flash 8 Video Encoder or the Video Import wizard. Each cue point consists of a name and the time at which it occurs. Specify cue point times in the format **hour:minute:second:frame**. You can specify cue point times with any frame rate and also express them in milliseconds rather than frame numbers.

You can also add and remove cue points through ActionScript with the **addCuePoint** and **removeCuePoint** methods. For more information, see "Media components (Flash Professional only)" in the "Using Components" section of Flash Help.

7 Drag the **playhead** until the timecode reads **00:00:05.546.** The video preview window lets you visually identify points in the video at which to insert cue points. (Use the left and right arrow keys on your keyboard to fine-tune the timecode setting). Click the **Add Cue Point** (+) button. Click inside the **Name** field and type **jump1**. Leave the **Type** setting to **Event**.

Flash Video Encoder embeds a cue point on the specified frame of the video and populates the cue point list with a placeholder including the name of the cue point and the time during playback when the event will be triggered. You can also specify the type of cue point you want to embed: navigation or event.

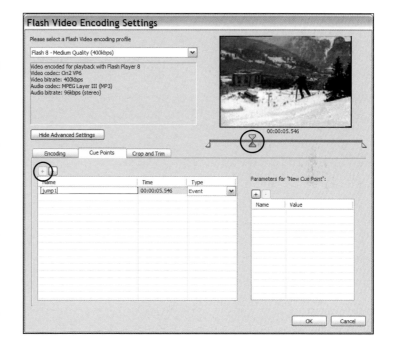

Navigation cue points insert a keyframe at that point in the video clip and are used for navigating or locating the specified point in the video clip. Event cue points are used to trigger ActionScript methods at the point the cue point is reached.

You can also establish parameters for each cue point. Parameters are sets of key-value pairs that are passed to the ActionScript method triggered by the cue point. You can use parameters to perform additional work such as indicating which text or graphic content should be displayed for each cue point.

---

8 Drag the **playhead** until the timecode reads **00:00:16.855**. (Use the left and right arrow keys on your keyboard to fine-tune the timecode setting). Click the **Add Cue Point** (+) button. Click inside the **Name** field and type **jump2**. Leave the **Type** setting to **Event**. Click **OK**.

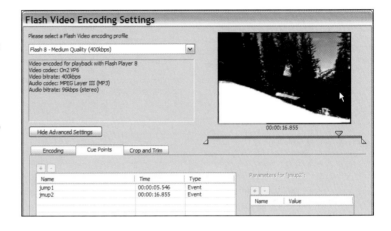

You now have established two event cue points in this video clip that you can use in a script for a variety of duties, such as triggering the display of addi-

tional content, playing audio, loading movie clips and much, much more. You can also change each to a navigation-type cue point and use them with ActionScript to locate and jump to any other navigation cue point in the list. For more information on these techniques, see the "Working with cue points" topic in the "Learning ActionScript 2.0" section of Flash 8 Online Help.

---

9 In the **Flash 8 Video Encoder** screen, click the **jumps.mov** clip and **Shift+click** the **shortJump.mov** clip to select each of the last three clips. Click the **Settings** button.

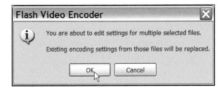

---

10 Flash displays a warning that you are about to edit the settings for multiple files and existing settings will be replaced. Click **OK** to acknowledge the warning.

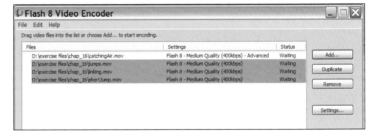

---

11 From the **Flash Video Encoding** pop-up menu, choose **Flash 8 – Low Quality (150 kbps)**. Click **OK**.

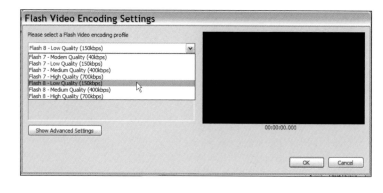

One advantage of using the Flash 8 Video Encoder instead of the Video Import wizard is that you can encode more than one video clip at a time, each with different encoding settings. You can also use a single encode set-ting on multiple clips at the same time, and batch process the entire group of video clips with a single click. You will batch process this group of clips next.

---

12 Click the **Start Queue** button. The Video Encoder starts batch processing the clips, starting with the first clip, **catchingAir.mov**. The progress of the encoding is displayed at the bottom of the screen, together with a preview of the video as it is being encoded. You can stop the batch process at any time by clicking the **Stop Queue** button. When the batch process is fin-ished, a **green check** appears for each clip that was successfully encoded. A **red exclamation point** appears if any errors were encountered during encoding, and an **Errors** dialog box provides more details.

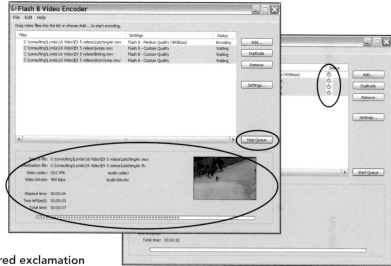

That's it! You have successfully encoded your first batch of video clips using the new stand-alone Video Encoder application. This is a fast and easy way to process multiple video clips.

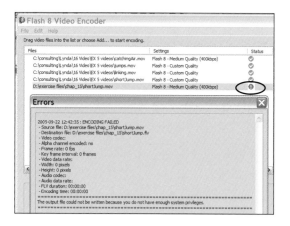

13 The encoded video clips are saved to the **chap_16** folder as Flash FLV files and are ready to be imported into your Flash files. No further processing or encoding is required (or will be performed by Flash when they are imported). Import the video using the same procedure detailed in Exercise 1. Close the **Flash 8 Video Encoder** application by clicking the **Close** button.

Nice job! You have made it through another chapter. Get ready for the next chapter—it is filled with useful information on how to publish your movies using the Publish and Export settings in Flash 8.

17

Publishing and Exporting

Prior to this chapter, you tested your movies in Flash 8 by choosing Control > Test Movie to generate a SWF file. This chapter shows you how to publish movies using the Publish settings. Testing and publishing both produce SWF files, but publishing offers many more options and greater control over the final output. As well, you'll learn how to generate an HTML file and a projector file from Flash 8. This chapter also teaches you how to export an image from a project file.

The Publish settings in Flash 8 are complex; you'll find a reference guide at the end of the chapter, which will show you additional settings that are more advanced than those covered by the exercises. In addition, you'll find a table providing a list of the file types you can export. The chapter concludes with a look at some helpful tips and tricks for optimizing your movies.

What Types of Content Can Flash 8 Publish?

In addition to the SWF file, Flash 8 can publish to several different file formats. This table describes many of the available publishing options:

Flash 8 Publishing Options	
Format	**Description**
Web delivery	If you plan to publish Web content, you can create an HTML file to embed the Flash 8 movie into. You'll learn how to generate this HTML code, and establish how the movie will appear, in this chapter.
CD-ROM delivery	If you want to run Flash 8 on a CD-ROM or other physical media, you can create a projector file, which you'll learn to do in this chapter.
Email attachment	If you want to create a Flash 8 movie you can easily attach to an email, you can create a projector file, which you'll learn how to do in this chapter.
QuickTime	You can generate a Flash track for QuickTime, which offers the opportunity to create Flash 8 controllers or buttons for QuickTime content. You learned how to do this in Chapter 16, "*Video.*"
Image file	If you want to publish an image file, such as a JPEG, PNG, or GIF, from your project file, you can use the Publish settings to create an image, which you'll learn how to do in this chapter.

This exercise walks you through the Publish settings interface to learn how to create the necessary HTML files for Web delivery of Flash 8 content. The following steps show you how changes you make in the Publish settings affect the way your movie is viewed in a Web browser.

---

1 Copy the **chap_17** folder from the **HOT CD-ROM** to your **Desktop**. Open **publish.fla** from the **publishTesting** folder in the **chap_17** folder. Choose **Control > Test Movie** to preview the movie. This is the finished version of the effects movie you created in Chapter 9, "*Bitmaps.*"

Notice the title publish.swf at the top of the window.

---

2 Leave Flash 8 for a moment and open the **chap_17** folder on your **Desktop**. Open the **publishTesting** folder.

Inside, you will see two files: one FLA file and one SWF file. When you chose Control > Test Movie, Flash 8 created the SWF file in the folder as well.

---

3 Return to Flash 8. Choose **File > Publish Preview > Default - (HTML)**, or press **F12**, to launch the default browser on your computer.

Notice the browser displays an HTML page with the SWF file embedded inside it. When you use the Publish Preview command, the Publish settings determine how Flash 8 decides to publish the documents. You will work with the Publish settings in just a few steps.

WARNING: | **Publish Preview Versus Test Movie**
The Publish Preview command gives you the most accurate representation of how your movie will look on the Web. The preview you see when you use Control > Test Movie does not always appear exactly the same as the published movie appears on a Web server. For example, sound in your movie may vary slightly, and complex animations may animate slightly slower when using the Test Movie command. To be safe, use the Publish Preview or Publish command to view the movie before you upload it to the Web.

---

4 Look in the **publishTesting** folder.

Inside you will now see three files: the FLA file, the SWF file, and the HTML file. When you preview your movie in a browser, Flash 8 creates an HTML file in the same folder where you saved your FLA file. Notice all three files have the same name. By default, Flash 8 names the additional files with the same name as the FLA file. You will learn how to change these names in the next few steps.

HTML file

5 Return to Flash 8 and choose **File > Publish Settings** to open the **Publish Settings** dialog box. Make sure the **Formats** tab is selected.

The Formats tab is used to specify which file formats Flash 8 will create when you publish the movie. Other tabs will appear or disappear according to which check boxes you select.

Tip: You can also access the **Publish Settings** dialog box by clicking the **Settings** button in the **Property Inspector**.

---

6 Make sure the **Flash** and **HTML** boxes are selected. Notice all the filenames are set to have the prefix **publish**. By default, Flash uses the name of the FLA as a basis for naming the other file types. Type **movie.swf** inside the **Flash File** field to change the name of the published SWF file. Type **webPage.html** inside the **HTML File** field.

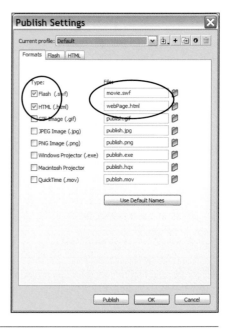

---

7 Click the **Publish** button to publish the SWF and HTML files with the names you just specified in Step 6. Click **OK** to exit the **Publish Settings** dialog box.

Flash 8 will create these new files and save them in the same folder as the original FLA file.

---

8 To make sure the new files have been published, look in the **publishTesting** folder.

Inside you will now see *five* files: the three files that were already there, each with the **publish** name, and two new files named **movie.swf** and **webPage.html**. Each time you click the Publish button in the Publish Settings dialog box (or you use File > Publish), Flash 8 writes and creates all of the files you selected in the Publish Settings dialog box (in this case, SWF and HTML). If you publish more than once with the same settings, Flash 8 will overwrite the existing files each time.

---

9 Return to Flash 8 and choose **File > Publish Settings**. In the **Publish Settings** dialog box, click the **Flash** tab. Choose **Top down** from the **Load Order** pop-up menu to load each layer in the movie from the top layer first and continue downward. Don't click **OK** or **Publish** just yet; you will change another setting in the next step.

Choosing the Top down option is a good habit to get into since, as you learned in Chapter 12, "*ActionScripting Basics and Behaviors,*" you should always place your actions on the top layer. When you choose Top down, your ActionScripting layer will always load first in the Macromedia Flash Player.

---

10 Select the **Generate size report** option and click **Publish** to open the **Output** panel and display the size report. Because you will be looking at the size report in a different manner, close the **Output** panel for now. Click **OK** to close the **Publish Settings** dialog box.

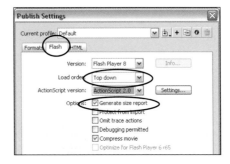

---

11 Look in the **publishTesting** folder.

Notice the new file report text file. Why is it named **movie Report.txt**? When you generate a size report, Flash creates a detailed report about the current SWF file. In this case, you renamed the SWF file movie, so the size report is named **movie Report.txt**.

---

12 Double-click the **movie Report.txt** file to open it. When you are done reviewing the file, close it.

Whenever you select Generate size report, Flash 8 creates a special text file giving a breakdown of the file size contributions of all of the symbols, fonts, and other elements in the movie. This is a handy tool when you want to know, frame by frame, how big the movie is, how many elements are present in the movie, and even which font faces you used and which font characters were embedded in the SWF file!

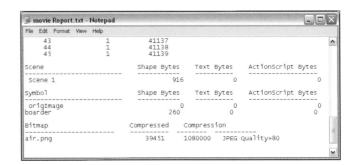

13 Return to Flash 8 and choose **File > Publish Settings** to open the **Publish Settings** dialog box. Click the **Flash** tab and select the **Protect from import** option.

Selecting this box prevents others from importing your SWF movie file into Flash and converting it back to a project file. Selecting the **Protect from import** option is not 100 percent secure. You can still import a protected movie into a Macromedia Director movie, and people "in-the-know" can also use third-party utilities to break into your Flash movie. To be safe, don't put highly sensitive information into Flash 8 movies, but do select the **Protect from import** option.

---

14 Click the **HTML** tab. Make sure **Dimensions: Match Movie** is selected. Click **Publish** to publish these changes, then click **OK** to close the **Publish Settings** dialog box.

The Match Movie option determines the movie's dimensions in the HTML tags. This value can be in pixels or can be a percentage of window size. As you will see in the next step, the Match Movie option publishes the movie at the same dimensions as the Stage and will not allow the SWF file to scale.

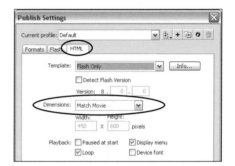

---

15 In the **publishTesting** folder, double-click **webPage.html** to open it. Click and drag the lower-right corner of the browser window to resize it.

Notice the SWF file doesn't scale with the browser window and, as you make the window smaller, the image cuts off. You'll fix this in the next step.

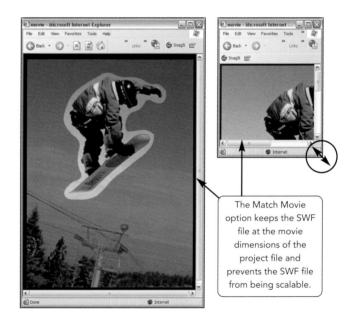

The Match Movie option keeps the SWF file at the movie dimensions of the project file and prevents the SWF file from being scalable.

16 Return to Flash 8 and choose **File > Publish Settings**. In the **Publish Settings** dialog box, click the **HTML** tab and choose **Dimensions: Percent**. Notice the default settings read **100%** for both **Width** and **Height**, which will keep both the width and height of the SWF file at 100% of the size of the browser. Click **Publish**, then click **OK** to

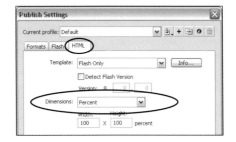

close the **Publish Settings** dialog box and to replace the **webPage.html** file you created in Step 14.

You need to click the Publish button if you want to preview the new settings you specified. Flash 8 will only update the HTML document with the new settings if you click the Publish button or choose File > Publish.

---

17 To see the difference this setting makes, open the file **webPage.html** file from the **publishTesting** folder. Resize the browser window. Notice the SWF file always matches the dimensions of the browser window.

Notice the SWF file scales this time! The Percent setting fills the browser window 100 percent by 100 percent, so that no matter how you resize the browser window, the movie will scale to fit the entire browser window and will not be cut off.

The Percent option sets the SWF file to be a percentage relative to the Web browser, therefore allowing the SWF file to be scalable.

NOTE: | **Important Uploading Advice!**

Flash 8 publishes the HTML file with the assumption the SWF file will be located in the same folder as the HTML file, so when you upload the HTML file to a Web server, make sure you put both files in the same directory.

---

18 Close **publish.fla**. You don't need to save your changes.

This exercise showed you many of the common Publish settings on the Flash and HTML tabs of the Publish Settings dialog box. For a more in-depth look at what each of the settings on these tabs can do, refer to the tables at the end of this chapter.

NOTE: | **Scalable Bitmaps and Vector Art**

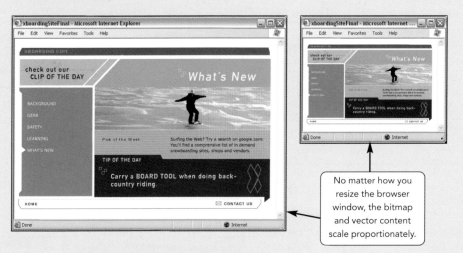

No matter how you resize the browser window, the bitmap and vector content scale proportionately.

Flash 8 is known for its vector capabilities, but its support of bitmap images is superb and far exceeds the support offered by HTML. Flash 8 lets you scale, animate, and transform (skew, distort, and so on) bitmaps without much image degradation. As a result, you can combine bitmap and vector images in your movies. When you create scalable content with bitmaps, make sure you import the bitmap at the largest size (although this can dramatically increase the final size of your SWF file) you plan to display it in your movie to ensure the best image quality without degradation.

2 | Creating Projectors

Have you ever received an email attachment with an .exe or .hqx extension and found when you opened it that it was a Macromedia Flash movie that played right in its own window without a browser? If you have, you may be more familiar with projector files than you think. Projector files are often sent via email because they are stand-alone files that can play without the Macromedia Flash Player on most computers. You can also distribute projector files via floppy disks or CD-ROMs, or show them from your hard drive without a browser (as a great PowerPoint substitute). This exercise teaches you how to create a projector file using the Publish Settings dialog box.

---

1 Open **projector.fla** from the **chap_17** folder.

In the following steps, you'll turn this Flash movie into a stand-alone projector file.

---

2 Choose **Control > Test Movie** to preview the movie and to create and save the SWF file in the same folder as the FLA file.

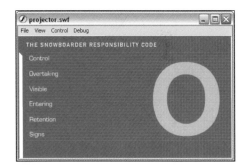

---

3 Close the **Preview** window. Choose **File > Publish Settings** to open the **Publish Settings** dialog box.

---

4 Deselect the **Flash** and **HTML** options. Select the **Windows Projector** and **Macintosh Projector** options. In the **Windows Projector File** field, type **wProjector.exe**. In the **Macintosh Projector File** field, type **mProjector.hqx**. Click **Publish**. Click **OK** to close the **Publish Settings** dialog box.

When you click Publish, Flash 8 automatically saves the projector files to the same folder as your FLA file.

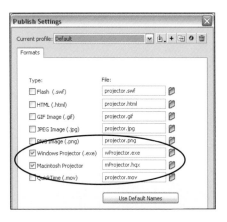

Missing Tabs in the Projector Publish Settings?

When you select the projector file types from the Formats tab in the Publish Settings dialog box, no additional tabs are available for you to alter the settings. However, you can control the way your projectors behave by using ActionScript and FSCommands.

5 Open the **chap_17** folder on your **Desktop**. Inside you'll see the two files you just generated, **mProjector** and **wProjector**.

Look for this icon on either platform as visual feedback that you can open this projector.

Note: Although you can create projectors for both Macintosh and Windows formats on either platform, you can't open a Mac projector (HQX) on a Windows machine, and likewise, you can't open a Windows projector (EXE) on a Mac computer. The format that works on your computer will display the icon shown in the illustration here.

6 If you're using Windows, double-click the file named **wProjector** to open it. If you're using a Mac, double-click the file named **mProjector** to open it.

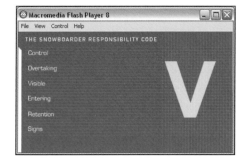

You have just created your first projector file. Notice that the sound and animation play. This is because the projector file takes the entire movie, sound and all, and displays it in its own player.

7 Keep **projector.fla** open for the next exercise.

3 | Modifying Projectors with FSCommands

In the last exercise, you learned how to create a projector file. This exercise shows you how to modify the original project file by adding ActionScript to control the stand-alone projector file. The following steps teach you how to use FSCommands to force the movie to take up the full screen of the computer and to disable the menu so that users cannot right-click or Ctrl+click the movie and see a list of menu items.

---

1 If you just completed Exercise 2, **projector.fla** should still be open. If it's not, go back and complete Exercise 2. Choose **File > Save As** to save a copy of the file. Name the file **fsProjector.fla**.

---

2 Click the **Insert Layer** button to add a new layer to the movie. Rename the new layer **actions**. Make sure this layer is on top of all the other layers.

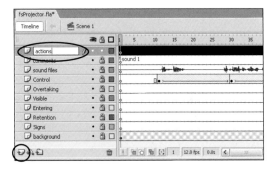

---

3 Click the first keyframe of the **actions** layer, and press **F9** (Windows) or **Option+F9** (Mac) to open the **Actions** panel.

Next, you will add the ActionScript to control the stand-alone projector file in this keyframe.

NOTE:

FSCommands as Frame Actions

It is usually most effective to add the FSCommands that control the window behavior to one of the first keyframes in the movie so your commands take effect immediately after the player opens.

FSCommands are actions that invoke JavaScript functions from within Flash 8. They include a command that is similar to an instruction, and an argument that checks to see if the command should be allowed (true) or not (false). A table at the end of this exercise describes the FSCommands for the stand-alone projector.

---

4 In the **Actions** panel, click the **Script Assist** button. Select **Global Functions > Browser/Network** and double-click the `fscommand` action to add it to the **Script** pane.

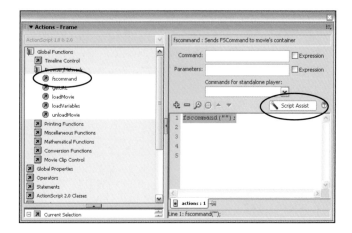

5 In the **Script Assist** pane, choose `fullscreen [true/false]` from the **Commands for standalone player** pop-up menu.

When the `fscommand` action is triggered (because it is on the first frame of the movie, it will be triggered when the movie is first launched), it will make the projector launch and completely fill the user's screen. The `fullscreen` command makes the player take up the whole screen and prevents screen resizing when the parameter is set to **true**.

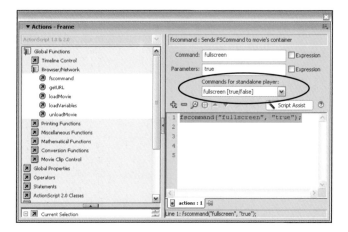

6 Choose **File > Publish Settings**. In the **Publish Settings** dialog box, rename the projector files **fsWprojector.exe** and **fsMprojector.hqx**, which will publish two new files without replacing the old projector files you created in the last exercise. When you are finished, click **Publish** to publish the projectors with the FSCommands added. Click **OK** to close the **Publish Settings** dialog box.

7 Open the **chap_17** folder on your **Desktop**. Inside you will see all the files you have created thus far. If you are using Windows, double-click **fsWprojector.exe** to open it. If you are using a Mac, double-click **fsMprojector.hqx** to open it. Now the projector will launch full screen! To exit the full-screen mode, press the **Esc** key.

8 Return to Flash 8. Make sure **Frame 1** is still selected in the **actions** layer. In the **Actions** pane, select **Global Functions > Browser/Network** and double-click **fscommand**. In the **Script Assist** pane, choose **showmenu [true/false]** from the **Commands for standalone player** pop-up menu. In the **Parameters** field, type **false**.

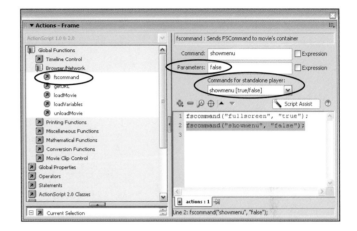

While a projector file plays, users can either right-click (Windows) or Ctrl+click (Mac) to view a list of menu items. If the projector is set to full screen, you may not want users to zoom in or out or manipulate the way the movie is presented. By disabling the menu (setting **showmenu** to **false**), you can limit the control users have.

9 Choose **File > Publish** to publish the changes you made (adding the new FSCommand) to the files you specified in the **Publish Settings** dialog box.

10 Open the **chap_17** folder on your **Desktop**. If you are using Windows, double-click the **fsWprojector.exe** file to open it. If you are using a Mac, double-click the **fsMprojector.hqx** file to open it. Try to **right-click** (Windows) or **Ctrl+click** (Mac) to access the shortcut menu and see the full list of menu items.

You can't do it! You should see only the About Macromedia Flash Player 8 and Settings menu items. Because you set **showmenu** to **false**, you're preventing users from seeing the full menu and using any of the options.

11 When you are finished testing the projector file, close any open files.

Understanding the Stand-Alone Projector FSCommands		
Command	Arguments	Function
`fullscreen`	true/false	Sets the movie to fill the full screen when set to **true**, and returns the movie to a normal window when set to **false**. Setting the movie to **fullscreen** without also setting **allowscale** to **false** can result in the movie changing scale in some cases.
`allowscale`	true/false	Enables or disables the user's ability to scale the movie. If the argument is set to **false**, the movie will always be presented at the original size and can never be scaled. It also prevents the scaling that occurs when the movie is set to **fullscreen**. It is important to note that this option refers to the Macromedia Flash movie itself and not the stand-alone projector window, since the user can still scale the player window larger or smaller by clicking and dragging an edge of it. However, the movie will remain at the original size if **allowscale** is set to **false**. Note also that if **showmenu** is not set to **false**, the user can still scale the movie by right-clicking (Windows) or Ctrl+clicking (Mac) to access the pop-up Options menu, which includes Zoom In and Zoom Out options.
`showmenu`	true/false	When set to **true**, enables a user to right-click (Windows) or Ctrl+click (Mac) the projector and have access to the full set of context menu items. When this command is set to **false**, it disables the user's ability to access any of the menu items except for the About Flash Player item.
`trapallkeys`	true/false	When set to **true**, enables the movie to capture keystrokes that the user enters on the keyboard.
`exec`	Path to application	Lets you launch another application file on the local system. For this to work properly, you must know the correct path and name of the application. You must type the correct path and name of the application in the Parameters field. If you are calling a file in the same directory, all you need is the filename.
`quit`	none	Quits the projector.

To Publish or to Export?

In addition to publishing files from Flash 8, you can also export files into other editable formats. Why would you want to do this? Sometimes you might want to use a frame of something you created in Flash 8 in another application, such as Adobe Photoshop or Adobe Illustrator. Many of the Export settings are very similar to the Publish settings, but the workflow for exporting files is different from publishing files. The following table documents the file formats you can export from Flash 8:

Export File Types Supported by Flash 8			
File Format	Extension	Windows	Mac
Adobe Illustrator 6.0, Adobe Illustrator sequence	.ai	x	x
Animated GIF, GIF image, GIF sequence	.gif	x	x
Bitmap and bitmap sequence	.bmp	x	
AutoCAD DXF image or DXF sequence	.dxf	x	x
Enhanced metafile and enhanced metafile sequence	.emf	x	
EPS 3.0 and EPS 3.0 sequence	.eps	x	x
Flash movie	.swf	x	x
JPEG image and JPEG sequence	.jpg	x	x
PICT and PICT sequence	.pct		x
PNG image and PNG sequence	.png	x	x
QuickTime video	.mov	x	x
WAV audio	.wav	x	
Windows AVI	.avi	x	
Windows metafile and Windows metafile sequence	.wmf	x	

In the last three exercises, you worked with the Publish settings in Flash 8 to publish different types of files. This exercise shows you how to use the Export settings to produce different file types from your project file. If you know you want to export only an image from your project file so you can work with it in another application, using the Export settings can be a great solution. You will learn how to export content from Flash 8 to create an Adobe Illustrator file in the steps that follow.

1 Open **exportingImages.fla** from the **chap_17** folder. Choose **Control > Test Movie** to preview the movie. When you are finished, close the preview window.

What if you also want to use the boarding logo as a static image for various printed pieces, such as a business card, letterhead, and envelope? In the following steps, you will learn how to export the logo as an Adobe Illustrator file.

2 On the **Stage**, click the logo to select it. Notice the setting in the **Property Inspector**—this is an instance of the movie clip named **mcOverAnim**.

3 Double-click the movie clip instance to open the movie clip's **Timeline**. Scrub the **playhead** to **Frame 20** of the animation, where the logo is in full color.

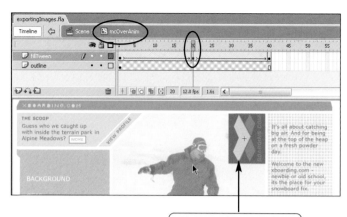

When you choose Export Image, you have several ways to decide what you're going to export. Flash 8 lets you export the frame the playhead is over (and all layers under that frame), export a selected frame (and all layers under and over that frame), or export a selected image (including the frame the image is on and all layers under and over that frame). Therefore, Flash 8 will export artwork based on what is selected or where the playhead is in the Timeline.

You are in the Movie Clip's symbol-editing environment.

4 Choose **File > Export > Export Image**. In the **Export Image** dialog box, navigate to the **chap_17** folder on your **Desktop**, name the file **logo**, and choose **Adobe Illustrator** from the **Save as type** pop-up menu. Click **Save**.

5 In the **Export Adobe Illustrator** dialog box, select the **Adobe Illustrator 6.0** option and click **OK**.

Adobe Illustrator 6.0 is the latest version Flash 8 can export to as an Illustrator file. Fortunately, you can open the exported file in Adobe Illustrator 6.0 and later.

6 Navigate to the **chap_17** folder on your **Desktop**. Double-click **logo.ai** file to open it in Adobe Illustrator.

You will see the logo all by itself, without any other images from the project file. Handy!

7 When you are finished, close this file. You don't need to save your changes.

More About the Publish Settings

The first three exercises in this chapter taught you firsthand how to use some of the Flash 8 Publish settings. I'm sure you noticed many settings that weren't covered in the exercises. You can change these settings at any point while developing or editing your project file (FLA).

Formats Tab

The first tab is the Formats tab. It lets you select the file formats that Flash 8 will publish. As each format is selected, additional tabs will appear to the right of the Formats tab, with the exception of the Windows Projector and Macintosh Projector types. Each tab holds settings specific to the selected format. The Formats tab also lets you modify the filename of each selected format that Flash 8 will publish.

Type

In the Type section under the Formats tab, you can select the type of files you wish to publish. Each of the types is covered in the pages that follow.

File

As you saw in Exercise 1, the default behavior is that all file formats will have the same name as the original project file. You can easily change the default by simply typing a new filename to the right of the corresponding file type. To revert back to the default name(s), simply click the **Use Default Names** button. You can also publish to another directory by targeting it in the name field, like this: **..:swfs/movie.swf**. By doing so, you can save and separate the project files (FLAs) from the movie files (SWFs) into their own folders and prevent clutter in your main directory.

Flash Settings

The Flash tab contains all of the settings that will be used for the SWF file, which is the file you have been viewing when you choose Control > Test Movie. The SWF file is embedded in the HTML document so that the movie can be seen properly in a Web browser. Here's a detailed description of each option:

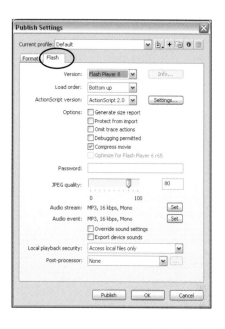

Flash Publish Settings

Name	Description
Version	Lets you export earlier formats of Flash SWF files. The real value of this feature is that it provides you the means to import (but not edit) work you did in Flash 8 into earlier versions of Flash, such as Flash 7.
Load order	Sets whether the layers will be loaded from the top down or the bottom up. For example, **Bottom up** means that the lowest layer will be shown first, the second lowest next, and so on. The reverse is true of **Top down**. This load setting takes place only when you have multiple elements loading in different layers in the same frame slot, and on a fast connection you may never see this happen. However, as you learned in Chapter 12, *"ActionScript Basics and Behaviors,"* you should always place your actions on the top layer. For this reason, you should select Top down so that your ActionScripting layer will load first. The frames (not layers) will always load in numeric order.
ActionScript version	From this pull-down menu, choose whether you used ActionScript 1.0 or ActionScript 2.0 in your movie. **Tip:** If you're unsure whether or not you used ActionScripting 1 or 2 in your Flash movie, just leave it set to ActionScript 2.0.

continues on next page

Flash Publish Settings *continued*

Name	Description
Generate size report	Creates a text file that contains detailed information about the size of all the elements in your movie. It will be published to the same directory as the rest of the files.
Protect from import	Prevents anyone from importing your SWF movie file into Flash and converting it back to a project file (FLA). This lets you protect your work. However, these protected files can still be imported into Macromedia Director and there are third-party applications that can break into any Flash movie, so to be on the safe side, don't put sensitive information into your Flash movies.
Omit trace actions	Blocks the Trace action (a debugging tool) from being exported with your movie. Select this option if you are using Trace actions and are producing a final cut of your movie.
Debugging permitted	Activates the debugger and allows the Flash 8 movie to be debugged remotely.
Compress movie	Compresses the Flash 8 movie to reduce file size and download time. This option is selected by default and works best when a movie has a lot of text or ActionScripting.
Optimize for Flash Player 6	If you're publishing a version 6 Flash movie, select this option to increase the playback performance of your movie. This performance increase will be realized only by those viewers who have Flash Player 6 r65 or later.
Password	Lets you set a password that prevents unauthorized users from debugging your movie.
JPEG quality	Lets you set the default image quality Export setting for all of the bitmap graphics in your movie. To retain greater control over your image fidelity and file size, ignore this setting and set the individual settings for each file in the Library instead.
Audio stream	Lets you set separate audio compression types and settings for all sounds in the movie that have a Stream Sync type and that have a compression type of Default.
Audio event	Lets you separately set the audio compression type and settings for all sounds in the movie that have a Start or Event Sync type and whose compression type is set to Default.
Override sound settings	Selecting this option lets you force all sounds in the movie to use the settings here, instead of using their own compression settings.

HTML Settings

The HTML tab lets you set values that determine how the HTML file is created for your movie. The HTML file is needed as a container to embed the SWF file if you plan to publish to the Web. By changing the settings under the HTML tab, you can change the appearance of your SWF file when viewed from a browser. The following table describes the available options:

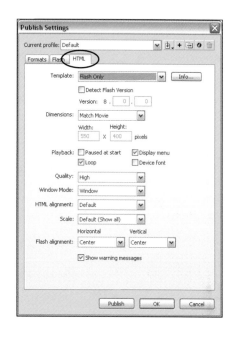

HTML Publish Settings

Name	Description
Template	Lets you choose from a list of HTML templates. Each of these templates was constructed to provide different types of support for the movie. If you don't choose a template, the default template will be used.
Detect Flash Version	Selecting this option will embed a Flash plug-in version detector into the HTML page. If the specified player is not found, users will be taken to an HTTPS server to download the required plug-in.
Dimensions	Lets you set the dimensions (in pixels or as a percentage of window size) the Macromedia Flash movie will be set to in the HTML tags. A setting of Match Movie will not allow the SWF file to scale in the browser. A percentage setting will allow the SWF content to scale if the user resizes the browser window.

continues on next page

HTML Publish Settings *continued*

Name	Description
Playback	Lets you define how the movie will act in the browser. You can select **Paused at start** to force the movie to start in a stopped position, without using a **Stop** action in the first keyframe. You can deselect the Loop check box to make the movie play only once. If you deselect the **Display menu** option, the Control menu will be disabled in the browser window. If you select **Device font**, the movie will use the local anti-aliased system font on the user's system instead of the font(s) embedded in the movie.
Quality	Sets whether the movie will be played back with emphasis on graphics quality or playback speed. High emphasizes graphics quality over speed; Low emphasizes playback speed over appearance.
Window Mode	Determines how the movie interacts in a DHTML environment. This setting has an effect only on browsers that are using absolute positioning and layering.
HTML alignment	Sets the horizontal alignment of the Macromedia Flash movie within the HTML page in a browser window.
Scale	Determines how the Macromedia Flash movie resizes within the movie window on the HTML page.
Flash alignment	Determines how the movie is aligned within the Macromedia Flash movie window. This determines how the movie will look if it is zoomed or cropped.
Show warning messages	Toggles whether or not the browser will display error messages that occur within the Object or Embed tags.

GIF Settings

You can use the GIF file format to produce animated graphics and static graphics—for example, an icon you want to save to use in other applications. By default, Flash will output the first frame of the movie as a GIF unless you specify a particular keyframe by entering the frame label **#Static** on the keyframe you select. Use caution, because Flash 8 will publish all the frames in the current movie as an animated GIF unless you designate a range of frames by entering the frame labels **#First** and **#Last** in the corresponding keyframes. The GIF settings are explained in detail in the table that follows:

GIF Publish Settings	
Name	**Description**
Dimensions	Lets you set the size of the GIF by entering the width and height into the corresponding fields. Selecting the **Match movie** option will generate a GIF that has the same dimensions as those in the Movie Properties dialog box in the project file.
Playback	Determines whether the GIF will be static or animated. If you select Static, the first keyframe of the movie will be used as the GIF image. If you would like a different keyframe to be used as the GIF image, you can add the label **#Static** to the selected keyframe, and Flash 8 will export the labeled keyframe instead. If you select Animated, Flash 8 will export the whole project file as an animated GIF. If you want to export only a selection of frames, add **#First** and **#Last** labels to the first and last keyframes. If you select **Loop continuously**, the GIF will repeat the animation over and over. If you select **Repeat**, you can manually enter the number of times you want the animated GIF to loop before it stops.

continues on next page

GIF Publish Settings *continued*	
Name	**Description**
Options	**Optimize colors:** Removes unused colors to decrease file size.
	Interlace: Makes the image appear in stages as it is downloaded.
	Smooth: Makes the GIF anti-aliased, which can increase file size.
	Dither solids: Matches colors that are not part of the 256-color palette as closely as possible by mixing similar colors.
	Remove gradients: Changes all gradients to solid colors, thereby reducing file size.
Transparent	**Opaque:** Makes the image's background appear solid.
	Transparent: Makes the background of the image appear invisible.
	Alpha: Controls the background and all shapes that have an alpha setting applied to them. Lets you set the threshold so that all colors above the specified amount will be solid, and all colors with an alpha setting below the specified amount will be transparent.
Dither	**None:** Matches any color that is not within the 256-color palette with the closest color from within the 256 colors, rather than using dithering.
	Ordered: Matches any color that is not within the 256-color palette, using dithering from a pattern of colors.
	Diffusion: Matches any color that is not within the 256-color palette, using dithering from a random pattern of colors. This creates the closest match of colors but also creates the greatest increase in file size of these three options.
Palette Type	**Web 216:** Creates a GIF file using the 216 Web-safe colors.
	Adaptive: Creates a custom color palette for this specific image. This palette type yields an image that is closest in appearance to the original thousands-of-colors or millions-of-colors image, but it also has a larger file size than the other palette types.
	Web Snap Adaptive: Similar to Adaptive, except Flash will substitute colors for Web-safe colors when possible.
	Custom: Lets you use a custom palette for the GIF file. When you select this option, the **Palette** option becomes active as well.

continues on next page

GIF Publish Settings *continued*	
Name	**Description**
Max colors	Determines the maximum number of colors created within the palette when you select either the **Adaptive** or **Web Snap Adaptive** option. The smaller the number, the smaller the file size, but this option can degrade the image quality by reducing the colors.
Palette	Lets you select your own custom color palette from your hard drive.

JPEG Settings

You can use the JPEG file format for images that have more detail than GIF images generally do, such as photographs. Although JPEG images cannot be animated (like an animated GIF), they can have an unlimited number of colors, rather than being limited to 256 colors. By default, Flash will output the first frame of the movie as a JPEG unless you specify a particular keyframe by entering the frame label **#Static** on the keyframe you select. The following table describes the available options for publishing a JPEG image:

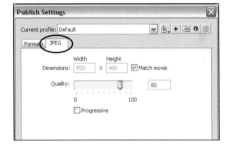

JPEG Publish Settings	
Name	**Description**
Dimensions	Lets you set the size of the JPEG by entering the width and height into the corresponding fields. If the **Match movie** option is selected, the JPEG will have the same dimensions as the project file's Movie Properties settings.
Quality	Sets the amount of compression, from **0** (lowest quality and smallest file size) to **100** (highest quality and largest file size).
Progressive	Lets the image appear in stages as it is downloaded.

PNG Settings

You can use the PNG file format to produce static graphics. Similar to the GIF format, the PNG format supports transparency. By default, Flash will output the first frame of the movie as a PNG unless you specify a particular keyframe by entering the frame label **#Static** on the keyframe you select. The PNG settings, which are similar to the GIF settings, are explained in detail in the following table:

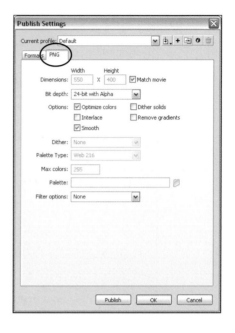

PNG Publish Settings

Name	Description
Dimensions	Lets you set the size of the PNG image by entering the width and height into the corresponding fields. Selecting the **Match movie** option will generate a PNG with the same dimensions as those set in the Movie Properties dialog box in the project file.
Bit depth	Sets the number of colors (bits per pixel) that will be used in the published file. As the bit depth increases, the file size increases as well. **8-bit:** Creates a 256-color image. **24-bit:** Creates an image using millions (16.7 million) of colors. **24-bit with Alpha:** Creates an image with millions of colors and allows transparency. (The higher the bit depth, the larger the file.)

continues on next page

PNG Publish Settings *continued*

Name	Description
Options	**Optimize colors:** Removes unused colors to decrease file size. **Interlace:** Makes the image appear in stages as it is downloaded. **Smooth:** Makes the PNG anti-aliased, which can increase file size. **Dither solids:** Matches colors that are not part of the 256-color palette as closely as possible by mixing similar colors. **Remove gradients:** Changes all gradients to solid colors, thereby reducing file size.
Dither	This option is available if the **Bit depth** is set to **8-bit**. **None:** Matches any color that is not within the 256-color palette with the closest color from within the 256 colors, rather than using dithering. **Ordered:** Matches any color that is not within the 256-color palette, using dithering from a regular pattern of colors. **Diffusion:** Matches any color that is not within the 256-color palette by dithering from a random pattern of colors, creating the closest match of colors, but with the greatest increase in file size of these three options.
Palette Type	**Web 216:** Creates a PNG file using the 216 Web-safe colors. **Adaptive:** Creates the PNG using a custom color palette for this specific image. This palette type yields an image that is closest in appearance to the original thousands-of-colors or millions-of-colors image, but it also has a larger file size than the other palette types. **Web Snap Adaptive:** Similar to Adaptive, except Flash will substitute colors for Web-safe colors when possible. **Custom:** Lets you use a custom palette for the PNG file. When you select this option, the **Palette** option becomes active as well.
Max colors	Determines the maximum number of colors created within the palette when either the **Adaptive** or **Web Snap Adaptive** option is selected.
Palette	Lets you select your own custom color palette (in the ACT format) from your hard drive.
Filter options	Lets you choose a filtering method that produces an image at the best quality and smallest file size.

Projector File Settings

You can also use Flash 8 to produce stand-alone applications for Windows or Mac machines.

Although there are no additional settings to choose from in the Publish Settings dialog box, you can select **Windows Projector** and **Macintosh Projector** in the Type options under the Formats tab. These projectors are self-contained files that can run on any computer, regardless of whether the user has the Flash 8 Player installed or not. You learned about projector files in depth in Exercises 2 and 3, earlier in this chapter.

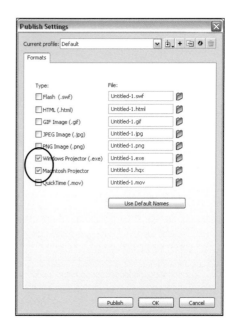

QuickTime Settings

The QuickTime settings let you publish the Flash 8 project file as a QuickTime 5 movie (MOV). The layers of the Flash 8 file will be converted to what is called the "Flash track" within the QuickTime movie. The table that follows explains the QuickTime tab options in detail:

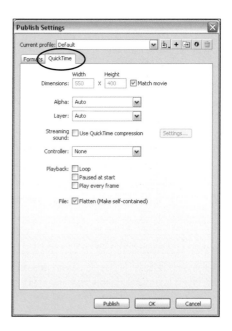

QuickTime Publish Settings

Name	Description
Dimensions	Lets you set the size of the QuickTime movie by entering the width and height into the corresponding fields. Selecting the **Match movie** option will generate a QuickTime movie that has the same dimensions as those set in the Movie Properties dialog box in the project file.
Alpha	Controls the transparency (alpha) of the Flash track in the QuickTime movie. **Auto:** Makes the Flash track opaque if it is the only track in the QuickTime movie or if it is located on the bottom of the other tracks. Makes the Flash track transparent if it is located on the top of other tracks. **Alpha Transparent:** Makes the transparent areas within the Flash track transparent. Other tracks below the Flash track will show through the transparent areas of the Flash track. **Copy:** Makes the Flash track opaque. Tracks below the Flash track will be masked.
Layer	Determines where the Flash track will reside relative to other tracks inside the QuickTime movie. **Top:** Positions the Flash track on top of all other tracks. **Bottom:** Positions the Flash track below all the other tracks. **Auto:** Positions the Flash track in front of the other tracks if Flash 8 content is placed in front of QuickTime content in the Flash 8 movie. Positions the Flash track behind the other tracks if Flash 8 content is placed in back of QuickTime content in the Flash 8 movie.
Streaming sound	Lets you convert all streaming audio in the Flash 8 project file into a QuickTime soundtrack.
Controller	Specifies the type of QuickTime controller that will be used to play the QuickTime movie.
Playback	**Loop:** When this option is selected, the movie starts over at the beginning after the end is reached. **Paused at start:** When this option is selected, the movie will start paused. When the user clicks a Play button, the movie will play. **Play every frame:** When this option is selected, all sound is disabled, and each frame plays without skipping.
File	**Flatten (Make self-contained):** Combines Flash 8 content and video content in one QuickTime movie. If this option is not selected, the Flash 8 file and video file will be referenced externally.

Saving Publishing Profiles

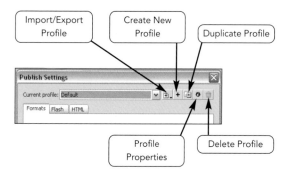

In the Publish Settings dialog box, you can set up the Publish settings the way you want and then save them as a Publish Profile. The benefits of saving your publishing settings is that you can easily use them later, or even pass them on to coworkers so that everyone has the same publishing settings as you do.

Current profile: Pop-up menu that lets you choose from a list of profiles you have created or imported.

Import/Export Profile: Lets you import a Publish Profile. You can also export (save) your current profile as an XML file you can store for later use or pass on to coworkers.

Create New Profile: Lets you save your current Publish settings as a new Publish Profile.

Duplicate Profile: Duplicates your currently selected profile. Duplicating a profile lets you use the profile settings as a starting point to make changes, while leaving the original profile unaltered.

Profile Properties: Lets you change the name of the currently selected Publish Profile.

Delete Profile: Deletes the currently selected profile.

Optimizing Movies

All movies in Flash 8 are not created equal. You can, however, use a few tricks and follow some simple guidelines to reduce the file size and increase the playback performance of your movie. The following list provides helpful tips to generate the best performance in your Flash 8 files:

Use symbols. Convert your artwork into a symbol, which makes it easier on a computer's processor since there is no raw data on the Stage. Also, if you use artwork multiple times in your project file, the symbol will only have to be downloaded once, and you can use it over and over without having any significant impact on file size.

Use solid lines wherever possible. Try to avoid using the dashed, dotted, or jagged line styles. Each dot, dash, or squiggle in these lines will be tracked as an independent object when the file is published. The jagged line style is the worst of the three. Lines using the jagged style contribute more than 100 times more bytes to the file size of your movie than do plain lines.

Use alpha sparingly. The more alpha, or transparency, you have in the movie, the slower the playback performance will be. Using alpha will not increase file size, but it can have a dramatic impact on playback performance. If you do use alpha, try not to have too many transparent elements stacked on top of one another.

Use gradients sparingly. Although their impact is not as serious as alpha, gradients can also slow down playback performance. Additionally, gradients that use alpha settings and are animated will significantly slow down playback performance. This combination of techniques is demanding on users' computer processors.

Use the Optimize command on your vector artwork. By selecting a vector object and using the **Modify > Shape > Optimize** command, you can reduce the file size of your movie.

Use vector graphics rather than bitmaps wherever possible. Vector graphics are usually significantly smaller than bitmaps, which can keep the file size down.

Be aware of complex objects in animation. The more complex your object is, the slower the playback performance of the animation will be.

Use device fonts where appropriate. When you use device fonts, Flash 8 will not embed the outlines for your movie's fonts, as it otherwise does by default. Instead, Flash 8 will display the text using a font on the user's machine that is closest to the specified font, saving file size.

Be cautious when looping streaming sound. When a sound's Sync option is set to Stream, it will play the sound at the same rate the animation is played. If you loop the streaming sound, Flash 8 will multiply the file size by the number of times you loop the sound; when the Sync is set to Stream and you specify a number of loops, Flash 8 actually adds frames to the Timeline—so be careful when adding looping to streaming sound.

Turn layers into guide layers. To prevent unwanted content from being exported, convert unwanted layers into guide layers. For example, if you have artwork you don't want to delete just yet, but also don't want a particular layer to end up in the movie, turn the layer containing the content into a guide layer. Guide layers are not

exported with the final movie, which may also save file size.

Use the individual compression settings. Use individual compression settings to compress imported bitmap graphics and sound files. By compressing each file individually, you can control the file size and image/sound quality, and often you can drastically reduce the image/sound file size from the original while keeping the image/sound quality relatively high.

Use the Load Movie command. Use the Load Movie command to break one large movie up into smaller pieces that only display content when needed or requested. With this command, rather than having one huge movie, you can create several smaller SWF files and load them into the main movie when the user requests the content by clicking a button.

Use the Generate Size Report and the Bandwidth Profiler features. Use these features to look at the breakdown of the SWF file, frame by frame. The report helps you identify places where you may be able to reduce the file size by compressing an image further, for example, the **Bandwidth Profiler** enables you to spot a frame that is significantly larger than other frames.

Be aware of platform performance. Flash 8 plays slightly faster (frames per second) on a Windows machine than it does on a Macintosh. Ideally, before you distribute Flash 8 files or upload them to a live Web site, test the files on both a Mac and a Windows-based machine to make sure the movie performs to your expectations on both platforms.

You have completed another chapter and should be ready to distribute your Flash 8 movies all over the world! Before you do, you may want to hang on and finish the last two chapters—*"Putting It All Together"* and *"Integration"*—because they contain some valuable information.

18

Putting It All Together

You may not realize it, but after working through the exercises in the previous chapters, you have actually created all the parts that make up a full, working Web site. This chapter takes you through the completed xboarding.com Web site and points out the elements in the site you've already created. You will then have a chance to rebuild sections of the site to enhance it even further, such as adding a preloader and creating draggable movies. Additionally, you will be introduced to several features in Flash 8 that allow you to maximize your production efficiency, including the Movie Explorer. Finally, you'll learn about the program's print capabilities.

1 | Understanding the Big Picture

This exercise introduces you to the completed xboarding.com Web site, which includes many of the exercise files you created in previous chapters in this book. As you look through the site, you'll see references to previous chapters in which you covered the associated technique. You might find you know more than you think you do!

---

1 Copy the **chap_18** folder from the **HOT CD-ROM** to your **Desktop**. Open **xboardingSiteFinal.fla** from the **siteFinal** folder in the **chap_18** folder.

We created this fully functional project file ahead of time for you, using many of the techniques you learned in this book.

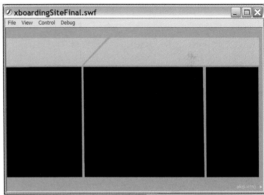

2 Choose **Control > Test Movie** to preview the movie.

Notice the animation of the outline being drawn and the snowboarder fading up. This is similar to the animation you created in Chapter 9, "*Bitmaps.*" Notice the next animation of the shapes turning into the interface. You created a piece similar to this in Chapter 5, "*Shape Tweening.*"

Missing Fonts

When you choose Control > Test Movie, you may see a dialog box that says, "One or more of the fonts used by this movie are unavailable. Substitute fonts will be used for display and export. They will not be saved to the Macromedia authoring document." This message tells you your computer does not have some of the fonts used to create the artwork in this file. Go ahead and click Use Default so your computer will pick a default font to replace the unrecognizable fonts in the movie.

When creating your own projects, you can avoid this missing font issue altogether by working with your designer to select fonts, such as Arial, Verdana, or Helvetica, that are common across multiple platforms. If you choose fonts that are likely to be included on all platforms, you will not see the "missing font" warning message. Also, please note that the user will not encounter this problem, because the font outlines are embedded in the movie to be viewed with the Macromedia Flash Player. The only time this error message will occur is when you try to view an FLA project file containing a font that is not installed on your computer.

3 On the **Welcome** screen, type your name and click **Enter**. On the next screen, click the **Click to Enter the Site** button to enter the Web site. You built a similar welcome screen in Chapter 13, "*Working with Text.*"

Notice the snowflake slowly falling down the screen. Does it look familiar? It is the same motion guide you created in Chapter 8, "*Motion Tweening and Timeline Effects.*" Notice the logo animating near the top of the screen. You created this in Chapter 11, "*Movie Clips.*"

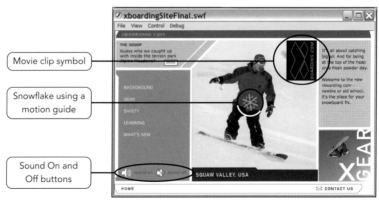

Movie clip symbol

Snowflake using a motion guide

Sound On and Off buttons

4 Click the **Sound Off** and **Sound On** buttons to stop and start the sound. You created similar buttons to control sound in Chapter 14, *"Sound."*

---

5 In the upper-left corner of the interface, click the **More** button.

This opens a browser window with the **thescoop.html** file embedded inside it. You created this file in Chapter 12, *"ActionScript Basics and Behaviors."* Close the browser window when you are finished previewing the file.

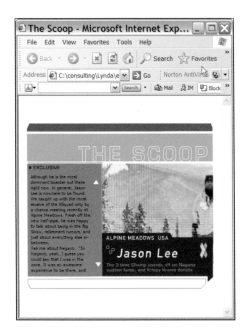

---

6 In the preview window, in the lower-right corner of the interface, click the **XGear** button to load an order form into a level in the Macromedia Flash Player. This form is similar to the file you created in Chapter 15, *"Components and Forms."* Go ahead and test the components and click the **Drag** button to drag the form around the window. When you are finished, click the **Close Window** button to unload the form from the Macromedia Flash Player.

You will learn how to make the form draggable and make the Close Window button work in a later exercise in this chapter.

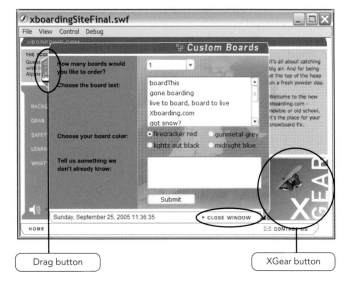

Drag button

XGear button

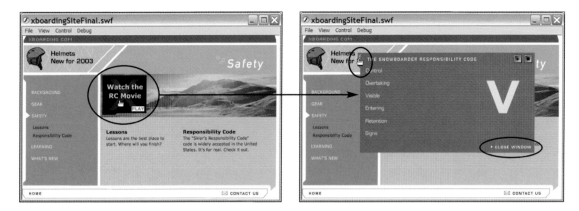

7 In the navigation menu, click the **Safety** button. You'll see the same drop-down menu you built in Chapter 12, "*ActionScript Basics and Behaviors.*" On the **Safety** page of the Web site, click **Play** on the **Watch the RC Movie** button to load the **Responsibility Code** movie you made in Chapter 14, "*Sound,*" into a level above the main **Timeline**. Click the **Drag** button to drag the movie around the screen, and click the **Close Window** button to unload the movie from the Macromedia Flash Player.

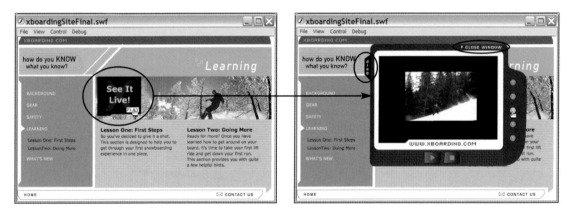

8 In the navigation menu, click the **Learning** button. On the **Learning** page of the Web site, click **Play** on the **See It Live** button to load a movie similar to the one you made in Chapter 16, "*Video,*" into a level above the main **Timeline**. Click the **Drag** button to drag the movie around the screen, click the buttons inside the movie to see the different snowboarders, and click the **Close Window** button to unload the movie from the Macromedia Flash Player.

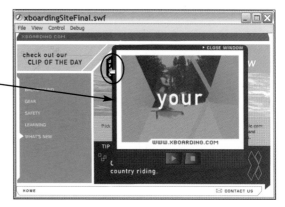

9 In the navigation menu, click the **What's New** button. On the **What's New** page of the Web site, click the **Check Out Our Clip of the Day** button to load a movie that has features similar to the file you made in Chapter 16, "*Video*," into a level above the main **Timeline**. Click the **Drag** button to drag the movie around the screen, click the **Start** and **Stop** buttons to play and stop the movie, and click the **Close Window** button to unload the movie from the Macromedia Flash Player.

Go ahead and explore this Web site to see how many other sections you recognize from lessons in this book. In later exercises of this chapter, you'll re-create parts of this project file to learn how to add some of the new sections, such as the draggable movies and Close Window buttons. When you are finished, keep the preview window open—you have one more area to look at next.

---

10 With the preview window still open, choose **View > Bandwidth Profiler**. Choose **View > Simulate Download**, which lets you see the preloader for the xboarding.com site.

A preloader is a short animation that plays while ActionScripting checks to see how many frames from the main movie have downloaded to the user's computer. This technique is often used as a "loading" screen while a large Flash movie downloads. You will build this preloader in Exercise 6 of this chapter. The Bandwidth Profiler is a feature in the test movie environment that lets you see how the movie streams based on different connection speeds.

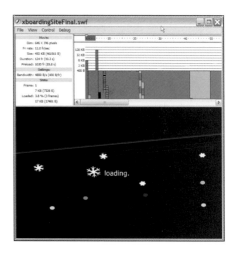

---

11 When you are finished, close the preview window, but keep the project file open for the next exercise.

It is now time to take a closer look at the FLA file to see how the Web site was put together. The next several exercises show you how the xboarding.com site was created, highlight certain workflow techniques, and introduce you to a few tools, including the Movie Explorer.

You can use scenes to organize large projects into smaller, more manageable pieces. By default, Macromedia Flash 8 will play all the scenes continuously in order unless you use ActionScript to tell it to do otherwise. If no ActionScripting is present in the main Timeline to stop the movie, the playhead will continue to the next scene and will play the frames in each scene, one after another, until it reaches the end or encounters a **stop** action. This exercise also demonstrates how scenes were employed in the **xboardingSiteFinal** project file.

---

1 If you just completed Exercise 1, **xboardingSiteFinal.fla** should still be open. If it's not, open **xboardingSiteFinal.fla** from the **chap_18** folder. In the edit bar, click the **Edit Scenes** button to reveal a menu listing the scenes within this project. Choose the **home** scene to open its **Timeline**.

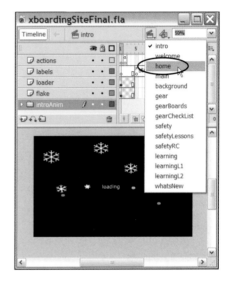

2 In the **home** scene, select **Frame 1** on the **actions** layer and press **F9** (Windows) or **Option+F9** (Mac) to open the **Actions** panel.

Notice there is a **stop** action in the Script pane, which prevents Flash 8 from playing one scene right after another.

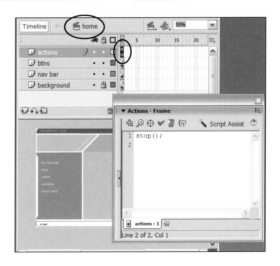

3 Click the **Edit Scenes** button and choose the **gear** scene to open its **Timeline**.

4 On the **actions** layer, click **Frame 1** to see another **stop** action.

This action causes Flash 8 to stop as soon as the playhead reaches this frame and wait until the user interacts with the buttons before it continues.

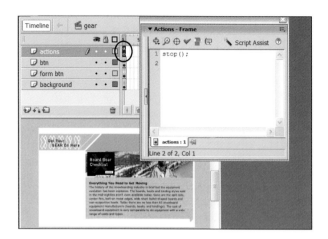

5 Use the **Edit Scenes** button to investigate each of the different scenes inside the **xboardingSiteFinal** project file.

The artwork in these scenes may look familiar to you. You used the SWF file for each of these scenes when you worked through the "Loading Movies" exercise in Chapter 12, "*ActionScript Basics and Behaviors.*" What you never saw in Chapter 12 was the FLA file that created them. Did you suspect that there was a different FLA file for each of the SWF files? Although the xboarding Web site could have been created that way, opening each of the 15 different FLA files to make changes would have been inefficient. Instead, I used a different scene for each different "page" of the xboarding Web site, exported each scene individually using the Test Scene command, and then used the `loadMovieNum` ActionScript, just as you did in Chapter 12, to load the correct page on demand when the user clicks a button.

6 When you are finished, keep **xboardingSiteFinal** open for the next exercise.

Managing Layers

Layers in Flash are similar to transparent sheets stacked on top of each other. Layers help you organize the content of the frames in the project file. For example, in Chapter 12, "*ActionScript Basics and Behaviors*," you learned to get in the habit of adding an action layer on top of all other layers so that you can always find your frame actions in the same place. In Chapter 14, "*Sound*," you learned to add a sound layer to the Timeline to keep the sounds consistently on the same layer and separate from others. Layers also play an important role in animation in Macromedia Flash 8. For instance, you learned in Chapter 5, "*Shape Tweening*," that if you want to tween multiple elements, each tweened element must be on its own layer. By default, all movies in Macromedia Flash 8 have at least one layer, although you can add as many layers as you need.

Adding and Removing Layers

You can add a new layer by choosing **Insert > Timeline > Layer** or by clicking the **Insert Layer** button. You can click the **Add Motion Guide** button to add a guide layer. You can click the **Insert Layer Folder** button to add a layer folder. You can remove a layer by clicking the **Delete Layer** button (the **Trash** icon).

Types of Layers

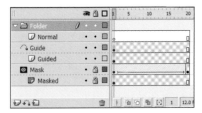

Throughout this book, you have worked with several kinds of layers in addition to a standard layer. There are three special types of layers:

- **Guide layers:** Guide layers come in two flavors: motion guide layers (guide layers) and guided layers. The difference between the two is that motion guide layers serve as a path for an object to follow, and guided layers contain the objects that follow the path.

  Motion guide layers are special layer types that are not exported when the movie is published or tested, and therefore they do not add to the size of the SWF file. These layers are visible only in the development environment. However, although artwork on a guide layer is not exported, actions on the layer are.

- **Mask layers:** Mask layers come in two flavors as well: mask layers and masked layers. A mask layer is a special layer that defines what will be visible (and invisible, or masked) on the layer (or layers) below it. The layers that are attached or indented under the mask layer are called masked layers. Only layers beneath the shapes in the mask layer will be visible.

- **Layer folders:** A layer folder is a special kind of layer that can hold other layers inside it. Layer folders can not contain artwork—the layer folder's sole purpose is to hold other layers so you can keep your Timeline compact and organized.

In the next exercise, you will see an example of both a motion guide layer and a layer folder in the **xboardingSiteFinal.fla** project file.

3 | Examining Layers

This exercise will provide more practice working with the layer controls in the Timeline.

---

1 In the **xboardingSiteFinal.fla** file, click the **Edit Scenes** button and choose the **intro** scene to open its **Timeline**.

Notice the layer folder, named **introAnim**, on the Timeline.

Note: The layers above the layer folder (actions, labels, loader, and flake) make up the preloader. You will re-create the preloader in Exercise 6 of this chapter. The section preceding Exercise 6 describes how to create layer folders and discusses how they can benefit your workflow.

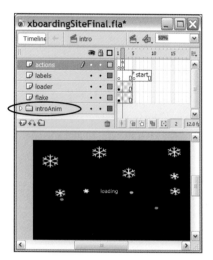

2 Click the triangle to the left of the layer folder to expand all of its layers.

Tip: You may have to resize the Timeline in order to view all of the layers. These layers make up the introductory animation you saw when you previewed the movie in Exercise 1.

Tip: You can choose **View > Magnification > Show All** to resize the **Stage** so you can see everything.

Click and drag down to expand the Timeline.

---

3 Click the **Edit Scenes** button and choose the **main** scene to open its **Timeline**.

---

4 Click the **snowflake** to select it. Notice the **motionGuide** layer is selected on the **Timeline**.

This snowflake travels down the motion guide you created in Chapter 8, "*Motion Tweening and Timeline Effects.*"

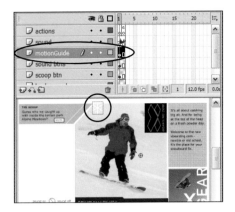

5 Double-click the **snowflake** instance to enter the movie clip's **Timeline**.

Once inside you will see the guide layer, Guide:trail (which contains the path the snowflake will follow) and the guided layer, flake (which contains the snowflake tween). This is very similar to the file you created in Chapter 8, "*Motion Tweening and Timeline Effects.*"

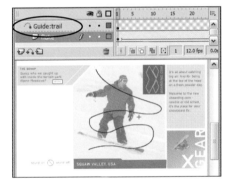

6 When you are finished, keep **xboardingSiteFinal.fla** open for the next exercise.

Organizing the Library

Throughout your production work on Flash 8 projects, you will frequently use the Library for a variety of purposes, including opening files, dragging sounds or movie clips out to the Timeline, renaming elements, finding elements within a project, and much more. Since you'll often use the Library, you need to keep it organized and use consistent naming schemes.

Organized Library

Disorganized Library

These two examples show an organized Library and a disorganized Library. Would you rather search for a movie clip symbol in the Library on the left, which has consistently named elements, or in the Library on the right, which is disorganized and uses many different naming schemes, as well as inconsistently placed items in the folders?

In addition to helping improve your efficiency, organizing your Library can also help others working on the project with you. Here are several basic "Library etiquette" guidelines to keep in mind:

- Be consistent in your naming conventions. There is no "right way" to name the items within your project file, but once you decide on a structure to follow, stick to it. Since the Library sorts elements alphabetically, I recommend using prefixes at the beginning of the item name. For example, use the prefix *btn* for buttons (as in btnHome) and use *mc* for movie clips (as in mcMenu). Again, there is no perfect way to name your elements. Instead, consistency is what matters.

- Choose brief, descriptive names, such as mcEffects, rather than meaningless letters, such as mef. By doing so, you can find it a lot easier, knowing you have given it an accurate, descriptive name.

- Use folders to organize the Library elements, and stay consistent with the folder names. You can create a folder by clicking the New Folder button. Short, descriptive names will help you navigate through the Library faster, and you will know what to expect inside each folder before you open it.

4 | Investigating the Library

This exercise will give you additional practice in working with the more important features of the Flash Library.

---

1 Press **Ctrl+L** (Windows) or **Cmd+L** (Mac) to open the **Library**. Double-click the folders to view the elements inside them. Notice all of the elements are named consistently and are located in the corresponding folders. Double-click a **Library** item to open its **Timeline**, or select an item and click the **Properties** button to open the **Properties** dialog box to learn more about the element.

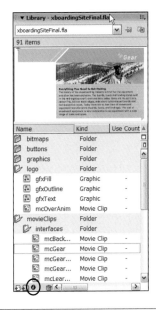

---

2 Continue to click around, expand and collapse the folders, and examine other elements in the **Library**.

---

3 Click the **Library Options** menu and choose **Collapse All Folders** to collapse all the folders in the **Library**.

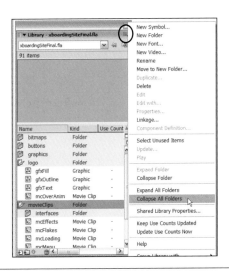

---

4 Notice the **bitmapLearning** file is not inside a folder. Click once on the **bitmaps** folder to expand it and reveal the files inside. Drag the **bitmapLearning** file that is outside the **bitmaps** folder into the **bitmaps** folder.

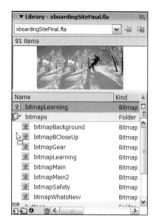

5 In the **Resolve Library Conflict** dialog box, select **Don't replace existing items** and click **OK**.

The library conflict resolution feature detects when you try to put two items with the same name into the same Library folder. If you choose not to replace the existing item, the new item will be given a slightly different name, keeping the original name and adding the word *copy* at the end.

Notice Flash 8 automatically renamed the file **bitmapLearning copy**. This feature is a great safeguard against accidentally writing over files!

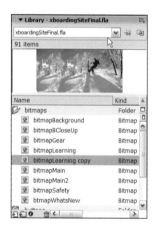

6 When you are finished, save **xboardingSiteFinal.fla** and keep it open for the next exercise.

5 | Using the Movie Explorer

The Movie Explorer is a handy tool that provides you with a visual representation of every aspect of the project file, organized into a hierarchical structure. You can use the Movie Explorer to view and locate just about every type of element within the project, including graphic symbols, button symbols, movie clip symbols, text, ActionScripts, frames, and scenes. This exercise introduces you to the basic features of the Movie Explorer while looking at the **xboardingSiteFinal.fla** project file.

---

1 In **xboardingSiteFinal.fla**, choose **Window > Movie Explorer** to open the **Movie Explorer**.

TIP: | **Why Use the Movie Explorer?**

You can use the Movie Explorer for a variety of purposes. For example, it can display a customized map showing all the text within a movie that uses the Verdana font, a list of all the graphic symbols in the project, or even all the sounds within a scene. Additionally, it can search for and locate a particular element when you know its name but not its location. The following steps take you through some of these examples.

---

2 Click the buttons next to **Show** to select the elements you want to see. After you have selected the categories you want to see, you can expand and collapse the folders within the display list window to reveal or hide the contents inside.

The Movie Explorer also lets you search for an item by name, including font names, symbols, ActionScript, and frame numbers. You'll search for a specific item next.

Show Video, Sounds, and Bitmaps

Show Frames and Layers

Customize which items to show

Options menu

Show Text

Show Buttons, Movie Clips, and Graphics

Show Action Scripts

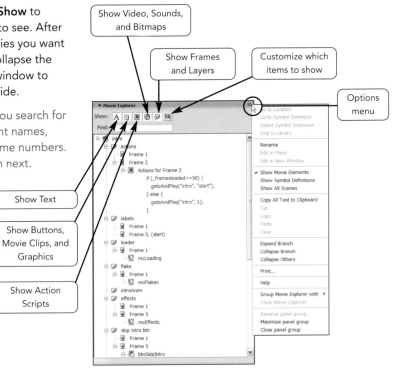

3 From the **Options** menu, choose **Show All Scenes** to reveal the categories for all of the scenes.

4 In the **Find** text box, type the item name **btnClipOfDay** to search for this element within the project file. When Flash finds the item, it will display it in the window.

Tip: Make sure that the **Show Buttons, Movie Clips, and Graphics** filter button is selected.

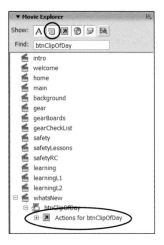

WARNING: Finding Files in the Movie Explorer

When you use the Find feature in the Movie Explorer, Flash 8 will search all the currently selected categories, not all the categories in the project file. If, for example, you are searching for a button, make sure you have the second button (Show Buttons, Movie Clips, and Graphics) selected. Otherwise, the Movie Explorer will not find the item you are searching for. When you open the Movie Explorer for the first time, by default, the first three buttons (including the Show Buttons, Movie Clips, and Graphics category) are selected for you.

The Movie Explorer will also reveal ActionScript applied to frames and objects within the project file. You will see this next.

5 If it is not already expanded, click the **plus** (+) sign next to the **Actions for btnClipOfDay** text to reveal more elements related to that object.

In this case, the Movie Explorer will reveal the actual ActionScript attached to the button instance. Using the Movie Explorer is a great way to learn how projects were built because you can drill down to the actual ActionScripting on any object in the movie.

6 When you are finished investigating the **Movie Explorer**, close the **xboardingSiteFinal** project file. You will be re-creating the preloader in the xboarding.com Web site in the next exercise.

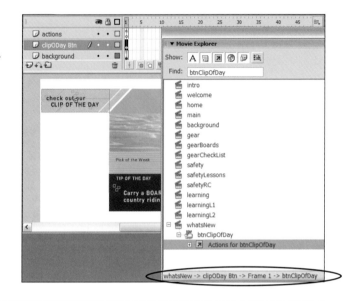

What Is a Preloader?

The SWF format is a streaming format, meaning the movie can begin playing before it is completely downloaded. In many cases, streaming is good for users because they don't have to wait for the whole movie to load before they see the beginning of the movie. On the other hand, there are times when you may not want the movie to begin until all the frames have been downloaded—to assure smooth playback or synchronization with sound and the animation, for example. Additionally, there is no way of knowing the users' bandwidth—dial-up, broadband, T1, or T3. Therefore, you may want to give users on a slower connection some type of visual feedback that the movie is being downloaded while they wait. One method of achieving both proper playback and giving visual feedback is to use a **preloader**.

A preloader can exist in the very first frames of the movie, in the first scene of the movie, or even at different points within the movie. It uses ActionScript to detect the progress of the SWF file download. After the whole movie (or an amount you specify) has downloaded onto the user's machine, the movie will play. You can put different artwork or animation into your movie to be displayed while the preloader is doing its detection work. The animation or artwork can keep users interested while they wait for the movie to download. The following exercise shows you how to create a simple preloader.

6 | Building a Preloader

As you build more complex projects in Flash 8, users may see the movie differently depending on their connection speed. Rather than allowing users to view a choppy animation or click a button that doesn't work yet because the movie is not completely downloaded, you can add a preloader that permits playback only after all the necessary frames have downloaded. This exercise shows you how to create a basic preloader so you can take control over what your users see and when they will see it.

---

1 Open **xboardingSite.fla** from the **siteInProgress** folder in the **chap_18** folder.

The **siteInProgress** folder contains all the files you need to re-create the xboarding.com Web site. Some files are already complete, and others have been partially created to get you started. You will complete these in the next few exercises.

---

2 In the project file, click the **Edit Scenes** button and choose the **intro** scene to open its **Timeline**. You will create the preloader in this scene.

The order of the scenes listed in the Edit Scenes list is the order in which they will play in the movie unless you tell the Timeline otherwise. When you have a preloader in the movie that will control the number of frames downloaded for the entire movie, the preloader needs to occur in the first scene.

---

3 In the **Property Inspector**, select **black** for the **Background** color.

Although the Stage looks black at first glance, it is actually white with a black graphic symbol over the top of it. Changing the Background color in the Property Inspector will temporarily change the background color of the movie to black so you can see the artwork in the new few steps.

In the next steps, you will be previewing movie clips in the Library that have white artwork and text. When the movie also has a white background, you cannot see the animation. Changing the background color of the movie temporarily will allow you to preview the animations.

---

4 Open the **Library**. In the **movieClips** folder, click the **mcLoading** movie clip to select it. In the **Library** preview window, click the **Play** button to preview the movie clip.

This movie clip will serve as the part of the looping animation that will play over and over until all the frames you specify are loaded.

5 In the **movieClips** folder, click the **mcFlakes** movie clip to select it. In the **Library** preview window, click the **Play** button to preview the movie clip.

Notice the falling snowflakes. This clip will serve as the background of the looping animation that will play until all the frames you specify are loaded.

6 Click the **Insert Layer** button to add a new layer to the **Timeline**. Name it **flake**.

When you insert a new layer on the Timeline, Flash automatically adds frames up to the current last frame on the Timeline. In this case, there are 100 frames in the **introAnim** folder, so Flash adds 100 frames to each new layer.

7 To delete the extra frames, select **Frames 2** through **100** and **right-click** (Windows) or **Ctrl+click** (Mac) and choose **Remove Frames** from the contextual menu.

8 From the **Library**, drag an instance of the **mcFlakes** movie clip onto the center of the **Stage**.

Tip: You can use the Align panel (Window > Align) to center the mcFlakes movie clip instance on the Stage. You can also use the Free Transform tool to stretch the mcFlakes movie clip instance so that it covers more of the Stage. When you are finished, lock the flake layer.

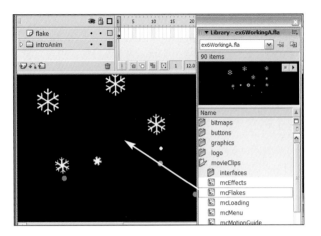

---

9 Click the **Insert Layer** button to add a new layer to the **Timeline**. Name it **loader**. Make sure the **loader** layer appears above the **flake** layer.

---

10 On the **loader** layer, select **Frames 2** through **100** and **right-click** (Windows) or **Ctrl+click** (Mac) and choose **Remove Frames** from the contextual menu.

---

11 From the **Library**, drag an instance of the **mcLoading** movie clip onto the center of the **Stage**.

Tip: You can use the Align panel to center the mcLoading movie clip instance on the Stage. When you are finished, lock the loader layer.

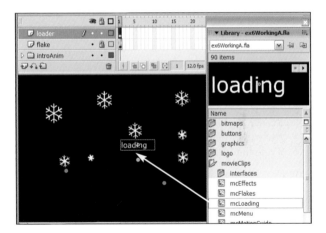

12 Shift+click **Frame 4** of the **loader** and **flake** layers to select **Frame 4** on both layers. Press **F5** to add frames up to **Frame 4** on both layers.

13 Click anywhere off the **Stage** to deselect everything, and in the **Property Inspector**, select **white** for the **Background** color, which changes the background color of the movie back to white.

14 Click the **Insert Layer** button to add a new layer to the **Timeline**. Name the new layer **labels** and move it above the **loader** layer. On the **labels** layer, select **Frames 2** through **100** and **right-click** (Windows) or **Ctrl+click** (Mac) and choose **Remove Frames**.

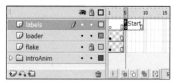

15 On the **labels** layer, select **Frame 5** and press **F7** to add a blank keyframe. In the **Property Inspector**, type **Start** in the **Frame** label field. Select **Frame 9** and press **F5** to add frames so you can see the **Start** label.

Why did you have to put the start label on Frame 5? Because the intro animation begins at Frame 5, and in the next few steps you will be adding ActionScript for the preloader that will check to see whether all the frames are loaded in the movie. If they are, the playhead will be sent to the start frame, and the intro animation (which begins at Frame 5) can play.

16 Click the **Insert Layer** button to add a new layer to the **Timeline**. Rename it **actions** and make sure it is above all the other layers on the **Timeline**. On the **actions** layer, select **Frame 2** and press **F7** to a blank keyframe to the **actions** layer. Select **Frames 3** through **100** and **right-click** (Windows) or **Ctrl+click** (Mac) and choose **Remove Frames** from the contextual menu.

17 On the **actions** layer, select **Frame 2**. Press **F9** (Windows) or **Option+F9** (Mac) to open the **Actions** panel. Click the **Script Assist** button to enter **Script Assist** mode. In the **Actions** panel, select **Statements > Conditions/Loops** and double-click the **if** action to add it to the **Script** pane.

The if action lets you set up a condition that tests whether or not something is true.

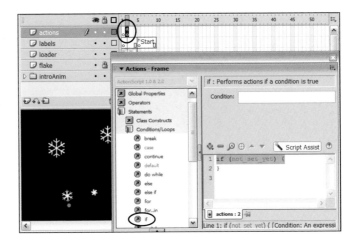

18 In the **Condition** parameter text field, type **_framesloaded>=_totalframes**.

This condition tells Flash 8 that if the frames loaded in the movie are greater than (>) or equal to (=) the total number of frames in the movie (in other words, if the move has completely loaded), then do "something." You will be adding that "something" in the next few steps.

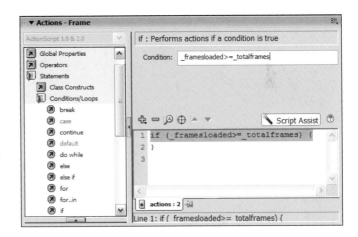

19 In the **Actions** panel, with the first line of text still selected, select **Global Functions > Timeline Control** and double-click the **goto** action to add it to the **Script** pane. Select the **Goto and play** option.

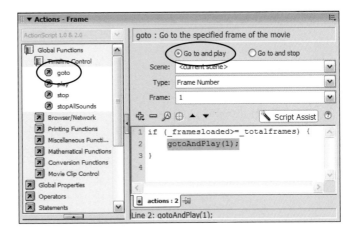

20 In the **Frame** text field, type **"intro"**, **"start"**.

This ActionScript tells Flash 8 to check to see whether the frames loaded into the movie are greater than or equal to the total frames in the movie. If they are, it should go ahead and play the intro scene, beginning at the start label.

You have just added ActionScript to have Flash 8 determine whether all the frames in the movie have been downloaded to the user's system. But what if the frames have not downloaded yet? You need to add one more condition to the ActionScript, which will make this command loop. You will do this next.

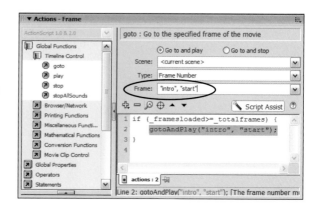

21 With the second line of script still selected, select **Statements > Conditions/Loops** and double-click the **else** action to add it to the **Script** pane.

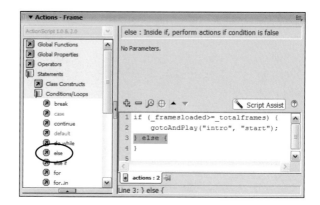

22 With the third line of code still selected, choose **Global Functions > Timeline Control** and double-click the **goto** action to add it to the **Script** pane. Select the **Go to and play** option.

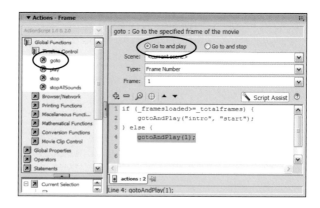

23 In the **Frame** text field, type **"intro", 1**.

This ActionScript tells Flash 8 that if the frames loaded are not greater than or equal to the total number of frames, it should go back to Frame 1, creating a loop that checks repeatedly to see whether all the frames are loaded. If they are not, the playhead will go back to Frame 1, but if they are, the playhead will go to the start label and play the intro animation.

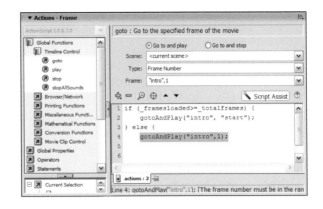

24 Choose **Control > Test Scene** to preview the movie. (Make sure you choose **Test Scene** and not **Test Movie**, since you need to test only the **intro** scene in this exercise.)

You may not see the preloader just yet. Why? Because all the frames may load so fast you can't even see the preloader in action. The next step will show you how use the Bandwidth Profiler to simulate the way the movie will appear on the Internet, so you can test the scripts by seeing the preloader hard at work.

Note: When you choose Control > Test Scene, you may see the "missing font" warning message. Go ahead and choose **Use Default** so your computer will pick a default font to replace the unrecognizable fonts in the movie.

NOTE:

What Is the Bandwidth Profiler?

The **Bandwidth Profiler** is a component in the test movie environment. It lets you see how the movie streams based on different connection speeds. You can use the Bandwidth Profiler to simulate how a user would view your movie using a a 56K modem, for example. You can also use the Bandwidth Profiler to view the preloader before the movie plays.

Feedback to tell you how much of the movie has loaded

Bars simulate frames, and bar heights simulate the size of the content within a frame.

SWF file

loading

25 With the preview window open, choose **View >
Bandwidth Profiler**, and choose select **View >
Download Settings > 56K (4.7 KB/s)**. Choose **View
> Simulate Download** to see your preloader work!

This setting lets you see the movie as it will appear
when streamed on a live 56K connection. Notice
the loading animation loops until all the frames are
loaded (you will see *Loaded: 100%* in the State section of the Bandwidth Profiler), and then the intro
animation begins.

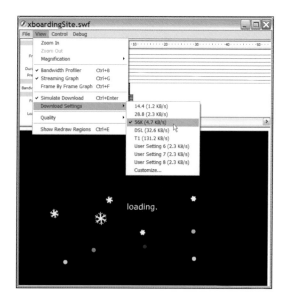

---

26 When you are finished previewing the preloader, choose **View > Bandwidth Profiler** to close it.

Note: What if you don't want all the frames in the movie to load before the intro animation begins? For
example, what if you want only 50 frames to load before the animation will play? If this is the case, your
ActionScripting on Frame 2 would instead look like this:

```
if (_framesloaded>=50) {

        gotoAndPlay("intro", "start");

} else {

        gotoAndPlay("intro", 1);

}
```

---

27 Nice work—you have made your first preloader! Save this file and keep it open for the next exercise.

---

7 | Printing from the Project File

Many Flash 8 users are unaware of the capability to print from inside the project file (the FLA file). You can use this feature to show a client the page layouts for a Web site or even your progress on a project. In the project file, you can choose to print all frames in the movie or just the first frame of each scene. This exercise shows you how to set up the parameters and print a section of the movie from inside the project file. Then, the following exercise shows you how to set up printing from inside the Macromedia Flash Player.

1 If you just completed Exercise 6, **xboardingSite.fla** should still be open. If it's not, go back and complete Exercise 6. Choose **File > Page Setup** (Windows) or **File > Print Margins** (Mac) to open the **Page Setup** (Windows) or **Print Margins** (Mac) dialog box.

2 From the **Frames** drop-down menu, choose **First Frame Only** to print the first frame in each scene.

Tip: The other option, All Frames, will print all the frames in the movie.

3 From the **Layout** drop-down menu, choose **Storyboard – Boxes**, which determines how the frames will appear on the printed page. Click **OK**.

4 In Windows, choose **File > Print** to preview how the printed page will look based on the settings you selected in the previous steps. On a Mac, choose **File > Print** and then click the **Preview** button, which generates a PDF of the preview page.

Note: Not all systems will have a preview option.

---

5 Choose **Print** from the **Print Preview** window to print the first frames of each scene from the project file.

This is a great way to quickly show a client the page layouts for a Web site or even your progress on a project without having to show your client the entire project file.

---

6 You have just printed your first document from inside Flash 8! Save **xboardingSite.fla** and keep it open for the next exercise.

Layout Settings

The Layout settings allow you to select from five layout options, which are described in the following table:

Printing Layout Options	
Option	**Description**
Actual Size	Prints the frame at full size
Fit On One Page	Increases or decreases the size of each frame so that it fills the print area of the page
Storyboard – Boxes	Prints multiple thumbnails on one page and creates a rectangle around each thumbnail
Storyboard – Grid	Prints multiple thumbnails inside a grid on each page
Storyboard - Blank	Prints multiple thumbnails on one page and prints only the artwork inside each thumbnail

Printing Flash 8 Content from a Browser

When a user is viewing a Web site created using Flash 8, different results occur when the user attempts to print the Web site, depending on the method used:

- If the user clicks the Print button in the browser window, the page of the Web site that he or she is currently viewing will be printed. Since you cannot control the user's browser, there is no way to completely control or disable printing inside the user's browser using Flash 8.

- If the user right-clicks (Windows) or Ctrl+clicks (Mac) and chooses Print from the contextual menu, every frame in the movie will print. However, you can change this by labeling certain keyframes as printable in the project file and thus restricting users to print only the frames you specify. You will learn to do this in the next exercise.

- If the user clicks a Print button created inside the Flash 8 movie, all the frames to which you have added a **#p** on the Timeline will print. (You will learn how to add this in the next exercise.)

Tip: You can also disable printing entirely in the Macromedia Flash Player by adding the label **!#p** to a keyframe. This label will make the entire movie nonprintable from the contextual menu in the Macromedia Flash Player.

Printing Platforms Supported by the Macromedia Flash Player

Flash players 6 and later can all print to both PostScript and non-PostScript printers. This includes most common printers, such as black-and-white and color, laser and inkjet, and PostScript and PCL printers.

In addition to printing files from within the project file, you can allow users viewing the movie in the Macromedia Flash Player to print Macromedia Flash content. By default, all the frames on the Timeline will print unless you either specify certain frames as printable by a user viewing the movie or disable printing altogether. This exercise shows you how to control printing by adding a special label to the chosen printable frames. It also shows you how to add ActionScripting to a button and set up the printing parameters for your users.

1 If you just completed Exercise 7, **xboardingSite.fla** should still be open. If it's not, go back and complete Exercise 7. In the project file, click the **Edit Scenes** button and choose **learningL1** to open its **Timeline**.

Note: If you receive the "missing font" message, click **Use Default** so your computer will pick a default font to replace the unrecognizable fonts in the movie.

2 Click the **Insert Layer** button to add a new layer to the **Timeline**. Name the layer **labels** and place it below the **actions** layer.

3 In the **labels** layer, select the first frame. In the **Property Inspector**, type **#p** in the **Frame Label** field to define that keyframe as printable.

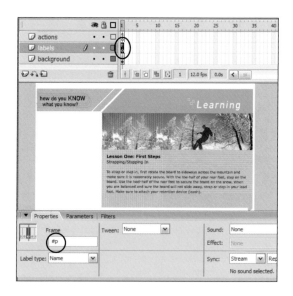

Printing from the Contextual Menu

You can permit your users to access the Print command from the contextual menu. The contextual menu will appear in the Macromedia Flash Player when a Windows user right-clicks or a Mac user Ctrl+clicks the movie.

By default, this Print command will print every frame in the movie. However, by labeling certain keyframes as printable in the project file (as you did in Step 3 by adding the **#p** label to the keyframe), you can restrict the users to printing only the frames you specify.

Further, you can also disable printing entirely in the Macromedia Flash Player by adding the label **!#p** to a keyframe. This label will make the entire movie nonprintable from the Macromedia Flash Player. Note that although you disable printing from the Macromedia Flash Player, the user can still choose the Print command from the browser. Since you cannot control the user's browser commands, there is no way to disable printing inside the user's browser using Flash 8.

4 Choose **Control > Test Scene**. (Make sure you choose **Test Scene** and not **Test Movie**, since you need to preview only the scene at this point.) **Right-click** (Windows) or **Ctrl+click** (Mac) the movie to access the contextual menu. Choose **Print** to print the frame you labeled in Step 3.

Note: After you have defined a keyframe as printable, when a user accesses the contextual menu and chooses Print, Flash will print only the frames labeled as #p.

In addition to allowing access to the contextual menu, you can allow the

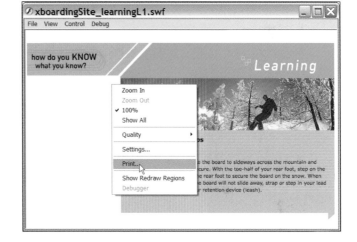

user to print frames within the movie by attaching ActionScript to a button that will print the frames you specify. To do this, you must first create the printable frame labels, as you did in the previous steps, and then you can create the button, which you will do in the steps that follow.

5 Lock the three existing layers on the **Timeline**. Click the **Insert Layer** button to add another new layer. Name this layer **print btn** and move it below the **labels** layer.

6 Choose **Window > Library** to open the **Library**. From the **buttons** folder, drag an instance of the **btnPrintMe** button onto the lower-right corner of the **Stage**.

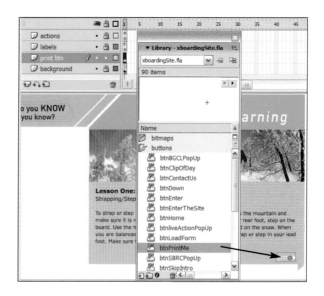

7 Make sure the **Print** button is selected on the **Stage**. Press **F9** or **Option+F9** (Mac) to open the **Actions** panel. Make sure **Script Assist** mode is deselected.

8 In the **Actions** panel, select **Global Functions > Movie Clip Control** and double-click the **on** action to add it to the **Script** pane. From the **Code Hint** menu that appears, choose **release** for the mouse event.

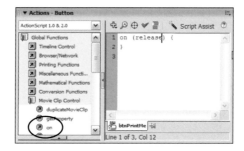

9 Place your cursor after the open curly brace and press **Enter** (Windows) or **Return** (Mac) to bring the cursor down to the second line.

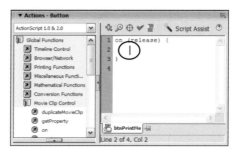

10 Select **Global Functions > Printing Functions** and double-click the `printAsBitmapNum` action to add it to the **Script** pane.

The `printAsBitmapNum` action will print all the content in the frame as a bitmap, honoring any transparency and color effects in the frame.

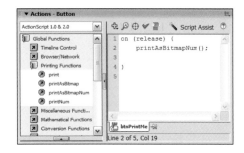

11 Between the parentheses, type **this, "bmovie"**.

When the ActionScript is attached to a button, `this` refers to the Timeline that contains the button. The `bmovie` sets the print area for all printable frames in the movie to the bounding box of the frame. In this case, Frame 1 will be printable since that Timeline is where you added the frame label **#p**.

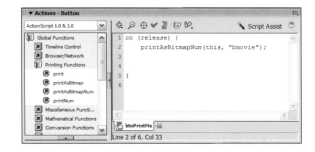

Note: By default, the print area is determined by the Stage size of the movie. Any movies loaded into levels will use their own Stage sizes as the print area unless you specify otherwise. Also, if any object is located off of the Stage, it will be cut off and will not print.

The table at the end of this exercise details all the available **print** action parameters.

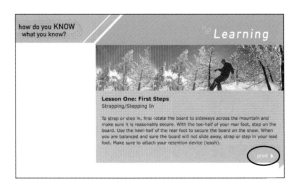

12 Choose **Control > Test Scene** and click the **Print** button to test it. Your printer will display a **Print** dialog box. Click **Print** to print the frame you labeled with **#p**.

Tip: You can use the **print** action to print frames in either the main Timeline or the Timeline of any movie clip or movie that is loaded into a level.

Note: For a movie clip to be printable, it must be on the Stage or work area, and it must have an instance name.

13 When you are finished, save **xboardingSite.fla** and keep it open for the next exercise.

		Print Action Parameters	
Option	**Setting**	**Description**
Print	As Vectors	Prints frames that do not use transparency (alpha) or color effects.
Print	As Bitmap	Prints frames that contain bitmap images, transparency, or color effects.
Location	Level	Specifies the level in the Macromedia Flash Player to print. By default, all of the frames in the level will print unless you specify otherwise. You can assign a **#p** frame label to print only specific frames in the level, rather than all the frames.
Location	Target	Identifies the instance name of the movie clip or Timeline to print. By default, all of the frames in the movie are printed. However, you can designate frames for printing by attaching a **#p** frame label to specific frames.

9 | Exporting Scenes

Now that you have created the preloader and identified the printable frames, you need to export the SWF file for each scene so that the site will work correctly. This exercise shows you how to do this by testing each scene in order to export its SWF file. You will then rename the scenes (with shorter names) so they can be loaded into the main Timeline on demand.

1 If you just completed Exercise 8, **xboardingSite.fla** should still be open. If it's not, go back and complete Exercise 8. Click the **Edit Scenes** button and choose **home** to open its **Timeline**.

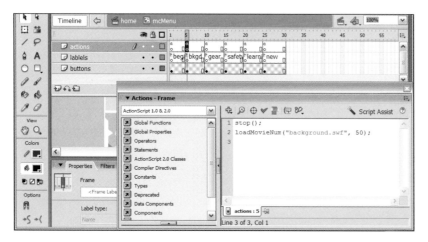

2 On the **Stage**, double-click the **menu** movie clip to open the **Timeline** for the movie clip. On the **actions** layer, select **Frame 5**. Press **F9** (Windows) or **Option+F9** (Mac) to open the **Actions** panel.

This is the same drop-down menu, and the same ActionScript, you created in Chapter 12, "*ActionScript Basics and Behaviors.*" The ActionScript stops the playhead when it reaches the frame where the ActionScripting resides (Frame 5), and it loads a movie named **background.swf** into Level 50.

In the following steps, you will create the **background.swf** file by exporting the background scene from this project file and rename it to match this ActionScripting. You will also create all the other interface SWF files that are loaded into levels.

3 Click the **Edit Scenes** button and choose **intro** to open its **Timeline**. Choose **Control > Test Scene**. As soon as you see the preview window, you can close it, because you do not need to spend time previewing the scene. Instead, the goal here is to export the SWF file for the scene.

Why Am I Choosing Control > Test Scene?

As you learned in Chapter 17, *"Publishing and Exporting,"* each time you choose Control > Test Movie, the SWF file of the entire movie is created in the same folder where the project file (FLA) is saved. Choosing Control > Test Scene also creates a SWF file, but it contains only the contents of the scene.

4 Keep the project file open and open the **siteInProgress** folder in the **chap_18** folder. Notice the **xboardingSite_intro.swf** file.

This is the file you just created in Step 3. When you choose Control > Test Scene, Flash 8 automatically names the exported file, using the name of the FLA file (**xboardingSite**) followed by an underscore and the name of the scene. Notice also the file named **xboardingSite_learningL1.swf**. This is the file you created in the last exercise. When you are finished, close the **siteInProgress** folder.

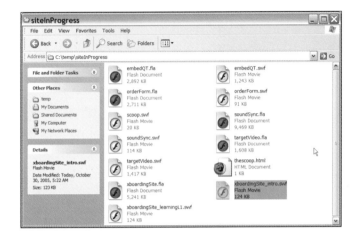

5 Click the **Edit Scenes** button and choose **welcome** to open its **Timeline**. Choose **Control > Test Scene**. As soon as you see the preview window, close it.

6 Repeat Step 5 to export a SWF file for each of the remaining scenes: **home**, **main**, **background**, **gear**, **gearBoards**, **gearCheckList**, **safety**, **safetyLessons**, **safetyRC**, **learning**, **learningL1**, **learningL2**, and **whatsNew**.

7 Open the **siteInProgress** folder again. You should now see 15 SWF files that start with the prefix **xboardingSite_**—one from each scene in the project file.

The last task to complete in order for the site to function properly is to rename the SWF files you just exported so that they match the ActionScripting in the drop-down menu you originally created in Chapter 12, *"ActionScript Basics and Behaviors."*

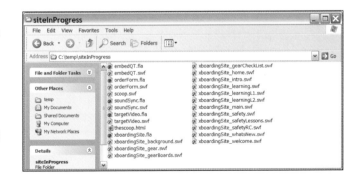

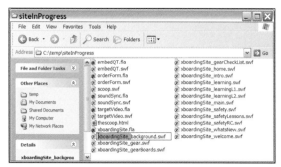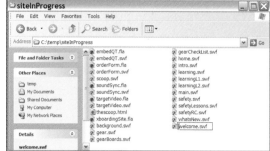

8 In the **siteInProgress** folder, rename each SWF file, deleting the **xboardingSite** name and the underscore so that it contains only the name of the scene.

You are renaming the files because the ActionScript that loads the SWF files does not include the xboardingSite name and the underscore. In order for the movie to work, the SWF names and the ActionScript need to match.

---

9 Choose **Control > Test Movie** (yes, **Test Movie** and not **Test Scene** this time) to preview the Web site. Type your name and click **Enter** to enter the site. Test all the menu buttons to make sure they work!

Tip: If you click one of the menu buttons and nothing happens, chances are you have somehow named the SWF file incorrectly. If this is the case, go back to the **siteInProgress** folder and check the name of the SWF file in question to make sure that its name is correct. Use the figure for Step 8 as a guide.

---

10 When you are finished, save this file and keep it open for the last exercise.

Note: Even though you can change the name of the SWF file by using the Publish settings, doing so changes the name of the SWF file for the whole movie, not just the scene. For example, if you choose the Control > Test Scene command after you have changed the name of the SWF file in the Publish settings to xSite, Flash will use the new name of the movie (xSite) followed by an underscore and the name of the scene.

---

10 | Creating Draggable Movies

When you load movies into levels, you can add functionality so that they not only will load but can also be dragged around the interface by the user. This exercise shows you how to do that. This exercise also shows you how to add the ActionScript and behaviors to allow the user to close the window when he or she is finished with it.

---

1 If you just completed Exercise 9, **xboardingSite.fla** should still be open. If it's not, go back and complete Exercise 9. Click the **Edit Scenes** button and choose **safety** to open its **Timeline**.

---

2 On the **Stage**, click the **Watch the RC Movie** button to select it. Press **F9** (Windows) or **Option+F9** (Mac) to open the **Actions** panel. This ActionScript has been created for you and tells Flash to load the movie named **soundSync.swf** into **Level 858** when the user clicks on the selected button.

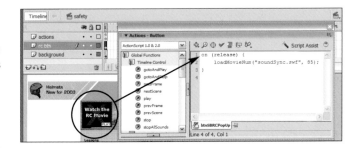

Why load **soundSync.swf** into level 85?
As you learned in Chapter 12, "*ActionScript Basics and Behaviors*," the current movies are loaded into Level 50, so in order to have **soundSync.swf** be visible, it needs to be loaded into a level higher than 50. Loading it into Level 85 gives you room to load other movies in between Levels 50 and 85 if you need to.

---

3 Close the **xboardingSite.fla** file. You do not need to save your changes.

In order to make the **soundSync.swf** file draggable, you need to modify the **soundSync.fla** file. You will do this next.

---

4 Open the **soundSync.fla** file from the **siteInProgress** folder. (We created this file to get you started. It is similar to the one you created in Chapter 14, "*Sound.*")

---

5 Choose **Control > Test Movie** to preview the file. Notice if you try to drag the movie, you can't. This is because no button or behaviors have been added to make the movie draggable. You will add the button and the behaviors in the following steps. Close the preview window.

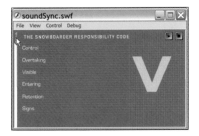

6 Click the **Insert Layer** button to add a new layer to the **Timeline**. Rename the new layer **btn invisible** and make sure it is just below the **labels** and **controls** layers.

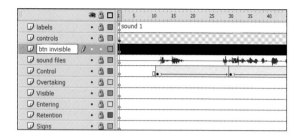

7 Press **Ctrl+L** (Windows) or **Cmd+L** (Mac) to open the **Library**. Click the **buttons** folder to expand it. Double-click the **btnInvisible** symbol to open the **Timeline**. Notice this button has only a Hit frame; therefore, it will serve as an invisible button in the movie.

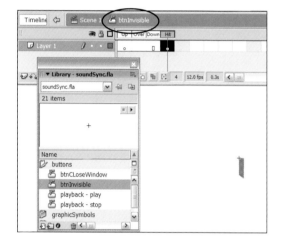

8 Click **Scene 1** to return to the main **Timeline**.

9 Drag an instance of the **btnInvisible** symbol onto the **Stage**. Position it so that it is on top of the tab on the upper-left side of the **Stage**.

You will add a behavior to make the button draggable next.

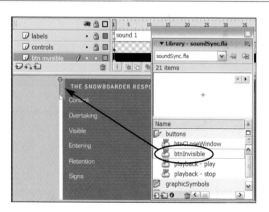

10 Choose **Window > Behaviors** to open the Behaviors panel. On the **Stage**, click the invisible button to select it. In the **Behaviors** panel, click the **Add Behavior** (+) button and choose **Movieclip > Start Dragging Movieclip**.

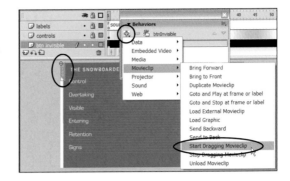

11 In the **Start Dragging Movieclip** dialog box, select **Relative** (the default), and click OK to accept the settings.

12 In the **Behaviors** panel, in the **Event** column double-click **On Release** and scroll down to **On Press**.

This behavior will allow the user to drag the movie while the mouse is pressed down. You will add the Stop Dragging Movieclip behavior next.

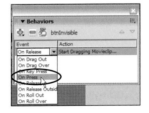

13 With the invisible button still selected, click the **Add Behavior** (+) button and choose **Movieclip > Stop Dragging Movieclip**.

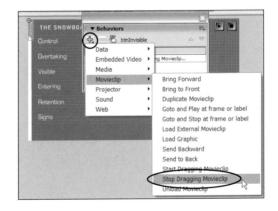

14 In the **Stop Dragging Movieclip** dialog box, click **OK**.

15 Choose **Control > Test Movie** to test the draggable button. Click the **Drag** button to drag the movie around the screen. When you are finished, close the preview window.

You will add the Close Window button next.

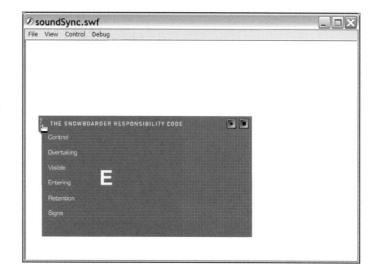

16 Click the **Insert Layer** button to add a new layer to the **Timeline**. Rename the layer **close btn** and move it below the **btn invisible** layer.

17 From the **Library**, drag an instance of the **btnCloseWindow** symbol onto the lower-right corner of the **Stage**.

You will add a behavior to this button next.

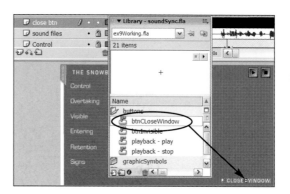

18 Click the **Close Window** button on the **Stage** to select it. In the **Behaviors** panel, click the **Add Behavior** (+) button and choose **Movieclip > Unload Movieclip**.

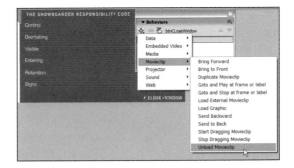

19 In the **Unload Movieclip** dialog box, select **Relative** (the default), and click OK to accept the settings.

20 Choose **Control > Test Movie** to test the **Close Window** button and to export the SWF file. Notice when you click **Close Window** it does just that, the window closes! Close the preview window.

You will test this movie in the actual project file next.

21 Save and close the **soundSync.fla** file. From the **siteInProgress** folder, double-click the **xboardingSite.swf** file to preview the site movie again.

22 In the navigation menu, click the **Safety** button.

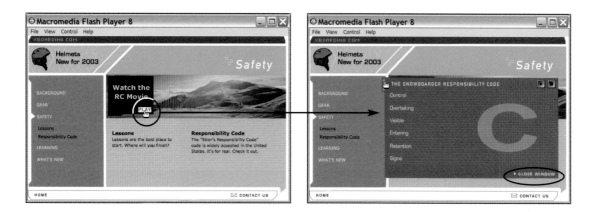

23 Click the **Watch the RC Movie** button and drag the **Snowboarder Responsibility Code** movie around the screen! Click the **Close Window** button to unload the movie!

---

24 When you are finished, close the preview window.

You have conquered another chapter! You should now have a more solid understanding of how the different pieces in this book come together to make a whole. Now there is only one more chapter left: Chapter 19, "*Integration.*"

19.

Integration

Although many designers work exclusively in Flash 8, the program doesn't have to be an island unto itself. There are many opportunities to combine it with other tools. The following hands-on exercises show how to use Fireworks, Illustrator, and Photoshop content with Flash 8. It also shows you how to incorporate Flash 8 content into a Web site designed in Dreamweaver 8. Keep in mind that in order to try these exercises, you must have these programs installed on your system. If you don't have the applications, you can download trial versions of Macromedia and Adobe products from their Web sites—**www.macromedia.com**, and **www.adobe.com**, respectively.

Importing Vector Files

You can import several different file types into Flash 8. The following chart lists the supported file types:

Vector File Types Supported by Macromedia Flash 8			
File Type	Extension	Windows	Mac
Adobe Illustrator 10 or earlier	.eps, .ai	X	X
AutoCAD DXF	.dxf	X	X
Enhanced Windows metafile	.emf	X	
Macromedia FreeHand	.fh8, .ft8, .fh9, .ft9, .fh10, .fh11	X	X
FutureSplash Player	.spl	X	X
Macromedia Flash movie	.swf	X	X
Windows metafile	.wmf	X	
PNG	.png	X	X

1 | Importing Fireworks Content

As you continue to develop your skills, you may want to use content created outside of Flash 8. Although there are many applications to choose from for creating artwork, you'll enjoy using Macromedia Fireworks content because colors and text can remain editable when you import the Fireworks 8 file into Flash 8. Or, if you choose to import flattened images, you can edit the artwork in Fireworks without ever leaving Flash 8! This exercise takes you through some basic techniques for importing and working with Fireworks PNG files as editable objects and text and as rasterized, flattened images.

Note: You must have Fireworks 8 installed in order to complete this exercise. You can download a trial version of Fireworks 8 from Macromedia's Web site at **www.macromedia.com**.

---

1 Copy the **chap_19** folder from the **HOT CD-ROM** to your **Desktop**. Open **fireworksFlash.fla** from the **chap_19** folder.

---

2 Choose **File > Import > Import to Stage**. Select the **gearSale.png** file in the **chap_19** folder and click **Open** to open the **Fireworks PNG Import Settings** dialog box.

Flash 8 automatically detects you are trying to import a Fireworks PNG file.

---

3 Select the following settings: **File Structure: Import into new layer in current scene**; **Objects: Keep all paths editable**; and **Text: Keep all text editable**. Click **OK** to import the PNG image onto a new layer and to allow the text and paths to be editable.

The Fireworks PNG Import Settings dialog box has a number of options. See the upcoming table for a description of each of the options in this dialog box.

Note: Importing a PNG file with editable paths and editable text allows all the vector information to remain as vector information and allows text to be editable. However, you will lose bitmap effects, such as bevels and glows. Also, if you are using an older version of Fireworks, you may notice some of the artwork aligns incorrectly upon importing.

Notice Flash 8 places the Fireworks PNG file on its own layer and even names it for you. Although you may not have realized it, you instructed Flash 8 to do so when you chose the **File Structure: Import into new layer in current scene** option in the Fireworks PNG Import Settings dialog box.

N O T E :

Understanding the Fireworks PNG Import Settings

The Fireworks PNG Import Settings dialog box offers a number of options. The following chart outlines each option:

	Fireworks PNG Import Settings	
Option	**Settings**	**Description**
File Structure	Import as movie clip and retain layers	Lets you import the PNG file as a movie clip with the layers and frames intact.
	Import into new layer in current scene	Lets you import the PNG file into a single new layer at the top of the stacking order. When you use this setting, the Fireworks layers are compressed into one single layer. The Fireworks frames are contained within the new layer.
Objects	Rasterize if necessary to maintain appearance	Maintains the appearance to preserve Fireworks fills, strokes, and effects.
	Keep all paths editable	Keeps all objects as editable vector paths, but fills, strokes, and effects may be lost on import.
Text	Rasterize if necessary to maintain appearance	Maintains the appearance to preserve Fireworks fills, strokes, and effects applied to text.
	Keep all text editable	Keeps all text editable, but fills, strokes, and effects may be lost on import.
Import as a single flattened bitmap		Turns the PNG file into a single flattened image.

4 Select the **Selection** tool from the **toolbar**. On the **Stage**, double-click the **GEAR** text, which will allow you to edit the text. Type the word **BOOT**. See how easy it is to make changes? Select the **Selection** tool from the toolbar again and reposition the **BOOT** text so it is centered above the **SALE** text.

---

5 Double-click the upper-right corner of the background artwork.

---

6 Click the object to select it. In the **Property Inspector**, choose a new color from the **Fill Color** box to change the background color.

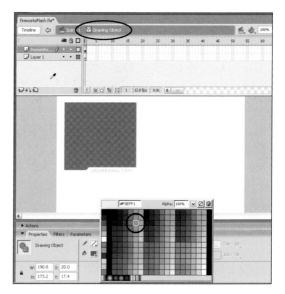

---

7 In the edit bar, click **Scene 1** to return to the main **Timeline** and see your changes!

You just learned how to import a Fireworks PNG file as a new layer using editable paths and editable text, which lets you modify object attributes such as the type and object color. Next, you will learn how to import the same Fireworks document as a flattened bitmap. However, with that method, you lose the ability to edit the object as a vector because it is imported as a bitmap graphic.

---

8 In the main **Timeline**, lock the **Fireworks PNG** layer and select **Frame 1** of **Layer 1**.

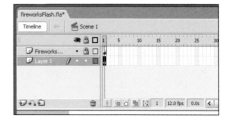

---

9 Choose **File > Import > Import to Stage** to open the **Import File** dialog box. In the **chap_19** folder, select the same **gearSale.png** file you imported earlier in this exercise. Click **Open** to open the **Fireworks PNG Import Settings** dialog box.

Again, Flash 8 automatically detects you are trying to import a Fireworks PNG file.

---

10 Select the **Import as a single flattened bitmap** option. Click **OK** to import the PNG image into **Layer 1** as a flat, bitmap graphic.

11 Click and drag the new bitmap graphic to the right of the **Stage** so you can see it better.

Tip: By default, Flash 8 automatically places imported artwork in the upper-left corner of the Stage. Since Layer 1 is below the Fireworks PNG layer, it will appear behind it in the stacking order.

12 Select the bitmap you just imported.

In the Property Inspector, notice the image you just imported is a bitmap. Also notice the glow around the artwork; this is visual feedback that the artwork has been imported as a bitmap. You imported the same file earlier in the exercise, but there was no glow. Why? When you import a Fireworks PNG file using editable paths and editable text, some fills, strokes, and effects may be lost. However, when you import a Fireworks PNG file as a flattened bitmap, you lose the ability to edit the text and paths, but glows and bevels

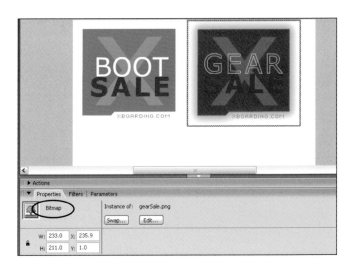

are preserved. What's best? It depends on what you want to do with the imported content. If you need to edit the vector artwork in Flash, import it using the technique you learned in Steps 2 and 3. If you want the image to look exactly the same as it did in Fireworks, use the technique you learned in Steps 9 and 10. What if you need to edit the content? Fortunately, you can edit the bitmap using Fireworks 8 without ever having to leave Flash 8. You'll learn how in the next steps.

13 Press **Ctrl+L** (Windows) or **Cmd+L** (Mac) to open the **Library**. Select the **gearSale** bitmap.

14 From the **Options** menu, choose **Edit with Fireworks** to open **gearSale.png** in Fireworks 8 automatically.

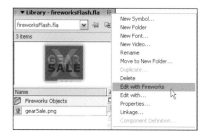

15 In Fireworks 8, select the **SALE** text. In the **Property Inspector**, choose **white** for the text color. When you are finished, click the **Done** button to close Fireworks 8 and return to Flash 8.

Note: The **Editing from Flash Basic** text provides a visual clue that you are editing directly from Flash.

Back in Flash 8, notice your file has been updated! As you can see, you can edit and update content created in Fireworks 8 easily!

16 Close **fireworksFlash.fla**. You don't need to save your changes.

NOTE: | **Learning Fireworks 8**

The purpose of these exercises was to show you how to import content created in Fireworks 8 into Flash 8. For more information about how to use Fireworks 8, use the **free 24-hour pass to the lynda.com Online Training Library** provided in the Introduction of this book and check out the following video-based training resources:

Fireworks 8 Essential Training

with Abigail Rudner

Studio 8 Web Workflow

with Abigail Rudner

2 | Integrating with Dreamweaver 8

Many designers create SWF files using Flash and then use Dreamweaver to integrate the SWF file with the required HTML documents. Dreamweaver 8 is also a great tool for managing large numbers of Web site files, and it provides a way to FTP the files to a Web server. This exercise shows how to combine HTML and Flash 8 using Dreamweaver 8. Why not just use the publishing features of Flash 8 for your HTML? It's fine for simple pages with only Flash content, but Dreamweaver 8 offers more control if you plan to integrate Flash content with several HTML pages, as you would want to do in a complicated Web site. After you import the SWF file into Dreamweaver, you can alter many attributes of the Flash 8 file, such as its size and positioning. You can even insert Flash content inside frames, tables, or layers within a Dreamweaver HTML document. The process is quite simple—this exercise shows you how.

Note: You must have Dreamweaver 8 installed in order to complete this exercise. You can download a trial version of Dreaweaver 8 from Macromedia's Web site at **www.macromedia.com**.

---

1 Open **homePage.fla** file from the **chap_19** folder.

---

2 Choose **Control > Test Movie** to produce the SWF file you will need in later steps for this exercise. Notice the animated logo.

---

3 Close the file when you are finished previewing it.

---

4 Open Dreamweaver 8. Choose **File > Open**, and select the **index.htm** file from the **chap_19** folder, which opens a document with a black background.

---

5 In the **Insert** bar, choose **Common** from the pop-up menu. In the **Common** panel, click the **Media** button, and then choose **Flash** from the menu.

6 In the **Select File** dialog box, locate the **chap_19** folder, select **homePage.swf**, and click **OK**. Make sure you choose the **SWF** file and not the **FLA** file.

Note: If Dreamweaver opens the Object Tag Accessibility Attributes dialog box, just click **OK** to ignore it for this exercise.

This is what the Flash content looks like in Dreamweaver.

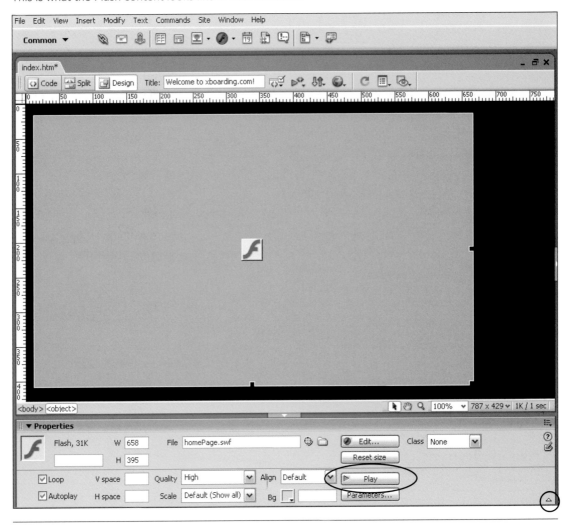

7 In the **Property Inspector**, click the small arrow in the lower-right corner to expand the **Property Inspector** (if it's not already expanded). Notice the green **Play** button. Click the **Play** button to preview the Flash file inside Dreamweaver.

8 Check the rollover functionality of the buttons (the caret appears to the left of the text when you roll your mouse over them). Notice the logo is animating also.

Using the Play button, you can have Macromedia Dreamweaver 8 preview graphic, button, and movie clip symbols inside your Flash 8 movie.

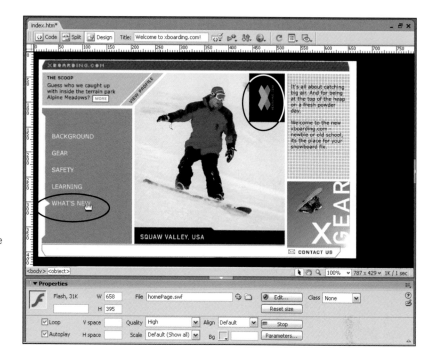

9 As you preview the file, notice that the green **Play** button in the **Property Inspector** changes to a red **Stop** button. When you're done previewing the file, click the **Stop** button to return to your work environment.

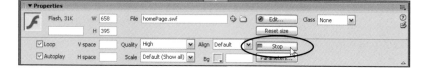

10 Make sure the SWF file is still selected, and then click the **Edit** button in the **Property Inspector**.

Tip: You can also **right-click** (Windows) or **Ctrl+click** (Mac) the SWF in Dreamweaver and then choose **Edit with Flash** from the contextual menu to open the file inside Flash 8.

11 Flash prompts you to locate the original source FLA file. Select **homepage.fla** and click **Open**.

12 Select the **Free Transform** tool and click and drag to rescale the logo smaller. When you are finished, click the **Done** button to return to Dreamweaver 8.

13 In Dreamweaver 8, click the **Play** button in the **Property Inspector**.

Notice that Dreamweaver 8 has automatically updated the SWF file inside the document to reflect the change you made to the logo. Cool!

Note: Using the Property Inspector in Dreamweaver 8 is an easy way to edit the FLA file, change the background color, change how the content will be aligned or how the movie will scale, and change plenty of other useful properties. Dreamweaver 8 offers a lot of control over how the content is displayed.

14 When you are finished, close all files in Dreamweaver 8 and Flash 8. Close Dreamweaver 8 and return to Flash 8 for the next exercise.

Importing Illustrator Content

Many digital artists are familiar with Adobe Illustrator and prefer to use its drawing capabilities over other vector illustration tools. Flash 8 supports direct import of Adobe Illustrator files. This exercise walks you through the process of importing an Adobe Illustrator file as keyframes into Flash 8 and how to import Adobe Illustrator content as separate layers in Flash 8.

---

1 In Flash 8, choose **File > New** to create a new document. Choose **File > Import > Import to Stage** and select the file **gearItems.ai** from the **chap_19** folder. Click **Open** to open the **Import Options** dialog box.

---

2 Select **Convert pages to: Keyframes** and **Convert layers to: Keyframes**. Deselect the **Include invisible layers** option. Click **OK**.

---

3 On the **Timeline**, scrub the **playhead** to see the content Flash imported as separate keyframes. Select a keyframe on the **Timeline.**

Notice the Frame label reflects the layer name from the original Illustrator file. As you can see, importing Illustrator files directly into Flash 8 makes creating Flash content very easy.

When you import Illustrator content as keyframes, all of your objects remain editable. You'll explore this further in the next few steps.

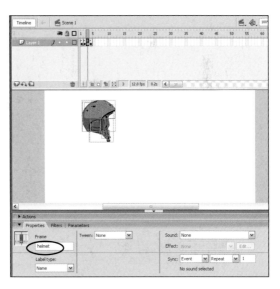

4 Move the playhead back to **Frame 1** and double-click the left side of the **snowboard** (between the two boomerang shapes) to open the group for this object.

Notice the content is editable.

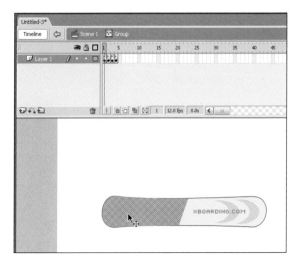

5 In the **Property Inspector**, choose a different **Fill Color**.

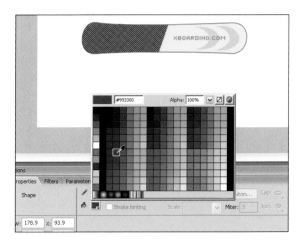

6 Click **Scene 1** to return to the main **Timeline** and check out your changes.

As you can see, content imported from Illustrator into Flash 8 remains as vector content, which you can edit directly in Flash 8.

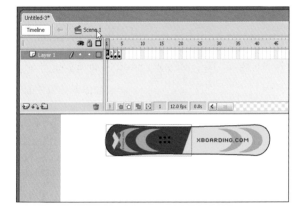

7 Choose **File > New** to create a new Flash document. Choose **File > Import > Import to Stage** and select **gearItems.ai** from the **chap_19** folder. Click **Open** to open the **Import Options** dialog box.

This is the same file you imported earlier in this exercise.

---

8 Select **Convert pages to: Scenes** and **Convert layers to: Layers**. Deselect the **Include invisible layers** option. Click **OK**.

On the Timeline, notice Flash imported the content as separate layers, and the names of the layers in the Illustrator file transferred over as well. You have successfully imported artwork from Illustrator into Flash and isolated each Illustrator layer on its own layer and frame on the Timeline. From here, you can do just about anything. Importing Illustrator files directly into Flash 8 makes creating Flash content from Illustrator content very easy!

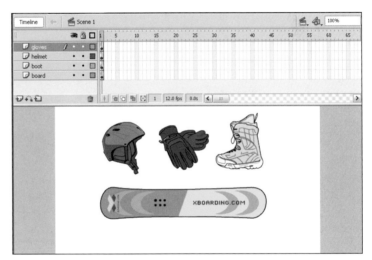

---

9 Close the file. You don't need to save your changes.

Note: Adobe Illustrator 10 and later and Adobe ImageReady CS and later can now export in the SWF file format, allowing you to import Illustrator and Photoshop content as SWF files. These versions provide you another possible workflow when integrating content from Adobe Illustrator and Adobe Photoshop.

Import Dialog Box for Illustrator, EPS, or PDF files

Flash can import Adobe Illustrator files in version 6 or later, EPS files in any version, and PDF files in version 1.4 or earlier. You can choose from the following options when importing Adobe Illustrator, EPS, or PDF files:

- Convert pages to scenes or keyframes.

- Convert layers to Flash layers or keyframes or flatten all layers.

- Select which pages to import.

- Include invisible layers.

- Maintain text blocks.

- Rasterize everything. Choosing this option flattens layers and rasterizes text, and disables options for converting layers or maintaining text blocks.

Note: The PDF version number is different from the Adobe Acrobat version number. Adobe Acrobat is a product used to author PDF files. PDF is the file format.

Illustrator, EPS, or PDF Import Dialog Box

Option Group	Setting	Description
Convert pages to	Scenes Keyframes	Controls how the PDF document pages are imported into Flash. If you select Scenes, each page will be transformed into a scene in Flash 8. If you select Keyframes, each page in your file will be transformed into a keyframe.
Convert layers to	Layers Keyframes Flatten	Controls how individual layers are imported into Flash 8 from your Illustrator or EPS file. Selecting Layers allows the layers in your file to remain as layers when imported into Flash. Selecting Keyframes allows Flash to convert the layers into keyframes. Selecting Flatten converts multiple layers into one layer in Flash.
Which pages to import	All From: To:	Lets you either import all pages from your PDF file or specify a range of pages to import into Flash.
Options	Include invisible layers	With this option selected, Flash will include all hidden layers from your Illustrator or EPS file.
	Maintain text blocks	With this option selected, Flash will preserve the text blocks in your Illustrator or EPS file so that they remain editable in Flash.
	Rasterize everything	Selecting this option flattens layers and rasterizes text, and disables options for converting layers or maintaining text blocks.
	Rasterization resolution	Lets you set the resolution for the rasterized file being imported.

4 | Importing Photoshop Content

This exercise introduces you to some of the techniques, challenges, and workarounds to importing Photoshop content info Flash 8.

Note: You must have Photoshop CS or Photoshop CS2, including ImageReady CS or ImageReady CS2, installed in order to complete this exercise. You can download a trial version of Photoshop CS2 from Adobe's Web site at **www.adobe.com**.

---

1 Open **photoshop.fla** from the **chap_19** folder.

---

2 Choose **File > Import > Import to Stage**. Select **snowboard.psd** from the **chap_19** folder and click **Open**.

Provided you have QuickTime installed on your computer, you can import a Photoshop file directly into Flash 8. Unfortunately, you are limited to working with a flat file. If you had multiple layers in the original Photoshop file, including vector-based shape and type layers, you won't be able to edit them individually in Flash 8 using this import technique, which in some cases may be acceptable. In other cases (most likely most cases), you'll

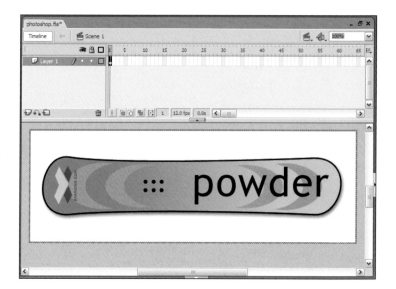

want to edit the contents of layers in Flash 8. Fortunately, you can work around this problem easily.

Photoshop ships with a second application, ImageReady, which is intended for designing and optimizing Web graphics. ImageReady CS and ImageReady CS2 include an Export to Macromedia Flash (SWF) feature that lets you export Photoshop files to the SWF file format. In turn, you can import the SWF file onto the Stage in Flash 8 and still work with layers. The next few steps show you how to do just that.

---

3 Choose **File > Revert** to return **photoshop.fla** to its original state.

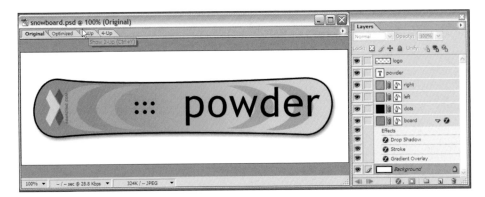

4 In ImageReady, open **snowboard.psd** from the **chap_19** folder. Make sure the **Layers** palette is visible. If it's not, choose **Window > Layers**.

Notice the image contains a series of layers, including type and shape layers and layer styles. Although Photoshop and ImageReady are predominantly bitmap-based editing programs, they contain vector-based features, specifically type and shapes. Wouldn't it be nice if you could edit each of these layers in Flash? Or, one better, wouldn't it be great if you could edit the vector-based type and shapes in Flash 8? In the next few exercises, you'll learn how.

5 Choose **File > Export > Macromedia Flash (SWF)**. In the **Macromedia Flash Export** dialog box, select the **Preserve Appearance** option, which will ensure sure the file looks exactly the same in Flash 8 as it did in ImageReady CS2. Make sure the **Generate HTML** and **Enable Dynamic Text** options are deselected, and choose **Lossless-32** from the **Format** pop-up menu. Click **OK**.

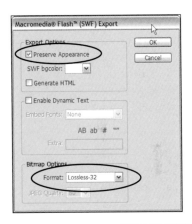

Lossless-32 is the same as PNG and will provide the highest-quality image when exporting SWFs from ImageReady CS2.

6 In the **Export as Macromedia Flash** dialog box, browse to the **chap_19** folder. Name the file **snowboard_pre-serve.swf** and click **Save**. A warning message appears, indicating one or more text or shape layers were flattened because **Preserve Appearance** was selected. Click **OK** to acknowledge the warning.

You'll learn more about what the warning means when you import the SWF file into Flash 8.

7 In Flash 8, choose **File > Import > Import to Stage**. Select **snowboard_preserve.swf** from the **chap_19** folder and click **Open**.

---

8 Press **Ctrl+A** (Windows) or **Cmd+A** (Mac) to select all. Choose **Modify > Timeline > Distribute to Layers**.

Notice the file looks exactly as it did in ImageReady CS2. Unfortunately, most, but not all, of the layers from the Photoshop file have been retained. Further, the type and shapes are no longer vector-based. Using the Preserve Appearance option in ImageReady CS2 ensures the files look identical when you import SWFs into Flash 8, but the files can lose some of the layers and lose the vector-based shape and type layers.

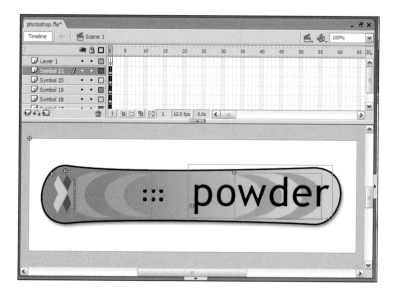

By choosing Preserve Appearance, you're telling ImageReady CS2 to keep the appearance of the file regardless of the impact on the layers and vector-based content in the file. In many cases, this approach might work for you. In some cases, you may want to have access to all the layers and be able to edit the vector content. Not to worry, you'll learn how in the next step.

---

9 Choose **File > Revert** to return **photoshop.fla** to its original state.

---

10 In ImageReady CS2, choose **File > Export > Macromedia Flash (SWF)**. In the **Macromedia Flash Export** dialog box, deselect the **Preserve Appearance** option. Make sure the **Generate HTML** and **Enable Dynamic Text** options are deselected, and make sure **Lossless-32** is selected from the **Format** drop-down menu. Click **OK**.

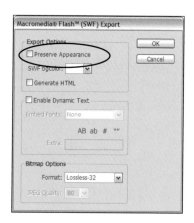

11 In the **Export as Macromedia Flash** dialog box, browse to the **chap_19** folder. Name the file **snow-board_no_preserve.swf** and click **Save**.

12 In Flash 8, choose **File > Import > Import to Stage**. Select **snowboard_no_preserve.swf** from the **chap_19** folder and click **Open**.

13 Press **Ctrl+A** (Windows) or **Cmd+A** (Mac) to select all. Choose **Modify > Timeline > Distribute to Layers**.

Notice all the layers were retained when you imported the SWF file. Next, you'll see how you can still edit the vector-based type and shape layers.

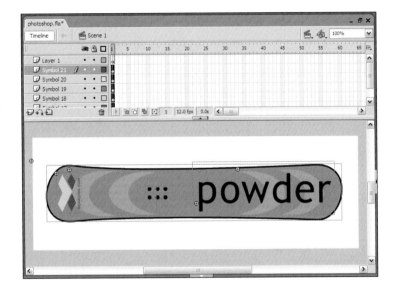

14 On the **Timeline**, click **Symbol 16**, the snowboard shape, to select it. Choose **Modify > Break Apart**.

Notice the dotted mesh over the shape.

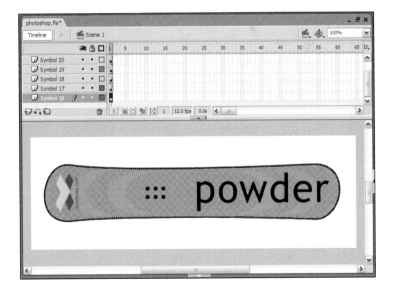

15 Click the **Stage** to remove the dotted mesh. Position your pointer at the edge of the shape until the pointer changes, as shown in the illustration here. Click and drag to reshape the snowboard.

As you can see, the snowboard remained as a vector-based shape, which is the reason you can edit it here!

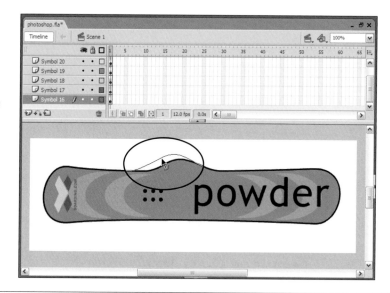

16 On the **Timeline**, click **Symbol 20**, the powder text, to select it. Choose **Modify > Break Apart**. Select the **Text** tool from the **toolbar**. Click inside the text.

Notice the text is now editable! Flash 8 retained the vector-based type from the original Photoshop file. You can edit the text and reformat the font, font size, or font color using the controls in the Property Inspector. Very cool!

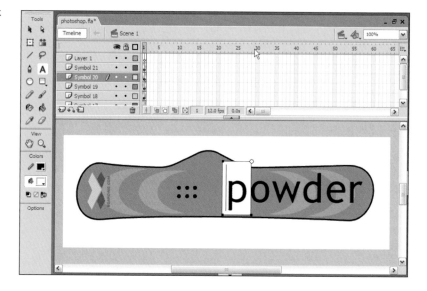

Although you kept the layers and the vector-based shape and type, you also lost a few things in the document. Specifically, you lost the drop shadow and gradient layer styles.

When you export SWFs from ImageReady CS2 and deselect the Preserve Appearance option, you tell ImageReady CS2 to keep the layers and vector-based content. Unfortunately, because Flash 8 cannot understand the layer styles in the Photoshop file, it drops them on import. Not to worry, you can create gradients easily in Flash 8, as you learned in Chapter 3, "*Using the Drawing and Color Tools,*" and you can now create drop shadows in Flash 8 using the new filters, which you learned about in Chapter 7, "*Filters and Blending Modes.*"

At this point, you might be wondering, when should you use Preserve Appearance and when should you not? The answer depends on what you plan to do with the SWF file when you import it into Flash 8. If the appearance of the file is more important than the layers and the vector-based content, and you want to be absolutely sure the file looks identical in Flash 8 as it did in Photoshop CS2 or ImageReady CS2, use Preserve Appearance. If maintaining the layers and editing the vector-based content is most important, do not use Preserve Appearance.

17 Close **photoshop.fla**. You don't need to save your changes.

NOTE:

Photoshop and Flash Integration

To learn more about Photoshop and Flash Integration, use the free 24-hour pass to the **lynda.com Online Training Library** provided in the Introduction of this book and check out the following resources:

Photoshop and Flash Integration
with Michael Ninness

Photoshop CS2 for the Web Essential Training
with Tanya Staples

5 | Creating Accessible Content

An increasing number of Web sites require accessible content, which means the content must be accessible and navigable by people who have disabilities. In Flash 8, you can make the content in your movie accessible to visually impaired people who have access to screen reader software. Screen reader software uses audio to describe what is on the screen. In order for the screen reader to read your content properly, you must set up the content in a certain way. This exercise shows you how to make content in your Flash 8 project files accessible.

System Requirements: The Flash 8 Player uses MSAA (Microsoft Active Accessibility) technology, which is technology that communicates with screen readers. This technology is available only on Windows operating systems. Also note the Windows Internet Explorer plug-in (ActiveX) version of the Macromedia Flash 6 Player (and higher) does support MSAA, although the Windows Netscape and Windows stand-alone players do not. Also, screen reader users will need to access Flash 8 content by using the Microsoft Internet Explorer browser, which is the only browser that supports MSAA.

1 Open the **accessibleContent.fla** file from the **chap_19** folder.

This file contains a background image, buttons, and text.

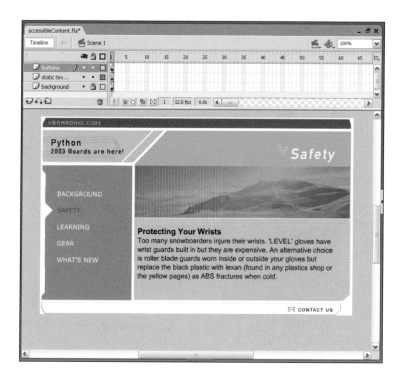

2 In the **Property Inspector**, make sure nothing is selected in the project file, and click the **Edit accessibility settings** button to open the **Accessibility** panel.

3 Select the **Make movie accessible** option. In the **Name** field, type **Safety Page**, and for the **Description** type **This page offers information about snowboarding safety.**

The **Make Movie Accessible** option makes the whole movie (which resides on one frame in the main Timeline) accessible to screen readers. The chart that follows describes the options in this panel.

4 When you are finished, close the **Accessibility** panel.

Accessibility Panel Options

Option	Description
Make movie accessible	Makes the movie readable by screen readers; this includes all text, input text fields, buttons, and movie clips. If this option is deselected, the movie will be hidden from screen readers.
Make child objects accessible	Makes the accessible objects (text, input text fields, buttons, and movie clips) located inside movie clips readable by screen readers. If this option is deselected, accessible objects within movie clips cannot be accessed by screen readers.
Auto label	Uses text objects, such as buttons or input text fields contained in the movie, as automatic labels for accessible content. If this option is deselected, screen readers will read text objects as text objects, not labels. (You will learn how to label individual items later in this exercise.)
Name	The title (name) for the movie, which the screen reader will read even if there is no other accessible content in the movie. This option is available only if you select the **Make movie accessible** option.
Description	The description of the movie, which will be read by the screen reader software. This option is also available only if you select the **Make movie accessible** option.

NOTE:

Accessible Objects

The Macromedia Flash 8 Player will include text, input text fields, buttons, movie clips, and entire movies as accessible objects that can be read by screen readers. However, individual graphic objects are not included as accessible objects, because graphics can't be easily turned into spoken words. On the other hand, movie clips are included as accessible objects, as are the objects inside movie clips, as long as they are text, input text fields, buttons, or other movie clips.

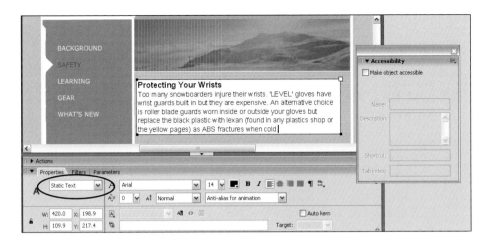

5 On the **Stage**, double-click the static text field to select the content. Choose **Window > Other Panels > Accessibility** to open the **Accessibility** panel again.

Even though you made your movie accessible in Step 3, you can have more control over what the screen reader will read, by filling out the fields in the Accessibility panel for this static text field, which you will do next.

Tip: You can open the Accessibility panel by choosing either **Window > Other Panels > Accessibility** or by clicking the **Edit accessibility settings** button in the **Property Inspector**.

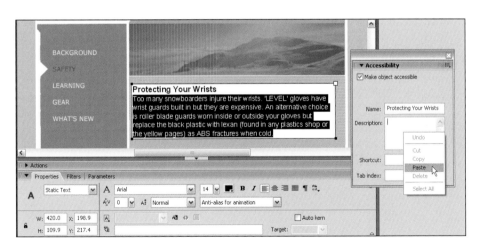

6 In the **Accessibility** panel, select the **Make Object Accessible** option. In the **Name** field, type **Protecting Your Wrists**. In the static text field on the **Stage**, select all the text below **Protecting Your Wrists** and **right-click** (Windows) or **Ctrl+click** (Mac) and choose **Copy** from the contextual menu. In the **Description** field, **right-click** (Windows) or **Ctrl+click** (Mac) and choose **Paste** from the contextual menu to paste the content.

Screen readers will read the text field name (Protecting Your Wrists) and then the description you just pasted.

It is very important that each accessible object in your movie have a name. The screen readers will identify an object by reading the object's name first and then the description of the object. Rather than allowing Flash 8 to name objects generically (by selecting the **Auto label** option in Step 3), name them yourself. Even though Flash Player automatically provides the names for static and dynamic text objects, you should rename them descriptively so they make more sense to your users.

7 On the **Stage**, select the **Background** button. In the **Accessibility** panel, make sure the **Make object accessible** option is selected. Type **Background button** for the **Name** and **This button takes you to the background page** for the **Description**. Close the **Accessibility** panel.

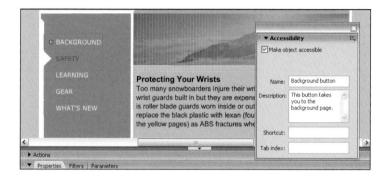

Again, rather than leaving it up to Flash to name your buttons (to avoid names like button 17), you should name your buttons individually.

Note: Even if you test your movie, unfortunately, it is not possible to test your movie's accessibility content using the Flash 8 test movie features. If you have access to a screen reader, however, you can test the movie's accessibility by playing it in a screen reader. Additionally, demonstration versions of screen reader software are available, so you can download one and test your movie that way.

TIP: | **Learning More About Accessibility**

If you are interested in learning more about Macromedia 8 and accessibility, a section on Macromedia's Web site will tell you all about it: **http://www.macromedia.com/macromedia/accessibility/**

8 Save and close this file. You are finished with the book!

Congratulations! You did it! I really hope this book helped you learn Macromedia Flash 8 quickly, and you are now armed and ready to create your own animated and interactive projects. I wish you the best of luck with all of your future Flashing!

Technical Support and Troubleshooting FAQ

If you run into problems while following the exercises in this book, you might find the answer in the Troubleshooting FAQ. If you don't find the information you're looking for, use the contact information provided in the Technical Support section.

Technical Support Information

The following is a list of technical support resources you can use if you need help:

lynda.com

If you run into any problems as you work through this book, check the companion Web site for updates:

http://www.lynda.com/books/HOT/fl8

If you don't find what you're looking for on the companion Web site, send me an email at: **fl8hot@lynda.com**.

We encourage and welcome your feedback, comments, and error reports.

Peachpit Press

If your book has a defective CD-ROM, please contact the customer service department at Peachpit Press:

customer_service@peachpit.com

Technical Support

http://www.macromedia.com/support/flash/

or

http://www.macromedia.com/support/email/cscontact/

If you're having problems with Flash Professional 8 unrelated to this book, please visit the first link to access the Macromedia Flash Support Center.

To contact Macromedia Technical Support, use the email form in the second link. They can help you with typical problems, such as an expired trial version.

You can also try to contact them directly by phone:

US and Canada: 1-800-470-7211 (toll-free)

Outside US and Canada: +1-415-553-7186

Frequently Asked Questions

Q: On the Macintosh, why can't I see any FLA files when I choose File > Open?

A: If the FLA file was created on a PC, you might experience a problem seeing the files when you try to open it on a Macintosh. You can correct this problem by changing the **Show** option to **All Files**.

Q: On the Macintosh, the FLA file won't open when I double-click it. Why?

A: If the FLA file was created on a PC, you might not be able to double-click it to open the file. If this is the case, open Flash 8 and choose **File > Open** to open the FLA file. If you don't see the FLA file listed when you choose **File > Open**, see the previous question. After you save the FLA file (originally created on a PC) on your Mac, you will be able to double-click the FLA to open it.

Q: My toolbar has disappeared. What should I do?

A: Choose **Window > Tools** to show/hide the toolbar. Chapter 2, "*Understanding the Interface*," explains the toolbar in detail.

Q: All of my panels have disappeared. What should I do?

A: Press the **Tab** key to show them and even hide them again. If you don't like their arrangement, you can restore them to their default onscreen positions by choosing **Window > Workspace Layout > Default**. This command is especially helpful when someone else has undocked and changed the combination of your panels. Chapter 2, "*Understanding the Interface*," describes each of the panels in detail.

Q: I undocked one of the panels, but I can't redock it again. Why?

A: To redock a panel, make sure you drag it over the location where you want dock it. When the black outline appears, release the mouse. Chapter 2, "*Understanding the Interface*," explains docking and undocking in detail.

Q: Why does Flash create extra files when I press F12 (Windows) or Cmd+F12 (Mac)?

A: Pressing **F12** (Windows) or **Cmd+F12** (Mac) is a shortcut for the **Publish Preview** command, which publishes the SWF file and an HTML file. Flash 8 creates these files in the same directory as the FLA file. If you want to preview your movie without publishing any other files, choose **Control > Test Movie** or **File > Publish Preview > Flash** to create only the SWF file. Chapter 17, "*Publishing and Exporting*," explains the publish features in detail.

Q: I tried to create my own shape tween, but it won't work, and the Timeline has a broken line. What does this mean?

A: A solid line with an arrow indicates that the tween is working properly. A dashed line in the **Timeline** indicates a problem with the tween, which could be caused by several things. First, you cannot create a shape tween using symbols, groups, or text blocks (text that hasn't been broken apart). Make sure you are using only objects that work with shape tweens. Second, make sure you have at least two keyframes in the layer you are trying to tween. In Chapter 5, "*Shape Tweening*," you will find a detailed list of the objects you can use to create shape tweens.

Q: Why do all of the objects on my Stage appear faded?

A: This occurs when you double-click a symbol instance or **right-click** (Windows) or **Ctrl+click** (Mac) a symbol instance and choose **Edit in Place**. This is a quick way to make changes to a symbol without having to access the **Library**; however, it can be confusing if that's not what you intended to do. In the edit bar, click **Scene 1** to exit this editing mode and to return to the main **Timeline**. In the picture shown here, **Scene 1** was renamed **main**. So, in this example, you would click the word **main** in the edit bar to return to the main **Timeline**.

Q: I tried to create my own motion tween, but it won't work. And the Timeline has a broken line. What does this mean?

A: You cannot create a motion tween using shapes or broken-apart text. A solid line with an arrow indicates that the tween is working properly. A dashed line in the **Timeline** indicates that there is a problem with the tween. Make sure you are using only objects that work with motion tweens. In Chapter 8, "*Motion Tweening and Timeline Effects*," you will find a detailed list of the objects you can use to create motion tweens.

Q: I tried to motion tween multiple objects, but it's not working. What could be wrong?

A: Motion tweening multiple objects requires that each different object exist on a separate layer. If you have all the objects on a single layer, the tween will not behave as expected. You can use the **Modify > Distribute to Layers** command to quickly distribute each object to its own layer. Also, make sure you are trying to tween objects that are capable of being motion tweened. Objects such as shapes and broken-apart text cannot be motion tweened. In Chapter 8, "*Motion Tweening and Timeline Effects*," you learned how to motion tween multiple objects; refer to this chapter for a review.

Q: I tried to change the alpha transparency of a shape using the Property Inspector, but Flash doesn't allow me to. What could be wrong?

A: To change the alpha transparency of a shape (dotted mesh), you need to use the **Color Mixer** panel. To change the alpha transparency of a symbol instance, you need to use the **Property Inspector**. You learned how to do this in Chapter 6, "*Symbols and Instances*." Refer to this chapter for a review.

Q: Why won't my movie clips play when I click the Play button?

A: You preview your movie clips on the main **Timeline** within the Flash 8 authoring environment. You can preview movie clips only within their own **Timeline**, in the **Library**, or by choosing **Control > Test Movie** to preview the movie clip in the Flash Player.

Q: I made an input text field, but when I test it using Control > Test Movie and I type inside it, nothing happens. Why?

A: When you created the text box, you most likely set the text color to the same color as the background of the movie. Try changing the text color and testing the movie again. Also, make sure that you have **Input Text** set for the **Text Type**.

Q: I want to learn more about the many actions in the Actions panel. How do I do this?

A: In the **Actions** panel, click the **Reference** button to open the **ActionScript 2.0 Language Reference** window. At the top of the window, click the **Index** link and then click the link representing the first letter of the action you want to learn more about. Scroll down the page to locate the action of interest and click on it. A complete description of the action will appear in the window.

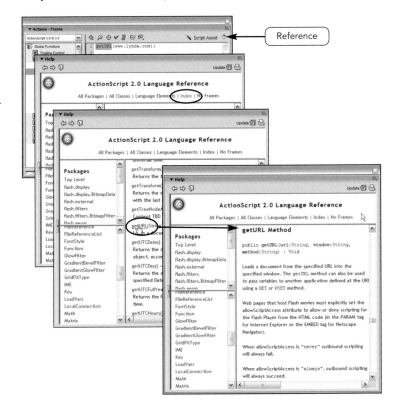

Flash Professional 8
Resources

There are many great resources for Flash users. You have ample choices among a variety of newsgroups, conferences, and third-party Web sites that can really help you get the most out of the new skills you've developed by reading this book. Here you'll find a list of the best resources for further developing your skills with Flash Professional 8.

lynda.com Training Resources

lynda.com

lynda.com is a leader in software books and video training for Web and graphics professionals. To help further develop your skills in Flash, check out the following training resources from **lynda.com**:

lynda.com Books

The **Hands-On Training** series was originally developed by **Lynda Weinman**, author of the revolutionary book, *Designing Web Graphics*, first released in 1996. Lynda believes people learn best from doing and has developed the **Hands-On Training** series to teach users software programs and technologies through a progressive learning process.

Check out the following books from lynda.com:

Flash Professional 8 Beyond the Basics
by Shane Rebenschied
lynda.com/books and Peachpit Press
ISBN: 0321293878

Dreamweaver 8 Hands-On Training
by Garo Green and Daniel Short
Lydna.com/books and Peachpit Press
ISBN: 0321293894

**Adobe Photoshop CS2 for the Web
Hands-On Training**
by Tanya Staples
lynda.com/books and Peachpit Press
ISBN: 0321331710

Designing Web Graphics 4
by Lynda Weinman
New Riders
ISBN: 0735710791

lynda.com Video-Based Training

lynda.com offers video training as standalone **CD-ROM** and **DVD-ROM** products and through a subscription to the **lynda.com Online Training Library**.

For a free, 24-hour trial pass to the lynda.com Online Training Library, register your copy of Flash Professional 8 Hands-On Training at the following link:

http://www.lynda.com/register/HOT/flash8

Note: This offer is available for new subscribers only and does not apply to current or past subscribers of the lynda.com Online Training Library.

To help you build your skills with Flash, check out the following video training titles from lynda.com:

Flash Video-Based Training

Flash Professional 8 Essential Training
with Shane Rebenschied

Flash Professional 8 New Features
with Shane Rebenschied

Flash Professional 8 Beyond the Basics
with Shane Rebenschied

Flash 8 User Experiences Best Practices
with Robert Hoekman Jr.

**Flash Professional 8 and Photoshop CS2
Integration**
with Michael Ninness

ActionScript 2.0 Video-Based Training

Learning ActionScript 2.0
with Joey Lott

Advanced ActionScript 2.0
with Joey Lott

Web Design Video-Based Training

Studio 8 Web Workflow
with Abigail Rudner

Photoshop CS2 for the Web Essential Training
with Tanya Staples

Fireworks 8 Essential Training
with Abigail Rudner

Flashforward Conference

Flashforward is an international educational conference dedicated to Macromedia Flash. Flashforward was first hosted by Lynda Weinman, founder of lynda.com, and Stewart McBride, founder of United Digital Artists. Flashforward is now owned exclusively by lynda.com and strives to provide the best conferences for designers and developers to present their technical and artistic work in an educational setting.

For more information about the Flashforward conference, visit **http://www.flashforwardconference.com.**

Online Resources

Macromedia Flash Developer Center
http://www.macromedia.com/devnet/flash

Macromedia has created a section of its Web site called the Macromedia Flash Developer Center. This is a one-stop shop for everything Flash. For example, you can read tutorials and articles on Flash 8, download sample applications, access links to other Flash resources, and even read the white papers written on topics related to Flash 8. This is the perfect link to use if you want to learn more about components or even video in Flash 8.

Macromedia Online Forums
http://www.macromedia.com/support/forums/flash

Macromedia has set up several Web-based online forums for Macromedia Flash. This is a great place to ask questions and get help from thousands of Flash users. These online forums are used by beginning to advanced Flash MX 2004 users, so you should have no problem finding the type of help you need, regardless of your experience with the program. A list follows describing several of Macromedia's online forums.

Flash General Discussion

Online forum for general issues related to using Macromedia Flash.

Flash Site Design

Online forum for design feedback on your Flash animations. This forum is dedicated to the discussion of Flash design and animation principles and practices. Other issues not specific to the Flash tools, yet important to Flash designers, are also discussed here.

Flash Actionscript

Online forum for discussion related to creating interactive Flash projects using Actionscripting.

Flash Remoting

Online forum that discusses issues involved with Flash Remoting. Flash Remoting supplies the infrastructure that allows users to connect to remote services exposed by application server developers and Web services. Examples of these are message boards, shopping carts, and even up-to-the-minute stock quote graphs.

Flash Exchange Extensions

Online forum for issues relating to Flash extensions, including how to use them and how to troubleshoot any problems with them. (See also the "Macromedia Exchange for Flash" section next.)

Macromedia Exchange for Flash

http://www.macromedia.com/exchange/flash/

Macromedia has set up another section of its Web site, called the Macromedia Flash Exchange. Here you'll find hundreds of free extensions written by third-party users and developers that can help you build new features into your Web site. These features are not part of the Flash 8 product, you can download them when you need them. Many of these extensions have features that normally would require an advanced level of ActionScripting. For example, some of these behaviors let you password-protect areas of your site and create pop-up menus, scroll bars, complex text effects, and so on.

The Macromedia site is not just for developers but for any Flash user who wants to take Flash to the next level. If you are a developer, this is a great place to learn how to write your own behaviors to share with the rest of the Macromedia Flash community.

You can also visit **http://www.macromedia.com/ support/forums/flash** and click the **Flash Exchange Extensions** link to access the online forum for Flash extensions.

Macromedia TechNote Index

http://www.macromedia.com/support/flash/ technotes.html

This section of the Macromedia Web site lists all the issues that have been reported and answered by Macromedia Flash staff.

Third-Party Web Sites

http://www.flashkit.com/
http://www.ultrashock.com/
http://virtual-fx.net/
http://www.actionscripts.org/
http://www.flzone.net/
http://flashmove.com/

http://flazoom.com/
http://www.were-here.com/
http://www.popedeflash.com/
http://www.macromedia.com/support/flash/
ts/documents/flash_websites.htm

Books

Macromedia Flash 8 Bible
by Robert Reinhardt and Snow Dowd
John Wiley & Sons, 2006
ISBN: 0471746762

Macromedia Flash MX 2004 ActionScript Bible
by Robert Reinhardt and Joey Lott
John Wiley & Sons, 2004
ISBN: 0764543547

Macromedia Flash 8 for Windows and Macintosh: Visual QuickStart Guide
by Katherine Ulrich
Peachpit Press, 2005
ISBN: 0321349636

Macromedia Flash 8 Advanced for Windows and Macintosh: Visual QuickPro Guide
by Russell Chun, H. Paul Robertson
Peachpit Press, 2005
ISBN: 0321349644

Macromedia Flash Professional 8 Training from the Source
by Tom Green, Jordan L. Chilcott
Publisher: Macromedia Press; 2005
ISBN: 0321384032

ActionScript for Flash MX: The Definitive Guide
by Colin Moock and Gary Grossman
O'Reilly & Associates, 2002
ISBN: 059600396X

Macromedia Flash MX Video
by Kristian Besley, Hoss Gifford, Todd Marks, and Brian Monnone
Friends of ED, 2002
ISBN: 1903450853

Teach Yourself VISUALLY Macromedia Flash MX 2004
by Sherry Willard Kinkoph
maranGraphics, 2003
ISBN: 0764543342

Macromedia Flash MX 2004 Magic
by Michelangelo Capraro
New Riders, 2003
ISBN: 0735713774

Flash MX 2004 Games Most Wanted
by Kristian Besley et al.
friends of ED, 2003
ISBN: 1590592360

Index

Numerals

D

Darken blend modes, 153

data action, Movie Clip events, 299

Debugger command (Window menu), 23

Debugger panel, 23
  keyboard shortcuts, 25

Default - (HTML) command (File menu), 97

Default command
  File menu, 495
  Window menu, 19

Default option (Sound Properties dialog box), 387

defaults
  browsers, 97
  document properties, 74

Delete Behavior panel, Behaviors panel, 289

Delete button, Library panel, 123

Delete command (Presets menu), 165

Delete Filter button, 164

Delete Layer button, 272
  layer controls, 16

Delete Preset dialog box, 165

Delete Shortcut button, 27

Deployment screen, 469

device fonts
  versus embedded fonts, 357–358
  static text, 353–357

Dim option, Bandwidth Profiler, 356

Distance setting, Drop Shadow filter, 215

Distribute to Layers command (Modify menu), 109

Distributed Duplicate command (Insert menu), 200

Distributed Duplicate dialog box, 200–201

Distributed Duplicate Timeline Effects dialog box, 202

docking
  panels, 18
  Timeline, 14–15
  toolbar, 17

document properties
  animation, 72–73
  defaults, 74

Document Properties dialog box, 72

document tabs, Flash 8 new features, 6

Document window, 13. *See also* Timeline

dot syntax, ActionScipt, 306

Down state, buttons, 243

Download Settings command (View menu), 548

download speeds, reasons to use Flash 8, 3

dragOut action, Mouse events, 298

dragOver action, Mouse events, 298

drawing models defined, 50

drawing tools, 28
  Brush tool, 37–39
  defining, 29–30
  fills, 31
  gradients, 57–59
  grouping objects, 55–56
  lines, 31
  merge drawing models
    creating shapes, 51–54
    defined, 50
    negative spaces, 54
  modifying paths, 65–69
  object drawing models, 50
    creating shapes, 51–54
    Flash 8 new features, 6
  Oval tool, 34–36
  Pen tool, 61–64
  Pencil tool, freehand line drawings, 32–33
  Rectangle tool, 34–36
  Selection tool, 40–45
  shapes, 31
  strokes, 31

Dreamweaver 8 integration, 575–578

Drop Shadow filter, 159
  animation, 212–214
  settings, 215

Duplicate dialog box, 26

Duplicate Scene button, 316

Duplicate Set button, 26

Duplicate Symbol dialog box, 256–257

Duration option, Bandwidth Profiler, 356

DV files, 451

dynamic text, 347–348
  HTML, 368–371
  loading external data, 364
  loading text, 362–367

E

Edit bar, 16, 20
  checking location, 130
  Document window, 13

Edit Bar command (Window menu), 20

Edit button, sound settings, 397

Edit Effects command (Modify menu), 203

Edit Envelope dialog box, 394, 397

Edit menu commands

F

Flash 8
    extending basic capabilities, 10–11
    file types, 9
    new features, 6–7, 60
    reasons to use, 3–5
Flash authoring tool, 8
Flash Basic 8, 3. *See also* Flash 8
Flash Document command (File menu), 51
Flash menu commands, Keyboard Shortcuts, 26
Flash Player, 8, 10
    affect on filters, 168
    printing from, 552–556
Flash Professional 8, 3. *See also* Flash 8
Flash Professional commands, Preferences, 17
Flash Projector, 8
    file format, 9
Flash Publish Settings dialog box, 511–512
Flash Type, 6, 359
Flash Video Encoding Settings dialog box, 486
Flashkit Web site, 11
Flip Vertical command (Modify menu), 234
FLV files, 453
Folder option (Layer Properties dialog box), 117
folders, layers, 115
Font attribute, Text tool, 349
Font Rendering Method attribute, Text tool, 350
Font Rendering Method menu, 356
Font Size attribute, Text tool, 350
fonts
    computer availability, 315
    device, static text, 353–357
    embedding outlines, 375
    kerning, 352
    missing, 526
formats
    file types, 9
    video imports, 451
forms, 428
    configuring components, 436–441
    creating, 431–435
    modifying themes, 442–447
Fr rate option, Bandwidth Profiler, 356
frame-by-frame animation, 77–81
Frame command (Insert menu), 75, 83
Frame option, Bandwidth Profiler, 356
frame rates
    recommendations, 82
    Timeline, 71
Frame view, Timeline, 14

Frame View menu, Timeline, 71
frames
    action layers, 296
    animation, 74–76
    copying, 87–89
    deleting, 83–86
    inserting, 83–86
    labels
        controlling videos, 468–477
        creating pop-up menus, 324–331
        defining, 323
    reversing, 87–89
Free Transform tool, 17
    features, 94
    onion skinning animation, 92
FSCommands
    modifying projectors, 503–506
    stand-along projector, 506
fullscreen command, 506
functions, assignment to objects, 302

G

General command, 17
General Preferences dialog box, 17
GIF files, 218
GIF Publishing Settings dialog box, 515–517
Global Functions category, Action panel, 293
Glow filter, 159
go action, controlling video, 465–467
Go to URL dialog box, 312
Go to URL Window Parameter options, 313
Go to Web Page behavior, Behaviors panel, 312–314
Go to Web Page command (Web menu), 289
goto action, 307–311
gotoAndStop action, 311
Gradient Bevel filter, 160
Gradient definition bar, Color Mixer panel, 57
Gradient Glow filter, 160
Gradient Transform tool, 17, 29, 58
gradients
    Color Mixer panel, 46–49
    drawing tools, 57–59
    Flash 8 new features, 6
graphic symbol Timeline, 121
graphic symbols, 119
    animated *versus* movie clip symbols, 274–277
    creating, 122–127

J–K

L

M

Q–R

W

X–Y–Z

Learn More for Less

@ the lynda.com Online Movie Library:

ONLY **$25**/mo FOR UNRESTRICTED ACCESS.

- Self-paced learning.
- 24/7 access.
- Over 33 of the latest software titles and technologies.
- Over 3,300 QuickTime Movies and growing monthly.
- Affordable pricing.
- Month-to-month option.
- Free online samples.

Visit http://movielibrary.lynda.com/

lynda.com

Hands-on Training Books, CDs, & Online Movie Library.

THIS SOFTWARE LICENSE AGREEMENT CONSTITUTES AN AGREEMENT BETWEEN YOU AND, LYNDA.COM, INC. YOU SHOULD CAREFULLY READ THE FOLLOWING TERMS AND CONDITIONS. COPYING THIS SOFTWARE TO YOUR MACHINE OR OTHERWISE REMOVING OR USING THE SOFTWARE INDICATES YOUR ACCEPTANCE OF THESE TERMS AND CONDITIONS. IF YOU DO NOT AGREE TO BE BOUND BY THE PROVISIONS OF THIS LICENSE AGREEMENT, YOU SHOULD PROMPTLY DELETE THE SOFTWARE FROM YOUR MACHINE.

TERMS AND CONDITIONS

1. GRANT OF LICENSE. In consideration of payment of the License Fee, which was a part of the price you paid for this product, LICENSOR grants to you (the "Licensee") a non-exclusive right to use the Software (all parts and elements of the data contained on the accompanying DVD-ROM are hereinafter referred to as the "Software"), along with any updates or upgrade releases of the Software for which you have paid on a single computer only (i.e., with a single CPU) at a single location, all as more particularly set forth and limited below. LICENSOR reserves all rights not expressly granted to you as Licensee in this License Agreement.

2. OWNERSHIP OF SOFTWARE. The license granted herein is not a sale of the original Software or of any copy of the Software. As Licensee, you own only the rights to use the Software as described herein and the magnetic or other physical media on which the Software is originally or subsequently recorded or fixed. LICENSOR retains title and ownership of the Software recorded on the original disk(s), as well as title and ownership of any subsequent copies of the Software irrespective of the form of media on or in which the Software is recorded or fixed. This license does not grant you any intellectual or other proprietary or other rights of any nature whatsoever in the Software.

3. USE RESTRICTIONS. As Licensee, you may use the Software only as expressly authorized in this License Agreement under the terms of paragraph 4. You may physically transfer the Software from one computer to another provided that the Software is used on only a single computer at any one time. You may not: (i) electronically transfer the Software from one computer to another over a network; (ii) make the Software available through a time-sharing service, network of computers, or other multiple user arrangement; (iii) distribute copies of the Software or related written materials to any third party, whether for sale or otherwise; (iv) modify, adapt, translate, reverse engineer, decompile, disassemble, or prepare any derivative work based on the Software or any element thereof; (v) make or distribute, whether for sale or otherwise, any hard copy or printed version of any of the Software nor any portion thereof nor any work of yours containing the Software or any component thereof; (vi) use any of the Software nor any of its components in any other work.

4. THIS IS WHAT YOU CAN AND CANNOT DO WITH THE SOFTWARE. Even though in the preceding paragraph and elsewhere LICENSOR has restricted your use of the Software, the following is the only thing you can do with the Software and the various elements of the Software: THE ARTWORK CONTAINED ON THIS DVD-ROM MAY NOT BE USED IN ANY MANNER WHATSOEVER OTHER THAN TO VIEW THE SAME ON YOUR COMPUTER, OR POST TO YOUR PERSONAL, NON-COMMERCIAL WEB SITE FOR EDUCATIONAL PURPOSES ONLY. THIS MATERIAL IS SUBJECT TO ALL OF THE RESTRICTION PROVISIONS OF THIS SOFTWARE LICENSE. SPECIFICALLY BUT NOT IN LIMITATION OF THESE RESTRICTIONS, YOU MAY NOT DISTRIBUTE, RESELL OR TRANSFER THIS PART OF THE SOFTWARE NOR ANY OF YOUR DESIGN OR OTHER WORK CONTAINING ANY OF THE SOFTWARE on this DVD-ROM, ALL AS MORE PARTICULARLY RESTRICTED IN THE WITHIN SOFTWARE LICENSE.

5. COPY RESTRICTIONS. The Software and accompanying written materials are protected under United States copyright laws. Unauthorized copying and/or distribution of the Software and/or the related written materials is expressly forbidden. You may be held legally responsible for any copyright infringement that is caused, directly or indirectly, by your failure to abide by the terms of this License Agreement. Subject to the terms of this License Agreement and if the software is not otherwise copy protected, you may make one copy of the Software for backup purposes only. The copyright notice and any other proprietary notices which were included in the original Software must be reproduced and included on any such backup copy.

6. TRANSFER RESTRICTIONS. The license herein granted is personal to you, the Licensee. You may not transfer the Software nor any of its components or elements to anyone else, nor may you sell, lease, loan, sublicense, assign, or otherwise dispose of the Software nor any of its components or elements without the express written consent of LICENSOR, which consent may be granted or withheld at LICENSOR's sole discretion.

7. TERMINATION. The license herein granted hereby will remain in effect until terminated. This license will terminate automatically without further notice from LICENSOR in the event of the violation of any of the provisions hereof. As Licensee, you agree that upon such termination you will promptly destroy any and all copies of the Software which remain in your possession and, upon request, will certify to such destruction in writing to LICENSOR.

8. LIMITATION AND DISCLAIMER OF WARRANTIES. a) THE SOFTWARE AND RELATED WRITTEN MATERIALS, INCLUDING ANY INSTRUCTIONS FOR USE, ARE PROVIDED ON AN "AS IS" BASIS, WITHOUT WARRANTY OF ANY KIND, EXPRESS OR IMPLIED. THIS DISCLAIMER OF WARRANTY EXPRESSLY INCLUDES, BUT IS NOT LIMITED TO, ANY IMPLIED WARRANTIES OF MERCHANTABILITY AND/OR FITNESS FOR A PARTICULAR PURPOSE. NO WARRANTY OF ANY KIND IS MADE AS TO WHETHER OR NOT THIS SOFTWARE INFRINGES UPON ANY RIGHTS OF ANY OTHER THIRD PARTIES. NO ORAL OR WRITTEN INFORMATION GIVEN BY LICENSOR, ITS SUPPLIERS, DISTRIBUTORS, DEALERS, EMPLOYEES, OR AGENTS, SHALL CREATE OR OTHERWISE ENLARGE THE SCOPE OF ANY WARRANTY HEREUNDER. LICENSEE ASSUMES THE ENTIRE RISK AS TO THE QUALITY AND THE PERFORMANCE OF SUCH SOFTWARE.

SHOULD THE SOFTWARE PROVE DEFECTIVE, YOU, AS LICENSEE (AND NOT LICENSOR, ITS SUPPLIERS, DISTRIBUTORS, DEALERS OR AGENTS), ASSUME THE ENTIRE COST OF ALL NECESSARY CORRECTION, SERVICING, OR REPAIR. b) LICENSOR warrants the disk(s) on which this copy of the Software is recorded or fixed to be free from defects in materials and workmanship, under normal use and service, for a period of ninety (90) days from the date of delivery as evidenced by a copy of the applicable receipt. LICENSOR hereby limits the duration of any implied warranties with respect to the disk(s) to the duration of the express warranty. This limited warranty shall not apply if the disk(s) have been damaged by unreasonable use, accident, negligence, or by any other causes unrelated to defective materials or workmanship. c) LICENSOR does not warrant that the functions contained in the Software will be uninterrupted or error free and Licensee is encouraged to test the Software for Licensee's intended use prior to placing any reliance thereon. All risk of the use of the Software will be on you, as Licensee. d) THE LIMITED WARRANTY SET FORTH ABOVE GIVES YOU SPECIFIC LEGAL RIGHTS AND YOU MAY ALSO HAVE OTHER RIGHTS, WHICH VARY FROM STATE TO STATE. SOME STATES DO NOT ALLOW THE LIMITATION OR EXCLUSION OF IMPLIED WARRANTIES OR OF INCIDENTAL OR CONSEQUEN-TIAL DAMAGES, SO THE LIMITATIONS AND EXCLUSIONS CONCERNING THE SOFTWARE AND RELATED WRITTEN MATERIALS SET FORTH ABOVE MAY NOT APPLY TO YOU.

9. LIMITATION OF REMEDIES. LICENSOR's entire liability and Licensee's exclusive remedy shall be the replacement of any disk(s) not meeting the limited warranty set forth in Section 8 above which is returned to LICENSOR with a copy of the applicable receipt within the warranty period. Any replacement disk(s)will be warranted for the remainder of the original warranty period or thirty (30) days, whichever is longer.

10. LIMITATION OF LIABILITY. IN NO EVENT WILL LICENSOR, OR ANYONE ELSE INVOLVED IN THE CREATION, PRODUCTION, AND/OR DELIVERY OF THIS SOFTWARE PRODUCT BE LIABLE TO LICENSEE OR ANY OTHER PERSON OR ENTITY FOR ANY DIRECT, INDIRECT, OR OTHER DAMAGES, INCLUDING, WITHOUT LIMITATION, ANY INTERRUPTION OF SERVICES, LOST PROFITS, LOST SAVINGS, LOSS OF DATA, OR ANY OTHER CONSEQUENTIAL, INCIDENTAL, SPECIAL, OR PUNITIVE DAMAGES, ARISING OUT OF THE PURCHASE, USE, INABILITY TO USE, OR OPERATION OF THE SOFTWARE, EVEN IF LICENSOR OR ANY AUTHORIZED LICENSOR DEALER HAS BEEN ADVISED OF THE POSSIBILITY OF SUCH DAMAGES. BY YOUR USE OF THE SOFTWARE, YOU ACKNOWLEDGE THAT THE LIMITATION OF LIABILITY SET FORTH IN THIS LICENSE WAS THE BASIS UPON WHICH THE SOFTWARE WAS OFFERED BY LICENSOR AND YOU ACKNOWLEDGE THAT THE PRICE OF THE SOFTWARE LICENSE WOULD BE HIGHER IN THE ABSENCE OF SUCH LIMITATION. SOME STATES DO NOT ALLOW THE LIMITATION OR EXCLUSION OF LIABILITY FOR INCIDENTAL OR CONSEQUENTIAL DAMAGES SO THE ABOVE LIMITATIONS AND EXCLUSIONS MAY NOT APPLY TO YOU.

11. UPDATES. LICENSOR, at its sole discretion, may periodically issue updates of the Software which you may receive upon request and payment of the applicable update fee in effect from time to time and in such event, all of the provisions of the within License Agreement shall apply to such updates.

12. EXPORT RESTRICTIONS. Licensee agrees not to export or re-export the Software and accompanying documentation (or any copies thereof) in violation of any applicable U.S. laws or regulations.

13. ENTIRE AGREEMENT. YOU, AS LICENSEE, ACKNOWLEDGE THAT: (i) YOU HAVE READ THIS ENTIRE AGREEMENT AND AGREE TO BE BOUND BY ITS TERMS AND CONDITIONS; (ii) THIS AGREEMENT IS THE COMPLETE AND EXCLUSIVE STATEMENT OF THE UNDERSTANDING BETWEEN THE PARTIES AND SUPERSEDES ANY AND ALL PRIOR ORAL OR WRITTEN COMMUNICA-TIONS RELATING TO THE SUBJECT MATTER HEREOF; AND (iii) THIS AGREE-MENT MAY NOT BE MODIFIED, AMENDED, OR IN ANY WAY ALTERED EXCEPT BY A WRITING SIGNED BY BOTH YOURSELF AND AN OFFICER OR AUTHO-RIZED REPRESENTATIVE OF LICENSOR.

14. SEVERABILITY. In the event that any provision of this License Agreement is held to be illegal or otherwise unenforceable, such provision shall be deemed to have been deleted from this License Agreement while the remaining provisions of this License Agreement shall be unaffected and shall continue in full force and effect.

15. GOVERNING LAW. This License Agreement shall be governed by the laws of the State of California applicable to agreements wholly to be performed therein and of the United States of America, excluding that body of the law related to conflicts of law. This License Agreement shall not be governed by the United Nations Convention on Contracts for the International Sale of Goods, the applica-tion of which is expressly excluded. No waiver of any breach of the provisions of this License Agreement shall be deemed a waiver of any other breach of this License Agreement.

16. RESTRICTED RIGHTS LEGEND. Use, duplication, or disclosure by the Government is subject to restrictions as set forth in subparagraph (c)(1)(ii) of the Rights in Technical Data and Computer Software clause at 48 CFR § 252.227-7013 and DFARS § 252.227-7013 or subparagraphs (c) (1) and (c)(2) of the Commercial Computer Software-Restricted Rights at 48 CFR § 52.227.19, as applicable. Contractor/manufacturer: LICENSOR: LYNDA.COM, INC., c/o PEACHPIT PRESS, 1249 Eighth Street, Berkeley, CA 94710.